Principles of Economics
MACRO

Principles of Economics
MACRO

Willis L. Peterson
University of Minnesota

Eighth Edition

IRWIN
Homewood, IL 60430
Boston, MA 02116

Senior sponsoring editor: Gary L. Nelson
Project editor: Jean Lou Hess
Production manager: Diane Palmer
Cover Designer: Russell Schneck
Compositor: TCSystems, Inc.
Typeface: 10/12 Times Roman
Printer: The Book Press, Inc.

Library of Congress Cataloging-in-Publication Data

Peterson, Willis L.
   Principles of economics.   Macro/Willis L. Peterson.—8th ed.
      p.   cm.
   Includes bibliographical references and index.
   ISBN 0-256-08538-2
   1. Macroeconomics.   I. Title.
HB172.5.P455 1991
339—dc20

90–45153

Printed in the United States of America
1 2 3 4 5 6 7 8 9 0 BP 7 6 5 4 3 2 1 0

Preface

Suggestions for Study

The social science called economics is commonly divided into two major subject matter areas: macro and micro. Macroeconomics, the topic of this book, deals mainly with the problems of unemployment and inflation: What causes these problems, and what can be done to mitigate or avoid them. In addition some related topics are covered at the end of the text. These include income redistribution and poverty programs, international trade and exchange rates, and economic growth and development. The latter areas focus mainly on the international economy. Microeconomics, covered in the companion micro text, deals largely with the spending decisions of households, the production decisions of business firms, and how prices and wages are determined in the product and resource markets.

The general objective of this text is to introduce you to the most important concepts in microeconomics, and to help you develop your skills in using these concepts to answer economic questions or make economic decisions. In other words, major emphasis is on concepts and their applications, as opposed to factual or descriptive material.

To gain a good understanding of the material and to do well in the course, the following procedure is recommended. First read the assigned chapter thoroughly. Don't try to speed-read as you would a magazine or a novel. The chapters are rather compact; most are designed to be read in 45 minutes to an hour. But each is packed with ideas or concepts. So take your time. After completing the reading of each chapter, read the summary paragraph at the end. This will give you an overview of the main ideas presented. Then look at the "You Should Know" items. Treat each one as a question. If there are some you cannot answer, refer back to the appropriate page to find out the answer. Then answer the end-of-chapter self-test questions without looking back at the material. Write your responses on a separate sheet so that you can go back over these questions later when preparing for an exam without being distracted by your first responses. Your instructor has the key to the self-tests. How you do on the self tests should be a good indication of your performance on in-class exams. Good luck and enjoy your exploration into economics.

Willis L. Peterson

CONTENTS

Principles of Economics
MACRO

Part I

Macro Foundations

Chapter 1

Introduction

OVERVIEW

This is a get-acquainted chapter. After setting out the distinction between macro- and microeconomics, the discussion turns to a few useful tips for studying macroeconomics. Be aware that macroeconomics has political overtones. This will become evident in later chapters. The remainder of the chapter provides some tips for economic reasoning.

"MICRO" VERSUS "MACRO" ECONOMICS

During its approximately 200-year history, economics has evolved into two major subdisciplines: microeconomics and macroeconomics. As its name implies, microeconomics is concerned mainly with small segments of the total economy—individual consumers and producers or groups of consumers and producers that are known as markets or industries. The subject matter of microeconomics deals in part with allocating resources to their most valuable uses so as to maximize the total output of the economy. Considerable emphasis also is placed on wage and price determination, which affects the distribution of a nation's output.

Macroeconomics, the topic of this book, is concerned mainly with economic aggregates, or the economy as a whole. The subject matter of macroeconomics deals to a large extent with the problems of unemployment and inflation. In large part, these problems also influence the total output of society and the distribution of this output.

The existence of unemployment implies that the total output of society is smaller than it need otherwise be. Unemployment also affects the distribution of society's output in that the unemployed suffer a reduction in income, which in turn means they cannot place as large a claim on society's goods and services. In regard to inflation, it is acknowledged that this phenomenon causes increased

3

uncertainty in the economy. If, as a result, investment is curtailed, future output is diminished from what it would otherwise be. Investment funds may also be diminished during inflation because of the disincentive that inflation places on saving, particularly if interest rates are held at artificially low levels by usury laws. Also, as will be pointed out in later chapters, attempts to reduce inflation invariably lead to increased unemployment, which reduces total output and alters its distribution. Inflation has other undesirable distributional effects as well. Those whose wages rise less rapidly than the price level lose relative to those who are able to maintain the purchasing power of their earnings. Perhaps the main distributional effect of inflation is that it reduces the real wealth of those who hold the major portion of their assets in the form of money while increasing the wealth of those who own assets, such as real estate, that rise in value during inflation. (The economic effects of inflation will be discussed in more detail in Chapter 6.)

One can say, therefore, that both micro- and macroeconomics deal with the size of society's output of goods and services and the distribution of this output. After completing the study of the micro and macro areas, however, one will see that the methods of analysis used in each differ to a considerable degree.

It should also be noted that macroeconomics can itself be divided into two major subdivisions. One is sometimes referred to as a study of income and employment theory; the other, as the study of monetary theory. The first deals to a large extent with the effects of government spending and taxation on the level of economic activity. The second is concerned mainly with the effect of the quantity of money and interest rates on the economy. As you might expect, then, the actions of government are important in the study of macroeconomics.

Macroeconomics also contains a number of related topics covered in Chapters 21 through 26. These include a discussion of antipoverty programs and problems, international trade and exchange rates, and economic growth and development with particular emphasis on the world's less-developed countries.

50 QUESTIONS

A better idea of what macroeconomics is all about can be obtained from the following 50 questions that you should be able to answer after completing the course.

1. What is opportunity cost?
2. How are prices determined and why do they change?
3. Who are the unemployed?
4. Why is the proportion of the adult population employed at an all-time high?
5. What is inflation and why is it bad?
6. What is gross national product (GNP) and how is it measured?
7. What proportion of the nation's output goes to the military?
8. Who were the first economists and what was their main concern?

9. What is Mercantilism? Laissez-faire? Say's Law? Ricardian rent? The labor theory of value?
10. Why is economics called the dismal science?
11. What are some of the objects that have been used as money, and why does the existence of money improve society's standard of living?
12. What is the relationship between money and prices?
13. According to the quantity theory, what causes inflation?
14. According to Keynes, what causes unemployment?
15. How can an extra dollar of spending by government, business firms, or consumers add more than one dollar of spending to the economy?
16. Why does unemployment increase when the government tries to stop inflation?
17. Is it possible to have stable prices and a low rate of unemployment at the same time?
18. Who says increased government spending can decrease unemployment, and who says it cannot?
19. How does the federal government print money to finance its deficit spending?
20. Should we worry about the national debt?
21. What is the difference between fiscal policy and monetary policy?
22. What are the two principles of taxation?
23. What are the main sources of government tax revenue, and what is the money spent on?
24. Is it possible for tax revenue to increase when tax rates are decreased?
25. What gives paper money purchasing power?
26. Does the increased use of credit cards mean we are evolving toward a moneyless society?
27. What are the benefits of holding money?
28. What is the cost of holding money?
29. In a balance sheet, why must assets always equal liabilities plus net worth?
30. How did banks evolve?
31. How is it possible for banks to lend part of the money deposited by their customers?
32. How do banks create money?
33. Why was the Federal Reserve System established, and what are its main functions?
34. What happens in the banking system when you write a check?
35. Can price and wage controls prevent inflation?
36. Why do incomes differ among people?
37. What are the characteristics of people that have the greatest chance of being poor?

38. How much does a college education add to a person's annual income?
39. Why do farm programs mainly benefit large, higher-income farmers?
40. Why do welfare programs promote the breakup of families?
41. What is a negative income tax, and how would it work?
42. How can international trade increase the output of all nations?
43. Why do most countries try to discourage international trade if it makes people better off?
44. "Buy American—Your Job Depends on It." Is this right?
45. What determines how many units of a foreign currency can be exchanged for a dollar?
46. How does the rate of exchange between dollars and other currencies influence the prices paid for imports and prices received for exports?
47. Who has the cleaner environment, poor nations or rich nations?
48. Are the poor nations catching up or falling further behind the rich nations in terms of per capita income?
49. What do the rich nations have that the poor nations lack?
50. What is the main reason over 40,000 people in the world die each day from the direct or indirect effects of malnutrition, and what can be done to alleviate this hunger problem?

POLITICS AND ECONOMICS—POLITICAL ECONOMY

In view of the importance of government in the study of macroeconomics, we should not be surprised to learn that politics and economics are closely related. Indeed, economics has been called the study of political economy. This was especially true during the 19th century. With the passage of time, political science and economics gradually emerged as separate, although closely related, disciplines.

We would expect, too, that much of the disagreement and controversy inherent in politics would carry over into economics, particularly in the macro area. This cannot be denied. People of a more conservative political outlook tend to prefer a society with a minimum of government intervention. Although it is unwise to generalize too much here, it seems reasonably safe to say that economists of a more conservative political philosophy also prefer a minimum of government intervention, particularly in the economic activities of society.

Virtually all economists probably would agree on the need for a certain amount of federal government intervention. For example, there is little question about the need for government regulation of the money supply or the provision for certain public goods such as national defense or roads. Moving toward the liberal pole (and we should recognize various degrees of liberalism or conservatism rather than an all-or-none situation), we find people who are willing to delegate more decision-making authority to government. Again, the more liberal economists tend to fall within this category. Although most economists make a sincere attempt at being objective or "scientific" in their profession, it is important to recognize that their political philosophies may, to some degree, carry over into their economic analyses.

POSITIVE VERSUS NORMATIVE ECONOMICS

Economists, recognizing that they have different political philosophies and that these divergent points of view may influence policy recommendations, have attempted to sort out as much as possible the *positive* from the *normative*. We can think of positive economics as "what is" and normative economics as "what should be." Positive economic statements commonly contain the words *if* and *then*. *If* a certain action is taken, *then* such and such will occur. For example, an economist may determine that *if* there is a tax increase, *then* X billions of dollars will be removed from the private sector of the economy. This is a positive statement. To say that an X-billion dollar tax increase should be enacted is a normative statement. Normative statements frequently call for some sort of action, whereas positive statements generally cite the consequences of a proposal or action. Most of the material in this book is "positive" in nature.

One should not conclude, however, that all positive statements are true. For example, it is sometimes stated that if there is an increase in the nation's money supply, then interest rates will decline. This is a positive statement. However, experience gained during the 1970s, when the money supply grew rapidly and nominal rates of interest increased to record heights, suggests that this statement is not correct, at least over long-run situations. In all sciences, there are ideas that at one time were regarded as true or correct but were subsequently rejected in light of new evidence or ideas. It is not necessarily true either that all positive statements are objective and devoid of value judgments. Deciding what is important involves some value judgment. Moreover, in conducting a study, the researcher must decide what data to collect, how to organize and analyze the data, and other procedures. Beware of the statement, "Let the facts speak for themselves." What the facts say depends a great deal on which facts are used and how they are presented.[1]

THE INDIVIDUAL VERSUS SOCIETY

Most of us are accustomed to looking at the world from the perspective of the individual. However, we find in our study of macroeconomics that what is true for the individual person need not hold true for society, or even for groups of people. Standing up to watch a touchdown run at a football game provides a good noneconomic example. If just one person stands up, that person can gain a much better view, but if everyone in the stadium stands up, no one is much better off.

---

[1] For an entertaining little book on the use of statistics, see Darrell Huff, *How to Lie with Statistics* (New York: W. W. Norton, 1954).

The distinction between the individual and society is especially important in monetary policy. Any individual would be considered better off if the amount of money earned were doubled, for this would mean the person now has access to twice the amount of goods and services. But if the total quantity of money in the entire economy were doubled, the total quantity of real goods and services available to the people would not necessarily change. As we go along, we will encounter other situations where circumstances are much different for the individual than for society.

CAUSE AND EFFECT

If two events happen in proximity to each other, there is a temptation to conclude that the second event was caused by the first. Whenever we observe two events such as these, we should always inquire whether there might have been a third event that caused both to occur. A good example is the stock market crash of 1929 and the ensuing Great Depression of the 1930s. This order of events has prompted some people to argue that the stock market crash caused the Great Depression. But as we shall see later, a third, independent event offers a better explanation for the Great Depression than does the stock market crash, although the crash probably contributed to the depressed state of the economy once unemployment began to increase.

The possibility of one event causing two other events to occur is illustrated by the diagram below. In this example, event A occurs first, and then events B and C occur as a consequence of A. If event C happens to take place after event B, one might be led to believe that B caused C, especially if event A is not evident or well publicized. Before concluding that one event has caused a later, second event, one should always ask, was there a third, less noticeable event that caused both to occur? Even if the answer turns out to be no, it is still a good idea to ask the question.

UNLEARNING PRECONCEPTIONS

One of the characteristics of studying economics, particularly macroeconomics, is that most people bring with them at the start at least some preconceived ideas of how the economy functions. In fact, it is almost impossible not to form economic opinions in view of the vast amount of reporting of economics by the news media. This is both good and bad. It is good because people are becoming more aware of the importance of government economic policy in their lives. But it is bad to the extent that people form erroneous ideas of how the economy operates and the effect of government policy. Unfortunately many myths, half-truths, and misconceptions about the economy appear in the news media almost every day.

One of the major reasons for this problem is that there are many influential people both in government and in the news who are carrying out economic analysis without the benefit of economics training. Few, if any, professional occupations can make this claim (or excuse). To practice law or medicine, one must have the appropriate degree from an accredited college. Indeed, to be a plumber or electrician a person must complete a number of years of apprenticeship training. Not so in economics. Economics is practiced by everyone, and the importance of one's practice increases with his or her influence over the nation's affairs. Nations have paid a dear price for having leaders who have had little or no understanding of economics.

Throughout this book, it is more than likely that you will come across ideas quite different from those you had previously learned and accepted. It is difficult to unlearn old ideas, but economics training will be of much greater value if you approach it with an open mind, allowing the new ideas you encounter to at least compete with your old preconceptions.

ECONOMIC THEORIES—A FRAMEWORK FOR THINKING

The economy is very complex. Each day millions of economic decisions are made by millions of people. Some of these decisions, especially those made by the government, have far-reaching and long-lasting consequences. To study each decision, however, even the major ones, would be a hopelessly complicated task. We would soon be bogged down in a maze of dull and uninteresting detail. Thus, economists have found it useful to construct theories of the economy. A *theory* is a statement (verbal, graphical, or mathematical) that contains the important information bearing on a decision or problem. As such, economic theories provide a framework for thinking. They help us to identify and separate the important information for making economic decisions from the trivial or unimportant.

In a sense, economic theories or models are similar to movies or stage plays in that they present only the important and necessary information. While watching a movie, we seldom see details or incidents that do not bear directly on the plot. For example, one never sees the leading character searching for a parking place, standing in line to check in baggage at an air terminal, going through customs, or sitting for extended periods in the plane. These details would be boring and uninteresting, adding nothing to the entertainment. Instead, we generally observe the plane taking off or landing, which in a few seconds can convey the idea of a several-thousand-mile journey. In other words, only the important and necessary information is presented. The same is true of an economic theory. For example, if we are interested in why the price of lettuce is changing, we do not consider the price of golf balls or umbrellas, because these prices have little, if any, bearing on the price of lettuce. Theories highlight the necessary and important information bearing on a decision or problem.

Theories are mainly used to explain past events and predict future events. If we can understand why an event happened at some point in the past, then, if the same causal factors should reappear, we should be able to predict the reoccurrence of the event.

We should point out, too, that just about everyone utilizes theory of one kind or another from the time he or she is old enough to think. To take a very simple example, we know that if we touch a hot stove we will burn a finger. Essentially this is a theory. In essence, the "hot stove theory" both explains and predicts. It explains why you might have a sore finger, and it predicts that should you touch another hot stove you will again burn a finger.

In the main, theories are developed by observing events and then generalizing from these events. Most of us formed the "hot stove theory" by touching a stove and observing (and feeling) what happened. From one or two observations we were able to generalize that touching all hot stoves results in burned fingers. Economic theories are developed in a similar manner. By identifying the prime causal factors of economic events, economists attempt to explain these events and thus predict future events.

It is common to hear people say that something is "all right in theory but not in practice." A little reflection will reveal, however, that such a statement is illogical. If a theory is correct, that is, if it can explain or predict events, then whatever the theory predicts will happen. Something cannot be correct and incorrect at the same time. If a theory does not predict or explain an event, then it is either incomplete or incorrect. Such theories need to be reformulated, perhaps by adding new, pertinent information so that they are consistent with reality. Theories are continually being tested as they are used. Those that stand the test of time and use generally are correct. Sometimes, however, a theory may appear to be incorrect if it is applied to a set of circumstances for which it was not intended.

In the use of economic theory, it is common to see the phrases *other things equal* and *other things constant*. In order to simplify reality, it is useful to consider the impact of one factor at a time, in effect holding everything else constant, conceptually at least. This practice allows us to focus our attention on a specific point of interest, pushing into the background other factors or bits of information, even though they may also be important and be a part of the theory. It is recognized that in the real world there may be a number of important factors operating simultaneously. But if we tried to incorporate all of them at once into the analysis, it soon would become too complex to be of much use. Thus the *other things equal* phrase is not an attempt to distort the real world but rather an attempt to better understand and predict the world's events by making the theory more manageable and at the same time more powerful.

Unfortunately the word *theory* has suffered from bad press for a long time. To students, the word often brings to mind abstract material devoid of any practical application. The feeling is probably justified if theory is learned purely for the sake of learning theory. But economic theory is not developed for its own sake; it is developed because it can be useful to explain and predict events. As we proceed, you will find that an attempt is made to apply the theories to real-world situations. Thus, if you do not find the world dull, you should not find theory dull.

Economic theories also are known as *principles, models, or hypotheses.* Essentially all three words mean the same thing. The word *principles* in the title of the book reflects the idea that it is basically a book on economic theories. Chapter 4 presents the theories of demand and supply; Chapter 9 discusses the original quantity theory of money; Chapters 10 and 11 present the Keynesian model; Chapter 12 covers the aggregate demand–aggregate supply model; Chapter 13 is on the rational expectations hypothesis; Chapter 17 focuses on the new quantity theory of money; and Chapter 23 presents the theory of international trade. These economic theories are intended to help explain and predict economic phenomena, principally unemployment and inflation. If the theories can do this, then they should be useful in helping the country avoid or at least minimize these two problems.

SUMMARY

Macroeconomics deals mainly with the problems of unemployment and inflation. Additional topics covered in this book include poverty and poverty alleviation programs, international trade, and economic growth and development. Because macroeconomics deals with government policy, it contains political overtones. Most of the content of this book can be described as positive economics, "what is," as opposed to normative economics, which advocates "what should be." The book also is largely conceptual or theoretical in nature. A theory is a statement that contains the important information bearing on a decision or problem. Theories are used to explain and predict events.

YOU SHOULD KNOW

1. The two major divisions of economics, and the main topics covered in each.
2. The difference between liberal and conservative viewpoints as they relate to economics.
3. The difference between normative and positive economics.
4. If what is true for the individual also holds true for society.
5. Why it is not necessarily correct to assume that when two events occur in succession, the first causes the second.
6. What a theory is, and why theory is useful.
7. How theories are formulated.
8. Other names for theory.

QUESTIONS

1. As noted, macroeconomics is concerned largely with the problems of unemployment and inflation. Why is society better off if these problems can be avoided or at least minimized?

2. How do liberals and conservatives differ on the following issues?
   a. power of the federal government.
   b. taxes.
   c. government regulation of business.
   d. military spending.

3. Indicate whether the following statements are normative or positive.
   a. If inflation is decreased, then unemployment will increase.
   b. The deficit should be reduced.

c. If interest rates decline, then people will spend more on houses and cars.

4. It has been observed that husbands who kiss their wives good-bye before leaving for work in the morning have fewer auto accidents than husbands who do not. Does this imply that kissing prevents accidents? Explain.

5. *a.* What is theory and why is it useful?
   b. In what way is a theory like a movie or stage play?

6. Why is the statement, "It's all right in theory but not in practice," incorrect?

7. What information is contained in the theory of starting a car?

SELF-TEST

1. As a field of study, economics has been in existence:
   a. since the beginning of time.
   b. a little over 200 years.
   c. since the early 1930s.
   d. since the end of World War II.

2. Macroeconomics is concerned mainly with:
   a. the important issues facing the government.
   b. allocating resources to their most valuable users.
   c. the problems of unemployment and inflation.
   d. the world economy.

3. Microeconomics is concerned mainly with:
   a. the small or unimportant issues facing society.
   b. allocating resources to their most valuable uses.

c. the problems of unemployment and inflation.
   d. state as opposed to national problems.

4. People with a more conservative political philosophy tend to prefer _____ role of government in the economic affairs of the country while those with a more liberal viewpoint _____ role of government.
   a. a more active; prefer to minimize the
   b. a more active; rule out
   c. to minimize the; rule out
   d. to minimize the; prefer a more active

5. Positive economics deals with _____ and normative economics deals with _____ .
   a. what is; what should be
   b. what is; what was
   c. what should be; what is
   d. what was; what is

6. One of the important lessons of macroeconomics is:

    a. what is true for the individual need not be true for society.

    b. what is true for the individual also is true for society.

    c. what is true for society also is true for the individual.

    d. *b* and *c.*

7. It has been observed that husbands who kiss wives before driving off to work in the morning have fewer auto accidents than those who do not. From this we can conclude:

    a. kissing prevents accidents.

    b. not kissing causes accidents.

    c. *a* and *b.*

    d. neither *a* nor *b.*

8. The discipline where formal training does not necessarily precede use:

    a. chemistry.   *c.* biology.

    b. physics.   *d.* economics.

9. A theory is a statement that contains the _____ information bearing on a decision or problem.

    a. entertaining.   *c.* irrelevant.

    b. important.   *d.* quantitative.

10. Economic theory is similar to a movie or stage play in that it:

    a. is entertaining.

    b. is fictional.

    c. is a mystery.

    d. contains necessary or important information.

11. Theories are used mainly to:

    a. explain and predict events.

    b. entertain.

    c. establish IQ scores.

    d. solve crimes.

12. The statement "it's all right in theory but not in practice":

    a. is intended to simplify reality.

    b. applies to correct theories.

    c. applies to all theories.

    d. is illogical.

13. The statement "other things constant" or "other things equal" is frequently contained in theories. They are intended to:

    a. simplify reality.

    b. distort reality.

    c. confuse reality.

    d. hide an error of an incorrect theory.

14. Which of the following words mean the same thing as theory?

    a. principle.

    b. model.

    c. hypothesis.

    d. all of the above.

Chapter 2

How to Read Graphs

OVERVIEW

Both micro- and macroeconomics make extensive use of graphs. A two-dimensional graph is a relationship between two variables. Two possible relationships exist—positive and negative. Two variables are positively related when both move in the same direction: up or down. A negative relationship exists when the two variables move in opposite directions: one moves up, the other moves down, or vice versa.

INTRODUCTION

In studying economics, graphs are frequently used to convey concepts or ideas. In a way, a graph is a picture of an idea. While the cliché "a picture is worth a thousand words" may exaggerate a bit, a graph provides a precise means of expressing an idea.

All graphs presented in this book are of two dimensions; they express a relationship between two variables. Therefore, each graph has two axes—vertical and horizontal. When drawing or viewing a graph, it is important to specify or ascertain what each axis represents.

A graph can convey either a positive or a negative relationship between the two variables. A positive relationship exists when both variables move in the same direction. Both either increase or decrease as illustrated by panels *A* through *C* of Figure 2–1. Positive relationships are graphed with upward-sloping lines. There is a negative relationship when the two variables move in opposite directions—one increases and the other decreases as illustrated by panels *A* through *C* of Figure 2–2. These graphs have downward-sloping lines.

FIGURE 2–1 Positive Relationships

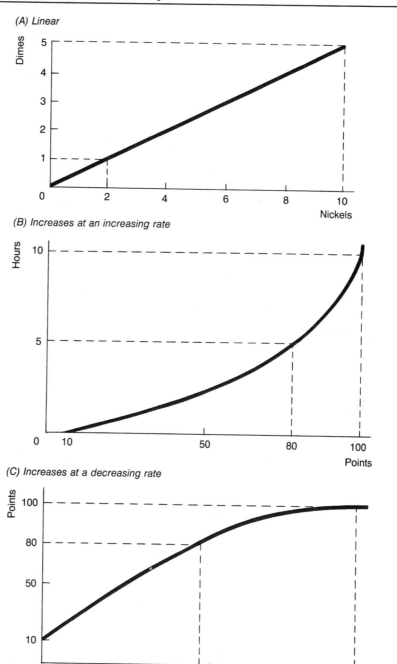

(A) Linear

(B) Increases at an increasing rate

(C) Increases at a decreasing rate

FIGURE 2–2   Negative Relationships

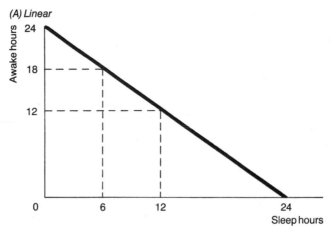

(A) Linear

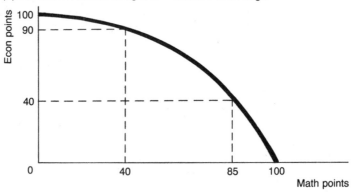

(B) Decrease at an increasing rate — concave to the origin

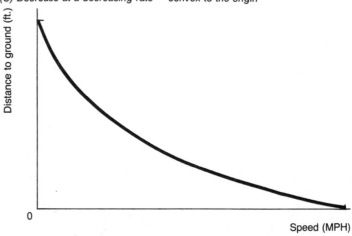

(C) Decrease at a decreasing rate — convex to the origin

POSITIVE RELATIONSHIP

A. Linear

Figure 2–1A illustrates a *linear positive relationship* between the two variables—nickels and dimes. The line represents the number of nickels and dimes that have equal value: one dime equals two nickels, and so on. In this graph, the upward-sloping line comes out of the origin. However, it is possible for such lines to begin at a point on either the vertical or horizontal axis.

B. Curvilinear

Panels B and C of Figure 2–1 represent a *curvilinear positive relationship* between the two variables—points obtained on an examination and the number of study hours used to prepare for the exam. In panel B, hours are on the vertical axis and points are on the horizontal axis. The graph shows that 10 points out of a maximum 100 are obtained with zero study; 5 hours yields 80 points, and a perfect score (100 points) is obtained with 10 hours of study. Also note that it takes more and more time to obtain each additional point the closer the student gets to a perfect score. In the first few hours of study, the easy material is learned, but a perfect score requires the mastery of the more difficult material that takes more time to grasp. While a graph cannot prove that this relationship holds true in all cases, it is reasonable to believe that it usually exists. Notice that in panel B the line increases at an increasing rate. When it reaches 100 on the horizontal axis, it becomes vertical. After 10 hours of study, more study time will not increase points because 100 is the maximum.

Panel C graphs the same two variables except the variable represented on each axis is switched—hours of study now are on the horizontal axis and points on the vertical axis. This line increases at a decreasing rate. After 10 hours and 100 points, the line becomes horizontal. Notice also that the same two variables can yield differently shaped graphs simply by changing the label on each axis.

NEGATIVE RELATIONSHIP

A. Linear

A *linear negative relationship* is illustrated between the two variables in panel A of Figure 2–2. The number of hours a person is awake each day is graphed against the number of sleep hours obtained. The two must add up to 24. At the point where the line intersects the vertical axis, the person is sleeping 24 hours and awake zero hours. The converse is true at the intersection of the horizontal axis. It is hard to imagine either extreme. Therefore, it is not necessary for a downward-sloping line to intersect the two axes. The relevant area may be only a portion in the middle of the line—say between 4 and 10 hours of sleep and 20 and 14 hours of awake time.

B. Curvilinear

Curvilinear negative relationships are illustrated by panels B and C of Figure 2–2. Panel B represents the relationship between points on an economics exam and points on a math exam. Let's say that both tests are given on the same day and that only 10 hours of study are available for the two. To have the graph intersect the two axes, assume that with zero hours of study, zero points are earned on each exam. Therefore, at the point of intersection on the vertical axis, 100 points are earned on the econ test and zero points on the math quiz. As the student takes a little time away from economics and devotes it to math, the math score rises by a larger amount than the econ score decreases. This is consistent with the example in panels B and C of Figure 2–1 where it took more time to learn the hardest material than the easiest. Therefore, if only one or two hours are taken away from econ and given to math, only a few points of the relatively hard econ material is given up but more points are earned on the math quiz because the easiest material is learned first. At the other extreme, the last few hours taken from econ causes a large loss of points compared to what is gained in math. A graph that bends out and away from the origin is called *concave to the origin*. Such a line decreases at an increasing rate.

Panel C of Figure 2–2 decreases at a decreasing rate. Such a line, which bends in toward the origin, is called *convex to the origin*. This line might represent a ski jumper coming off a ski jump. At the point where the line intersects the vertical axis, the ski jumper is ready to push off. Distance to the ground is at a maximum and speed is zero. Coming down the slide, distance to the ground decreases rapidly at first, and then decreases at a decreasing rate. At the point where the skier first touches the ground, speed is at a maximum. It is not necessary for the graph of a line convex to the origin to intersect either or both axes, although in this example, it does.

Graphs may or may not imply a cause-and-effect relationship between the two variables. In panels B and C of Figure 2–1, and panel B of Figure 2–2, it was implied that the amount of study time influences the grades on examinations. In other words, study is a cause and grades are an effect. The other panels just show a relationship between two variables. Most of the graphs used in economics imply some kind of cause-and-effect relationship.

GRAPHING NUMBERS

The preceding sections illustrated how specific values of the variables represented on the two axes can be determined from a graph or diagram. It should be stated, however, that the graphs are determined from numbers rather than the other way around. That is, one must obtain or be given specific values of the two variables before a graph can be drawn. In this section the numerical relationships that give rise to the various graphs discussed above are presented.

A. Positive Relationships

1. Linear.
An example of numbers that yield a linear positive relationship is given below.

Vertical axis	0	2	4	6	8
Horizontal axis	0	4	8	12	16

The preceding numbers would graph an upward-sloping line starting at the origin. (It is not necessary that all such lines start at the origin.) Notice that both variables move in the same direction—both go up or both go down. Because the difference between the numbers on both axes remains constant over the array, the graph will be a straight line. The vertical axis variable changes by two units each step, and the variable shown on the horizontal axis changes by four units. Both variables do not have to change by the same number of units each step, but the change of each variable must remain constant in each step over the array.

2. Slopes Up at an Increasing Rate.

Vertical axis	2	4	7	11	16
Horizontal axis	0	4	8	12	16

In this example, the vertical axis variable increases by larger and larger increments each successive step, while the horizontal axis variable increases by a constant amount. Hence, the line slopes up, or rises, at an increasing rate.

3. Slopes Up at a Decreasing Rate.

Vertical axis	1	6	10	13	15
Horizontal axis	0	4	8	12	16

In this example, the vertical axis variable increases by successively smaller increments each step, while the variable on the horizontal axis increases by a constant amount. Therefore, the line slopes up at a decreasing rate.

B. Negative Relationships

1. Linear.   Recall that a negative relationship exists when the two variables move in opposite directions—one up, the other down. The relationship is linear (straight line) if both change by constant amounts as shown below.

Vertical axis	20	15	10	5	0
Horizontal axis	0	4	8	12	16

2. Slopes Down at an Increasing Rate.

Vertical axis	20	18	14	8	0
Horizontal axis	0	4	8	12	16

In this case, the vertical axis variable decreases by larger and larger increments each step while the variable represented on the horizontal axis increases by a constant four units. Therefore, the line slopes down, or falls, at an increasing rate.

3. Slopes Down at a Decreasing Rate.

Vertical axis	20	12	6	2	0
Horizontal axis	0	4	8	12	16

Notice in this case, the vertical axis variable decreases by smaller and smaller increments, while the horizontal axis variable continues to increase by a constant four units. Consequently, the line decreases at a decreasing rate.

To summarize, there are two general classes of relationships—positive and negative. And within each of these there are three subclasses: linear, increasing rate, and decreasing rate.

SLOPE OF A LINE

The slope of a line is obtained by dividing a given change along the vertical axis by the corresponding change along the horizontal axis as shown in Figure 2–3. Change along the vertical axis is ΔV, and change along the horizontal axis is denoted by ΔH. An easy way to remember the numerator and denominator is to

FIGURE 2–3   Slope of a Line

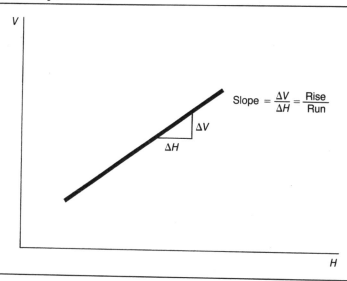

think of ΔV as the rise of the line and ΔH as the run. Thus slope is rise over run. Upward-sloping lines have a positive slope, and downward-sloping lines have a negative slope.

The slope of a straight line, linear positive or linear negative, remains constant at all points along the line. The slope of a curved line changes at different points along the line. The slope of an upward-sloping line that increases at an increasing rate becomes larger and larger at points higher on the line. If the line should become vertical, the slope becomes infinite. Conversely, the slope becomes successively smaller at points higher on an upward-sloping line that increases at a decreasing rate. If the line should become horizontal, the slope becomes zero.

As mentioned, the slope of a downward-sloping line is negative. The change from a larger to a smaller number is a negative change. When dividing a negative number by a positive value, or vice versa, the answer is always negative. Hence, the slope of a downward-sloping line is negative.

SUMMARY

A two-dimensional graph expresses a relationship between two variables. A positive relationship is expressed by an upward-sloping line and a negative relationship by a line that slopes downward. Both relationships can be either linear or curvilinear. The slope of a line is obtained by dividing the change along the vertical axis by the change along the horizontal axis: rise/run. The slope of a linear line is constant at all points along the line, whereas the slope of a curvilinear line changes at different points along the line.

YOU SHOULD KNOW

1. The shape of a graph expressing a linear positive relationship between two variables.
2. The shape of graphs expressing the two possible curvilinear positive relationships.
3. The shape of a graph expressing a linear negative relationship between two variables.
4. The shape of graphs expressing the two possible curvilinear negative relationships.
5. How to determine the shape of a graph from a table.
6. How to calculate the slope of a line.

QUESTIONS

1. On a graph, show the likely relationship between hours of study and points on an exam. Show points on the vertical axis and hours of study on the horizontal. Would the line be different for an average student than for a brilliant student? Explain.

2. *a.* Graph the relationship between earnings per week from part-time employment and average scores on exams during the term using the numbers in the following table:

Earnings	Points
$300	0
200	50
100	75
0	80

   Graph points on the vertical axis and earnings on the horizontal.
   b. Connect the points. What are the three ways of describing the shape of the line?
   c. What is the meaning of the line?

3. *a.* Draw an upward-sloping line that first increases at an increasing rate and then increases at a decreasing rate.
   b. Draw a downward-sloping line that first decreases at an increasing rate and then decreases at a decreasing rate.

4. Which of the two graphs in question 3 most accurately describes the relationship between hours of study per week on economics and average points on the examinations? Let points be on the vertical axis and hours of study on the horizontal.

5. *a.* What is the meaning of a vertical line that intersects the horizontal axis?
   b. What is the meaning of a horizontal line that intersects the vertical axis?

6. *a.* What is the slope of the line in panel A of Figure 2–1? What would be its slope if nickels were graphed along the vertical axis and dimes on the horizontal?
   b. Does the slope of an upward-sloping, straight line change at different points along the line? Explain. What about a downward-sloping, straight line?
   c. How does the slope of a line that is concave to the origin change as you move from points high on the curve to lower points?
   d. What are the slopes of the lines referred to in questions 5*a* and 5*b*?

SELF-TEST

1. A two-dimensional graph expresses the relationship between _____ variables.
   a. two
   b. three
   c. one or more
   d. an unlimited number of

2. A positive relationship between two variables exists when the variables move in:
   a. all directions.
   b. opposite directions.
   c. the same direction.
   d. a circular motion.

3. Two variables that exhibit a positive relationship are graphed by _____ line.
   a. an upward-sloping
   b. a downward-sloping
   c. a straight
   d. a curvilinear

4. A negative relationship between two variables exists when the variables move in:
   a. all directions.
   b. opposite directions.
   c. the same direction.
   d. a circular motion.

5. Two variables that exhibit a negative relationship are graphed by _____ line.
   a. an upward-sloping
   b. a downward-sloping
   c. a straight
   d. a curvilinear

6. A linear positive relationship is graphed by a _____ line.
   a. straight downward-sloping
   b. straight upward-sloping
   c. curvilinear upward-sloping
   d. curvilinear downward-sloping

7. A line that slopes up at an increasing rate expresses a _____ relationship between two variables.
   a. curvilinear positive
   b. curvilinear negative

   c. linear positive
   d. linear negative

8. A line that slopes up at a decreasing rate expresses a _____ relationship between two variables.
   a. curvilinear positive
   b. curvilinear negative
   c. linear positive
   d. linear negative

9. A line that slopes down at an increasing rate expresses a _____ relationship between two variables.
   a. curvilinear positive
   b. curvilinear negative
   c. linear positive
   d. linear negative

10. A line that slopes down at a decreasing rate expresses a _____ relationship between two variables.
    a. curvilinear positive
    b. curvilinear negative
    c. linear positive
    d. linear negative

11. A graph of the two variables shown below yields a line that slopes _____ at a(n) _____ rate.

Vertical axis	2	4	6	8	10
Horizontal axis	4	8	12	16	20

   a. upward; increasing
   b. upward; constant
   c. downward; increasing
   d. downward; constant

12. A graph of the two variables shown below yields a line that slopes _____ at a(n) _____ rate.

Vertical axis	5	4	3	4	1
Horizontal axis	1	2	3	4	5

a. upward; constant
b. upward; increasing
c. downward; constant
d. downward; decreasing

13. A graph of the two variables shown below yields a line that slopes ———— at a(n) ———— rate.

Vertical axis	100	95	80	50	0
Horizontal axis	0	20	40	60	80

a. downward; decreasing
b. downward; increasing
c. upward; decreasing
d. upward; increasing

14. A graph of the two variables shown below yields a line that slopes ———— at a(n) ———— rate.

Vertical axis	100	60	30	10	0
Horizontal axis	0	20	40	60	80

a. downward; decreasing
b. downward; increasing
c. upward; decreasing
d. upward; increasing

15. The slope of a line is obtained by dividing:
    a. the vertical axis by the horizontal axis.
    b. the change in the vertical axis by the change in the horizontal axis.
    c. the horizontal axis by the vertical axis.
    d. the change in the horizontal axis by the change in the vertical axis.

16. What is the slope of the line in question 14 of the segment extending from 100 to 60 on the vertical axis and 0 to 20 on the horizontal axis?
    a. −2   c. −1/2
    b. 2   d. 1/2

17. What is the slope of the line in question 14 of the segment extending from 10 to 0 on the vertical axis and 60 to 80 on the horizontal axis?
    a. −2   c. −1/2
    b. 2   d. 1/2

Chapter 3

Opportunity Cost

OVERVIEW

If one were to send a questionnaire to economists asking them to rank the 10 most important concepts in economics, opportunity cost would rank high on the list. After defining opportunity cost, this chapter presents the related ideas of the production possibilities schedule and the production possibilities curve, and it illustrates how they are useful for making economic decisions at all levels.

OPPORTUNITY COST DEFINED

Opportunity cost is defined as what has to be given up to obtain more of something else. Opportunity cost exists because resources are scarce. We cannot produce everything we want or would like. Thus, if we want more of something, we must be willing to settle for less of something else. Opportunity cost can be measured in either monetary or nonmonetary units.

The idea of opportunity cost was already introduced in Chapter 2, Figure 2–2, panel B, without calling it such. Recall that 10 hours were available to study for two exams—economics and mathematics. In that case, time was the scarce resource. Twenty hours of study could have yielded a perfect score in both. But only ten hours could be spared from other courses or activities. Thus, to obtain more points in one exam, a lower score must be accepted on the other.

PRODUCTION POSSIBILITIES SCHEDULE

The exact relationship between the two exam scores can be more easily seen with a *production possibilities schedule*. This is a table showing alternative combinations of two goods (exam scores) that can be produced from a given amount of resources (10 hours of study time).

Possibility	Economics Points	Mathematics Points
I	100. . .A	0. . .F
II	90. . .A	50. . .C
III	50. . .C	85. . .B
IV	0. . .F	100. . .A

From this table, it is possible to compute how much of one good must be given up to obtain an additional unit of the other good. Let us begin with possibility I and move to II. A useful formula to calculate the cost of each additional math point obtained is:

$$\text{Give up/Get} = 10/50 = 1/5 = .20$$

The ratio of two numbers gives the units of the top number per unit of the bottom number. Therefore, moving from I to II, each additional math point obtained costs 0.20 of an econ point. The opportunity costs of moving down the table among the other combinations are given below:

Possibility	Econ Points Given up for Each Math Point Obtained
I–II	.20
II–III	1.1
III–IV	3.3

One could begin with possibility IV and move up the table. In this case, more econ points are obtained by giving up math points.

Possibility	Math Points Given up for Each Econ Point Obtained
IV–III	.30
III–II	.88
II–I	5.0

Notice the increase in the size of the above numbers moving from one extreme to the other. At first, just a fraction of an econ point must be given up to obtain one more math point. This figure becomes successively larger in the next two steps. The same is true moving to higher econ scores. This example represents *increasing opportunity cost.* The cost of each additional unit of whatever is being increased becomes larger and larger as one approaches the maximum output of that item. Increasing opportunity cost occurred in that case because it became more time-consuming to add points the closer one came to the maximum 100; the hard material took longer to learn than the easy material.

Before leaving this example, you might ask, which combination of econ and math points (or letter grades) would the student choose? The two extremes where an F is obtained on one or the other exam most likely would be avoided. Aside from that, it is hard to tell. If the student wished to maximize grade points, possibility II is the best—a grade of A in econ and a C in math. However, if the student were a math major and wished to avoid a C in math, possibility III might be chosen—C in econ and a B in math. It is important to remember that when moving from one possibility to another, move only if what you get is worth more than what you give up.

PRODUCTION POSSIBILITIES CURVE

Plotting the numbers from a production possibilities schedule yields a *production possibilities curve,* as illustrated in Figure 3–1. This is a line showing various combinations of two goods that can be produced from a given amount of

FIGURE 3–1 Production Possibilities Curve Showing Increasing Opportunity Cost

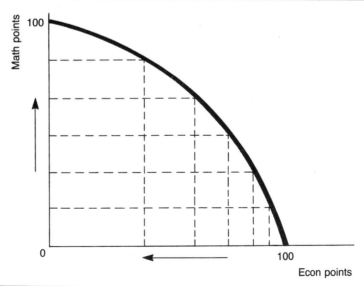

FIGURE 3–2 Production Possibilities Curve Showing Constant Opportunity Cost

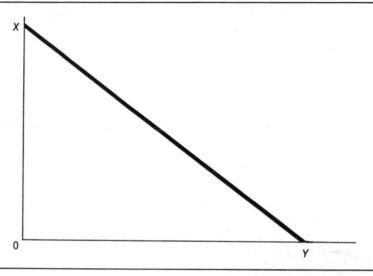

resources. Increasing opportunity cost always yields production possibility curves that are concave to the origin—they bend out. This can be seen by starting at the zero math/100 econ point combination and move up by equal increments along the math axis. The first block of math points obtained requires giving up only a small number of econ points. Notice, however, that each additional step up the math axis requires giving up a larger and larger number of econ points. This is increasing opportunity cost. The same holds true if one begins at the 100 math/zero econ combination and moves out by equal increments along the econ axis. You might try this with a diagram of your own.

It is virtually impossible to come up with realistic examples of *constant opportunity cost* where the cost of adding a unit of one good in terms of another good given up does not change over the entire range of observations. If such an example did exist, it would be characterized by a straight downward-sloping production possibilities curve such as in Figure 3–2.

SOCIAL CHOICES   Dividing the output of society

The production possibility curve is a useful device for illustrating choices that must be made by every society. Three important choices are: (1) the share of resources devoted to military goods versus nonmilitary production, often called "guns and butter," (2) public versus private goods, and (3) consumption versus investment.

FIGURE 3–3   War and Peace

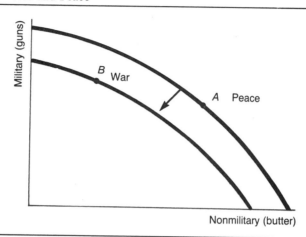

A. Guns versus Butter

Military goods are commonly referred to as "guns" and nonmilitary goods as "butter." A nation that needed to maintain a large military establishment or went to war with another nation would be located at point *B* on its production possibilities curve, as opposed to point *A* in Figure 3–3. The opportunity cost of the military is the nonmilitary goods and services given up. War also destroys resources—people and property. In countries ravaged by war, the production possibilities curve also shifts inward because of the loss of resources, as illustrated by the lower line in Figure 3–3.

B. Public versus Private Goods

Public goods are goods produced and/or distributed by government. In contrast to private goods, which are consumed by the individuals or families that purchase them, public goods are consumed by the society-at-large. Examples include public parks, streets and highways, the military, and police and fire protection. Governments also may subsidize certain kinds of private goods such as education, housing, food, and medical care, with the objective of helping low-income people attain the basic necessities of life.

The amount of public goods available to a society depends on its willingness to levy taxes to pay for these goods, and the wealth or total resources owned by a nation. Figure 3–4 illustrates the case where people living in a rich nation enjoy

FIGURE 3–4   Public versus Private Goods

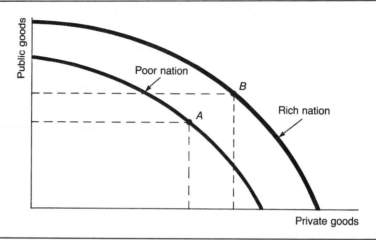

more of both public and private goods than the inhabitants of a poor nation. But given the wealth of a nation, the decision to produce more public goods must cause a reduction in private goods, and vice versa.

C. Consumption versus Investment

A third way to divide up the output of a society is between consumption and investment. Investment goods are capital such as buildings and machines that increase the total resources of a society. Investment is possible only if society is willing to forgo some consumer goods. However, in the long run, as a nation's stock of capital increases, the total resources of the country also increase. This in turn enables society to increase its production of consumer goods, leading to a higher standard of living. This phenomenon, called *economic growth,* is discussed in more detail at the end of this chapter and in the last two chapters of the book. The investment versus consumer goods trade-off can be illustrated with a diagram similar to Figure 3–4.

TRANSFERABILITY OF RESOURCES

Virtually all production possibilities curves drawn to illustrate social choices are concave to the origin. Recall that this implies increasing opportunity cost. This phenomenon is thought to exist for every society because resources are not equally productive in all uses. As a nation moves toward the extremes—the intersection of the curve with either axis—resources must be pressed into tasks for which they are not well-suited. Or, perhaps they cannot be used at all. For

FIGURE 3–5   Production Possibilities or Transformation Curve

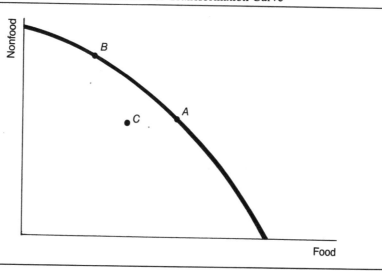

example, as a nation moved up and to the left past point *B* in Figure 3–5, farmland and machinery would become redundant. Thus, a small increase in nonfood output causes a large reduction in food production.

When a nation moves in small increments somewhere in the middle of the curve, *increasing* opportunity cost is not so evident. In this region, the resources that are suited to just one kind of production can be utilized in that area. The smaller incidence of increasing opportunity cost is especially true when time is allowed for resources to adjust to their new uses. For example, time allows farm people to acquire skills that are necessary for other occupations.

The production possibilities curve is also known as the *transformation curve.* As a nation moves along the curve, it transforms one kind of output into another. Moving from point *A* to point *B* in Figure 3–5 transforms food into other goods.

EFFICIENCY AND FULL EMPLOYMENT

When drawing a production possibilities or transformation curve, two implicit assumptions must be made: (1) resources are used efficiently, and (2) resources are fully employed. Much of the material in microeconomics deals with the attainment of maximum efficiency in resource use; reducing unemployment is an important issue in macroeconomics. If these assumptions are not met, the nation will be at a point below the surface of the curve—such as point *C* in Figure 3–5. By reducing unemployment or increasing efficiency, the nation can increase the output of both goods and improve its standard of living.

FIGURE 3–6 Production Possibilities Curve Illustrating Economic Growth

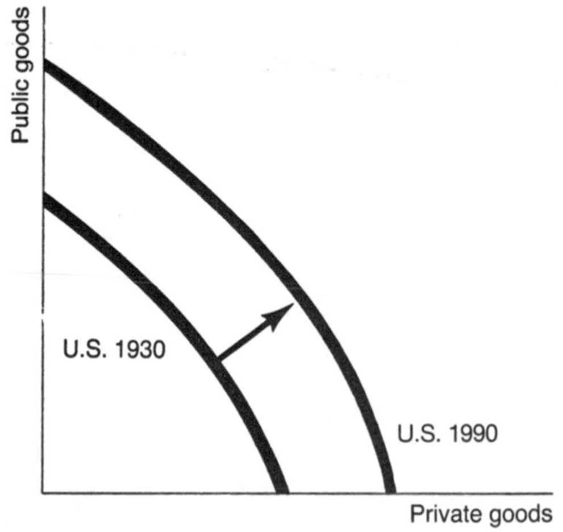

ECONOMIC GROWTH

An increase in the output of goods and services over time is known as *economic growth*. Sustained economic growth is attained only by an increase in a nation's resources. In recent history, nations have increased their resources mainly by producing more capital—both nonhuman and human. *Nonhuman capital* includes machines, tools, computers, buildings, roads, communications facilities, and so on. *Human capital* is the increase in knowledge made possible by research and education. Both forms of capital enhance the productivity of labor—thereby increasing society's per capita output.

Economic growth is illustrated by an outward shift of a nation's production possibilities curve, as in Figure 3–6. The increase in total resources increases the nation's ability to produce. The curve drawn in Figure 3–6 refers to *total* output of society. While an increase in total output is an acceptable definition of economic growth, standard of living will increase only if total output increases at a faster rate than population.

SUMMARY

Opportunity cost is defined as what has to be given up to obtain more of something else. It is measured by the formula: give up/get. A production possibility schedule lists alternative combinations of two goods that can be produced from a given quantity of resources. A production possibilities curve is a graph of a production possibilities schedule. Increasing opportunity cost occurs because resources are not equally productive in all uses. To be on the surface of its production possibilities curve, a nation must employ its resources efficiently and have full employment. To achieve economic growth, a nation must increase its resources. This is accomplished mainly through investment that produces more human and nonhuman capital.

YOU SHOULD KNOW

1. The definition of opportunity cost.
2. The meaning of a production possibilities table.
3. How to calculate opportunity cost from a production possibilities table.
4. The meaning of increasing opportunity cost.
5. The meaning of a production possibilities curve.
6. The shape of a production possibilities curve that expresses increasing opportunity cost.
7. The two requirements for being on the surface of a production possibilities curve.
8. What is required for economic growth to occur and how this is represented by a production possibilities curve.

QUESTIONS

1. Consider the following production possibilities schedule for a college student:

Possibility	Earnings from a Part-Time Job	Grade Points
I	$ 250	60
II	500	50
III	750	32
IV	1,000	4

   a. Calculate the opportunity cost of increasing earnings moving from possibility I to IV, one step at a time.
   b. Do the same calculation for increasing grade points moving from IV to I.
   c. What is the shape of the production possibilities curve drawn from these figures? What does it illustrate?
2. a. Would you expect increasing opportunity cost to be important in your allocation of time? Consider, for example, spending more of your time on economics and less on other subjects.
   b. In allocating an extra hour of study to a certain subject, what should be true of the return to this activity in comparison to the return to all other activities that could be done at the same time?
3. Consider the following production possibilities schedule:

Points on Econ Quiz	Points on Math Quiz
0	200
25	180
50	140
75	80
100	0

a. What is the opportunity cost of increasing econ points from 25 to 50? From 75 to 100? (Present your answer in terms of each econ point obtained.)

b. What is the opportunity cost of increasing math points from 80 to 140? From 180 to 200? (Present your answer in terms of each math point obtained.)

c. Does this example represent constant or increasing opportunity cost? Explain.

d. Represent this production possibilities schedule by a production possibilities curve.

4. Suppose that later in the day you have an hour available for anything you wish to do. What factors should you consider in deciding how to spend that hour?

5. *a.* What is the opportunity cost to you of this economics course?

b. What can be inferred from your decision to take this course rather than doing something else with your time and money?

6. Why is increasing opportunity cost a normally expected phenomenon in the economy?

7. Is it possible for a nation to increase the production of both goods represented on a transformation curve without adding to its stock of resources? Explain and illustrate.

8. Using a production possibilities curve, illustrate the following:

a. a nation goes to war.

b. a drought reduces food production.

c. economic growth.

d. unemployment.

SELF-TEST

1. Opportunity cost is:

a. the cost of producing opportunities.

b. $4.98.

c. what has to be given up to obtain more of something else.

d. what is obtained when a unit of something else is given up.

2. A production possibilities schedule is a table showing various possible combinations of two:

a. goods that can be produced by a fixed quantity of resources.

b. goods that yield a given level of satisfaction.

c. resources that can produce a given level of output.

d. resources that cost a given amount of money.

Answer questions 3–7 from the following production possibilities schedule.

Possibility	Hours Worked per Week on a Part- Time Job	Grade Points
I	0	60
II	10	50
III	20	30

3. The opportunity cost of increasing hours of work from 0 to 10 is _____ grade points per hour.

a. 5   *c.* 10

b. 1/5   *d.* 1

4. The opportunity cost of increasing hours of work from 10 to 20 is _____ grade points per hour.

a. 20   *c.* 2

b. 1/2   *d.* 1/10

5. The opportunity cost of increasing grade points from 30 to 50 is _____ hours per grade point.
   a. 2
   b. 10
   c. 1/2
   d. 20

6. The opportunity cost of increasing grade points from 50 to 60 is _____ hours per grade point.
   a. 1/10
   b. 10
   c. 5
   d. 1

7. This example depicts _____ opportunity cost.
   a. constant
   b. increasing
   c. decreasing
   d. zero

8. A production possibilities curve is a line showing various possible combinations of two:
   a. resources that will produce a given output.
   b. goods that cost a given amount.
   c. goods that can be produced from a given quantity of resources.
   d. resources that cost a given amount.

9. A production possibilities curve representing increasing opportunity cost is:
   a. convex to the origin.
   b. concave to the origin.
   c. a straight, downward-sloping line.
   d. a straight, upward-sloping line.

10. The two axes of a production possibilities curve represent:
    a. resources of inputs.
    b. dollars of resources or inputs.
    c. goods or outputs.
    d. dollars of goods or output.

11. When moving from one possibility to another, a person should make the move only if:
    a. what is obtained is worth more than what is given up.
    b. what is given up is worth more than what is obtained.
    c. nothing has to be given up.
    d. forced to do so.

12. Constant opportunity cost is depicted by a production possibilities curve that is:
    a. concave to the origin.
    b. convex to the origin.
    c. a straight, upward-sloping line.
    d. a straight, downward-sloping line.

13. When a country goes to war, the point at which the country is located on its production possibilities curve moves _____ if "guns" are represented on the vertical axis and "butter" on the horizontal. If the country also is ravaged by a war, the entire curve shifts _____ .
    a. up; out
    b. down; out
    c. up; in
    d. down; in

14. The production possibilities curve of a rich nation is _____ that of one for a poor nation. If either nation wishes to increase the amount of public goods it produces, it must give up _____ goods.
    a. inside; private
    b. inside; military
    c. outside; private
    d. outside; military

15. If a nation devotes most of its resources to the production of consumption goods, it cannot produce many _____ goods. As a result, the country _____ increase its output very much in the future.
    a. public; will not
    b. investment; will not
    c. public; will
    d. investment; will

16. Virtually all production possibilities curves are drawn _____ to the origin, which represents _____ opportunity cost. This situation is expected to prevail because resources _____ equally productive in all uses.
    a. convex; increasing; are not
    b. convex; decreasing; are
    c. concave; increasing; are not
    d. concave; decreasing; are

17. To be on the surface of its production possibilities curve a nation must:
    a. utilize its resources efficiently.
    b. have full employment.
    c. have stable prices.
    d. a and b.

18. Unemployment can be represented by a _____ of the production possibilities curve.
    a. point inside
    b. shift inward
    c. point outside
    d. shift outward

19. Economic growth is made possible by _____ and is represented by _____ of the production possibilities curve.
    a. investment; a point outside
    b. investment; an outward shift
    c. consumption; a point outside
    d. consumption; an outward shift

Chapter 4

Introduction to Demand and Supply

OVERVIEW

About half of the material in the introductory micro course is devoted to constructing and using the concepts of demand and supply. This chapter provides an introduction to demand and supply, and how they serve to determine prices in a market economy. This introduction should be sufficient to understand the material in this book that requires the use of these concepts.

DEMAND DEFINED

Let us begin with demand. We can define *demand* as a negative relationship between price and quantity. That is, when price is relatively high, the quantity of an item that people buy per week, per month, or per year will tend to be relatively low. Conversely, if price is relatively low, the amount that people buy tends to be somewhat greater.

The idea that people buy less of an item when its price is high and more when its price is low has a certain intuitive appeal. There are two reasons for this behavior. First, a relatively high price prompts people to look for lower-priced substitutes. For example, when the price of beef is high, people tend to cut back on beef consumption and eat more pork, chicken, fish, cheese, and other substitutes. On the other hand, when the price of beef is low, it becomes a substitute for other, relatively more expensive protein sources. A second reason people buy less of an item when its price increases is because their incomes do not go as far. In a sense, a higher price forces people to make do with a little less of the item. Conversely, if an item's price declines, people may use some of their increased purchasing power to buy more of the item.

FIGURE 4-1 A Demand Curve

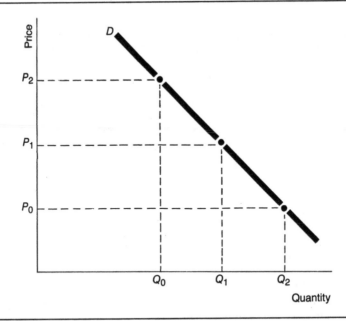

Economists often illustrate this relationship with a diagram. Price is placed on the vertical axis and quantity on the horizontal axis. By choosing various possible prices and observing the amounts people will buy at these prices, we can trace a downward-sloping line, as illustrated by Figure 4–1. For example, if price is high, say at P_2, quantity will be low at Q_0. As price declines to P_1 and P_0, quantity increases to Q_1 and Q_2, respectively. If we assume that the same relationship holds between these points as on the points, we can connect them and obtain a downward-sloping line. Economists call this a *demand curve*, even though it is often drawn as a straight, downward-sloping line.

SUPPLY DEFINED

Let us turn next to the concept of supply. Supply is defined as a positive relationship between price and quantity. When price is relatively high, the quantity of an item that producers or sellers will place on the market tends to be relatively large. Conversely, when price is relatively low, the quantity supplied also will be low.

The idea that producers will place more on the market when price is high and less when price is low also is intuitively appealing. In this case, a high price

FIGURE 4–2 A Supply Curve

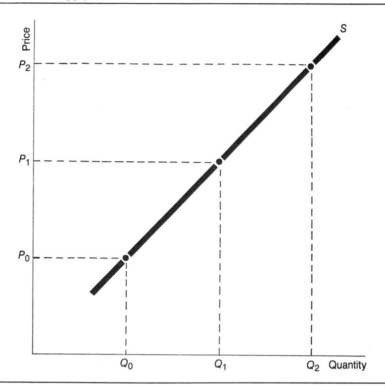

provides an incentive for producers to increase output because their profits will be greater than when price is low, other things being equal. And the prospect of relatively high profits tends to result in producers' cutting back on less profitable activities and increasing the output of the high-priced item. For example, if shoes are high priced, shoe manufacturers may build more manufacturing capacity for shoes and cut back on the production of other items. Also, there will be a tendency for producers of other less profitable items to switch to shoes in an effort to "get a piece of the action." The opposite occurs if shoe prices are low relative to prices of other goods and services. Some shoe manufacturers may get out of the shoe-manufacturing business entirely, while others may cut back shoe production in an attempt to expand output of more profitable things.

As in the case of demand, economists often illustrate the supply relationship with a diagram, again placing price on the vertical axis and quantity on the horizontal axis. With a positive relationship between price and quantity, the observed points trace out an upward-sloping line, as illustrated by Figure 4–2. For example, if price is relatively high, say at P_2, quantity supplied also will be high, as indicated by Q_2. As price declines to P_1 and P_0, quantity supplied also declines to Q_1 and Q_0, respectively. Economists call the line that is traced out by this price-quantity relationship a *supply curve,* even though it is often drawn as a straight, upward-sloping line.

EQUILIBRIUM PRICE AND QUANTITY

It is important to recognize that demand alone, or supply alone, cannot tell us which price and quantity will actually exist. They only tell us the various possible prices and quantities that might prevail. But when we combine the two concepts, the exact market price and quantity can readily be determined. The demand and supply curves are something like two blades of a scissors; both are necessary to do the job.

The process of price and quantity determination can best be understood by superimposing the demand and supply curves on the same diagram, as shown by Figure 4–3. This is possible because both have price on the vertical axis and quantity on the horizontal axis.

Perhaps the easiest way to see which price will prevail is to begin with a

FIGURE 4–3   Determination of Equilibrium Price and Quantity

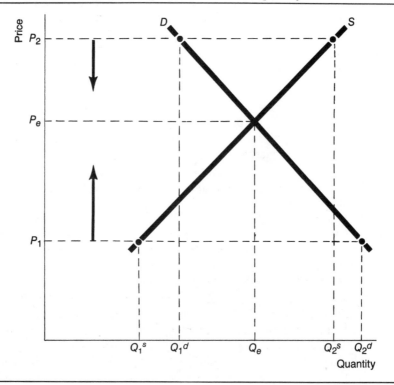

price that would not be likely to prevail, at least for long, say the high price P_2. At this price, consumers buy a relatively small amount, Q_1^d, but producers supply a relatively large amount, Q_2^s. As you can see, the outcome of this situation would be a surplus of unsold goods or services. As a result, there would be a downward pressure on price. Some buyers, seeing the glut in the market, may press sellers to lower the price. And some sellers, seeing the buildup of inventories, may initiate some price reductions in an effort to entice buyers to take a larger amount of their output.

Alternatively, let's see what happens if price is relatively low, say at P_1. In this case, quantity demanded, as shown by Q_2^d, is larger than quantity supplied, Q_1^s. Now there will be a shortage of the item as demanders indicate a willingness to buy more than suppliers wish to sell. At this low price, some buyers are not able to obtain all they would like to buy, while some sellers are experiencing empty shelves or are drawing down their inventories. As a consequence, some buyers will be likely to offer sellers a higher price in order to obtain some of the scarce good. Also, we can be quite sure that at least some sellers will ask for a higher price as long as they can be sure of selling their entire stock.

So far, we have seen that neither the high price P_2 nor the low price P_1 could long prevail in the market. Forces are present to drive P_2 down or P_1 up. By now it is probably evident that there is only one price, P_e, that can prevail without the presence of downward or upward pressure, for at price P_e buyers are willing to take off the market exactly the same quantity that sellers are willing to offer. In other words, the market is in equilibrium. For this reason, P_e and Q_e often are referred to as equilibrium price and quantity, respectively.

One might conclude at this point that once a market gets into equilibrium, price and quantity should remain unchanged for all time to come. Right? Wrong! What happens in virtually all markets is that the demand and supply curves themselves are continually shifting or changing positions. Once they are in a new position, equilibrium price, quantity, or both are likely to be different. Once this occurs, the equilibrating process must start over again.

SHIFTS IN DEMAND

The two possible shifts in demand are illustrated in Figure 4–4. The shift to the right from D_1 to D_2 represents an *increase* in demand. This means buyers are willing to take a larger quantity off the market at any given price. On the other hand, a shift to the left from D_1 to D_0 is referred to as a *decrease* in demand. In this situation, buyers decrease the quantity they will take off the market at any given price. The reasons demand may increase or decrease are discussed briefly in the section on demand shifters.

Notice the effects of shifts in demand on the equilibrium price and quantity. When demand increases, both price and quantity increase. Intuitively this makes sense. When people want to buy more of something they will generally bid up the price of the item, and producers are likely to respond by increasing its production

FIGURE 4–4 Shifts in Demand

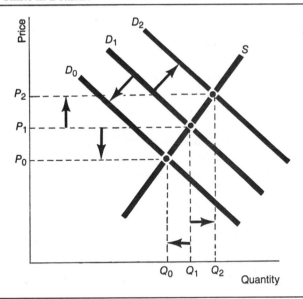

as it becomes more profitable. Conversely, when demand decreases, the equilibrium price and quantity both decrease. In this case, the decrease in the desire of buyers to purchase the product causes a decrease in its price, and producers respond by decreasing the output of this item because it now has become less profitable.

SHIFTS IN SUPPLY

Figure 4–5 is intended to illustrate the two possible shifts in supply. The shift to the right from S_1 to S_2 represents an *increase* in supply. This means sellers become willing to place a larger quantity on the market at any given price. On the other hand, a shift to the left from S_1 to S_0 is a *decrease* in supply. In this situation, sellers decrease the quantity they will place on the market at any given price. The reasons supply may increase or decrease are discussed briefly in the section on supply shifters.

Notice the effects of the shifts in supply on the equilibrium price and quantity. When supply increases, quantity increases but price decreases. As sellers place a greater quantity of the item on the market, it becomes more plentiful, and its price declines. As price declines, buyers now find this item a better buy, and as a result they become willing to take more off the market. Conversely, a decrease in supply causes an increase in price because the good in question becomes less plentiful. The higher price discourages people from buying it, so quantity decreases.

Before turning to the factors that cause demand and supply to shift, a distinction

FIGURE 4–5 Shifts in Supply

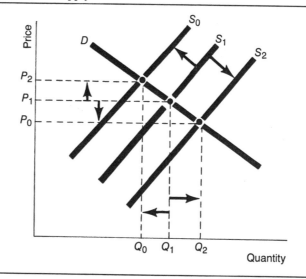

should be drawn between a change (shift) in demand or supply and a change in the quantity demanded or supplied. For example, an *increase in demand* refers to a shift to the right by the demand curve, whereas an *increase in quantity demanded* refers to a movement downward along a given demand curve. The latter would be caused by an increase in supply. The same distinctions should be made between a *decrease in demand* and a *decrease in quantity demanded*. The latter would be caused by a decrease in supply.

The same terminology should be applied to the supply side. For example, an *increase in supply* refers to a shift to the right by the supply curve, whereas an *increase in quantity supplied* refers to a movement upward along the supply curve. This movement would be caused by an increase in demand. The same is true for a *decrease in supply* and a *decrease in quantity supplied*.

 Keep in mind that a change in price does not cause a change (shift) in demand or supply. Because price is shown on the vertical axis of the demand-supply diagram, a change in price just causes a movement up or down along the same demand and supply curves. Let us now briefly consider the main factors that cause shifts in the demand and supply curves. There are five demand shifters and five supply shifters that apply to most goods and services.

DEMAND SHIFTERS

1. Changes in Prices of Related Goods or Services. The demand for a good, say pork, will increase if the price of a substitute good, such as beef, increases. Consumers, in an attempt to avoid buying as much of the higher-priced beef, increase their purchases of pork, thereby increasing the demand for pork, that is, shifting the demand for pork to the right. The opposite would, of course, hold true if the price of a substitute good declined.

2. Changes in Money Incomes of Consumers.   The demand for most goods and services tends to increase or shift to the right as the money income of consumers increases.[1] Again, this is reasonable to expect; when we have more money to spend, we are able to increase our purchases of certain items. By the same token, a decrease in consumer incomes, say because of an increase in unemployment, tends to decrease the demand for many items, that is, shift it to the left.

3. Changes in Expectations of Consumers Regarding Future Prices and Incomes.   If consumers expect the price of an item to increase in the future, they are likely to attempt to increase their rates of purchase of the item in order to stock up before the price rise. Similarly, if people expect their future incomes to be larger than their present incomes, we can expect them to buy more at the present than if they expected "hard times" ahead. The opposite would be true, of course, for expected lower prices or incomes in the future.

4. Changes in Tastes and Preferences.   Sometimes people will step up their purchases of an item if they suddenly take a liking to it. For example, the demands for motorcycles and blue jeans have increased in recent years. On the other hand, yo-yos and bobby socks no longer are "in."

5. Changes in Number of Consumers.   The total market demand for an item will be greater as the number of consumers in the market increases. Nationwide, the demand for most goods and services has been shifting to the right because of population growth. Of course, in places where population has declined, such as in rural areas and small towns during the 1950s and 1960s, the demand for most goods and services also declined.

These five demand shifters include those that apply to most goods and services. There may be other demand shifters that occur because of special circumstances. For example, if the purchase of a good or service is illegal and subject to a stiff penalty, people may decide the risk is not worth taking and therefore refrain from buying it. The markets for illegal goods and services are discussed in greater detail in Chapter 13 of the companion micro text.

SUPPLY SHIFTERS

1. Changes in the Prices of Resources.   A decrease in the price of resources (hence a decrease in production costs) increases the supply of the item produced, that is, shifting its supply to the right. As costs decline, producers can sell an item

---

[1] Some exceptions include cold-water flats, old-fashioned washboards, and starchy foods.

for a lower price and still retain their previous profit margins. (Bear in mind that an increase in supply also means producers are willing to supply a given quantity for a lower price.) An increase in resource prices has the opposite effect, namely, to decrease supply, or shift it to the left.

2. Changes in Prices of Alternative Items that May Be Produced.

If there is a decrease in the prices of other goods or services that require about the same kinds of resources to produce, then we can expect the supply of the item in question to increase. For example, a firm that is producing both footballs and basketballs will likely increase its supply of footballs if the market price of basketballs decreases. On the other hand, an increase in the price of an item can be expected to decrease the supply of alternative goods or services.

3. Changes in Expectations of Producers Regarding Future Prices.

If producers expect the prices of their products to decrease in the future, they may sell part of their inventories, thereby increasing the present supply, in order to take advantage of favorable prices at the present. Accordingly, if producers expect higher prices in the future, they may decrease their present supplies in order to have more to sell when price is expected to be higher.

4. Changes in Technology.

A change in technology always increases the supply of the item being produced because it lowers production costs. If the new technology did not lower production costs, producers would not adopt it.

5. Changes in Number of Producers.

The total market supply of an item will increase if the number of producers increases, assuming the average size of the producers remains constant. Finally, the supply of a good or service will decline or shift to the left with a decrease in the number of producers, again assuming no change in the average size of producers.

These five supply shifters include those that apply to most goods and services. There may be other supply shifters that occur because of special circumstances. For example, in the production of food, changes in weather or growing conditions represent an important supply shifter. Unusually good weather should bring forth an increase in the supply of these products. However, unfavorable conditions, such as drought, likely will decrease supply, that is, shift the supply curve to the left.

SUMMARY

Demand is defined as a negative relationship between price and quantity. When the price of an item increases, other things equal, people buy less of it because the item is now more expensive relative to substitute goods and because their income doesn't go as far. Supply is defined as a positive relationship between price and quantity. Sellers place more on the market when the price is high, other things equal, in a desire to increase their income or profits. Equilibrium price and quantity correspond to the intersection of the demand and supply curves. They change in response to shifts in demand, supply, or both.

YOU SHOULD KNOW

1. The definition of demand.
2. The two reasons why people buy more of a product when its price declines.
3. The definition of supply.
4. Why suppliers place more of a product on the market when its price increases.
5. What equilibrium price and quantity are and how to represent them on a diagram.
6. The meaning of a shift or change in demand.
7. The meaning of a shift or change in supply.
8. The five demand shifters.
9. The five supply shifters.

QUESTIONS

1. *a.* What is demand?
   b. Why do people tend to buy less of a good when its price increases and more when its price decreases? Illustrate this relationship with a demand curve.
2. *a.* What is supply?
   b. Why do producers tend to produce more when price increases and less when price decreases? Illustrate this relationship with a supply curve.
3. Under what conditions will there be a surplus of a product? A shortage?
4. *a.* According to the theory of demand, is it possible for consumers to want to buy more of a product at a given price? Explain.
   b. According to the theory of supply, is it possible for a producer to want to sell more of a product at a given price? Explain.
5. Explain how each of the following circumstances would affect the demand for U.S. automobiles. Also indicate what would happen to the equilibrium price and quantity of this product, assuming no change in supply.

   a. The price of foreign cars increases.
   b. The money incomes of consumers increase.
   c. Consumers expect higher prices next year.
   d. Consumers change their preference toward European styling.
   e. Population increases.
6. Explain how each of the following circumstances would affect the supply of cookies. Also indicate what would happen to the equilibrium price and quantity of this product, assuming no change in demand.
   a. The price of labor increases.
   b. There is an increase in the price of doughnuts, an alternative product that can be produced.
   c. Producers expect higher prices next month.
   d. New, more efficient cookie-forming machines become available.
   e. There is an increase in the number of cookie-producing firms of a given size.

SELF-TEST *check All*

1. Demand is a _____ relationship between _____ and _____ .
   a. positive; price; quantity
   b. positive; income; purchases
   c. negative; price; quantity
   d. negative; income; purchases
2. The diagram depicting a demand curve has _____ on the vertical axis and _____ on the horizontal axis.
   a. price; quantity
   b. income; quantity
   c. quantity; price
   d. quantity; income
3. A demand curve is drawn _____ sloping because when price is high, other things equal, quantity demanded will be relatively _____ .
   a. upward; low
   b. downward; high
   c. upward; high
   d. downward; low
4. When the price of a good increases people purchase less of it because:
   a. they attempt to purchase lower-priced substitutes.
   b. their income doesn't go as far.
   c. of inflation.
   d. a and b.
5. Supply is a _____ relationship between _____ and _____ .
   a. positive; price; quantity
   b. position; profits; production
   c. negative; price; quantity
   d. negative; profits; production
6. The diagram depicting a supply curve has _____ on the vertical axis and _____ on the horizontal axis.
   a. price; quantity
   b. quantity; price
   c. profits; quantity
   d. quantity; profits
7. A supply curve is drawn _____ sloping

because when price is high, other things equal, quantity supplied will be relatively _____ .
   a. upward; low
   b. downward; high
   c. upward; high
   d. downward; low
8. When the price of a good increases, producers tend to place more of it on the market to:
   a. increase their profits.
   b. decrease their costs.
   c. decrease their profits.
   d. increase their costs.
9. If actual price is higher than the equilibrium price, there will be a _____ causing the actual price to _____ .
   a. shortage; decrease
   b. shortage; increase
   c. surplus; decrease
   d. surplus; increase
10. If actual price is below the equilibrium price, there will be a _____ causing the actual price to _____ .
   a. shortage; decrease
   b. shortage; increase
   c. surplus; decrease
   d. surplus; increase
11. An increase in demand refers to a situation where the entire demand curve shifts to the _____ , which means people will purchase _____ of the item at any given price.
   a. right; more
   b. right; less
   c. left; more
   d. left; less
12. An increase in demand causes equilibrium price in the market to _____ and quantity to _____ .
   a. increase; decrease
   b. increase; increase

c. decrease; decrease

d. decrease; increase

13. An increase in supply refers to a situation where the entire supply curve shifts to the _____ , which means sellers will place _____ quantity on the market at any given price.
    a. right; more   c. left; more
    b. right; less   d. left; less

14. An increase in supply causes equilibrium price in the market to _____ and quantity to _____ .
    a. increase; decrease
    b. increase; increase
    c. decrease; decrease
    d. decrease; increase

15. An increase in demand causes an increase in _____ while an increase in supply causes an increase in _____ .
    a. supply; demand
    b. quantity supplied; quantity demanded

c. supply; quantity demanded

d. quantity supplied; demand

16. Which of the following would cause an increase in demand for new American-made cars?
    a. increase in price of European-made cars
    b. decrease in price of Japanese-imported cars
    c. increase in money incomes of car buyers
    d. a and c

17. Which of the following would cause an increase in supply of personal computers?
    a. increase in prices of typewriters, an alternative product that can be produced
    b. increase in the price of personal computers
    c. improvement in technology for producing personal computers
    d. b and c

Part II

The Macro Economy

Chapter 5

Unemployment

OVERVIEW

This and the following chapter are intended to provide background information on the two main problems that justify the study of macroeconomics: unemployment and inflation. This chapter focuses on unemployment—how it is measured, some problems of its measurement, the magnitude of the problem, who are the unemployed, and the duration of unemployment.

FULL EMPLOYMENT DEFINED

Perhaps the best way to begin the discussion of unemployment is to define the meaning of full employment. *Full employment* exists when everyone who is willing and able to work at the prevailing wage rate can find a job in the line of work for which he or she is qualified.

There are several points worth noting in this definition. First, full employment, or unemployment, as used in the context of macroeconomics generally refers to people rather than capital, that is, buildings, machines, land, and other supplies. As a rule, society has not been as concerned with the unemployment of nonhuman inputs as with the unemployment of human beings. It is not difficult to understand why. Machines or buildings do not become hungry or cold if their income stops, nor do they suffer from the psychological ills of being idle. Yet we should not dismiss the problem of unemployed capital entirely. For one thing, the employment of human beings is often tied to the employment of capital. This is illustrated by the increase in unemployment brought on by the closing of a factory or mine, especially in a small community. We should also bear in mind that all capital is owned by human beings. Hence, a reduction in the earnings of capital means a reduction in the earnings of the owners of capital. Moreover we should not lose sight of the fact that capital, as well as labor, contributes to the total output of society. Thus, if some capital is unemployed, the total output that is available to society will be less than maximum.

51

A second point to note about the definition of full employment is that at full employment not every adult need be gainfully employed. For example, full-time college students, homemakers who choose not to work outside the home, and retired people would not be considered employed. This is not to say that these people are idle or "nonproductive"; it is just that they are not considered part of the labor force. Also, there are a few people who have decided that work is too distasteful and have removed themselves from the labor force.

A third subtle but fairly important point in the definition of full employment relates to the willingness of people to take jobs that are available. For example, consider the case of a $500-per-week construction worker who is laid off. If no other construction jobs are available in the area, the worker files for unemployment insurance and is considered unemployed. The fact that this person is unemployed, however, does not mean he or she is unemployable. There may be other jobs available that the construction worker would be qualified for, such as factory worker, but chooses not to accept. Rather than work in a different occupation, this person chooses to be unemployed.

This is not intended to be a criticism of the construction worker or anyone who decides on this action. For the individual, it can be the most rational thing to do. If a person expects to be back at work again in a few weeks, it may not pay to seek another job. Certainly if a person's unemployment compensation approaches the take-home pay of another, lower-paying job, there is not much incentive to take such a job. Of course, if a person is unemployed for a prolonged period so that unemployment payments run out, then the unemployed person might be more willing to accept a less desirable job. The main point is that a certain amount of unemployment may refer to unemployment from a specific job or line of work rather than not being able to find any job at all.

We should also be aware that some unemployed people probably would be willing to work at their previous jobs for a lower wage rather than be out of work altogether. For example, the construction worker may be willing to work for $300 per week rather than being forced to accept, say, $150 per week in unemployment compensation or $250 per week at an alternative job.

Unfortunately for the unemployed, wage rates tend to be rather inflexible on the down side. If a choice is to be made between an across-the-board wage cut and a layoff of the most recently hired people, both employers and labor unions tend to favor the latter alternative. A reduction in wages affects all employees of a firm or industry and, needless to say, does not make them very happy. And both employers and labor unions are reluctant to antagonize the rank and file of the labor force. No firm with disgruntled employees can prosper, and a labor union cannot be a very effective bargaining agent if its members have the feeling of being sold out. The other alternative, laying off the youngest and least-skilled workers, affects only a small part of the labor force. Once they have left, they are no longer disgruntled employees who can cause disruptions in production. Nor do these people have much power within labor unions; many are not even members.

The main point to remember here is that there is something of a built-in incentive for both employers and labor unions to choose unemployment over lower wages. At least some unemployed people would probably choose to work at their old jobs at less than the prevailing wage rather than be unemployed, but they seldom have the opportunity to make this choice. Of course, when unemployment in a firm or industry becomes so long-term and severe that a company's survival comes into question, wage reductions do occur. During the Great Depression of the 1930s, virtually all money wages declined. Wage reductions also occurred in the early 1980s when unemployment again became abnormally high, especially in the auto industry. It is nice to have a job at high wages, but when it comes to the choice of having no job versus one at lower wages, workers generally accept the latter, particularly when unemployment compensation runs out.

The unemployment that results from the stickiness or inflexibility of wages can be illustrated by a demand and supply diagram for labor. If an industry or an economy experiences a decrease in sales, the demand for labor will decrease, as illustrated by the shift down and to the left of the demand for labor in Figure 5–1. If the actual wage declined from W_1, to W_0, there would be no increase in unemployment. Everyone who wanted to work at this wage could find a job.

FIGURE 5–1   Wage Stickiness and Unemployment

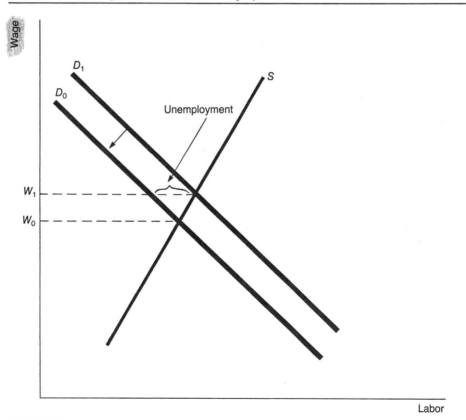

However, as explained above, employers and unions are reluctant to lower wages, thereby antagonizing employees. If the wage remains at W_1, the difference between the quantity of labor demanded and the quantity supplied represents the unemployed.

The reluctance of workers to accept lower wages is understandable. But unemployment or the threat of unemployment is not appealing either. One method of reducing the severity of the unemployment problem when sales and the demand for labor decline is to provide a share of labor earnings through profit sharing. This means that an employee's guaranteed or base wage would be lower than with a pure wage arrangement, but the remainder would be made up by sharing in the profits of the firm. In the event of a decline in the firm's sales, total employee compensation would decrease because of lower profits. This would lower costs and enable the firm to decrease the price of its product and maintain a larger quantity of sales than without the price cut. Once the market recovered, higher profits would restore employee compensation to the former higher level automatically.

This system also would be advantageous during an inflationary time when hourly wages may initially lag behind cost-of-living increases, precipitating strikes. During inflation, part of the higher profits resulting from higher product prices would automatically be distributed to employees, allowing them to maintain their standard of living without negotiated wage increases.

Another advantage of profit sharing is the increased incentive of employees to work hard and do their best to maximize the firm's efficiency, product quality, and profits. By doing so, the employees help themselves as well as their employer.

THE UNEMPLOYMENT RATE

Figures on the number of unemployed people in the United States are gathered each month by the Bureau of Labor Statistics from a sample of about 60,000 households. Living quarters rather than people are selected for the survey. About 15,000 groups of addresses, each including about four dwellings that are relatively close together, are selected to be representative of the entire country. The occupants of a selected dwelling are visited by an interviewer for eight months—four consecutive months in the current year and the same four months in the following year.

In order to determine the unemployment rate, figures must be gathered on both employed and unemployed individuals. *Employed* people include those 16 years of age or older who:

1. Did any work at all during the survey week as paid employees.
2. Worked in their own businesses or professions.
3. Worked 15 hours per week or more as an "unpaid" member of a family farm or business.
4. Were temporarily absent from their jobs for reasons such as illness, vacation, strike, or bad weather.

TABLE 5–1   U.S. Population and Labor Force Statistics, 1989

Noninstitutional population, 16 and over	186.4 million
Labor force*	125.6 million
Employed	119.0 million
Unemployed	6.6 million
Unemployed rate	5.3 percent

* Includes armed forces.

Source: *Economic Report of the President,* 1990, p. 330.

To be counted among the *unemployed,* an individual 16 years or older must have:

1. Not worked during the survey week.
2. Made specific efforts to find work within the past four weeks of the survey.
3. Been available for work during the survey week.

The labor force is defined as the sum of the employed plus unemployed:

$$\text{Labor force} = \text{Employed} + \text{Unemployed}$$

The *unemployment rate* is computed by dividing the number of unemployed people by the number in the labor force and multiplying by 100 to convert to a percent:

$$\text{Unemployment rate} = \frac{\text{Unemployed}}{\text{Labor force}} \times 100$$

The figures in Table 5–1 provide an indication of the relative size of each of these groups in the United States in 1989. At that time, the labor force (employed plus unemployed) made up about 67 percent of the total noninstitutional population over the age of 16. This number is referred to as the *labor force participation rate*.

FRICTIONAL UNEMPLOYMENT

From the discussion thus far, it might appear that any unemployment at all is undesirable and that we should not be satisfied until we attain a goal of zero unemployment. Would such a goal be reasonable or even desirable? Probably not. We should bear in mind that the economy is continually changing and adapting to new opportunities. Very few business activities continue to remain unchanged month after month, much less year after year. As a result, we may observe a temporary loss of work for certain employees because of short-term fluctuations in business activity, changes in employment opportunities, or a voluntary termination of work because of a desire to change jobs. Unemployment resulting from the above circumstances is called *frictional unemployment,* reflecting the idea that changes in the economy require adjustments that do not occur immediately or without some cost in terms of unemployment.

We know that many occupations experience busy and slack seasons during the year. Construction work, for example, typically has experienced a seasonal decline during the winter. People who work in this industry expect temporary layoffs, and their salaries during the busy season generally compensate them for this. Another example occurs in the auto industry, where a company may lay off part of its labor force for a week or two in order to bring its inventory back to a desired level.

It is a common occurrence as well in a dynamic, growing economy for employment opportunities to change. Because of changes in consumer demand, some firms or industries decline and fade away, only to be replaced by others. Workers who find themselves in declining industries or firms must relocate to other growing industries. Even though there may be other comparable jobs available, most people prefer to take some time to search out the best.

Related to this is the unemployment brought about by employees who quit their jobs in order to seek more desirable ones. In many cases, people cannot take time off to interview and search while holding a full-time job. Anyone who has gone through a job search knows that it can be very time-consuming. Sometimes a new job requires traveling, buying and selling a house, or finding a different apartment. Probably most people who quit a job for one reason or another are reasonably certain of finding another. And in most cases, they succeed within a few weeks. Their earnings may have been temporarily interrupted, but in the long run they are able to make up the loss in their new and better jobs.

Frictional unemployment appears to have increased during the 1960s and 1970s. In the early 1960s, the most frequently quoted figures tended to be in the range of a 3 to 4 percent unemployment rate. In more recent years, figures in the 5 to 6 percent range are commonly quoted. There are a number of possible reasons for the increase. One is the increase in part-time employment of high school and college students. Because these people tend to enter and leave the labor force more frequently than full-time workers, a greater proportion of the labor force will be looking for jobs at any given time, and a higher unemployment rate will result. In addition, an increase in unemployment compensation and welfare benefits is likely to increase the unemployment rate because people can be more selective in taking new jobs after they have been laid off. Indeed, some welfare programs require people to be unemployed to collect benefits; by meeting the requirements of the program, the beneficiaries increase the unemployment rate.

One might expect the state of the economy itself also to influence the level of frictional unemployment. If the economy is sluggish and jobs are hard to find, we would expect the time it takes a person to relocate in a new job after being laid off from a declining business—or voluntarily leaving a former job—to be longer than when the economy is booming and the labor market is tight. For example, during World War II, the total U.S. unemployment rate dipped to between 1 and 2 percent.

The main point to be drawn from this section is that some fraction of the labor force, normally between 5 and 6 percent, can be expected to be temporarily out of work because of adjustments in the economy and movement between jobs. For purposes of economic policy, the economy can be considered at or near full employment if the rate of unemployment is at this order of magnitude. Our main interest in the discussion relating to unemployment will be with situations where the total economy experiences a slowdown in economic activity and the overall unemployment rate rises above the 5 to 6 percent range.

U.S. UNEMPLOYMENT RECORD

Looking back over the past half-century, we observe substantial variations in the U.S. unemployment rate. As shown in Table 5–2, with an unemployment rate of 3.2 percent, 1929 was a year of relatively full employment. Then came the crash. Four years later, in 1933, the United States, in the depth of the Great Depression, suffered from an astronomical unemployment rate of 24.9 percent. We will have more to say about the Great Depression in later chapters.

The Great Depression was no overnight sensation, however; it lasted all the way through the 1930s. In 1939, just before the U.S. entry into World War II, unemployment still was as high as 17.2 percent. Then, at the height of World War II, 1944, unemployment fell to an almost unbelievable low of 1.2 percent. The drain of manpower into the military and the strong demand for labor undoubtedly contributed to this low figure.

TABLE 5–2   U.S. Unemployment Rates, Selected Years, 1929–1989

Year	Unemployment Rate	Year	Unemployment Rate
1929	3.2%	1980	7.1%
1934	21.7	1981	7.5
1939	17.2	1982	9.5
1944	1.2	1983	9.5
1949	5.9	1984	7.4
1954	5.5	1985	7.2
1959	5.5	1986	7.0
1964	5.2	1987	6.2
1969	3.5	1988	5.5
1974	5.6	1989	5.3
1979	5.8		

Source: *Economic Report of the President*, 1990, p. 330.

The return to a peacetime economy was accompanied by a rise in unemployment, reaching 5.9 percent in 1949. During the Korean conflict, the unemployment rate again declined, reaching a low of 2.9 percent in 1953. Toward the end of the 1950s, the country found itself in the "1958 recession" with an unemployment rate of 6.8 percent.[1] Unemployment tended to drift downward during the 1960s, particularly during the Vietnam buildup toward the latter part of the decade. However, coinciding with the U.S. troop withdrawals from Vietnam and attempts to reduce inflation, the U.S. unemployment rate exhibited a sharp upswing during the early 1970s, rising to 8.5 percent in 1975. After a slight dip during the late 1970s, the unemployment rate exhibited another increase in the early 1980s, coinciding with the Reagan administration's attempt to reduce inflation and the size of the federal government.

It is fairly evident from these figures that war and low rates of unemployment tend to be positively correlated. During the periods when the United States was involved in World War II, Korea, and Vietnam, the onset of hostilities was followed by a decrease in unemployment, while the return to peacetime was accompanied by a rise in unemployment.

Is war therefore a necessary condition for full employment? We will be better able to answer this question in later chapters. For now, it is sufficient to say that large increases in military personnel and spending no doubt contribute to reducing unemployment and increasing inflation. After each war, the release of military personnel and reduction in military spending along with government efforts to control inflation are likely to increase unemployment. One might argue, therefore, that war causes both inflation and unemployment but at different times.

DURATION OF UNEMPLOYMENT

So far we have been concerned mainly with the total amount of unemployment in the economy. But we should also consider how long the unemployed are out of work. It is one thing to be out of work for two or three weeks but quite another to lose one's main income for a year or more. The first case might result in a strained budget, but the second could mean the loss of home or car, or even hunger for the family. Thus, we should be as concerned about the duration of unemployment as about the unemployment rate.

Figures showing the average number of weeks the unemployed were out of work in 1989 are presented in Table 5–3. It is somewhat encouraging to see that 49 percent of those who were laid off in 1989 were unemployed for less than five weeks—a relatively short time. Although such an interruption in earnings may put a crimp in a family's budget, it is not likely to deprive the family of essentials such

---

[1] The question is sometimes asked: What is the difference between a recession and a depression? It has been said that it is a recession when your neighbor is out of work and a depression when you yourself are out of work; that is, a depression is worse than a recession.

TABLE 5–3   Duration of Unemployment, 1989

Duration of Unemployment	*Percent of Unemployment*
Less than 5 weeks	49
5–14 weeks	30
15–26 weeks	11
27 weeks or more	10
	100

Source: *Economic Report of the President,* 1990, p. 340.

---

as food and housing, particularly when unemployment compensation makes up part of the loss.

As might be expected, when the overall level of unemployment increases, the duration of unemployment also increases. For example, in 1983, when the unemployment rate was 9.5 percent, 24 percent of the unemployed were out of work for 27 weeks or more, while only 33 percent were jobless for less than 5 weeks.

We should bear in mind, too, that even at fairly low levels of unemployment, some people will be out of work for long periods. These might include people from depressed areas or those who have few skills to offer in the job market. Unfortunately, it is not likely that government policies or programs to stimulate the entire economy can do much for these people. Instead, programs are needed to improve employment opportunities in specific geographic areas or to help people relocate to areas where jobs are available. Many of the long-term unemployed lack the skills demanded in the job market. Job training programs to increase marketable skills may be of some help to these people.

DISGUISED UNEMPLOYMENT

We should also be aware that employment figures may disguise a certain amount of unemployment. Consider the case of an aeronautical engineer who is laid off and accepts employment as a parking lot attendant, which may be the best alternative at least for the immediate time. Although he is no longer unemployed, his income and his contribution to society's output are considerably less than they might otherwise be. When people have no choice but to work in jobs that do not fully utilize their capabilities, they are in part unemployed, or *underemployed,* as economists might say. Thus, a reduction in unemployment accomplished by the taking of less desirable jobs may in fact overstate the true reduction that takes place.

The manner in which unemployment statistics are collected also may result in a downward bias to the true unemployment figure. Recall that for a person to be unemployed, that individual must have made specific efforts to find employment in the past four weeks. For a person who has been out of work for months and has been turned down repeatedly in the quest for work, there will likely come a time when he or she gives up looking, at least until some concrete opportunity presents itself. A person who has given up trying to find a job would, according to the unemployment survey, not be included in the labor force and would not be considered unemployed. However, that person still would not be working. This phenomenon is known as the *discouraged worker effect*. Both the underemployment phenomenon and the discouraged worker effect contribute to *disguised unemployment*. And disguised unemployment causes the official unemployment statistics to understate the extent of the unemployment problem.

WHO ARE THE UNEMPLOYED?

Although average unemployment figures such as 5 or 6 percent are useful in providing an indication of the seriousness of the unemployment problem, they do not tell us anything about the differences in employment among individuals or groups in society. As you might expect, not all employees face an equal chance of being laid off or finding a new job.

As shown in Table 5–4, unemployment is more prevalent among the young and the least skilled. Note that in 1989, when the overall unemployment rate in the United States averaged 5.3 percent of the labor force, young males between the ages of 16 and 19 experienced an unemployment rate of 15.9 percent. Part of this group came from high school and college dropouts and part from 1989 high school graduates who were not able to find a job immediately after graduation. Females in this age group experienced a slightly lower unemployment rate, 14.0 percent, although this figure is still over twice the national average rate.

There probably are a number of reasons for the relatively high unemployment rate among teenagers. Recent high school graduates or dropouts require some

TABLE 5–4   Unemployment Rates by Groups, 1989

All workers	5.3%
Males, 16 to 19 years	15.9
Females, 16 to 19 years	14.0
Males, 20 years and over	4.5
Females, 20 years and over	4.7
Married men	3.0

Source: *Economic Report of the President,* 1990, p. 338.

time to find their first full-time jobs. Because of lack of experience and skills, jobs for these people probably are the most difficult to find. Also, studies have shown that minimum wage laws are at least partly to blame for this problem. If the hourly wages of new, inexperienced workers are fixed higher than their contribution to output, employers will lose money by hiring them; hence, they will not do so.

In general, the more skills a person has, the less chance he or she has of being laid off. We would expect employers to be reluctant to lay off a person who cannot be replaced easily. The employer who lays off a skilled person runs the risk of not getting that person back when business conditions improve. If the individual does not come back, then the firm must bear the expense of finding a suitable replacement and retraining or "breaking in the new employee." For this reason, a firm may actually choose to lose money on a skilled person for a few months rather than lay that person off. The unskilled person, however, is more easily replaced; so there is a greater tendency on the part of an employer to let such an individual go as soon as the person is not producing the value of his or her wage.

Note the relatively low level of unemployment among married men (3.0 percent) as opposed to other groups. Part of the explanation may be the longer seniority on the job, since married men as a group are older than single people. In addition, married men with families to support are likely to look harder for another job when laid off and also to be more willing to accept less desirable employment on a temporary basis.

COSTS OF UNEMPLOYMENT

From the standpoint of the individual, the economic cost of unemployment is, of course, the loss or reduction in income from being out of work. Granted, a large share of U.S. workers now are eligible for unemployment compensation, which eases the problem somewhat. However, during 1989 the average weekly unemployment check was about $150. For a family accustomed to a $500- or $600-per week wage or salary, this reduction in income comes as a severe shock to the family budget.

We must leave to the psychologists and sociologists the identification and measure of the mental and social problems that result from unemployment. In spite of how much we dislike trudging off to work or school on Monday mornings, most people find a life of idleness even more distasteful, especially when they have little or no income to buy recreation. Living off the "dole" may keep one alive, but it does not lead to a very enjoyable or interesting life.

It is necessary as well to look at the economic costs of unemployment from the standpoint of the total economy or society. Unemployment means the economy is producing a smaller amount of real output of goods and services than it could otherwise enjoy. For this reason, nearly everyone loses from unemployment because there is a smaller output to be distributed among the members of society. Payment of unemployment compensation to the unemployed does not reduce the loss in total output. However, it is a method of redistributing the claims to society's output. Essentially, by introducing unemployment compensation, society is saying that employed people are willing to give up a part of their claims on the output of the economy and share it with their less fortunate neighbors who are out of work.

THE EMPLOYMENT RATE

The discussion so far in this chapter has focused largely on the negative state of the economy, that is, the extent of unemployment. An alternative view of the economy can be obtained by looking at the *employment rate,* which can be defined as the percent of the adult population aged 16 to 64 that is employed:

$$\text{Employment rate} = \frac{\text{Employed}}{\text{Population, 16–64}} \times 100$$

Figures on the U.S. employment rate for selected years from 1929 to 1989 are presented in Table 5–5. Perhaps the most interesting aspect of this table is the pronounced upward trend in the employment rate over the period. In 1944, a year with an exceptionally low unemployment rate (1.2 percent), the employment rate was only 59 percent. In contrast, during 1983, when the unemployment rate averaged 9.5 percent, the employment rate was up to 69 percent. The employment

TABLE 5–5   U.S. Employment Rates, Selected Years, 1929–1989

Year	Employment Rate	Year	Employment Rate
1929	62%	1974	66%
1934	50	1979	68
1939	53	1983	66
1944	59	1984	68
1949	60	1985	69
1954	60	1986	70
1959	62	1987	71
1964	62	1988	72
1969	65	1989	73

Note: From 1929 to 1944, the employment figures consist of all persons 14 years of age and older in civilian occupations, whereas the 1949–89 figures are for people 16 years and older in these occupations.

Source: *Economic Report of the President,* 1990, pp. 329–30.

rate continued to increase during the 1980s. In 1989, the nation's employment rate reached an all-time high of 73 percent. Much of the increase in the employment rate is due to the increased participation of married women in the labor force.

There are several reasons the employment rate may be a better measure of the state of the economy than the more commonly used unemployment rate. First, the unemployment rate may increase not because of a slowdown in the economy but rather because of an increase in the number of people who desire to become members of the labor force. For example, during the 1970s, the unemployment rate was higher than it was during the 1960s. Yet the employment rate also increased during the 1970s. Thus, the economy probably was not quite so sluggish during the 1970s as the unemployment rate might lead us to believe. As mentioned, much of the increase in the employment rate during the 1970s was the result of the increased participation of women and students in the labor force. In 1969, 43 percent of women 16 years old and over held jobs outside the home; by 1989, this figure had increased to 57 percent.

A second advantage of the employment rate is that it is not biased by changes in the desirability of being in the labor force. It has been argued that in recent years the unemployment rate is biased upward because, in order to qualify for benefits under certain welfare programs, some people have to declare themselves unemployed. In other words, these people have an incentive to be declared unemployed. This phenomenon would not affect the employment rate because the total number of employed people would not change.

A third advantage of the employment rate is that it is not biased by the discouraged worker effect. People who quit looking for work and go off the unemployment rolls reduce the measured rate of unemployment when in fact nothing has changed. Such action does not change the employment rate.

SUMMARY

Full employment is defined as a situation where everyone who is willing to work at the prevailing wage can find a job for which he or she is qualified. To be counted among the unemployed, a person must (1) have not worked during the survey week, (2) have made specific efforts to find work during the preceding four weeks, and (3) have been available for work during the survey week. The unemployment rate is obtained by dividing the number of unemployed by the number of people in the labor force and multiplying by 100. Frictional unemployment is due to growth and decline of firms and industries and to people changing jobs. In recent years, a 5 to 6 percent unemployment rate is considered a normal level of frictional unemployment. Generally, the highest unemployment rate is experienced by teenagers and the lowest by married men. The employment rate, defined as the percent of the adult population aged 16 to 64 who are working, has been higher in recent years than during World War II. This is mainly because of the increased participation of married women and students in the labor force.

YOU SHOULD KNOW

1. The definition of full employment.
2. Who the employed are.
3. Who the unemployed are.
4. How the unemployment rate is computed.
5. Who is included in the labor force.
6. The meaning of frictional unemployment.
7. The U.S. unemployment record, 1929–1989.
8. The two sources of disguised unemployment.
9. What groups exhibit the highest unemployment rates.
10. What is the employment rate, and why it has increased over time.

QUESTIONS

1. Which of the following people, if any, would be considered unemployed?
   a. a Midwestern cash-grain farmer spending the winter in Arizona because there is nothing to do on the farm
   b. a homemaker working 20 hours per week as a salesclerk but who would like to work 40 hours as a secretary
   c. a salesclerk who has been fired after being caught taking items home and is seeking another job
   d. A new Ph.D. driving a taxi because of an inability to obtain a teaching job
   e. A young woman who has quit her job in New York in order to move to California where she has not yet found a job
   f. a 62-year-old man laid off a year ago who has quit looking for work because of a lack of opportunities
2. Which of the following people, if any, would be included in the labor force?
   a. the owner and operator of a service station
   b. a homemaker who works 20 hours per week as a hospital volunteer
   c. a full-time college student
   d. a college student working 10 hours per week on a part-time job
   e. a construction worker, laid off because of lack of work, attempting to find another job
   f. a recent high school graduate who is looking but has not yet found a job
3. In a free society, is it reasonable to expect zero unemployment? Explain
4. a. In what way does the official unemployment rate understate the unemployment problem?
   b. In what way does the official unemployment rate overstate the unemployment problem?
   c. Would the use of the employment rate as a measure of unemployment reduce these biases? Explain.
5. Why do teenagers exhibit an unemployment rate that is about five times higher than that of married men?
6. Is it possible for both the unemployment rate and the employment rate to increase at the same time? Explain.

SELF-TEST

1. Full employment exists when everyone:
   a. is working.
   b. who wants to work is working at the

   job he or she desires.
   c. who wants to work at the prevailing wage rate is working at the job he or

she desires.

d. who wants to work at the prevailing wage rate is working at a job for which he or she is qualified.

2. The main concern of unemployment is with _____ , although unemployed _____ also reduces total output of the country.

    a. capital; labor

    b. labor; capital

    c. capital; land

    d. land; capital

3. During times of depressed economic activity, there is a tendency for _____ to choose _____ over _____ in the short run.

    a. employers; unemployment; lower wages

    b. employers and unions; unemployment; lower wages

    c. employers; lower wages; unemployment

    d. employers and unions; lower wages; unemployment

4. To be counted among the unemployed, a person 16 years of age or older must have:

    a. not worked during the survey week.

    b. made specific efforts to find work within the past four weeks.

    c. been available for work during the survey week.

    d. all of the above.

5. Which of the following people would be included among the unemployed?

    a. a 62-year-old woman laid off a year ago who has quit looking for work because of a lack of opportunities

    not looking

    b. a Midwestern cash-grain farmer spending the winter in Florida because there isn't anything to do on the farm

    c. a salesclerk fired for dipping into the till who is looking for another job

    d. a new Ph.D. driving a taxi because of an inability to obtain a teaching job

6. The unemployment rate is determined by dividing the _____ by the _____ and multiplying by 100.

    a. population; number of unemployed

    b. labor force; number of unemployed

    c. number of unemployed; population

    d. number of unemployed; labor force

7. The labor force consists of:

    a. the employed.

    b. the adult population, age 16 and over.

    c. the adult population, age 21 and over.

    d. the employed plus the unemployed.

8. Which of the following people would be included in the labor force?

    a. a full-time college student

    b. an unemployed mine worker who has given up looking for another job

    c. a college student working 10 hours per week on a part-time job

    d. a homemaker putting in 15 hours per week as a nursing home volunteer

9. A decrease in sales causes the _____ labor to decrease. If wage rates remain constant, _____ will occur.

    a. supply of; unemployment

    b. demand for; unemployment

    c. supply of; inflation

    d. demand for; inflation

10. In the United States, the labor force amounts to about _____ of the adult population, age 16 and over.

    a. 100 percent   *c.* one half

    b. two thirds   *d.* one third

11. Frictional unemployment stems from:

    a. disagreements between employers and labor unions.

    b. people changing jobs.

    c. growth and decline of firms and industries.

    d. b and c.

12. The rate of frictional unemployment that is expected to prevail in the United States is now in the range of _____ percent.

    a. 3 to 6   *c.* 6 to 7

    b. 5 to 6   *d.* 7 to 8

13. Frictional unemployment is thought to have _____ in recent years because of the _____ labor force participation of students and increased welfare benefits.
    a. increased; decreased
    b. decreased; increased
    c. decreased; decreased
    d. increased; increased

14. During the late 1980s, the U.S. unemployment rate hovered around _____ percent, which was about _____ what is was during the Great Depression.
    a. 3; one fourth
    b. 5; four times
    c. 3; four times
    d. 5; one fourth

15. The Great Depression lasted from:
    a. 1930 to 1934.
    b. 1930 to 1939.
    c. 1939 to 1946.
    d. 1980 to 1984.

16. During the 1980s, the largest group of unemployed were out of work:
    a. less than 5 weeks.
    b. 5–14 weeks.
    c. 15–26 weeks.
    d. 27 weeks or more.

17. The underemployed are included among the _____ . These are people who are _____ for their jobs.
    a. employed; overqualified
    b. employed; underqualified
    c. unemployed; overqualified
    d. unemployed; underqualified

18. Discouraged workers include those who have _____ . They _____ counted among the unemployed.
    a. retired; are not
    b. given up trying to find a job; are
    c. retired; are
    d. given up trying to find a job; are not

19. Disguised unemployment includes:
    a. discouraged workers.
    b. the underemployed.
    c. those who will not admit to friends they are unemployed.
    d. a and b.

20. In the United States, the unemployment rate is lowest for:
    a. male teenagers.
    b. female teenagers.
    c. females, 20 years or older.
    d. married men.

21. The employment rate is obtained by dividing the _____ by _____ and multiplying by 100. It was _____ in 1989 than it was during World War II.
    a. employed; adult population, 16–64; higher
    b. employed; adult population, 16–64; lower
    c. adult population, 16–64; employed; higher
    d. adult population, 16–64; employed; lower

22. An increase of new entrants in the labor force will likely cause the unemployment rate to _____ and the employment rate to _____ .
    a. increase; decrease
    b. decrease; increase
    c. increase; increase
    d. decrease; decrease

Chapter 6

Inflation

OVERVIEW

This chapter focuses on the second major problem of macroeconomics: inflation. After defining inflation, the discussion turns to the consumer price index (CPI), the main device used to measure inflation. The reasons the CPI is likely to overstate the inflation problem also are discussed. The discussion then turns to the economic effects of inflation—who gains and who loses. The chapter ends by drawing a distinction between the nominal and real rates of interest.

THE CONSUMER PRICE INDEX

We now turn to the second major problem area of macroeconomics: inflation. *Inflation* is defined as a sustained increase in the general price level. The most commonly used measure of the general price level in the United States is the *consumer price index* (CPI). The CPI is constructed by the U.S. Department of Labor, Bureau of Labor Statistics. As its name implies, the CPI is intended to reflect the prices of goods and services purchased by consumers. Basically, the CPI measures the cost of a "bundle" or "market basket" of selected goods and services in a given year as compared to the cost of the same bundle in a base year.

The goods and services in the market basket reflect the buying habits of people across the country. The types and quantities of goods included in the market basket are revised about once every 10 years. The 1982–84 market basket is currently used to construct the CPI. Compared to the 1972–73 mix, used previously, expenditures on legal fees, takeout meals, exercise and stereo equipment, and cable television were increased while expenditures on red meat, gasoline, sugar and sweets, and dry cleaning were decreased.

In calculating the cost of the bundle, the price of each good or service is multiplied by its quantity purchased during the specified period. As a result, the items that make up a large share of an average family's budget weigh more heavily in computing the cost of the bundle than items purchased in small amounts. For example, the quantity of safety pins purchased by an average family during a year is likely to be small compared to food or housing. Even if the price of safety pins should double, the overall price level as measured by the CPI would show only a small increase because safety pins make up such a small part of the budget. On the other hand, doubling the price of transportation or housing would cause a greater increase in the CPI because these items loom large in the family budget.

In order to obtain a better understanding of how the CPI is constructed, it will be useful to construct one from a simple example. Consider just three items: a loaf of bread, a jug of wine, and a theater ticket—items that might be used to represent the cost of eating, drinking, and being merry.

What we want to do is construct a number that will tell us how much, if at all, the prices of these items have changed over a period of time. Essentially we will represent three prices by just one number. The official CPI, of course, represents the prices of several thousand items with just one number, but the technique of construction is the same. Assume that the time period we are interested in is from 1970 to 1990. Let 1970 be the so-called base year—the year we use for comparison. The average prices of the three items for 1970 and 1990 are shown below:

Item	1970 Price	1970 Quantity	1990 Price
Loaf of bread	$0.25	50	$0.65
Jug of wine	1.75	10	5.00
Theater ticket	1.85	20	6.00

The next thing we must determine is the quantity of each item that is consumed. If we just add raw prices, then the theater ticket, for example, carries nearly 10 times more weight than the loaf of bread. This could be misleading if the person did not go to the theater very often. Therefore, in constructing a price index, we have to assign a quantity to each item so that the budget reflects its importance.

The Department of Labor CPI uses base-year quantities; let us do the same. Some plausible quantities of these items that might have been consumed by an average person during 1970 are shown in the middle column of the above table.

The next step is to multiply price times quantity of each item for each year. The results are shown below.

Item	1970: $P \times Q$	1990: $P \times Q$
Bread	$12.50	$ 32.50
Wine	17.50	50.00
Tickets	37.00	120.00
Total	$67.00	$202.50

These figures tell us that the same bundle of goods and services that cost $67.00 in 1970 sold for $202.50 in 1990. We can represent this change as an index by dividing the 1990 cost by the 1970 cost and multiplying by 100. We obtain:

$$1990 \text{ index} = \frac{202.50}{67.00} \times 100 = 302$$

The 1990 index of 302 tells us that the price of this bundle of goods and services increased over threefold or 202 percent from 1970 to 1990.[1] Recall that a percent change is computed by finding the change in the number between the base year and the current year and then dividing by the base-year figure. In the CPI, the base year is always equal to 100. To convert to a percent, the answer is then multiplied by 100. In this example the percent change is equal to

$$\frac{302 - 100}{100} \times 100 = 202$$

The CPI allows us to combine the movement of many prices into a single number.

The general formula for constructing this index is as follows:

$$CPI = \frac{\Sigma_i Q_{0i} P_{1i}}{\Sigma_i Q_{0i} P_{0i}}$$

where Q_{0i} and P_{0i} represent the base-year quantity and price of the ith good or service, and P_{1i} represents the current-year price of the ith good or service. The Σ_i instructs us to sum all the $P \times Q$'s as we did above. This formula is essentially the one used by the Department of Labor to construct the CPI for each year. The formula is sometimes known as the Laspeyres formula, after the man who popularized it.

BIASES IN THE CPI

A. Quality Changes

When using the CPI to measure the change in the general level of prices, we should be aware of some possible biases that tend to creep in. Perhaps most important is the bias caused by improvements in the quality of goods and services over time. In constructing the CPI, the Department of Labor attempts to hold quality as constant as possible. For example, in comparing automobile prices, it chooses prices of comparably equipped cars. It would not be meaningful to take the price of a car without air conditioning in 1970 and compare it with the price of one with air conditioning in 1990, for example.

---

[1] This figure is only an example and is not intended to reflect the actual price change of the items listed.

However, there are certain quality changes that are difficult to hold constant. The engine in a 1990 car may run 100,000 miles, while a 1970 engine may stand up for only 75,000 miles before a major overhaul. This type of quality change cannot be easily measured. Because most durable goods have undergone some quality improvements over the years, many of which are difficult to measure, the CPI probably overstates the true rise in prices that can be attributed purely to inflation. In other words, part of any price rise might be attributed to better quality and part to pure inflation.

B. Environmental Regulations

An even more difficult problem of measuring quality change relates to the environment. Because of environmental regulations, business firms have had to spend billions of dollars on installing pollution-control devices and filing reports to federal and state governments. Some of the pollution-control devices are included in the products, such as catalytic converters on cars, while others, such as "scrubbers" in smokestacks, become part of the manufacturing establishments. In either case, the cost of these devices along with the cost of preparing reports must be borne by consumers through higher prices for the goods they buy. If prices of the affected goods did not go up, resources would leave these industries and go where they could earn more. The main point is that the higher prices are picked up by the CPI and imply inflation. Yet, if pollution-control devices do improve the quality of the environment, then people are buying higher-quality products, because they are buying cleaner air and water along with the conventional goods.

C. The Index-Number Problem

Another bias can stem from a change in the relative prices of items purchased. Notice in the above example that the price of theater tickets increased relatively more than the price of bread or wine. When the price of a good or service rises more than other prices, there is a tendency on the part of consumers to economize on the higher-priced items by substituting more of the cheaper items for it. In our example, the consumer may substitute drinking wine in place of attending the theater.

In the construction of the 1990 price index, it was assumed that the consumer bought the same relative amounts of the items in 1990 as in 1970. If, in fact, the consumer bought fewer theater tickets and more wine, because of the relative increase in the price of tickets, then the 1990 cost, $202.50 in our example, overstates the true cost of the bundle of goods that the consumer actually bought. This second bias, often called the "index-number problem" by statisticians and economists, also tends to make the CPI overstate the "true" rise in prices.

D. List versus Actual Prices

In times of increased unemployment such as occurred during 1982 and 1983, prices of many consumer items sell at a discount. For example, automobile dealers and manufacturers marked down car prices or gave rebates in an attempt to increase sales during those years. Because the CPI measures list prices rather than actual discounted prices, it is likely to overstate the rise in the price level during periods of depressed business activity.

PRODUCER PRICE INDEX

A second but less commonly used index to measure the change in the general price level is the producer price index, formerly known as wholesale price index (WPI). This index, also constructed by the Department of Labor, is the same type of index as the CPI except that it reflects prices at the wholesale level of both consumer goods and industrial products. The producer price index excludes prices of personal services, however. Except for a brief period during the 1970s, prices of services have increased relative to the prices of goods. Therefore, the consumer price index has risen more than the producer price index during the post-World War II era.

U.S. INFLATION RECORD

Although most people are aware that prices have been rising in recent years, it will be useful to briefly review the U.S. inflation record over the past half-century (starting with the Great Depression) in order to see more clearly the periods in which inflation has been most prevalent. The U.S. CPI from 1929 to 1989 is presented in Table 6–1. In this table, 1989 is used as the base year, that is, the year the CPI = 100.

In comparing the size of the CPI in 1934 with the 1989 figure it becomes evident that the general price level has increased more than ninefold in the United States over the six decades falling within the 1934–89 period. In other words, it took $9.09 in 1989 to buy what $1 bought in 1934.

Of course, the CPI did not increase at a steady rate. As shown in Table 6–1, the price level actually declined between 1929 and 1939. Moving into World War II, prices exhibited some increase, but the largest jump came during the 1944–49 period. After 1954, the price level increased at a rather modest rate (at least by present standards) until the mid-1960s. Then from 1964 to 1989 the CPI increased four-fold.

Although the observed changes in the CPI provide an indication of the inflationary tendency of the economy, a somewhat more direct method of measuring inflation is by determining the annual percent change in the price level. This measure is called the *rate of inflation* or, simply, the *inflation rate*. The most

TABLE 6-1 U.S. Consumer Price Index, Selected Years, 1929–1989 (1989 = 100)

Year	CPI	Year	CPI
1929	14	1974	39
1934	11	1979	59
1939	11	1984	84
1944	14	1985	87
1949	19	1986	88
1954	22	1987	92
1959	24	1988	95
1964	25	1989	100
1969	29		

Source: *Economic Report of the President*, 1990, p. 359.

accurate measure of the rate of inflation during a given year is obtained by finding the change in the CPI from the end of the preceding year to the end of the year in question (December to December), dividing by its initial value, and multiplying by 100 to convert to percent. For example, the 4.6 percent inflation rate for 1989 is computed as follows (the CPI figures are based on 1982–84 = 100):

$$\frac{126.1 - 120.5}{120.5} \times 100 = 4.6 \text{ percent}$$

Annual inflation rates for the United States, five-year averages, are presented in Table 6–2. The negative value for the 1930–34 period indicates a decline in the general price over this period. Note that the highest rates of inflation occurred in

TABLE 6-2 U.S. Annual Inflation Rates, Five-Year Averages, 1930–1989

Period	Average Inflation Rate	Period	Average Inflation Rate
1930–34	−4.7%	1960–64	1.2%
1935–39	0.8	1965–69	3.4
1940–44	4.9	1970–74	6.1
1945–49	6.4	1975–79	8.2
1950–54	2.5	1980–84	6.6
1955–59	1.6	1985–89	3.7

Source: *Economic Report of the President*, 1970, p. 229, and 1990, p. 363.

the years immediately following World War II and during the 1970s and early 1980s. The explanation of why the inflation rate was relatively high during these years constitutes a major part of the chapters to follow.

THE ECONOMIC EFFECTS OF INFLATION

During years of relatively high inflation, the attention of wage earners is usually drawn to the race between wages and prices. If prices rise faster than wages, it is obvious that wage earners are harmed by inflation. Yet it may come as a surprise to learn that during the 1947–89 period, in only 10 of those 43 years did prices rise faster than average hourly earnings of all private nonagricultural workers in the United States.[2] Those years were 1959, 1974–75, 1979–81, 1985, and 1987–89. During these years, real wages declined about 11 cents per hour per year on the average. Granted, these overall average figures no doubt cover up instances where specific individuals or groups have suffered losses in other years. Nevertheless, it does not appear that wage earners have suffered large-scale reductions in their real wages on account of inflation.

One reason people may think inflation diminishes their standard of living is that they see how much less each dollar they earn will buy. But one should also bear in mind that part of the increase in wages that people have obtained was to keep pace with inflation. It is not correct to assume that nominal wages would have increased as much as they did if the price level had remained stable. Although each dollar does not go as far during inflation, people can still be as well or even better off if they have more dollars.

The preceding discussion is not intended to play down the effects of inflation, but rather to turn our attention away from earnings toward assets, where inflation tends to have a greater effect on the average person. People own assets of various forms, including cash and checking account money, money in savings accounts, stocks and bonds, and real or physical assets such as land, buildings, automobiles, appliances, clothing, and jewelry. The form in which a person holds his or her assets in large part determines how inflation affects the individual.

 The asset that suffers the most from inflation is cash and checking account money. Because a dollar is always a dollar regardless of what happens to the price level, an increase in prices reduces the purchasing power of money. For example, a person who held $1,000 during 1979, when the price level increased 13.3 percent, suffered a $133 loss in the purchasing power of this money. At the end of the year, the $1,000 would buy only $867 worth of goods and services. And this loss goes on year after year as long as inflation persists.

One might ask, why don't people exchange their money for assets that go up in value with the price level, such as real estate? Some people, if they expect inflation, will make an effort to do so. But it is important to recognize that every dollar that

---

[2] *Economic Report of the President,* 1990, p. 344.

exists always has to be held by someone. So if one person draws down his or her money holdings, someone else must end up holding more. Hence, inflation always takes its toll. Essentially, inflation is a tax on money.

Because the exact rate of inflation rarely, if ever, can be predicted with certainty, inflation also tends to redistribute income and wealth. For example, if a union contract is written with the expectation that prices will increase by 6 percent over the year, and then prices actually increase by 13 percent, this wage increase will not be enough to stay abreast of inflation. In this case, there is some redistribution of income away from employees to employers. Of course, the opposite is likely to occur if inflation is less than is expected. Real wages may go up more than was intended by both employers and employees, and as a result employees, at least those who keep their jobs, gain at the expense of employers.

Gains and losses also may occur in pension plans. Workers who contribute money to a pension plan that does not pay out at higher rates in the event of inflation tend to lose, to the benefit of the organizations that administer the plans, mainly firms and labor unions. Much of the money that is paid into pension plans is invested in assets that increase with the price level. When the assets are sold and the pensioners are paid off in so-called cheap dollars, the organization may end up with a considerable amount left over. In this case, the pensioners end up receiving considerably less than they expected to receive in terms of real purchasing power. This has not been true of the social security program, however, where payments have more than kept pace with inflation.[3] Still, the depreciation in the value of money has hit retired people relatively hard because many kept a large part of their savings in savings accounts where the rate of interest has not been high enough to offset the adverse effect of inflation.

Bonds and life insurance policies have redistributive effects similar to pension plans that do not adjust their payments for inflation. In this case, people purchase bonds and insurance policies with relatively valuable dollars but are paid back in dollars with less purchasing power. This occurs because bonds and insurance policies have a fixed face value, regardless of the price level that exists when they mature. Again, if the funds received from the sale of bonds and insurance policies are invested in real assets, such as real estate, that go up with the price level, the organizations issuing the bonds and insurance policies gain at the expense of those who buy them. Traditionally stocks have been considered a better hedge against inflation because their market value can increase with the price level, although in short-run situations stock prices may decline during inflationary times. Consequently, stocks are best used as a long-run inflation hedge.

In view of the decrease in the value of money along with the losses suffered through retirement plans, bonds, and insurance policies, one might ask how an average person can protect himself or herself against inflation. The answer is that it is very hard. For the average household, the family dwelling (if owned) is probably

---

[3] Between 1950 and 1989, the average real monthly social security payment to retired persons more than doubled.

the surest hedge against inflation, since real estate prices are highly responsive to price-level changes. Beginning in the late 1970s, the higher interest paid by the money market funds provided some protection against the loss in the purchasing power of money. However, income taxes reduced this rate, particularly for middle- and high-income people. For a young person, investment in education is a fairly good inflation hedge because the extra earnings that education makes possible increase with the price level. If a person borrows to buy a house or obtain more education, inflation may bring about some additional gains that are discussed in the following section.

Not only does an unexpected increase in the rate of inflation redistribute income and wealth, but an unexpected slowing down or decrease in the rate of inflation has similar effects. After inflation has been experienced for a number of years, and people come to expect it in the future, the prices of real assets such as real estate and precious metals (gold and silver) are bid up as wealthholders attempt to get out of money and into real assets. Also, nominal or money rates of interest tend to be high during such a period. If the rate of inflation begins to decline and people come to expect a return to more stable prices, the demand for real assets also will decrease, causing a decline in their prices. In turn, people who purchase these assets with the expectation that inflation will continue, suffer losses. The losses are compounded if the assets were purchased with borrowed funds carrying a relatively high rate of interest. The above situation describes what happened to many young farmers and land speculators during the late 1970s. Some were unable to make even the interest payments on their land in the early to mid-1980s and were forced to sell at a loss. Bringing inflation under control, particularly if the decrease is unexpected, can hurt people as much as an unexpected increase in inflation. Clearly, it is better that the inflation would have not occurred in the first place.

THE NOMINAL VERSUS THE REAL RATE OF INTEREST

The existence of inflation also has an important impact on the borrowing and lending of money. A simple example will illustrate the point. Suppose you borrow $1,000 for one year at an interest charge of 10 percent. Also suppose that the rate of inflation that occurs during the year is also 10 percent. When you repay the loan at the end of the year, you pay back the original $1,000 plus $100 in interest for the use of the money. But notice also that at the end of the year it takes $1,100 to buy the same goods that $1,000 could have bought at the beginning. In other words, the loan is paid back in cheap dollars. The lender had no more real purchasing power at the end of the year than at the beginning. This in turn means that, if you had used the money to purchase real property or education that increased in value with the price level, you would have borrowed the money "free of charge." The $1,100 that you paid back at the end of the year was worth the same in real purchasing power as the $1,000 at the beginning. By the same token, the lender made the loan "free of charge"because that person did not have any more in real purchasing power at the end of the year than at the beginning.

The only way that lenders can protect themselves during inflation is to charge higher rates of interest. Of course, borrowers are willing to pay higher rates because they know that loans will be paid back with dollars of less purchasing power. During times of inflation, both lenders and borrowers should be as interested in the real rate of interest as in the nominal rate. The nominal rate of interest is simply the rate that is quoted on a loan or savings account. The real rate of interest reflects the "real" returns from a loan or savings account after inflation has been deducted. It is calculated as follows:

$$r = i - \%\Delta P$$

where r is the real rate of interest, i is the nominal rate, and $\%\Delta P$ is the percent change in the price level, that is, the rate of inflation. For example, if the nominal rate is 8 percent and the rate of inflation is 8 percent, the real rate is zero. Because the exact rate of inflation cannot be predicted with certainty, the real rate may turn out to be negative. For example, the real rate would be -4 percent if inflation were 12 percent and the nominal rate 8 percent.

It is possible that even if most people correctly anticipate the rate of inflation, the money rate may not be able to increase enough to fully offset the effects of inflation. This may occur because of usury laws that place a ceiling on how high the money rate can go. For example, during 1979 usury laws prohibited the money rate of interest on savings accounts to even approach the 13.3 percent inflation rate. As a result, the real rate of interest paid on savings accounts during 1979 turned out to be negative, meaning that savers has less real purchasing power in the bank at the end of the year than at the beginning. To make matters worse, the purchasing power of savings is reduced even more because of the income tax on interest earnings. One might ask, If the real rate is negative, why did people put money in savings accounts? The answer is that even though people lose some purchasing power by placing money in a savings account and earning a negative real rate of interest, they lose less than if they held the money as cash or left it in their checking accounts. As mentioned, money market funds became a better place for savings because they could pay higher nominal rates of interests than passbook savings accounts.

Because of the difficulty of predicting when inflation will occur, together with usury laws that place limits on how high money rates of interest can go, there has been a tendency for real rates to be low when inflation was increasing and vice versa. As shown in Table 6–3, during the early 1930s, when the nation was sliding into the Great Depression and the price level was declining, the real rate of interest was higher (7.0 percent) than it was during the next 50 years. Conversely, during and immediately after World War II, when the nation experienced relatively high rates of inflation, the real rate of interest was negative. In years of relatively stable prices, such as the 1950s and early 1960s, the real rate of interest became positive once again in the neighborhood of 1 to 2 percent. Then as inflation speeded up in the 1970s, the real rate declined, turning negative in the 1975–79 period. The unusually high money rates of interest of the 1980–84 period caused the real rate to turn positive again during those and later years.

TABLE 6–3 Real Rates of Interest in the United States, Five-Year Averages, 1930–1989

Period	Real Rate of Interest	Period	Real Rate of Interest
1930–34	+7.0	1960–64	+2.3
1935–39	0.0	1965–69	+2.4
1940–44	−4.3	1970–74	+1.0
1945–49	−5.3	1975–79	−1.3
1950–54	−0.5	1980–84	+5.0
1955–59	+1.6	1985–89	+3.9

Note: Rates are computed by subtracting the average inflation (or deflation) rate during each period from the average interest rate paid on four- to six-month prime commercial paper during the corresponding period.

Source: *Economic Report of the President*, 1990, p. 376.

SUMMARY

Inflation is defined as a sustained increase in the general price level. It is commonly measured by the consumer price index (CPI). The CPI is constructed by dividing the cost of a specified bundle of goods and services in the year in question by the cost of the same bundle in a base year, and multiplying by 100. The CPI measure of inflation will be biased upward if there are unmeasurable quality improvements in goods over time and if there are changes in the relative prices of goods and services (the index-number problem). Money is the asset most hurt by inflation. Inflation is a tax on money. The real rate of interest is obtained by subtracting the rate of inflation from the nominal rate of interest. Physical assets such as real estate and precious metals are hedges against inflation but are not good assets to own when the inflation rate is declining.

YOU SHOULD KNOW

1. The definition of inflation.
2. How the consumer price index is constructed.
3. How to calculate the rate of inflation from the CPI.
4. The reasons the CPI might give a biased picture of inflation.
5. The U.S. inflation record, 1929–1989.
6. The assets most hurt by inflation.
7. The assets that provide a hedge against inflation.
8. Why a decrease in the rate of inflation also can be harmful.
9. The difference between the nominal rate of interest and the real rate of interest.
10. Why the real rate of interest can be negative, and when this is most likely to occur.

QUESTIONS

1. Construct a simple consumer price index from the following data. Use 1970 as the base year. (These data are for illustrative purposes only and are not based on actual figures.) What does the computed index number mean?

Item	1970 Price	1970 Quantity	1990 Price
Dormitory room	$800.00	1	$2,000.00
Cafeteria meal	1.00	600	4.00
Books	5.00	20	20.00

2. How might the consumer price index provide a biased picture of inflation? In your answer, state the direction of the biases.

3. *a.* If money is not a good asset to hold during inflation, why doesn't everyone convert this money to nonmonetary assets such as real estate?
   b. Would you expect the price of real estate to increase more or less than the general price level during the early stages of inflation? Explain.

4. Who benefits and who is harmed by an unexpected *increase* in the rate of inflation?

5. Who benefits and who is harmed by an unexpected *decrease* in the rate of inflation?

6. *a.* Why are nominal rates of interest high during inflation?
   b. Is it possible for the real rate of interest to be negative? Explain.

SELF-TEST

1. Inflation is defined as a _____ increase in _____ .
   a. sustained; the price level
   b. temporary; the price level
   c. sustained; the prices of necessities
   d. temporary; the prices of necessities

2. The CPI measures the cost of _____ in a given year relative to the cost of _____ in a base year.
   a. necessities; those purchased
   b. luxuries; those purchased
   c. a market basket of goods; that purchased
   d. a market basket of goods; the same goods

3. In constructing the CPI, those items that make up a large fraction of consumers' budgets will have _____ influence on the index.
   a. a large
   b. a small
   c. no

Answer questions 4 and 5 from the following table.

Item	Base Year Price	Base Year Quantity	Current Year Price
Bread	$ .20	100	$ .50
Circuses	10.00	1	15.00

4. The CPI for the current year when the base
   year = 100 is:
   a. 46   c. 175
   b. 217   d. 117

5. The index tells us that the price of
   this bundle of goods increased by
   _____ percent between the base year
   and current year.
   a. 46   c. 217
   b. 75   d. 117

6. If the quality of goods included in the market basket has improved over time, the
   CPI will _____ the true increase in the
   price level.
   a. accurately measure
   b. understate
   c. overstate

7. More stringent environmental regulations
   have the effect of _____ the CPI
   and _____ the true rate of inflation.
   a. decreasing; overstating
   b. increasing; overstating
   c. decreasing; understating
   d. increasing; understating

8. The index-number problem stems from a
   change in _____ . During inflation it
   causes the CPI to _____ the increase in
   prices.
   a. relative prices; understate
   b. relative prices; overstate
   c. the price level; understate
   d. the price level; overstate

9. In the United States, the highest rates of
   inflation occurred during the:
   a. 1950s   c. 1970s
   b. 1960s   d. 1980s

10. The asset that is most hurt by inflation is:
    a. real estate   c. gold
    b. stocks   d. money

11. Bonds _____ a desirable asset to own
    during inflation because their face
    value _____ .
    a. are; remains constant
    b. are not; remains constant

c. are; increases with the price level
d. are not; decreases with the price level

12. For the average family _____ is (are) a
    good hedge against inflation.
    a. government bonds
    b. a savings account
    c. the family home
    d. cash in the bank

13. If the nominal rate of interest does **not**
    increase in proportion to the increase in
    prices during inflation, this is a good time
    to be a _____ .
    a. lender   c. saver
    b. borrower   d. a and c

14. The real rate of interest equals
    the _____ rate minus the _____ rate.
    a. inflation; nominal
    b. nominal; inflation
    c. inflation; CPI
    d. CPI; nominal

15. If the nominal rate of interest is 8 percent
    and the inflation rate is 3 percent, the real
    rate of interest is _____ percent.
    a. 11   c. −11
    b. 5   d. −5

16. Negative _____ rates of interest are
    most likely to be experienced during times
    of high _____ .
    a. nominal; inflation
    b. real; unemployment
    c. nominal; unemployment
    d. real; inflation

17. During the early 1930s, the real rates of
    interest:
    a. equalled the nominal rates.
    b. exceeded the nominal rates.
    c. were relatively high.
    d. b and c.

18. During the early 1980s, real rates of in-
    terest:
    a. equalled the nominal rates.
    b. exceeded the nominal rates.
    c. were relatively high.
    d. b and c.

Chapter 7

Measures of National Income and Output

OVERVIEW

In the study of macroeconomics, it is necessary to utilize some measure of the total output or income of the economy. The measure that probably is most widely known is gross national product (GNP). This chapter is intended to provide an understanding of what GNP is and how it is measured. Special emphasis is given to the biases contained in GNP when it is used as a measure of economic well-being. At the end of the chapter, some additional measures of national income or output that can be derived from GNP are presented. However, before turning to the discussion of GNP, it will be useful to provide a simplified picture of what is being measured by means of an economic flowchart of the economy.

AN ECONOMIC FLOWCHART

The simplified economy depicted by Figure 7–1 contains two sectors: the household sector and the business sector. Two types of goods are produced: consumption goods and investment goods. In reality some of these goods are purchased and distributed by the government, but, conceptually at least, all goods provided by the government can be included in one or the other of these two broad categories.

Notice in Figure 7–1 that there are two sets of circular flows. The clockwise, or outer, flow represents money income and expenditures. The counterclockwise, or inner, flow represents real resources and consumer goods and services. As shown in the upper part of the diagram, households supply resources (labor, capital, and management) and in return receive income in the form of wages, interest, rents, and profits. The lower part of the diagram illustrates the fact that households in turn spend part of their income for consumer goods and services.

FIGURE 7–1 The Flow of Income and Output in an Economy

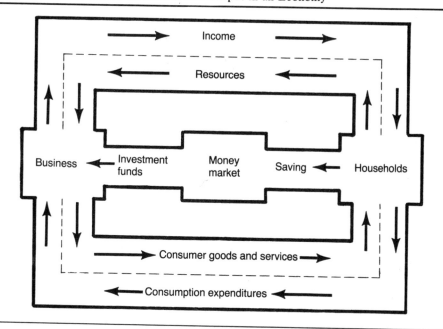

We know that most people do not spend all of their income; part is saved. This is illustrated in Figure 7–1 by the savings flow coming out of the household sector. The two flows coming out of the household sector represent the idea that people can do two things with income: they can spend it, or they can save it.

The fact that people do not spend all their income on consumption goods and services (i.e., part is saved) frees part of the nation's resources for the production of investment goods—buildings, factories, machines, roads, and so on. If society insisted on spending every dollar of its income on consumption goods, no resources would be available to produce investment goods. In other words, the value of the nation's resources employed in the production of goods and services is equal to the income of households (see Figure 7–1). If all income was spent on consumer goods, then by definition all resources would be used to produce consumer goods. The act of saving releases some resources from the production of consumer goods and allows them to be used in the production of investment goods, that is, capital. This is an important use of resources because it adds to the total stock of capital in the economy and makes possible economic growth.

The flow of savings that comes out of the household sector is funneled into a so-called money market, where it becomes available to business firms to use for the purchase of resources to produce investment goods. Business firms also provide an important source of savings in the economy by retaining part of their earnings to "plow back" into the firms, that is, reinvest. Thus, savings from both households and business firms provide the wherewithal to invest.

To summarize briefly, the income generated by the production of consumption and investment goods flows into the household sector, where part is used by households for the purchase of consumption goods and part (the savings) is available to be used by business firms for the production of investment goods.

We should not be led to believe from Figure 7–1, however, that there are two separate groups in the economy—one producing and the other consuming. Certainly everyone must be a consumer to stay alive, but at the same time almost every person is also a producer. Those who are part of the labor force produce goods and services in business places; others, such as homemakers, produce goods and services for themselves and their families at home. Students of all ages also are producers by building up their stock of human capital. Schooling is an investment that increases society's stock of capital; in this case, human capital. Both nonhuman and human capital increase the productive capacity of the economy.

The measures of national output that we will now consider represent the value of the annual flow of consumption and investment goods and services coming out of the business sector. As mentioned, some of these goods are purchased (or produced) and distributed through the government. Because of the difficulty of separating the goods and services purchased and distributed by the government into the consumption and investment categories, such goods generally are included in a separate government category (we will come back to this point later in the chapter). Therefore, the total output of the economy generally includes three broad categories of goods: (1) consumer goods, (2) investment goods, and (3) goods purchased and distributed by the government. Let us now turn to the primary measure of this national output: gross national product.

GROSS NATIONAL PRODUCT DEFINED

Gross national product (GNP) is defined as the total value of all final goods and services produced in the economy during some period of time. There are several points worth noting in this definition. First, GNP is a dollar figure. Because of the thousands of diverse goods and services produced in the economy, it is necessary when combining them to utilize some kind of common denominator. As we learned in the first grade, we cannot add together unlike items such as apples and oranges, or bobby pins and battleships.

However, if we assign a monetary value to each item, we are able to use the dollar, or any other kind of monetary unit, as a common denominator. The next question is: What money value should each item be assigned? Two possibilities come to mind: (1) market value and (2) cost of production. The Department of Commerce in measuring GNP has decided upon using market value whenever possible. The decision to use this criterion is not completely arbitrary, however. The market value of a good or service is an indication of how much the item adds to the well-being or satisfaction of society. If a packet of bobby pins sells for 60 cents and a new pair of shoes sells for $60, we can infer that the pair of shoes contributes about 100 times more satisfaction to society than the bobby pins, or else people would not be willing to pay 100 times more for the shoes.

One major problem of using market price as a measure of satisfaction is that not everything that is produced is bought and sold through the market. Military expenditure is one important category of nonmarket production. In this case, the Department of Commerce in computing GNP is forced to use cost of production rather than market price. If a missile system costs $5 billion to produce, it is implicitly assumed in the GNP computations that the missiles contribute $5 billion worth of satisfaction to society. Of course, some people would disagree with this assumption. To some, assigning $5 billion to missiles is much like assigning $60 to a packet of bobby pins that may have cost that much to produce using a very inefficient method of production. But few women would likely receive $60 worth of satisfaction from the $60 bobby pins. As a result, the product probably would go off the market and not even enter GNP. Thus, cost of production may be a misleading indicator of the satisfaction received from a product.

Another major nonmarket item included in GNP is the rental value of owner-occupied housing. Even though an owner does not pay rent, satisfaction nevertheless is obtained from the dwelling. However, it is somewhat easier to estimate the rental value of a house than that of a missile system. There is an established rental market for homes and apartments, and the Department of Commerce is able to utilize the resulting figures in estimating the dwellings' worth to society. A third major nonmarket item that is included in GNP is food produced and consumed on farms. Here again, these prices are estimated from those of comparable items sold by farmers.

The second point to note about GNP is that it is the market value of all *final* goods and services. Thus, GNP excludes the value of goods and services produced for resale or further processing. We might inquire: Why doesn't the Department of Commerce include these items? Surely the steel that goes into an automobile or the leather that goes into a pair of shoes contributes to the well-being of society. The reason for excluding these so-called intermediate goods and services is that they are already included in the market price of the final product.

A simple example will help make this clear. Consider the various stages in the manufacture of a dozen cookies. The raw materials for the ingredients (flour, shortening, sugar, and so on) are produced by the farmer. Assume the value of these raw materials is 25 cents. The processor buys the raw materials for 25 cents, turns them into cookie ingredients, and sells the ingredients to the baker for 45 cents. In other words, the processor adds 20 cents to the raw materials. The 20 cents is called value added. *Value added* is equal to the sales of a firm minus the purchases from other firms.

To continue the example, the baker turns the ingredients into cookies that are sold to a wholesaler for 75 cents, meaning the baker adds another 30 cents

(75 − 45 cents). The wholesaler sells and delivers the dozen cookies to the retailer for 80 cents, adding 5 cents to the value of the dozen cookies. The retailer sells them for 90 cents, adding another 10 cents (90 − 80 cents). The steps in the production and sale of the dozen cookies are summarized below:

Step	Sale	Value Added
Farmer	$ .25	$.25
Processor	.45	.20
Baker	.75	.30
Wholesaler	.80	.05
Retailer	.90	.10
Total	$3.15	$.90

The value of sales in the five steps of the cookie sample is $3.15, but this is not a meaningful number. It can be changed for the same product simply by changing the number of different involved firms in the overall production process. For example, if the processor and baker merged to become one firm, the 45-cent sale from the processor to the baker would not show up, reducing the sum to $2.70. Because of this problem, the Department of Commerce measures GNP as value added by each industry (the sales of the industry minus the purchases from other industries). Notice that the sum of the value-added figures for the various firms (industries) equals the retail price of the product.

A third point to note about GNP is that it excludes "pure exchange" transactions, which include such things as the purchase and sale of securities, gifts, and secondhand sales. These transactions are omitted from GNP because nothing new is produced. If you buy a $100 stock certificate, for example, the person who sells it to you gains the $100 and you gain the certificate. From the standpoint of the total economy, nothing has changed. It must be admitted, though, that after the transaction, both you and the seller should be better off than before it; if not, there would be no sense in carrying out the transaction. The value added by the brokerage industry that brings buyers and sellers together is included in GNP, however.

About the same reasoning applies to donations and gifts. Here also, nothing new is produced or created, so they should not enter GNP computations. Of course, one could argue here as well that both the giver and receiver are better off after a gift is made than before, or else it would not be made. But it is difficult if not impossible to measure this kind of satisfaction, so it is simplest to leave it out of GNP.

A fourth and final point to note about GNP is that it is a "flow" figure as opposed to a "stock." Flows are always given per unit of time, whereas a stock has no time dimension. As a rule, GNP is given in billions of dollars per year. It is virtually impossible, though, to imagine the magnitude of a billion dollars. If you were a billionaire, for example, and invested your money in a money market fund at 8 percent, you would draw $80 million per year just in interest.

GNP AS A MEASURE OF ECONOMIC WELL-BEING

An important use of the GNP figure is to compare the standard of living or economic well-being of people within a nation over a period of time or between nations at a point in time. The presumption is that the higher the GNP (the greater the output of goods and services), the better off people are. The use of GNP to gauge economic well-being presumes that people prefer more goods to less. This presumption is not unreasonable. Given the choice between $15,000 per year of goods and services and $20,000 per year (at the same price level), it is likely that most people would choose the latter.

BIASES IN GNP

When using GNP to compare the economic well-being of a society from one year to another or to compare that of two societies, one should be aware of a number of possible biases that can cause GNP to be a distorted measure of economic well-being. Fortunately the major biases can be removed.

A. Change in the Price Level

Because GNP is a monetary figure, any change in the price level causes a change in GNP that is not the result of a change in real output. For example, the sixfold increase in the price level from 1929 to 1989 caused the measured growth in GNP to overstate the growth in real goods and services. In other words, if the price level had not changed over this period, the dollar value of GNP would have grown considerably less than it did.

The effect of changes in the general price level can be removed by "deflating" the GNP by the consumer price index.[1] Recall from Chapter 6 that the CPI measures the increase in the general price level. GNP is "deflated," or adjusted for changes in the general price level, by dividing the GNP figure by the CPI and multiplying by 100. For example, suppose we would like to know the value of 1989

---

[1] The Department of Commerce constructs a separate price index designed specifically for deflating GNP. It is called the *implicit price deflator*. Although the implicit price deflator is likely to be a more accurate deflator for GNP, we will continue to use the CPI because it is the index discussed in Chapter 6 and is most familiar.

GNP if the 1929 price level had existed in 1989. The figures in the following table provide the necessary information.

Year	GNP Current Year Prices ($ Billions)	CPI
1929	103	100
1989	5,233	714

In this case, the 1989 GNP figure ($5,233 billion) is divided by the 1989 CPI (714) and the result multiplied by 100. The answer, $733 billion, is what 1989 GNP would have been if the 1929 price level had still prevailed in 1989. Thus, it is evident that the growth in real goods and services was considerably less than the raw, unadjusted GNP figures might first imply.

One might also ask what 1929 GNP would have been if 1989 prices had prevailed back then. In this case, the answer can be obtained by dividing 1929 GNP by the CPI, only now the CPI must show 1989 as the base year. In other words, the 1989 CPI must equal 100.

Although the CPI figures are published in several sources, it may not always be in the base year that is desired. It is easy to change the base year: Simply divide all the CPI figures by the CPI of the year you wish to turn into the base, and multiply by 100. Now the base year you want will be 100.

The preceding calculations are illustrated below.

a. *Deflating 1989 GNP by 1989 CPI (1929 = 100):*

$$\frac{5233}{714} \times 100 = \$733$$

b. *Changing the base year of the CPI from 1929 to 1989:*

$$1929 \text{ CPI: } \frac{100}{714} \times 100 = 14.0$$

$$1989 \text{ CPI: } \frac{714}{714} \times 100 = 100$$

c. *Deflating 1929 GNP by 1929 CPI (1989 = 100):*

$$\frac{\$103}{14.0} \times 100 = \$736$$

After adjusting the GNP for changes in the general price level, we obtain what is known as GNP in "constant dollars." If 1929 is used as the base year, it would be "constant 1929 dollars." If 1989 is used as the base, it would be "constant 1989 dollars." Value figures that are not adjusted for changes in the price level should be labeled as "current-year dollars." When viewing a time series of value figures, it is important to know whether the figures are in current or constant dollars or prices. As illustrated above, the figures can be grossly different in the two cases. The unadjusted GNP became more than 50 times larger between 1929 and 1989, whereas GNP in constant dollars increased by a multiple of 7.36. Of course, the same deflating procedure could be carried out on all the intervening years' GNP figures to obtain the growth in real GNP over an extended period, as shown in Table 7–1. Also, the same deflating procedure could be done on any value figure, such as wages, military spending, gasoline prices, or tuition.

Although deflating GNP by the CPI removes the major part of the bias or distortion in GNP caused by changes in the general price level, we should remember that the CPI itself can be biased. As mentioned in the previous chapter, it is difficult if not impossible to hold the quality of items constant when comparing prices over time. If, as is likely, the quality of many items has increased over time, the measured rise in the CPI is likely to overstate the "true" increase.[2] Thus,

TABLE 7–1   United States GNP, Five-Year Intervals, 1929–89

Year	GNP Current-Year Prices ($ Billions)	GNP Constant 1989 Prices ($ Billions)	GNP per Person 1989 Prices
1929	$ 103	$ 723	$ 6,160
1934	65	597	4,722
1939	91	835	6,138
1944	210	1,474	10,553
1949	257	1,332	8,786
1954	365	1,676	10,259
1959	484	2,063	11,345
1964	632	2,513	13,022
1969	930	3,171	15,243
1974	1,413	3,587	16,764
1979	2,414	4,115	18,690
1984	3,661	4,369	18,461
1989	5,233	5,233	21,035

Source: *Economic Report of the President*, 1990, p. 294.

---

[2] If you doubt that quality has increased, look through a Wards or Sears catalog from the 1930s, 1940s, or 1950s.

when we deflate and compare current-year GNP to GNP in years past, we in effect understate current-year GNP in relation to GNP long ago. A similar bias creeps in to the extent that changes in relative prices bring about changes in the mix of goods and services purchased. As explained in Chapter 6, this "index-number problem" tends to make the measured CPI overstate the true rise in prices. Again, the effect is to bias the growth in real GNP downward.

B. Population Growth

If population is growing, as is the case in most countries, including the United States, growth in total GNP even in constant dollars can overstate the true improvement in economic well-being of the individual. Thus, it is desirable to compute GNP per person by dividing GNP by total population. By dividing 1929 and 1989 U.S. GNP (constant 1989 dollars) by the population in those two years, we obtain a per capita GNP of $6,160 and $21,035 for 1929 and 1989, respectively. Thus, the real output per person increased more than threefold from 1929 to 1989. The results of removing the bias caused by an increase in the price level and by the increase in population are presented in Table 7–1.

To summarize briefly, the more than fiftyfold growth in total current-dollar GNP is reduced to about a sevenfold growth between 1929 and 1989 when adjusted for price-level changes. After dividing through by population, we obtain about a threefold increase in real GNP per capita between 1929 and 1989.

C. Nonmarket Activities

A third source of bias in GNP as a measure of economic well-being can occur because GNP does not include many nonmarket activities in the economy. In a previous section we noted that in measuring GNP, the government attributes a value to food produced and consumed on farms and to owner-occupied housing. There are, however, other things that people value that are not in GNP.

An important nonmarket item is leisure time. Even though it is not bought and sold in the market, there can be little doubt that people place a value on it. But the value of leisure is not included in GNP. In itself, the omission of the value of leisure from GNP need not bias GNP as a measure of well-being as long as the amount of leisure remains constant over time, or among countries. But if the amount of leisure time increases, measured GNP will not grow as rapidly as it would have if people were receiving larger paychecks for working the extra hours.

The amount of leisure time can be approximated by the length of the workweek. The shorter the workweek, the more leisure time is available. As shown in Table 7–2, in all manufacturing industries in the United States, the average length of the workweek declined from 44.2 hours in 1929 to 41 hours in 1989. However, most of this decline came during the 1930s. After increasing to 45.2 hours in 1944, the workweek in manufacturing settled down to about 40 hours after World War II and has remained there ever since. In contrast, the workweek in retail trade has

TABLE 7–2   Length of Workweek, U.S. Manufacturing and Retail Trade, Selected Years, 1929–89

Year	Manufacturing (hours)	Retail Trade (hours)	Year	Manufacturing (hours)	Retail Trade (hours)
1929	44.2	—	1964	40.7	37.0
1934	34.6	—	1969	40.6	34.2
1939	37.7	43.4	1974	40.0	32.7
1944	45.2	41.0	1979	40.2	32.6
1949	39.1	40.4	1984	40.7	30.0
1954	39.6	39.2	1989	41.0	29.2
1959	40.3	38.2			

Source: *Economic Report of the President,* 1969, p. 260, and 1990, p. 344.

declined substantially from World War II to the present. However, part-time jobs have become quite common in retail trade, so the measured decline is not a true indication of the length of the workweek for full-time workers. It is probably safe to say that the leisure-time bias should not be a problem unless we are comparing current GNP with pre-1930 figures, or if we are comparing U.S. GNP with the GNP of nations with longer workweeks, mainly the less-developed countries. In these cases, the current U.S. GNP will understate the true current well-being.

Related to the leisure-time bias, but operating in the opposite direction, is the bias caused by the entry of women into the labor force. With the coming of laborsaving devices in the home, together with higher educational levels and increased job opportunities for women, a larger proportion of the nation's females now hold full- or part-time jobs than was true 40 or 50 years ago. For example, in 1940 about 28 percent of all women in the United States participated in the labor force, whereas in 1989 this figure more than doubled to 57 percent. Instead of making clothes, baking bread, watching the children, washing dishes, and so forth, more women are now using part of their salaries to purchase these services in the market. The purchases of ready-to-wear clothing, convenience foods, restaurant meals, child-care services, appliances for cleaning and food preparation, and so on are included in the GNP measure. When the tasks performed by these purchases were done by women in the home, they were not reflected in the GNP measure. Some offset to this bias occurs because of the decrease in employment of maids, housekeepers, and gardeners over the past 50 years. The services of these people were a part of GNP. At any rate, it appears that the movement of women from the home to factories and offices has caused our current GNP to look better than it really is in comparison to GNP 50 years ago. This is not because the goods and services produced by women are of little value to society. The bias is due to the increase in household activities that pass through the market and are therefore caught by the GNP measure. It has been estimated that 7 percent of the increase in real per capita GNP that occurred between 1950 and 1982 was due to the monetization of household activities previously carried out in the home.[3]

The bias caused by leaving out nonmarket activities also becomes important when a society changes from a rural, self-sufficient economy to an urban, market-oriented economy. Years ago, rural people were much more self-sufficient than either rural or urban people are today. They built and repaired their own utensils and tools, wove cloth, sewed their own clothes, built some of their own furniture, and grew their own fuel for transportation (feed for horses). Even though many of these goods and services never came through the market and hence were not caught by GNP, the people living in those days nevertheless benefited from their use.

The effect on GNP of the transformation from a self-sufficient, rural economy to a monetized, market-oriented economy is especially important for the developing nations. By catching a growing proportion of daily activities in the GNP measure, a nation can exhibit an impressive rate of economic growth that may overstate the true growth in real output.

D. Military Expenditures

The inclusion in GNP of military expenditures together with police and fire-protection costs represents a potential source of bias when using GNP to measure economic well-being. During wars or times of military conflict, the government increases its spending on national defense. Since military goods cannot be consumed or invested, the production of these items does not contribute to economic well-being, at least directly. Granted, if the country were defeated or destroyed by a foreign power, economic well-being as well as personal freedoms would decline drastically. Thus, most people would probably argue that some military spending is necessary. But military spending will cause a bias in GNP as a measure of changes in well-being if the percent of GNP devoted to the military changes. For example, between 1939 and 1944, the percent of GNP devoted to military spending increased from just over 1 percent to more than 40 percent (see Table 7–3). Even though GNP increased greatly over this five-year period, economic well-being did not increase in proportion. The same phenomenon occurred during the Korean and Vietnam wars, although the bias in these cases was less pronounced than during World War II. In general, wars cause GNP to overstate the growth in economic well-being.

With the exception of the Korean and Vietnam wars, the proportion of GNP devoted to military spending has followed a long-term downward trend in the United States since World War II (see Table 7–3). This trend causes a slight downward bias in the growth of economic well-being as measured by GNP. It is a

---

[3] David L. Hammes, Jean-Jacques Rosa, and Herbert G. Grubel, "The National Accounts, Household Service Consumption, and its Monetization," *KYKLOS* 42 (1989), pp. 3–15.

TABLE 7–3 U.S. Military Spending as a Percent of GNP, 1939–1989

Year	Percent	Year	Percent
1939	1.3	1969	8.2
1944	41.6	1974	5.5
1949	5.2	1979	4.6
1954	13.0	1984	6.1
1959	9.5	1989	5.8
1964	7.9		

Source: *Economic Report of the President*, 1969, p. 227, and 1990, p. 295.

relatively easy task to remove any bias caused by military spending by subtracting this amount from GNP to arrive at nonmilitary GNP, as shown in Table 7–4. This figure provides a more accurate measure of how many goods and services are available for consumption and investment purposes. In 1989, for example, the subtraction of military spending reduced per capita GNP by $1,222, or 5.8 percent.

Whether the amount spent on the military is too large, about right, or too small is a matter of opinion. Those who argue for increased military spending believe it is cheaper in the long run to be strong militarily if doing so forestalls potential aggressor nations from stirring up trouble around the world and creating situations

TABLE 7–4 U.S. Military Expenditures, Total and Nonmilitary GNP, Five-Year Intervals, 1939–1989 (constant 1989 dollars)

Year	Military Expenditures		Per Capita GNP	
	Total ($ Billions)	Per Person ($)	Total ($)	Nonmilitary ($)
1939	$ 11	$ 872	$ 6,160	$ 5,288
1944	608	4,401	10,553	6,152
1949	71	445	8,786	8,341
1954	189	1,154	10,259	9,105
1959	190	1,074	11,345	10,271
1964	193	1,001	13,022	12,021
1969	253	1,253	15,243	13,990
1974	193	912	16,764	15,852
1979	190	859	18,690	17,831
1984	264	1,116	18,461	17,345
1989	303	1,222	21,035	19,813

Source: *Economic Report of the President*, 1990, p. 295.

that may pull the country into war. The long-run downward trend in the military's share of GNP no doubt was a factor in the Reagan administration's decision to build up the military during the early 1980s. Those who favor a smaller military believe that spending billions in this area amounts to a sheer waste of resources and, if anything, increases the chances of war by creating situations where nations resort to military solutions to problems. There is no way of knowing who is right. Most everyone wants peace; the question is, What is the best way to attain it?

E. Distribution of Output

Although this item is not strictly a bias, we should be mindful of the importance of the distribution of a nation's output on the economic well-being of the average person. When we computed per capita GNP, we simply divided total GNP by the number of people in the country. We obtain the same figure regardless of how GNP is distributed. But most people probably believe that society as a whole is better off if everyone is able to share in the nation's output as opposed to the case where the nation's income and wealth are concentrated in the hands of a few very rich and powerful families. The oil-rich kingdoms of the Middle East provide a good example of the latter case.

In Chapters 21 and 22 we will study in more detail some of the major problems and issues in the areas of poverty and income distribution. For now, it is sufficient that we become aware that the per capita GNP figure does not tell us anything about how the GNP is distributed. We might say, however, that this problem is less severe in the United States than in many other countries of the world. Although U.S. output is by no means shared equally, neither is it concentrated in the hands of a select few. Also, the United States has not experienced a drastic change in income distribution during its history.

The biases inherent in GNP and their effect on GNP as a measure of the growth of economic well-being in the United States from 1929 to the present are summarized below.

Bias	Effect on GNP As a Measure of Well-being
Inflation	Overstates
Population growth	Overstates
Increased leisure time	Understates
Entry of women in labor force	Overstates
Decrease in maids and housekeepers	Understates
Less self-sufficiency	Overstates
Relative growth of the military	Overstates

EXPENDITURE COMPONENTS OF GNP

In the discussion relating to the flowchart of the economy in Figure 7–1, it was pointed out that the total output of the economy consists of consumption goods, investment goods, and goods purchased and distributed by the government. In this section, we will take a somewhat more detailed look at what is included in each category.

A. Personal Consumption Expenditures

As the name implies, this category includes the expenditures of individuals and households on all consumer items. It is common to further divide this category into (*a*) consumer durables such as automobiles, refrigerators, and television sets and (*b*) consumer nondurables, which include both goods (meat, bread, clothes, beverages, cosmetics, etc.) and services (medical and dental care, barber and beauty shop services, repair services, etc.).

One large item that is perhaps conspicuous by its absence is the purchase of newly constructed residential housing. The Department of Commerce includes this item in the investment category. However, the Commerce Department does compute the annual rental value of owner-occupied housing and adds this amount to consumer expenditures, along with actual rental payments on apartments and houses. Also, as mentioned, the purchases of secondhand items are not included, mainly because they represent a transfer of assets rather than a net addition to output.

B. Gross Private Domestic Investment

Investment as used in this context refers to the expenditures on construction of physical capital or facilities, mainly buildings, machines, and tools. It does not include the purchase of stocks or bonds, or money placed in a savings account. We sometimes refer to the purchase of these items as an "investment." But this does not constitute investment as defined in the national accounts, mainly because it involves a mere transfer of assets from one party to another and not an addition to the nation's stock of physical capital.

The distinguishing feature of investment goods as defined in the national accounts is that they yield a stream of services or returns over a long period of time. This is in contrast to consumer goods, which tend to be used up over a shorter period. One might argue that consumer durables, such as automobiles and appliances, yield their services over a long period, too. But the line between consumer durables and investment goods had to be drawn somewhere. Recall, however, that the construction of residential housing is included as an investment good.

In addition to machines, tools, and buildings, the investment component of GNP includes any change in inventories held by business firms. In order for GNP to accurately reflect the nation's output for a given year or time period, it is necessary to add any net *increase* in inventories that has taken place. In this case, the output or production of goods and services is greater than sales. Of course, a large part of the nation's inventories are consumer goods, but the main thing is that they are included somewhere. By the same token, a net *decrease,* or drawing down, of inventories is subtracted from the investment figure to reflect the fact that sales of final goods and services exceeded their production.

Some explanation is in order in reference to the modifiers "gross private domestic" in the heading of this subsection. *Gross* refers to the total new investment during a given year. It does not contain any deduction for the amount of capital that has been used up or depreciated during the year. Hence, gross investment will overstate the true increase in the nation's capital. Later we will discuss the measure of output when depreciation of capital has been deducted. *Private* denotes investment by the private sector as opposed to government investment. Finally, *domestic* refers to investment in the United States as opposed to investment in other nations. In future discussion we will refer to only gross or net investment, with the understanding that the "private domestic" adjectives also apply.

C. Government Spending

This category of expenditures includes the purchases of goods and services by all levels of government—federal, state, and local. Included are such items as expenditures on military hardware and personnel, police and fire protection, public school operation, roads, and public parks. However it does not include so-called transfer payments. By and large these are transfers from taxpayers to welfare and social security recipients. As such, these payments do not represent a net addition to output; hence, they are not counted in GNP. Of course, the expenditure of these funds by the recipients on either consumption or investment goods is reflected in GNP.

To summarize briefly, we have identified the three major components of GNP from the standpoint of expenditures on final goods and services: (1) consumption, (2) investment (gross), and (3) government spending. Traditionally, these components have been identified as C, I_g, and G, respectively. Thus, an easy way to remember the makeup of GNP is to call to mind the simple formula:

$$GNP = C + I_g + G$$

Figures showing the percent of GNP accounted for by each of these three expenditure categories for selected years from 1929 to 1989 are presented in Table 7–5. During the post-World War II period, the shares going to the three groups have been relatively constant.

TABLE 7-5 Percent of Each of the Three Major Expenditure Categories in GNP, 1929–1989

Year	Consumption	Investment	Government
1929	75%	16%	9%
1934	79	5	16
1939	74	10	16
1944	52	3	45
1949	69	14	17
1954	65	14	21
1959	64	16	20
1964	63	15	22
1969	62	16	22
1974	63	15	22
1979	63	17	20
1984	64	17	19
1989	66	15	19

Source: *Economic Report of the President*, 1990, p. 294.

INCOME COMPONENTS OF GNP

Although we will be interested mainly in the three expenditure components of GNP in later chapters, it should be mentioned that GNP also can be viewed from the income side. In other words, instead of measuring the expenditures on final goods and services, we can measure the income derived from the production of these goods and services. It is a bit easier to grasp the idea of this dual measure of GNP if we remember that every dollar spent on a good or service is income to somebody; that is, for every dollar of expenditure, there is a dollar of income. Thus, if we measure income, we should obtain exactly the same figure as when we measure expenditures.

Traditionally, the Department of Commerce has divided the nation's income into four categories: (1) wages, (2) interest, (3) rents, and (4) profits. The first category, wages, represents the income of wage and salary workers. Interest and rents represent income earned by the owners of capital (machines, buildings, land, etc.). The fourth category, profits, is a residual representing what is left for producers after paying wages, interest, and rents. One can view profits as payments to owners of firms for the capital they have contributed as well as a reward for taking risks in initiating and carrying on production. Of course, there is no guarantee that profits will always be positive, at least for the individual firm.

Measuring GNP in terms of income is useful in that it tells us how much of the nation's output is enjoyed by each category of resource owner. The division between wages and the other three categories is of particular interest in that it provides an indication of labor's share of national output in relation to capital's share. Of course, workers also own a substantial share of the nation's capital, particularly when we consider that pension funds, which account for over 35 percent of the stock invested in corporations, are in fact owned by workers.

Dividing income into the above four categories is generally referred to as the "functional distribution" of income. As the name implies, this distribution categorizes income by the function of its recipients—workers, owners of capital, and management. Income also can be categorized according to its "personal distribution." In this case, income is divided according to the income level of its recipients. It tells us, for example, what share of the nation's income flows to the upper 10 percent of the nation's income recipients, what share flows to the next 10 percent, and so on. We will study the personal distribution of income in more detail in Chapter 21.

The relative shares of these four income categories are presented in Table 7–6. Over the 1929–89 period, wages have accounted for the major share of the nation's income, between 81 and 85 percent in most years. Although the data do not reveal any long-run trends in the share of income going to each category, there is some year-to-year variation. Note that during the years shown when unemployment was the highest—1934, 1939, and 1984—profits were the lowest in

TABLE 7–6   Relative Shares of National Income, Five-Year Intervals, 1929–1989

Year	Wages*	Interest	Rents	Profits†
1929	76%	5%	6%	12%
1934	85	8	3	3
1939	83	5	4	9
1944	83	1	3	13
1949	81	1	4	14
1954	82	1	4	13
1959	81	2	4	13
1964	81	3	3	13
1969	83	4	3	10
1974	85	6	2	7
1979	82	7	1	10
1984	81	8	2	9
1989	82	11	1	6

* Includes compensation of employees, business and professional income, and farm income.
† Includes corporate profits before taxes with inventory evaluation adjustment.

Source: *Economic Report of the President,* 1970, p. 191, and 1990, pp. 320–21.

relative terms. Thus, it is in the interest of both management and labor to maintain full employment. Also, the increase in interest rates during the 1980s increased the interest share at the expense of the profit share, which was the lowest in 1989 of any time since the Great Depression.

GOVERNMENT AS A SEPARATE SECTOR

The traditional breakdown of GNP from the standpoint of expenditures includes government purchases of goods and services as a separate item or sector. Although the three-way division of GNP into consumption, investment, and government spending turns out to be useful in future discussion, one should guard against a complete separation of government from the rest of the economy. By treating government as a separate entity, it is easy to regard the goods and services purchased by the government as neither consumption nor investment goods, and as such unavailable to the general public. But this is not true.

With the possible exception of purchases for the military, all goods and services purchased by the government can be classified as either consumption or investment goods. For example, expenditures on public parks and school lunches could be considered consumption goods. Government expenditures on roads and flood-control projects could be considered investment goods. The main point is that people benefit from government consumption and investment expenditures, as they do from private expenditures, on these two kinds of goods. Even though we will follow the convention of separating government from private-sector expenditures in the remainder of this book, we should not be led to believe that government goods and services are lost or unavailable to the people. Aside from the cost of running the government bureaucracy, it does not "consume" any goods or services; the people do.

It is equally important to recognize that the government does not pay for anything either. All the money that the government spends must first come from taxpayers; and taxpayers are individual people. Even the so-called taxes on business, such as the corporation income tax, are ultimately borne by individuals through higher prices for goods and/or lower dividends received by stockholders. Strictly speaking, there is no such thing as federal funds or even state funds; all government funds come from individuals. It is true that if certain goods are paid for by taxes collected by the federal government, different individuals may end up paying for the goods than if they were purchased by state or local governments, or by the people who benefit from the goods.

NET EXPORTS IN GNP

Although the three expenditure items, consumption, investment, and government spending, comprise the major share of GNP, to be strictly correct we should include a fourth item—net exports. *Net exports* are defined as total exports minus total imports. For example, if the country sells $50 billion worth of goods and services to foreign countries and buys $48 billion in return, net exports are $2 billion.

It is somewhat unfortunate that foreign trade enters GNP in this manner, particularly if we wish to use GNP as a measure of economic well-being, for it implies that the more we can sell to foreign countries and the less we buy from them, the better off we are. But, again, this is not true. Goods and services we use that are produced abroad benefit us as much as things produced in this country.

The effect of subtracting imports from GNP is reduced to an absurdity if we use an extreme example. Suppose we (the United States) were able to sell everything we produced to other countries but did not buy anything in return, that is, zero imports. In this case, we would not be able to enjoy any of the fruits of our labor because we would have sold them all abroad. The apparent desirability of exports probably stems from the extra business and employment generated by foreign sales. Yet we should keep in mind that in order for other countries to buy from us they must have dollars, which they obtain by selling goods to us; international trade is a two-way street. Perhaps the main point here is that both exports and imports are good if they add to the total output available to the people. We will see in Chapter 23 how international trade can result in more total goods available to people of all nations.

The reason exports are added to GNP and imports subtracted is to obtain a measure of production rather than consumption. Recall that GNP measures the output or production of final goods and services. When we refer to economic well-being we are really talking about consumption. This is another reason GNP is not a perfect measure of economic well-being.

NET NATIONAL PRODUCT

In addition to gross national product, the Department of Commerce computes a number of other measures of national output or income. A second measure is net national product (NNP). Net national product differs from GNP in that the depreciation of capital (*D*) is subtracted. Depreciation of capital is often referred to as *capital consumption allowances*. In a sense, it is the capital that is worn out or used up during the year in the production of goods and services.

$$NNP = GNP - D$$

As stated in a previous section, GNP is the total expenditure on final goods and services by consumers, investors, and government agencies. These expenditures generally are abbreviated by $C + I_g + G$, where I_g stands for gross investment.[4] Net national product, on the other hand, is denoted by $C + I_n + G$, where I_n represents net investment. Net investment equals gross investment minus depreciation.

---

[4] Net exports are deleted to simplify the discussion.

$$\text{GNP} = C + I_g + G$$

$$\text{NNP} = C + I_n + G$$

NNP is considered to be a more accurate measure of the true output of the economy than GNP. If a nation uses up its capital to produce goods and services (as the United States did during World War II), it may have a large output temporarily, but sooner or later output will decline as the stock of capital in the country is depleted. NNP reflects how much is produced over and above that required to keep the nation's stock of capital intact.

NATIONAL INCOME

National income (NI) is equal to NNP minus indirect business taxes (T_{IB}). By and large, these are the sales, excise, and property taxes. National income is supposed to be a more accurate measure of income to labor and owners of capital because these taxes are siphoned off by the government. It should be remembered, however, that the national income measure became institutionalized before the income tax was very important or was deducted from paychecks; so years ago it was a more accurate indicator of incomes to resource owners than is the case now.

PERSONAL INCOME

Personal income (PI) is defined as the income received by households before personal income taxes. It is computed by subtracting social security taxes (T_{ss}), corporate income taxes (T_{CI}), and corporate saving (S_c) from NI and adding transfer payments (T_R) to this figure. Transfer payments represent income payments from government to individuals other than for services rendered, that is, gifts. Because personal income requires four adjustments to national income, it will be useful to summarize what we have done:

$$\text{PI} = \text{NI} - T_{ss} - T_{CI} - S_c + T_R$$

DISPOSABLE INCOME

Disposable income (DI) is equal to PI minus personal income taxes (T_{PI}). This measure represents the income that people have to spend or save. In other words, there are only two things that people can do with their disposable income; they can spend it, or they can save it. The Department of Commerce separates these two components of DI and publishes the annual expenditure on consumption and personal saving:

$$\text{DI} = \text{PI} - T_{PI}$$

$$\text{DI} = C + S$$

TABLE 7–7 U.S. per Capita Disposable Income, Selected Years, 1929–1989 (constant 1989 dollars)

Year	Income	Year	Income
1929	$4,926	1969	$10,521
1939	4,817	1974	11,736
1949	6,600	1979	12,423
1954	7,111	1984	12,998
1959	8,137	1989	15,194
1964	9,179		

Source: *Economic Report of the President,* 1990, p. 325.

Although people no doubt value the public goods component of GNP, the figure that most people probably consider the most revealing of their own economic well-being is disposable income—what they have left after taxes to spend on themselves or their families, or to save. Figures giving the per capita disposable income for people in the United States from 1929 to 1989 (in constant 1989 dollars) are in Table 7–7. Notice the decline that occurred from 1929 to 1939, but the more than threefold growth of real per capita DI from 1929 to 1989.

SUMMARY OF OUTPUT OR INCOME MEASURES

In this chapter, five different measures of the nation's output or income have been presented. They tend to be confusing and difficult to remember, but a brief summary might be helpful.

	Gross national product
Less:	Depreciation of capital
Equals:	**Net national product**
Less:	Indirect business taxes
Equals:	**National income**
Less:	Social security taxes
	Corporate income taxes
	Corporate saving
Plus:	Transfer payments
Equals:	**Personal income**
Less:	Personal income taxes
Equals:	**Disposable income**

SUMMARY

All income received by resource owners is either spent on consumer goods or saved. Saving provides the wherewithal to produce investment goods. Gross national product (GNP) is the value of all final goods and services produced in the economy during a specific period, usually a year. It is measured by summing the value added of all industries. The effect of inflation on GNP can be removed by dividing nominal GNP by the consumer price index of the corresponding year. The result gives GNP in constant prices of the base year. Although the effects of population growth and inflation on GNP can be easily removed, other biases, such as the increased participation of women in the labor force, make GNP less than a perfect measure of economic well-being. Two other commonly used measures of national income or output are net national product (NNP) and disposable income (DI).

YOU SHOULD KNOW

1. The two real flows and the two monetary flows in the economy.
2. The definition of gross national product.
3. How GNP is measured.
4. Why GNP is measured by value added rather than total sales.
5. Why GNP can give a biased picture of economic well-being.
6. How to deflate GNP using the CPI.
7. How to change the base year of the CPI.
8. How nonmarket activities cause GNP to give a biased measure of economic well-being.
9. The relative importance of military spending in GNP.
10. The three expenditure components of GNP.
11. The four income components of GNP.
12. How imports and exports influence GNP.
13. How net national product and disposable income are computed.

QUESTIONS

1. *a.* According to the simple flowchart of the economy, income received by households must equal expenditure by households on consumer goods and services. True or false? Explain.
   b. Why is it necessary to have saving in order to have investment?

2. What is GNP? How is it measured? Why is GNP measured in value-added terms rather than as total sales?

3. Which of the following would be included in GNP? Explain.
   a. Used-car sales.
   b. Stock market transactions.
   c. Rental value of owner-occupied housing.
   d. Welfare payments.
   e. Transactions in the "underground economy."
   f. Laundry done at home.
   g. Laundry done by commercial laundries.

4. State whether each of the following circumstances causes GNP to overstate or understate growth in economic well-being between 1929 and the present and explain why.
   a. An increase in the general price level.
   b. An increase in population.
   c. An increase in leisure time.
   d. An increase in meals purchased in restaurants relative to meals eaten at home.
   e. An increase in the proportion of women in the labor force.
   f. An increase in the "underground economy."
   g. An increase in military spending.
   h. An increase in expenditures for police protection because of an increase in crime.

Answer question 5 from the following information.

Year	GNP per Capita (Current Dollars)	CPI (1967 = 100)
1930	$ 735	50
1960	2,852	89
1989	21,035	371

5. a. Calculate GNP per capita in constant 1967 dollars.
   b. Calculate GNP per capita in constant 1989 dollars.

6. Exports are added to GNP and imports are subtracted. It follows that the more we export and the less we import the better off we will be because GNP will be larger. True or false? Explain.

7. Which of the measures of national income or output would most accurately reflect:
   a. the total value of output of final goods and services.
   b. how much is produced over and above that which is required to maintain the nation's stock of capital intact.
   c. how much money people have to spend or save.

SELF-TEST

1. Conceptually, all production in an economy can be divided into _____ goods and _____ goods.
   a. investment; public
   b. private; consumption
   c. public; consumption
   d. investment; consumption

2. Income received by households is payment received for _____ supplied to the business sector.
   a. labor
   b. consumer goods
   c. capital
   d. resources

3. In the economic flowchart, income received by households equals _____ by households.
   a. expenditures on consumer goods
   b. investment on capital goods
   c. expenditure on consumer goods plus saving
   d. investment on capital goods plus saving

4. If all the nation's resources were devoted to the production of consumer goods, there would be no production of _____ goods. Therefore, _____ provides the wherewithal to _____ .
   a. investment; spending; invest
   b. future; saving; spend
   c. investment; saving; invest
   d. future; spending; save

5. In the economy, saving is done by:
   a. households.
   b. business firms.
   c. government.
   d. a and b.

6. Gross national product (GNP) is the total value of _____ in the economy during a given year.
   a. sales
   b. final goods produced
   c. consumer goods produced
   d. investment goods produced

7. In the measurement of GNP, wherever possible _____ are used to assign value.
   a. market prices
   b. costs of production
   c. government-controlled prices
   d. government agencies

8. In measuring GNP, the Department of Commerce adds up the _____ by all the industries in the economy.
   a. value of final goods produced
   b. sales
   c. value added
   d. value of consumer goods produced

9. The sum of _____ by all firms engaged in the production of a product equals selling price of the final product.
   a. sales
   b. production costs
   c. expenditures
   d. value added

10. Value added of a firm equals _____ minus _____ .
    a. sales; expenses
    b. expenses; sales

c. sales; purchases from other firms
d. purchases from other firms; sales

11. Which of the following would *not* be included in GNP?
    a. value of food produced and consumed on farms
    b. value of leisure time
    c. value of owner-occupied housing
    d. a and c

12. Which of the following would be included in GNP?
    a. value of leisure time
    b. value of time used to prepare meals at home
    c. value of time to prepare meals eaten in restaurants
    d. a and b

13. Using GNP to measure economic well-being presumes that people:
    a. do not value public goods.
    b. place no value on the finer things in life such as the arts and theater.
    c. prefer more to less.
    d. are driven by the desire for material gain.

14. The existence of inflation causes nominal GNP to _____ the growth in economic well-being. This bias can be removed by dividing each year's GNP by _____ and multiplying by 100.
    a. overstate; population
    b. understate; population
    c. overstate; the CPI
    d. understate; the CPI

Answer questions 15–17 from the following table.

Year	GNP	CPI
1	100	100
2	500	250

15. GNP in year 2 in constant year 1 prices:
    a. $100   *c.* $250
    b. $500   *d.* $200

16. The CPI for year 1 when year 2 is the base year is:
    a. 100   *c.* 40
    b. 250   *d.* 25

17. GNP in year 1 in constant year 2 prices:
    a. 100   *c.* 250
    b. 500   *d.* 400

18. Real GNP per capita in the United States increased over _____ fold between 1929 and 1989.
    a. two   *c.* four
    b. three   *d.* five

19. The _____ in the length of the work-week between 1929 and the present causes real GNP per capita to _____ the growth in economic well-being.
    a. decrease; overstate
    b. increase; overstate
    c. decrease; understate
    d. increase; understate

20. The increased participation of women in the labor force causes GNP to _____ growth in economic well-being because _____ .
    a. overstate; more consumer goods and services are purchased rather than produced at home
    b. overstate; women earn less than men
    c. understate; more consumer goods and services are purchased rather than produced at home
    d. understate; women earn less then men

21. Subtracting military spending from GNP reduces measured economic well-being in the United States by about _____ percent.
    a. 50   *c.* 12
    b. 25   *d.* 6

22. Which of the following is *not* included among three expenditure components of GNP?
    a. personal consumption expenditures
    b. wages
    c. gross private domestic investment
    d. government purchases of goods and services

23. Which of the following is *not* among the four income components of GNP?
    a. wages   *c.* rents
    b. interest   *d.* pensions

24. An increase in exports _____ GNP but _____ the amount of goods available for consumption.
    a. decreases; increases
    b. increases; decreases
    c. decreases; decreases
    d. increases; increases

25. NNP equals GNP _____ .
    a. minus government spending
    b. minus depreciation of capital
    c. plus government spending
    d. plus depreciation of capital

26. The amount of money people have to spend or to save is:
    a. national income.
    b. disposable income.
    c. personal income.
    d. wage income.

Part III

Classical Economics

Chapter 8

The Classical Economists

OVERVIEW

The objective over the next six chapters is to present the main tenets of macroeconomic thought in chronological order. We begin in 1776 with the work of Adam Smith and the classical economists and follow them into the 19th century. The next chapter addresses in more detail one of the main theories of classical economics—the quantity theory of money. The discussion then turns to the work of John Maynard Keynes whose ideas are still influential in modern macroeconomic thought. Keynes's major book, *The General Theory of Employment, Interest, and Money,* appeared in 1936. This is followed by a discussion of the main schools of thought that evolved after World War II.

INTRODUCTION

Although the main emphasis of this text is on contemporary economic principles and problems, some understanding of early economic thought and how it evolved over time will be helpful in understanding the current material. Over the remainder of the text, it will be interesting to observe the similarities and differences between current economic thought and that which existed in the early years of the discipline. It may come as a surprise to see that many of the ideas and issues of 200 years ago are still alive and fresh today. Understandably, it is not possible in a single chapter to present in detail a body of literature encompassing many thousands of pages. One should view this chapter as an appetizer rather than a full meal in one's economic food for thought.

The early economic writers have come to be known as classical economists—a name coined by Karl Marx. Most were from Great Britain, although there were some from France, Germany, Sweden, and Austria. Their period in history is generally regarded to extend from about 1776 to the 1870s, although some writers have placed all economic literature before the 1930s in the classical school.

GREAT BOOKS

This chapter is organized along the lines of concepts and issues rather than books or writers. But it will be helpful to have a brief introduction to the major writers of the period and their work in order to provide a frame of reference for the discussion to follow. Also, the early economists built upon each other's work, as is true of all sciences even now. By virtue of the constraints of space and time, coverage of classical thought must be selective and not highly detailed. Several excellent books summarize and critique the works of the classical economists.[1]

Any discussion of classical economics must begin with Adam Smith, who is widely regarded as the founding father of economics. His best-known book, *An Inquiry into the Nature and Causes of the Wealth of Nations* (1776), is commonly referred to by just the last four words of the full title—*The Wealth of Nations*. The major emphasis of the book was on economic growth. In general, Smith was fairly optimistic about England's chances of achieving economic growth provided changes were made in government policy that he prescribed and that will be explained in more detail in later sections.

The optimistic tone of *The Wealth of Nations* regarding future improvements in the standard of living of people became the accepted mode of economic thought over the last quarter of the 18th century. But in 1798 there appeared a book titled *An Essay on the Principle of Population as It Affects the Future Improvements of Society,* by the Reverend Thomas Malthus. In short, Malthus argued that any gains achieved by economic growth would be wiped out by population growth, leaving mankind in a long-run state of poverty and hunger. As Malthus's bleak picture of the future became widely known in the years following the publication of his essay, Thomas Carlyle, a Scottish writer and historian, dubbed economics the "dismal science," a name that still sticks today.

As we move into the 19th century, the rate of publication of new books on economics picks up considerably; and we do something of an injustice to the many early writers for not mentioning them all. But it is necessary to limit the discussion to the books that have become best known. The next book, *Traité d'Économie Politique* (Treatise on Political Economy) (1803) by Jean-Baptiste Say, a French economist, is probably not so well known as one of the ideas contained therein. The idea has come to be known as Say's law. In simple terms, Say's law can be interpreted to mean that supply creates its own demand. Say put forth this idea in response to those who argued that if a nation experienced economic growth, there would eventually come a "general glut" of goods on the market that could not be sold as people reached a level of total satiation. The concern was that, when the

---

[1] See, for example, Thomas Sowell, *Classical Economics Reconsidered* (Princeton, N.J.: Princeton University Press, 1974); D. P. O'Brien, *The Classical Economists* (Oxford: Clarendon Press, 1975); and Mark Blaug, *Economic Theory in Retrospect* (Cambridge: Cambridge University Press, 1978). For an entertaining book on the lives and times of the classical economists, see Robert L. Heilbroner, *The Worldly Philosophers* (New York: Simon & Schuster, 1972).

general glut of goods appeared, not everyone who wanted to work would be able to find a job, leading to a permanent state of unemployment.

David Ricardo's *Principles of Political Economy* (1815) is often compared to Adam Smith's *Wealth of Nations*. The consensus seems to be that as an exercise in rigorous economic reasoning, Ricardo's *Principles* is superior, but from the standpoint of breadth of coverage and insights into the workings of society, Smith is still the master. Ricardo is probably best known for his work on the pricing of factors of production, particularly on land rent, and for providing an economic basis for trade between two nations even when one of the countries is more productive than the other in all areas of production. The latter idea will be explained in Chapter 23 on international trade.

John Stuart Mill's two-volume work, also titled *Principles of Political Economy* (1848), represents another milestone in early economic thought. The purpose of the book, as Mill stated in the preface, was to update *The Wealth of Nations,* "adapted to the more extended knowledge and improved ideas of the present age." Clearly Mill underestimated his accomplishment. Over 50 years later, the book was still the dominant textbook in introductory economics courses in both British and American universities. If one were to rank the books that most shaped early economic thought, Smith's *Wealth of Nations,* Ricardo's *Principles,* and Mill's *Principles* would be high on the list.

Gradually the classical school of thought gave way during the last quarter of the 19th century to a new school that has come to be known as neoclassical economics. Risking the danger of oversimplifying, one might say that the primary emphasis of the classical school was on macroeconomics, including the issues of economic growth, unemployment, control of the money supply and prices, over-population, taxation, and international trade, along with the determination of wages and the prices of other resources, mainly land. The neoclassical school focused more on microeconomics. Neoclassical writers made significant advances in the theory of consumer behavior, the theory of the firm, and the theory of markets, with more emphasis on relative prices as opposed to the absolute level of prices. It is probably not coincidental that neoclassical writers developed the idea of the marginal or extra unit as opposed to the total or average measures. The coming of neoclassical thought is sometimes referred to as the "marginalist revolution." Stanley Jevon's *The Theory of Political Economy* (1871) marks the beginning of the new marginal analysis as well as the extensive use of mathematics. However, A. A. Cournot's *Recherches* (1838) was the first to develop the theory of the firm in mathematical terms. Walras's *Elements* (1874) also was highly mathematical in its approach.

While it would not be correct to include Karl Marx in either the classical or neoclassical school, his book *Das Kapital* (1867), which provides the basis for the Communist ideology, looms large, not only in the last half of the 19th century, but also in present-day thought, at least in the Communist nations. Some of the mainstreams of Marxist thought are presented later in this chapter.

As neoclassical theory developed, writers strove to make greater applications of economics to the everyday problems and decisions of individuals. P. H. Wicksteed's *The Common Sense of Political Economy* (1870) is a good example of these attempts. His discussion of how much train schedules could be speeded up by the shortening of family prayers, or how the value of a mother-in-law could be measured by how high a cliff one would dive off to save her, provide examples of economics in practice.

Another giant among neoclassical works is Alfred Marshall's *Principles of Economics* (1890). From the standpoint of longevity and influence, this book rivals Smith's *Wealth of Nations* and Mill's *Principles*. Indeed, Marshall may be regarded as the father of modern economics. The concepts of demand and supply presented in Chapter 4, for example, were more fully developed by him. Again, in the neoclassical tradition, Marshall's book is primarily micro in nature.

MERCANTILISM

At the time Adam Smith's *Wealth of Nations* appeared, mercantilism was the dominant mode of thinking, which in turn influenced much of government policy. *The Wealth of Nations* was written as an attack upon mercantilism. Thus, in order to understand the classical arguments, it is necessary to have some knowledge of mercantilistic thought.

One main tenet of mercantilist thought was that a nation's wealth depended primarily on the amount of gold or bullion a nation could accumulate. Wealth was associated with gold. One method of accumulating more gold, in addition to expropriating it from the New World, was to sell more goods to other countries than were bought from them. Thus, government policies were designed to encourage exports, particularly manufactured goods, and discourage imports. Colonization policies provided expanded markets for manufactured goods as well as jobs for government administrators. The Corn Laws, which taxed the imports of agricultural products, reduced imports and maintained favorable prices for large landowners. Labor unions were outlawed as conspiracies under the Combination Laws; their intended effect was to keep wages low so that British goods would have an advantage in the world market.

Whether the mercantilists really believed that their policies that facilitated the accumulation of gold were in the best interest of British society is something we cannot answer. We can be sure, however, that mercantilist policies enhanced the power and wealth of government, business interests, and large landowners at the expense of the great mass of poor people. This is not to say that the wealthy lacked social conscience, but it was somewhat warped, at least by present Western standards. The rich defended their lavish standard of living in the midst of extreme poverty by arguing that it was better for them to spend their money on luxury goods rather than give it to the poor. Giving money to the poor would just lead to idleness, which in turn would lead to all sorts of depravity. By producing luxuries for the rich, the poor would earn a little money and be kept busy.

It is interesting to note also that some of the mercantilists' ideas and policies contradicted each other. They wanted more gold and lower prices at home. But, as will be explained later, an increase in gold will lead to higher prices, which in turn will discourage exports. In fairness to the mercantilists, it should be pointed out that Britain imported a considerable amount of goods from the East Indies and the Baltic states but sold little in return to them. Hence, there was a continual concern over obtaining sufficient gold to pay for these imports. In such cases, it would have been more convincing to use this reason in their arguments rather than the one that viewed gold as good for its own sake.

THE WEALTH OF NATIONS

As mentioned, Adam Smith's *Wealth of Nations* was in part an attack on mercantilist ideas and government policies. Smith argued that it was the real output of goods and services that determined the true wealth of nations rather than the amount of money or gold a country was able to produce or accumulate. To Adam Smith and the other classical economists, money was a "veil." If removed, it would reveal the true wealth of a country—the flow of real goods and services. This is not to say that they viewed money as unimportant. They recognized the value of money as a medium of exchange, and they also were aware of the relationship between the quantity of money in existence and the price level. But the classical argument is in sharp contrast to mercantilist thought, which viewed money as an end in itself.

Smith and the other classicists stressed the creation of new wealth rather than its transfer between people and nations. In mercantilist doctrine, there was conflict between classes and nations; what one class or nation gained, the other lost. The classicists instead emphasized the existence of harmony between social classes and nations, while at the same time recognizing areas of conflict. In matters of commerce, according to classical thought, both trading partners gained rather than having one gainer and one loser.

In *The Wealth of Nations* and later classical writings, there is a genuine concern for poor people, and much emphasis is placed on bettering their lot. Smith argued that no nation can flourish if a greater part of the people is poor and impoverished. The classical economists condemned slavery on both moral and economic grounds. In the latter area, they argued that slavery's inherent weakness was the lack of incentives for the workers. Ricardo worked for the repeal of the Corn Laws, which established tariffs on the imports of wheat and other agricultural products that kept the price of food artificially high. These laws were especially hard on poor people. The classical economists also crusaded for the repeal of the Combination Laws, which outlawed labor unions. Some favored progressive taxation, in which the rich would pay a larger percent of their income as taxes than would the poor. The classicists also favored publicly funded education so that the children of poor families would have a better chance to break out of the cycle of poverty.

LAISSEZ-FAIRE

The term *laissez-faire* has come to be associated with the classical economists. It is defined as a policy whereby the government exercises minimum control over industry and trade. The classical economists preferred to allow competition rather than have government regulate the economy. They, of course, saw the necessity of a central government to enforce a system of laws, to provide for the national defense, and to supply certain public goods such as highways. While they were not pacifists, the classicists viewed wars as popularly supported adventures. They were not so naive as to believe that all wars were thrust upon the people by leaders seeking power and glory. Smith, for example, advocated a negotiated peace with America in 1776. The classical economists argued also that wars should be financed by current taxes rather than borrowing so that the people would know immediately the full economic cost of war and would therefore be less inclined to enter into armed conflict. Indeed, in all areas of government spending, they favored a balanced budget, or pay-as-you-go approach.

To support the concept of laissez-faire, Adam Smith developed the idea of the "invisible hand." Here Smith argued from the powerful motive of self-interest. It is not to the benevolence of the baker that we owe our bread, he argued, but rather to the baker's self-interest. The gist of Smith's argument is that businesspeople will produce those goods that provide them with the greatest rewards. But the goods that are most profitable to produce are those goods most desired by society, else they would not be so high priced and profitable. Thus, Smith argued that an economy is capable of regulating itself by this "invisible hand"; there is no need for the government to intervene. Indeed, Smith and the other classical economists maintained that government intervention promoted waste and inefficiency while supporting the vested interests of the wealthy and privileged classes.

It should also be noted that Smith and the later classical writers were as critical of private monopolies as they were of government. They interpreted monopoly very broadly as any case where a seller could influence the price of the product sold. They saw monopoly as being directed against the public good, resulting in higher prices for goods and services and distortions in the mix of goods that would be produced under a system of competition. In general, the classicists were distrustful of both big business and big government.

It has been argued that the idea of laissez-faire grew out of a society characterized by laissez-faire. But this is not correct. The idea grew out of a society greatly influenced by both big government and private monopoly. In reality, it was an idea designed to take away their privilege and power.

While the concept of laissez-faire has been used primarily to explain how an economy is capable of allocating resources to promote the public good without the intervention of government, the idea can also be extended to the problem of unemployment. Unemployment was a problem in classical times, and the classical economists were both aware of and concerned about its existence. For the most part, the classical economists saw unemployment coming from an overproduction of specific goods rather than a general overproduction of all goods, although

Ricardo thought that new technology might produce general unemployment. At any rate, the classical writers did not believe that depressions would be permanent. They argued that an economy contained mechanisms that, given time to work, would restore full employment. These mechanisms were flexible interest rates, wages, and prices.

To see the classical argument in more detail, consider a situation where there is a reduction in investment spending, which might occur because of a less optimistic attitude among businesspeople regarding future business conditions. The sudden reduction in investment would cause a surplus of funds in the so-called money market. As a result, there would be downward pressure on the interest rate, just as there is for the price of any good when a surplus exists. The decrease in the interest rate would counteract the pessimistic attitude of businesspeople by making it more profitable to invest. Also, because of the lower interest rate, consumers would find it less costly to borrow funds for large purchases, which in turn would stimulate their spending on such items. Thus, the classical economists argued that the likely decrease in interest rates resulting from the decrease in investment spending would set up counteracting forces to stimulate spending and restore full employment.

The classical economists used similar reasoning with regard to wages and prices. If unemployment appeared in the labor market, there would be a tendency for wages to fall as workers competed for the available jobs. The reduction in wages would in turn serve as an incentive for employers to hire more labor and for some people to drop out of the labor market, thereby lowering unemployment. The market for goods and services would behave similarly. The resulting surplus of unsold investment and consumer goods would result in downward pressure on these prices, restoring the purchasing power of lower wages and giving investors and consumers an incentive to step up their purchases, again stimulating the economy. Thus, the classical economists argued that an economy, if left alone, would return to a state of full employment in the event of temporary downturns in economic activity. One might call this the laissez-faire solution to unemployment.

SAY'S LAW

The classical economists were concerned with two kinds of unemployment: (1) that which occurs because of temporary overproduction in specific industries and (2) that resulting from a general overproduction of nearly all goods and services, commonly referred to as a general glut. The early classical writers admitted the possibility of the first type of unemployment but argued against the likelihood of the second. Actually, the first hint of what has come to be known as Say's law can be found even before *The Wealth of Nations* in the work of an early French economist, Mercier de la Rivière, a physiocrat. (The physiocrats argued that the only true net increase in wealth came from the soil; all other activities just passed the wealth around.) Rivière in his book *L'order naturel* (1767) pointed out that the value of all things sold must be equal to the value of all things bought. There are two ways of interpreting this idea. One interpretation is that it's simply a definition—

the value of sales must be equal to the value of purchases. But it is clear from Rivière's book that he had something more profound in mind. The second interpretation is that the proceeds from sales provide the wherewithal to engage in purchases. Adam Smith, also writing before Say, developed the idea a little further. Smith argued that money did not have any value in and of itself but was only useful as a means of purchasing goods and services. Therefore, he argued, when people receive money from the production of goods and services, they will almost immediately turn around and spend the money on either the same things or on other goods. Thus, the money earned from production (supply) provides the means to buy (demand). It is this interpretation that has given rise to the popular phrase used to describe Say's law—"Supply creates its own demand."

The crucial element of this argument is that money is valuable only as a medium of exchange. This being the case, there is no reason to hold on to money that is earned other than to make purchases. James Mill, also writing before Say, made a similar argument. Say in his book was openly contemptuous of the earlier writers who put forth essentially the same argument he expanded on. But for some reason, perhaps because Say made the argument more widely known and precipitated much controversy, it came to be associated with him. At the time of Say's book, there was much popular concern over whether a growing economy would eventually reach a state of general glut and as a consequence be unable to provide employment for a growing population.

Some of the disagreement over Say's law among the classical economists probably came from different interpretations of the law itself. Some writers appeared to give it the first of the two interpretations mentioned above, namely that the value of purchases equals the value of sales. There can be no disagreement over this interpretation, because it is always true. Later this idea came to be known as Say's Identity. It was over the second interpretation that the main disagreement arose: Will the payments made to resource owners, mainly labor in those days, enable them to buy all that is produced, thereby preventing a general glut of goods and services? Even here the classical writers had trouble defining a common ground. When they wrote about glut, some referred to the question of whether it would be general or particular, that is, in specific industries. Others posed the question of whether the glut would be permanent or temporary. Virtually all classical writers rejected the idea that a general glut could be permanent. The question that received the greatest attention was whether there could be a temporary general glut so that there would be widespread unemployment. This would be much worse than a glut in particular industries. If Say's law were valid, an economy should not experience even a temporary general glut.

The controversy and different interpretations of Say's law prevailed for over 30 years. In 1844, J.S. Mill, in his *Essays on Some Unsettled Questions of Political Economy*, put his finger on the key issue. In Mill's words, "Although he who sells, really sells only to buy, he need not buy at the same moment when he sells; and he does not therefore necessarily add to the immediate demand for one commodity when he adds to the supply of another." With these words, J. S. Mill explained how it would be possible for at least a temporary general glut to occur, thereby leading to widespread unemployment. People may earn money to spend it, but if they grow apprehensive of the future, they may not spend it right away. Thus, Say's law was shown to be invalid. This is not to say that the classical economists also rejected the idea of a self-correcting economy that would restore full employment after a time, as explained in the preceding section.

TAXES AND THE NATIONAL DEBT

Lest with the current concern over taxes and the national debt we think that we live in unusual times, it is instructive to see that the classical economists were also concerned over these issues. Even though the classical economists preferred a minimum of government and therefore a low level of taxation, they recognized the necessity of government and the problems of financing it. Ricardo went so far as to say that economics is useful only when "it directs government to right measures of taxation." This view probably stemmed from the fact that he regarded laissez-faire as the proper policy (or lack of it) elsewhere in the economy.

The classical economists were very much against deficit spending for a number of reasons. For one thing, they felt that if taxpayers did not have to pay for wars with current taxes they would be more inclined to enter into military action. If people saw their taxes rising immediately with a military buildup, they would more likely decide the cost was not worth the returns. There is evidence from classical literature that the requirement of pay-as-you-go financing of government would serve as a brake on government spending in general. It is also true that during the classical period foreigners held a substantial amount of the bonds issued by the British government. The necessity of paying off these bonds would therefore transfer wealth from Britain to other countries. A third reason for arguing against deficit financing was that the economy would suffer distortions and disincentive effects when taxes were raised to pay off the debt.

The classical economists in general and Ricardo in particular opposed deficit spending on something close to moral grounds, arguing that the practice "tends to make us less thrifty." Ricardo also recognized that government bonds outstanding are equivalent to taxes owed, raising the question, What is the difference if a man leaves an estate to an heir charged with a given tax or leaves a smaller fortune free of taxes? By this question, he implied that there is no difference.

THE MALTHUSIAN DOCTRINE

Adam Smith's *Wealth of Nations* saw the future in a rather optimistic light. Smith argued that the division of labor, which he defined very broadly as including all manner of technological improvements, would lead to increased per capita output and a growing standard of living for the people. This line of thought was in harmony with the general philosophical views of the times, which saw the eventual perfectibility of society. Malthus's ideas were in sharp contrast to the notion that the world would get better.

In essence, the Malthusian doctrine states that population growth will inevitably outrun any growth in food supplies, leaving mankind in a desperate state of poverty and hunger. Malthus went on to argue that there is either a "preventive" or a "positive" check on population at all times. By the preventive check, Malthus had in mind the moral restraint of people, which may counteract the strong desire to reproduce. However, Malthus viewed mankind, especially the masses, as being rather indolent, and he felt that the desire to reproduce would outweigh the brake of moral restraint. If there were a moral restraint, he argued, it would most likely stem from a fear of starvation. Among the positive checks on population Malthus included all manner of vice, disease, and pestilence. And if these checks didn't do the trick, there was always the ultimate check of food shortages and famine.

Probing deeper into his argument, Malthus postulated that population would grow geometrically, or at a compound rate, while food production would only grow arithmetically. In other words, population growth would take the form of the progression 1 2 4 8 16 32 64 . . . , while food production increased as 1 2 3 4 5 6 7. . . . It is easy to see, or, as Malthus said, even "a slight acquaintance with numbers will show," that even a small number growing at a compound rate will overwhelm a large number growing at an arithmetic rate. Given these assumed rates of growth, Malthus, of course, was right. But he offered no evidence that this is actually how population and food do grow. Surprisingly, his numbers were accepted as "gospel" (recall that he was a preacher!). No one bothered to compute, as did an American physicist at a later date, that if the human race had started with one couple living in 10,000 B.C. and had grown at a modest rate of 1 percent per year (biologically humans can increase at a maximum rate of about 5 percent per year), the earth would now be a ball of flesh several thousand light years in diameter and expanding outward faster than the speed of light. Never in history has there been a growth of any population of the magnitude feared by Malthus. Perhaps the willingness of the public to accept Malthus's numbers at that time was because of a rapid spurt in British population growth during the Industrial Revolution. However, there is little evidence that Malthus made much use of the British population census.

To strengthen his argument, Malthus brought in the now well-known "law of diminishing returns." Rigorously defined, it states that, as more and more of a variable input is added to one or more fixed inputs, beyond some point the extra output forthcoming from each additional unit of the variable input will become less and less. In Malthus's scheme, land was the main fixed input and population or labor the main variable input. Malthus did use the law rather loosely, however. He argued, for example, that man-made capital and technical improvements could not offset the limits on production set by natural resources. But it is not evident that the production of new technology is subject to the law of diminishing returns, because no one can prove that the potential stock of knowledge is finite.

Malthus went on to lay out the implications of his theory. For one thing, he argued that all deliberate attempts to improve the living conditions of the poor by government welfare programs will end in failure. Such programs just remove the positive checks to population increase, freeing people temporarily from bearing the consequences of their own improvidence, that is, the urge to reproduce. Not only were such ideas harsh, but Malthus also chose the most biting language he could muster, almost to the point of deliberately offending the sensitive reader.

Luckily for the human race, Malthus was wrong. His population theory is not taken seriously anymore, by professional demographers at least. There probably are some who argue that Malthus was right in reference to the less developed countries and that it will only be a matter of time before all countries are driven down to a level of subsistence. However, if Malthus's theory is correct, we should observe a high rate of population growth in the rich nations, due to a lack of positive restraints, and a low rate of population growth in the poor countries, because of the arithmetic nature of the growth in food production. In fact, we observe just the opposite.

The Malthusian doctrine became widely known and gained many believers during the 19th century. Indeed, economics became known as the "dismal science" because of Malthus's dire predictions. However, most present-day economists and demographers are not nearly as pessimistic about the future as were Malthus and his followers.

RICARDIAN RENT

As defined by Ricardo, "Rent is that portion of the produce of the earth which is paid to the landlord for the use of the original and indestructible properties of the soil." Later it was modified to include payment not only for the original properties, but also for any permanent improvements. Ricardo and other classical writers of the time utilized the idea of differential land quality to illustrate why rent existed. The poorest land cultivated at any given time would be that whose yield just covered the cost of the labor and capital with nothing left over for rent. All land of superior quality that employed the same amount of capital and labor would by definition yield a greater output. The difference in the output of the good land over the poor land would be the rent earned by the good land.

In Ricardo's analysis, land is assumed to be fixed in quantity and to have no alternative use other than agriculture. This being the case, it follows that the amount of rent is determined by the price of the product. As Ricardo put it, "Corn is not high because a rent is paid, but rent is paid because corn is high." Ricardo made good use of this conclusion to argue against the Corn Laws, which restricted the import of wheat and increased the domestic price of wheat. Higher prices of agricultural products result in higher rents for landlords—money that they obtain without any effort on their part. Thus, Ricardo was able to show that the effect of the Corn Laws was to enrich landlords. Another policy implication of Ricardian rent is that the earnings from land can be taxed without reducing the production of agricultural products or distorting the output mix of the country.

The notion that rent is unearned income precipitated other policy recommendations as well. Henry George advocated a "single tax" on land rent to finance the government. After Ricardo's book was published, it was clearly "open season" on landlords. Also, the Fabian Socialists, spearheaded by George Bernard Shaw, were able to enlist popular support in their efforts to establish a socialist state because of widespread moral indignation over this unearned income. In a socialist state, the government owns the land and reaps the "unearned increment." Even today in Britain, so-called unearned income from land or capital is taxed at a higher rate than labor earnings, or even the winnings from lotteries.

CLASSICAL VALUE THEORY

One of the questions that the classical economists wrestled with was, What determines the value or price of an object? Why do some things fetch a high price, while others sell for a small sum? This question occupied the attention of the classical economists during the entire classical era. Adam Smith began the analysis with an example of a primitive society where land is free and labor the only scarce, hence valuable, input. He reasoned that in such a society of hunters, if it takes twice as much labor to catch a beaver as to kill a deer, then one beaver will exchange for two deer. At first glance, this example appears to depict a labor theory of value whereby the value of an object is determined by the amount of labor expended to produce it. But it would be more correct to call Smith's idea a cost-of-production theory of value. The value of an object is determined by the cost of producing it; since beaver cost twice as much to produce as deer, they sell for twice as much. He makes clear the distinction between a labor theory and a cost-of-production theory by arguing that the value of a commodity is the sum of the normal amounts paid to all resources used in making it. Some preclassical writers had suggested something close to a labor theory of value, but Smith pointed out that this theory would be valid only in the special and artificial conditions of an "early and rude state of society."

It has been pointed out by later writers that Smith's argument represents a *measure* of the cost of production rather than a *theory* of value because he did not explain how resources or inputs obtain their value. In a sense, he explained prices by prices. In fairness to Adam Smith, it should be pointed out that he was mainly interested in determining long-run values, or prices under conditions of constant costs, that is, where the supply curve is perfectly horizontal. Under these conditions, the value of an object is determined entirely by the cost of production or supply, while the quantity sold is determined by demand. Of course Smith still did not have an apparatus to determine short-run prices or prices when costs are not constant. For this we have to turn to supply and demand.

There was considerable disagreement among the classical economists regarding the importance of supply and demand in the determination of value. J. S. Mill treated cost of production and supply and demand as two separate theories, saying that supply and demand determine prices where the cost of production is inoperative. Now we know that supply is determined from the cost of production and that both supply and demand determine value. Part of the early controversy probably stemmed from different writers giving different meanings to the same words. To Ricardo and J. S. Mill, supply and demand meant quantities bought and sold.

Malthus in his *Principles* book defined supply and demand as we do now—as schedules or relationships between price and quantity rather than fixed amounts. He was the first to distinguish between the "extent" (quantity) of demand and the "intensity" of demand (position of the demand curve). Unfortunately, J. S. Mill's popular *Principles* text overshadowed the insights of Malthus on supply and demand for several decades. They were later developed by neoclassical writers.

MARX AND THE LABOR THEORY OF VALUE

Although Karl Marx is not generally considered to have been a classical economist, he did draw upon and modify many classical ideas. And even if one disagrees with Marxist or communist ideology, it is important to be somewhat familiar with the source of these ideas. Unlike most economic writers both before and after him, Marx in his book *Das Kapital* (1867) tried to incorporate historical, sociological, and economic forces in a single theoretical framework. Marx was highly critical of the classical economists for being too specialized, referring to them as those "vulgar economists." No doubt his dislike of the classical economists also was motivated by their distrust of government and advocacy of laissez-faire.

In addressing the age-old question of what determines value, Marx argued that commodities are exchanged in proportion to the labor utilized in production. This is the labor theory of value. The more labor is embodied in a good, the higher its value. Recall that this is the same basic idea as that presented in Adam Smith's deer and beaver example, except that Marx deals with an economy having both labor and capital. In Marx's world, capital is indirect labor.

Marx also argued that profit is "surplus value" produced by labor. That is, laborers produce a larger value for their employers than they receive as wages. He did not argue, however, that this condition stems from the heartlessness of employers who have the power to determine wages and decide to set wages at a subsistence level. Quite the contrary, Marx asserted: Because capital has come into the hands of a relative few, labor has become a commodity traded on the market as any other, at a price determined by the labor time required to produce it. In other words, the price of labor (wage) is equal to the labor time necessary to produce the wage goods that go to maintain labor. The "reserve army of the unemployed" and competition in the labor market maintain the wage at the subsistence level. Since labor is able to produce more than the cost of its subsistence, the remainder goes to employers as surplus value. To Marx, surplus value is unpaid labor, meaning that employers receive the excess of sales over wages as unearned income. In the Marxist framework, employers pay for the exchange value of labor but receive its use value, which is greater. Notice that Marx had to have the labor theory of value in order to obtain surplus value; the two go together. Because of this alleged unearned surplus reaped by employers, Marx advocated state ownership of the means of production.

Marx's argument, however, does not stand up under empirical scrutiny, nor is it logically sound. Marx asserted that surplus value per worker is the same in every industry. This is consistent with the labor theory of value, which states that products of equal quantities of labor will sell for equal quantities of money. But it is a known fact that capital per worker varies between industries. If profits, or surplus value per worker, are the same across industries, it follows that the rate of profit per unit of capital is smaller the larger the amount of capital per worker. In other words, the higher the degree of mechanization, the lower the rate of profit. This implies that employers have an incentive to discard machines in order to increase profits—just the opposite of what is observed in capitalist economies. Thus, Marx's theory is not empirically verified.

With the failure of central planning and the communist economic model, it is easy to be critical of Karl Marx and his ideas. However one should be mindful of the times when he wrote *Das Kapital*. During this period, capitalism was a harsh system. Wages were at the subsistence level, working conditions were bad, and there was no unemployment compensation for people who had lost their jobs. Also, there were no food stamps, welfare, or public assistance for the hungry, the sick, and the destitute. Young children labored long hours in factories and mines instead of receiving an education. And women were denied opportunities in many professions. Meanwhile, the upper classes lived in ostentatious luxury. It is possible that the threat of an alternative system, namely communism, helped move capitalism toward a more humanistic mode. It is unfortunate that Marx's alternative was so extreme. The recent developments in Eastern Europe and the Soviet Union suggest that a Communist system can be replaced or at least moved toward a middle ground with markets, private property, and the personal freedoms that exist in the Western democracies.

SUMMARY

The era of the classical economists began in 1776 with the publication of Adam Smith's book *The Wealth of Nations*. The book was written as an attack on mercantilism, which describes a set of government policies that gave special privilege to the wealthy business and land-owning classes. Adam Smith and later classical writers preferred a less active role of government in the economy, advocating a policy of laissez-faire. With the exception of Thomas Malthus, who thought world population growth would outrun food supplies, classical writers were optimistic about the ability of nations to achieve economic growth provided governments followed laissez-faire policies. Karl Marx represented a radical departure from the classical economists, advocating public ownership of the nation's resources.

YOU SHOULD KNOW

1. The author and title of the first major book in economics.

2. The authors of the other major books in economics that were written during the classical period.

3. The main tenets of mercantilism.

4. The main ideas of classical economics as put forth by Adam Smith and later writers.
5. The meaning of laissez-faire.
6. How the economy could solve an unemployment problem without government intervention.
7. The meaning of Say's law.
8. How the classical economists viewed taxes and deficit spending.
9. What the Malthusian doctrine is.
10. What Ricardian rent is and why it exists.
11. How the classical economists explained the difference in prices among goods.
12. What the labor theory of value put forth by Karl Marx is.

QUESTIONS

1. Contrast the views of Adam Smith and the other classical economists with the earlier mercantilist traditions.
2. Did the classical economists think unemployment could be a problem for a market economy? Explain.
3. *a.* What is Say's Identity, and how does it differ from Say's law?
   b. Was Say's law accepted by all classical economists? Elaborate.
4. What did the classical economists think of deficit spending by the government?
5. How did the thinking of Thomas Malthus differ from that of Adam Smith?
6. According to David Ricardo, "Is wheat high because rent is high, or is rent high because wheat is high?" If Ricardo was correct, who were the main beneficiaries of the Corn Laws?
7. How did Adam Smith explain why some products sold for higher prices than other products?
8. *a.* What is Karl Marx's labor theory of value?
   b. Why was the labor theory of value necessary to obtain surplus value?

SELF-TEST

1. The first major economics book was authored by:
   a. Karl Marx.
   b. John Maynard Keynes.
   c. Adam Smith.
   d. Thomas Malthus.
2. The first major economics book appeared in:
   a. 1976.   *c.* 1776.
   b. 1876.   *d.* 1676.
3. The work of the early economists has come to be known as _____ economics.
   a. voodoo
   b. classical
   c. neoclassical
   d. supply side
4. Which of the following economists are included among the classical group?
   a. Thomas Malthus
   b. David Ricardo
   c. John Stuart Mill
   d. all of the above
5. The mercantilists believed that a nation's wealth was determined by:
   a. its output of goods and services.
   b. its land area.
   c. the amount of gold it possessed.
   d. its merchant fleet.

6. In contrast to the mercantilists, Adam Smith and the classical economists argued that the true wealth of a nation was:
   a. the quantity of money in the economy.
   b. the amount of gold it possessed.
   c. its output of goods and services.
   d. its merchant fleet.

7. The Corn Laws established tariffs on agricultural _____ and were _____ by the classical economists.
   a. exports; advocated
   b. exports; opposed
   c. imports; advocated
   d. imports; opposed

8. According to Adam Smith, it _____ to the benevolence of the baker that we owe our bread but rather to his _____ .
   a. is not; self-interest
   b. is not; concern for poor people
   c. is; self-interest
   d. is; concern for poor people

9. Laissez-faire is a policy _____ by the classical economists that calls for _____ intervention in the economy by the government.
   a. advocated; minimum
   b. advocated; maximum
   c. opposed; minimum
   d. opposed; maximum

10. In regard to the problem of unemployment, the classical economists thought:
    a. it did not exist.
    b. it could occur but not persist because of flexible interest rates, wages, and prices.
    c. it could occur but only because of government intervention.
    d. it would result from an overproduction of goods—a general glut.

11. According to the classical economists, the existence of unemployment would cause prices, interest rates, and wages to _____ thereby causing a(n) _____

in spending and a(n) _____ in unemployment.
   a. increase; increase; increase
   b. decrease; increase; increase
   c. increase; decrease; decrease
   d. decrease; increase; decrease

12. According to Say's law:
   a. supply creates its own demand.
   b. demand creates its own supply.
   c. the value of purchases equals the value of sales.
   d. the value of purchases equals income of consumers.

13. According to Say's Identity:
   a. supply creates its own demand.
   b. demand creates its own supply.
   c. the value of purchases equals the value of sales.
   d. the value of purchases equals income of consumers.

14. _____ found the flaw in Say's law, pointing out that people:
   a. Thomas Malthus; will reproduce faster than they can increase food production.
   b. J. S. Mill; may not wish to buy at the same time as they sell.
   c. Karl Marx; are exploited by capitalists.
   d. David Ricardo; benefit from the Corn Laws.

15. The classical economists _____ deficit spending, arguing that it:
   a. favored; stimulated the economy.
   b. opposed; caused a reduction in government spending.
   c. favored; prevented inflation.
   d. opposed; eventually increased taxes and made the country poorer.

16. Thomas Malthus argued that:
   a. the developed countries would be plagued by agricultural surpluses.
   b. population growth would outrun food supplies leaving mankind in a state of hunger and poverty.
   c. the increase in resources from the new

world and new technology would lead to economic growth.

d. man evolved from lower forms of life.

17. Economics is sometimes called the "dismal science" because:
    a. of Thomas Malthus's predictions.
    b. it is so dry and uninteresting.
    c. economists typically are pessimistic about the future.
    d. it came into being in Scotland, which is dark and cloudy in the winter.

18. Ricardo demonstrated that _____ benefited from the Corn Laws.
    a. consumers
    b. the colonies
    c. land owners
    d. the less developed countries

19. According to Ricardo:
    a. corn is high because rent is paid.
    b. rent is paid because corn is high.
    c. rent is paid because land varies in quality.
    d. b and c

20. In Adam Smith's primitive society where land is free and labor is the only scarce input; the price of products is determined by:
    a. demand and supply.
    b. cost of production.
    c. deer and beaver.
    d. the labor theory of value.

21. According to Karl Marx, a term paper that embodies 40 hours of work is _____ as good as one that took 20 hours to prepare.
    a. one half   c. four times
    b. twice   d. 20 times

22. Karl Marx argued that wages would:
    a. be equal to what people could subsist on.
    b. be determined by the demand and supply of labor.
    c. increase as employers utilized more capital-intensive techniques.
    d. be determined by the government.

Chapter 9

The Quantity Theory
of Money

OVERVIEW

This chapter presents one of the main theories put forth by the classical economists—the quantity theory of money. Essentially, this theory says that if the quantity of money in a country grows more rapidly than real output, the country will experience inflation. Later, in Chapter 17, some refinements will be made to the original quantity theory.

INTRODUCTION

The problem of inflation ranked high on the agenda of economic problems for the classical economists, who argued that the primary cause of inflation was an excessive growth of a nation's money supply. The classicists were particularly concerned that the use of paper money rather than gold could lead to inflation. The basic idea of the quantity theory is that given the level of output, the general level of prices moves in the same direction as changes in the quantity of money.

MONEY DEFINED

Before proceeding, it is necessary to define what is included in the measure of the nation's money supply. There are two widely used definitions of money: (1) the narrow definition commonly referred to as M_1 and (2) M_2, the broad definition. The narrow definition of money includes currency outside of banks and checking account balances. The broad definition includes M_1 plus savings account bal-

TABLE 9–1   Quantity of Money in the United States and Corresponding Velocities, Selected Years, 1929–1989 ($ billions)

Year	M_1	M_2	V_1	V_2
1929	$ 26	$ 46	3.9	2.2
1939	36	51	2.5	1.8
1949	111	148	2.3	1.7
1959	141	298	3.5	1.6
1969	206	590	4.6	1.6
1974	278	909	5.2	1.6
1979	389	1,499	6.2	1.6
1984	554	2,376	6.6	1.5
1985	627	2,567	6.4	1.6
1989	798	3,217	6.6	1.6

Sources: 1929–39: Milton Friedman and Anna Schwartz, *A Monetary History of the United States, 1897–1960* (Princeton, N.J.: Princeton University Press, 1963), Table A–1; 1949–1989: *Economic Report of the President*, 1990, p. 371.

ances. The latter includes money deposited in money market funds. The U.S. M_1 and M_2 figures for selected years are presented in the first two columns of Table 9–1. Notice that the M_2 figure in recent years is four times larger than M_1.

GRESHAM'S LAW

It is possible, of course, for a society to utilize more than one form of money, providing both are accepted by the people. A curious situation can prevail, however, when one form of money becomes less valuable than another. For example, consider the case where both gold coins and paper are used as money. Now suppose the quantity of paper money expands relative to the amount of gold coins. If the government attempts to hold the value of paper money constant relative to that of gold, people, sensing that paper is becoming more plentiful and less valuable, will likely attempt to get rid of their paper money and hold on to their gold. Consequently, gold will tend to disappear from circulation. This phenomenon is known as Gresham's law—bad money drives out good money. In order for Gresham's law to be valid, however, it is necessary for the government to maintain a fixed rate of exchange between the "good" and "bad" money. If paper were allowed to find its own rate of exchange with gold in the market, becoming less valuable as its supply increased, then both gold and paper would continue to be exchanged because people would be willing to part with gold if its value increased—that is, they could obtain more paper money per ounce of gold.

VELOCITY OF MONEY

The cornerstone of the quantity theory is the velocity of money. In general terms, the velocity of money can be thought of as the average number of times each dollar is spent each year. Two definitions of velocity have evolved: (1) transactions velocity and (2) income velocity.[1]

1. *Transactions velocity* Transactions velocity (V_T) is equal to the total sales (transactions) of an economy divided by the money supply.

$$V_T = \text{Sales/Money}$$

Although this measure of velocity coincides with the definition given above, the average number of times each dollar is spent each year, the total value of sales in an economy is not a commonly used figure. Recall from Chapter 8 that GNP is a value-added or income figure rather than a sales figure. Thus, transactions velocity figures are rarely computed.

2. *Income velocity* As its name implies, income velocity (V_I) is equal to a measure of a nation's income such as GNP divided by the nation's money supply.

$$V_I = \text{Income/Money}$$

Although V_I cannot be interpreted literally as the number of times each dollar changes hands each year, there will be a fairly close correlation between changes in V_T and V_I. The higher the V_I, the larger the average number of times each dollar is spent.

The velocity of money for the United States using the two measures of money is presented in the last two columns of Table 9–1. Velocity using M_1 (V_1) has increased in recent times, at least in comparison to the pre-World War II period. Velocity according to M_2 (V_2) is, of course, smaller because GNP is divided by a larger number. Of greater interest is the fact that it has not changed much over the post-World War II period. An explanation of why velocity can change is given later in Chapter 17.

MONEY AND PRICES

An intuitive idea of how the quantity of money and prices are related can be obtained by considering a simple economy that produces one product, say 1,000 loaves of bread per year. Also assume that this simple economy has 1,000 pieces of paper in existence that it calls money. Finally, assume that *all* the money in existence is exchanged once each year for *all* the bread produced annually. (This is what money is for—to be used in exchange for goods and services.) Under these assumptions, each loaf of bread will be changed for one piece of paper called a dollar bill. In other words, the price of bread in this case must be $1 per loaf.

---

[1] Irving Fisher, *The Purchasing Power of Money,* (New York: MacMillan, 1913).

Under these assumptions, there is no way the price of bread could be any different than $1.

Now suppose that the quantity of money in existence doubles to $2,000, but the quantity of bread produced remains the same at 1,000 loaves. Under the conditions stipulated in the preceding paragraph, where all money is exchanged once for all the bread that is produced, two pieces of paper called dollar bills will now be exchanged for each loaf of bread. In other words, the price of bread now must be $2 per loaf. The relationship among the quantity of money, the output of bread, and the price of bread is summarized in the following table.

Quantity of Money	Output of Bread	Price of Bread
$1,000	1,000	$1
2,000	1,000	2

THE QUANTITY EQUATION OF EXCHANGE

The quantity theory of money is best expressed by the quantity equation of exchange. This equation says that the quantity of money in the economy (M) times velocity (V) equals the total value of income or output in the economy (GNP). (Since the distinction between transaction velocity and income velocity is not of critical importance here, velocity will be denoted simply by V.) It will be helpful to divide the measure of income, or GNP, into two components: price and quantity; that is, the total value of output (or income) in the economy is equal to the price of each final good and service times its quantity. Using P to represent the prices of all goods and services and Q to represent all the quantities, we can write the expression for calculating velocity, as follows:

$$V = \frac{GNP}{M} \text{ or } V = \frac{P \times Q}{M}$$

By multiplying both sides of the computational formula given on the right by M, we obtain:

$$M \times V = P \times Q$$

The resulting formula is commonly known as the *quantity equation of exchange*. It says that the quantity of money in the economy multiplied by its velocity equals the total value of income (or output) in the economy during a given year. The equality always holds true because velocity is free to take on any value that satisfies the equation. As a result, the equation is often called an *identity* because the right side always equals the left side.

PREDICTIONS BASED ON THE QUANTITY THEORY

The quantity equation of exchange has long been used by economists to illustrate what happens to prices (P) and/or value of output ($P \times Q$) when there are changes in the quantity of money (M) or in velocity (V). A few examples will illustrate the point. Using some specific numbers, suppose we start with a situation where $M = 500$, $V = 2$, $P = 1$, and $Q = 1,000$.

1. Double M, No Change in V and Q.   This situation corresponds somewhat to the simple bread economy example given in a previous section, except in that example the velocity is assumed to be 1. If money is doubled to 1,000, velocity remains constant at 2, and Q stays at 1,000; the only thing that can happen is for P to double, as shown below:

	M		V		P		Q
a.	500	×	2	=	1	×	1,000
b.	1,000	×	2	=	2	×	1,000

This example could represent an economy at full employment where M is increased but Q cannot increase because resources are being fully utilized.

2. Half M, No Change in V.   In this case, all that can be said is that the right-hand side of the expression will decline by half. In cases where the quantity of money has decreased, such as during the Great Depression, the first effect seems to be a decline in output (Q). Then as surpluses of goods and services build up and unemployment drags on, prices and wages begin to fall:

	M		V		P		Q
a.	500	×	2	=	1	×	1,000
b.	250	×	2	=	500		

3. Double V, No Change in M and Q.   This case is similar to case 1 above in that a doubling in the rate at which people spend money has the same effect as a doubling of the quantity of money—that is, to double the price level:

	M		V		P		Q
a.	500	×	2	=	1	×	1,000
b.	500	×	4	=	2	×	1,000

A decrease in velocity would have the same effect on the value of output as a decrease in the quantity of money (case 2), so it is not necessary to restate this case.

Probably the most serious limitation of using the quantity equation of exchange to predict price and output changes from changes in the quantity of money is the necessity of assuming a constant velocity. For example, if M doubles as in case 1 above and V declined by one half, nothing has to change on the right-hand side ($P \times Q$). Or, if a decrease in M is offset by an increase in V, again, there need be no change in $P \times Q$.

While the classical economists did not argue that *V* was an absolute constant, they did not believe that changes in *V* would be large enough to nullify any prediction made about changes in $P \times Q$ resulting from a change in the money supply. This assumption was later challenged by other economists, and as a result much of the work on monetary theory in the immediate post-World War II period centered on attempts to explain why and in what direction velocity can change. The outcome of this work is called "the new quantity theory," which will be discussed in Chapter 17.

SUMMARY

The classical economists are perhaps best known for their quantity theory of money. In short, this theory predicts that the price level will increase if the quantity of money increases at a faster rate than the output of real goods and services. The quantity theory is best expressed by the quantity equation of exchange: $M \times V = P \times Q$. It says that the quantity of money times velocity must always equal the monetary or nominal value of output in the economy during any given year.

YOU SHOULD KNOW

1. What the classical economists viewed as the primary cause of inflation.

2. The narrow and broad definitions of money.

3. The meaning of Gresham's law.

4. What the velocity of money is, the two ways it can be computed, and which is the most common.

5. The relationship between money and prices.

6. What the quantity equation of exchange is and how to derive it.

7. What the quantity equation predicts will happen if the money supply is increased, other things constant.

8. What the quantity equation predicts will happen if the money supply is decreased, other things constant.

9. What the quantity equation predicts will happen if velocity increases, other things constant.

QUESTIONS

1. According to the quantity theory, how is the quantity of money and prices related?

2. What are two ways of defining money?

3. What are two ways of defining velocity?

4. *a.* Derive the quantity equation of exchange from the computational formula for velocity.

b. What is the meaning of the quantity equation of exchange?

c. Why does the right-hand value of the formula always equal the left side?

5. According to the quantity equation of exchange, what should happen if:

a. the quantity of money is increased during a time of full employment?

b. the quantity of money is increased during a time of unemployment?

c. the quantity of money is decreased?

6. *a.* If the predictions made in Question 5

above are to be correct, what must be assumed about velocity?

b. Stipulate how changes in velocity could negate the changes in the money supply.

SELF-TEST

1. The quantity theory of money predicts that if the quantity of money increases more rapidly than real output in the economy, _____ will occur.
   a. unemployment
   b. inflation
   c. bankruptcies
   d. a shortage of gold

2. The classical economists were concerned mainly with the problem of:
   a. unemployment.
   b. inflation.
   c. food surpluses.
   d. scarcity of land.

3. M_1, the narrow definition of money, includes:
   a. cash.
   b. cash plus checking account balances.
   c. cash plus checking plus savings account balances.
   d. M_2 plus savings account balances.

4. M_2, the broad definition of money, includes:
   a. cash.
   b. cash plus checking account balances.
   c. cash plus checking plus savings account balances.
   d. M_1 plus cash.

5. In recent years in the United States, M_2 is about _____ as large as M_1.
   a. twice
   b. three times
   c. four times
   d. 10 times

6. According to Gresham's law:
   a. bad money drives out good money.
   b. good money drives out bad money.
   c. supply creates its own demand.
   d. rent is paid because wheat is high.

7. The velocity of money is a measure of:
   a. how many times each dollar is spent each year.
   b. the number of times a dollar has to be spent to generate a dollar of income.
   c. how many dollars of income it takes to generate a dollar spending.
   d. how many dollars are spent for each 100 dollars of income.

8. Transactions velocity is obtained by _____ by _____ .
   a. dividing sales; money
   b. multiplying sales; money
   c. dividing money; sales
   d. multiplying money; sales

9. Income velocity is obtained by _____ by _____ .
   a. dividing money; income
   b. multiplying money; income
   c. dividing income; money
   d. multiplying income; sales

10. Other things equal, an increase in the quantity of money causes prices to _____ proportion to the increase in money.
    a. increase in
    b. increase more than in
    c. decrease in
    d. decrease more than in

11. The quantity equation of exchange is obtained by _____ both sides of the velocity formula by _____ .
    a. dividing; M
    b. multiplying; M
    c. dividing; V
    d. multiplying; V

12. The quantity equation of exchange is:
    a. $M \times V = P$
    b. $M \times V = Q$
    c. $M \times V = P \times Q$
    d. $M = P \times Q$

13. If V is held constant, the quantity equation of exchange predicts that P will _____ if M is doubled and full employment prevails.
    a. triple
    b. increase by one half
    c. double
    d. remain constant

14. If V is held constant, the quantity equation of exchange predicts that _____ will decline if M declines.

    a. P
    b. Q
    c. $P \times Q$
    d. both P and Q

15. According to the quantity equation of exchange, a doubling of V during a time of full employment causes _____ to _____ .
    a. P; double
    b. Q; double
    c. $P \times Q$; increase fourfold
    d. $P \times Q$; decrease by one half

16. When using the quantity equation of exchange, the classical economists assumed _____ was constant.

    a. P
    b. Q
    c. $P \times Q$
    d. V

Part IV

The Simple Keynesian Model

Chapter 10

Building Blocks of the Simple Model

OVERVIEW

The material in this and the following chapter has come to be known as the simple Keynesian model. It is called *simple* to distinguish it from a somewhat more complete model that incorporates money and interest rates. The more complete model will not be presented. This chapter focuses on the three main components of the simple model—consumer spending, investment spending, and government spending. Most of the discussion is on consumer spending.

INTRODUCTION TO JOHN MAYNARD KEYNES

Until the early 1930s, the classical economists' view of an automatically adjusting economy was the predominant view held by economists. But then came the Great Depression. Astronomical unemployment rates of 15 to 20 percent persisted year after year in the United States. The Depression dragged on toward the mid-1930s, and the economy did not seem able to adjust to regain full employment. Granted, money rates of interest declined and prices and wages fell, but still severe unemployment persisted.

Needless to say, many economists began to voice disenchantment with the classical theory. One English economist in particular, John Maynard Keynes, was especially influential. In 1936, Keynes came out with a book titled *The General Theory of Employment, Interest and Money,* which presented a view of a market economy that was somewhat different from that espoused by his classical counterparts. Basically Keynes argued there was no guarantee of full employment in a market economy. He maintained that in such an economy there is always the possibility that the "effective" demand for consumer and investment goods might not be sufficient to take off the market the entire supply that would be forthcoming from a full-employment economy.

The implication of Keynes's theory, then, is that a market economy can find itself in a sort of equilibrium in which the level of aggregate demand for consumer and investment goods is not sufficient to generate full employment of the labor force. Keynes argued, therefore, that the government may be needed to influence or augment the level of aggregate demand so as to ensure full employment.

You will note, therefore, a basic difference between the classical economists and Keynes. The classicists argued that a market economy, even though it might experience short-term unemployment, would through flexible interest rates, wages, and prices return to a state of full employment without government intervention. Keynes put less faith in market forces and argued instead for more direct government intervention. In summary, one can say that the classical economists took full employment as given and concentrated their attention on the problem of inflation. In contrast, Keynes took the price level as given and focused on unemployment.

THE CONSUMPTION FUNCTION

The heart of the simple Keynesian model is the aggregate expenditure (AE) function. The AE function consists of three components: **(1)** consumer spending, **(2)** investment spending, and **(3)** government spending. Let us look first at consumer spending.

Keynes argued that consumption is determined mainly by income. This is a plausible argument. People with a $30,000-per-year income can be expected to spend more than a $20,000-per-year family, on the average. In addition, Keynes argued that, as a family's income increased, its consumption increased but not quite as much as the growth in income.

Again this is reasonable. In order to maintain a bare minimum of food, clothing, and shelter, low-income people may have to spend their entire income and then some. College students are a good example. Many students probably consume more than their income, with the difference made up by gifts or borrowing. However, as incomes rise to the $30,000- to $40,000-per-year figure and beyond, families can satisfy their basic needs and in addition put something away for a "rainy day." The relationship between income and consumption has come to be known as the "consumption function"—consumption depends on or is a function of income.

In Figure 10A, we represent the two ideas or hypotheses that Keynes put forth regarding the relationship between income and consumption. First, the upward-sloping line tells us that if disposable income increases, then consumption also increases. For example, if disposable income is $8,000 per year, the consumption function tells us that consumption is $15,000 per year. Then as we move out along the income axis, say to $32,000 per year, consumption increases to $25,000 per year.

Keynes's second hypothesis, namely, that consumption does not increase as much as income, is represented by the fact that the consumption function does not rise as rapidly as the 45-degree line. (This line is so named because it bisects the

FIGURE 10–1   Relation of Income, Consumption, and Saving

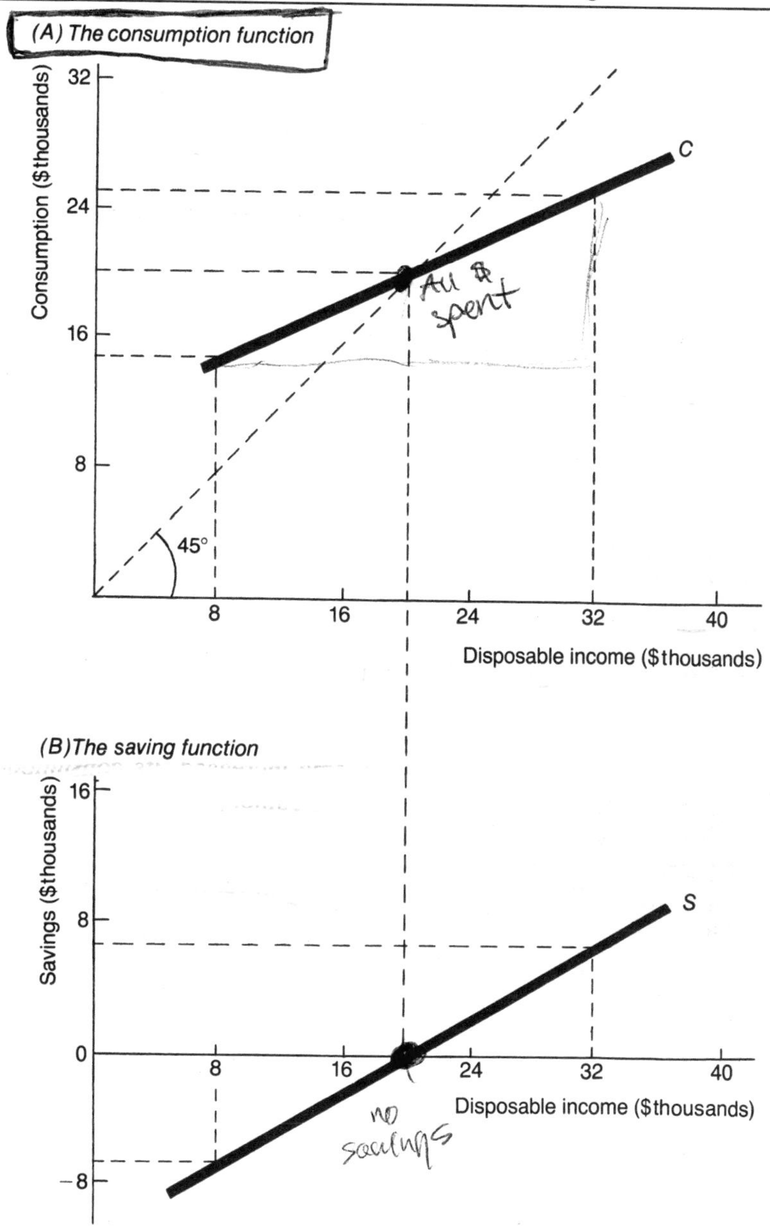

(A) The consumption function

(B) The saving function

90-degree angle made by the diagram.) Notice that anywhere on the 45-degree line, income equals consumption. Thus, if consumption increased dollar for dollar with income, the consumption function would be the same as the 45-degree line. The idea that consumption increases less rapidly than disposable income is reflected by a consumption function that is somewhat "flatter" than the 45-degree line.

The relationship between income and consumption also tells us what kind of relationship exists between income and saving. As noted earlier, there are only two things people can do with their disposable income: spend it or save it. Hence, if we know income and consumption, we can easily derive saving. This is illustrated in Figure 10–1B, where the distance between the consumption line and the 45-degree line represents the amount saved at the particular level of income. We can, as shown in Figure 10–1B, represent the distance between the 45-degree line and consumption on a separate diagram. The resulting line is called the saving function. It tells us how much is saved at a given level of income.

Also notice the relationship between diagrams A and B in Figure 10–1. At the point where the consumption function intersects the 45-degree line in diagram A, consumption is equal to income; that is, people spend all they take in. Saving, therefore, is equal to zero at this level of income, and this is shown in diagram B where the saving function intersects the horizontal axis. In this particular example, savings equal zero, or C equals DI, at the $20,000 income level. To the left of this intersection, consumption is greater than income, and saving is negative. And to the right of the intersection, consumption is less than income, so saving is positive.

AVERAGE PROPENSITY TO CONSUME

We can further our understanding of the relationship between consumption and income by developing the concepts of the average propensity to consume (APC) and marginal propensity to consume (MPC). The *average propensity to consume* is defined as the proportion of disposable income spent on current consumption of goods and services. It is computed as follows:

$$APC = \frac{C}{DI}$$

If we wish, we could multiply the resulting answer by 100 and express it as a percentage figure—the percent of DI that is spent on consumption goods and services.

One interesting thing to note about APC is that it becomes smaller and smaller the farther we move along the consumption function, as shown in Figure 10–1A. In the region to the left of the intersection of the consumption and 45-degree lines, APC is greater than one. In other words, consumption is greater than DI. At the intersection, APC equals one, and to the right, APC becomes progressively less than one.

The figures to compute APC for the United States are readily available. The results of the computations are shown in Table 10–1. With the exception of the Great Depression and World War II, two highly atypical periods, the APC in the

TABLE 10–1   Average Propensity to Consume in the United States, Five-Year Intervals, 1929–1989*

Year	APC	Year	APC
1929	0.93	1964	0.92
1934	0.98	1969	0.91
1939	0.95	1974	0.90
1944	0.80	1979	0.92
1949	0.93	1984	0.91
1954	0.91	1989	0.92
1959	0.92		

* Computed by dividing consumption expenditures by personal disposable income.

Source: *Economic Report of the President,* 1990, p. 324.

United States has been in the range of 0.90 to 0.95; that is, people have been spending about 90 to 95 percent of their incomes and saving 5 to 10 percent. Notice also that there does not appear to be a discernible long-run trend in the size of the APC over this period.

You might reasonably ask at this point, If disposable income in the United States has been increasing over the years, is it not logical to expect that we would be moving out along the consumption line, so that APC should be steadily declining? Yet in Table 10–1 we see that APC has remained relatively constant during a time when incomes have grown substantially.

It should be pointed out that the consumption function we are dealing with in the Keynesian model reflects *short-run* changes in consumer spending in response to short-run fluctuations in disposable income. Empirical evidence suggests, and it is reasonable to expect, that people do not change their spending habits in direct proportion to short-run changes in income. For example, if a family breadwinner is unemployed for six months and suffers, say, a 40 percent reduction in annual income, it is not likely that the family will reduce its spending by a full 40 percent during that year. The family may reduce consumer spending by 10 to 20 percent by cutting down on purchases of items they find least essential (restaurant meals, travel, entertainment, dental work, and so on) but not the full 40 percent. The deficit may come out of savings or possibly even from borrowing. The family does not cut back by the full 40 percent because it does not expect the reduction in income to be permanent. By the same token, a family that experiences a large increase in income during a given year, say because of an above-average amount of overtime or an inheritance, will probably increase its spending some during that year but not by the full amount of the extra income.

The idea that people regulate their long-run spending habits in accordance with long-run expected income was first advanced by Milton Friedman, recipient of the

FIGURE 10–2   Upward Shifts in the U.S. Consumption Function

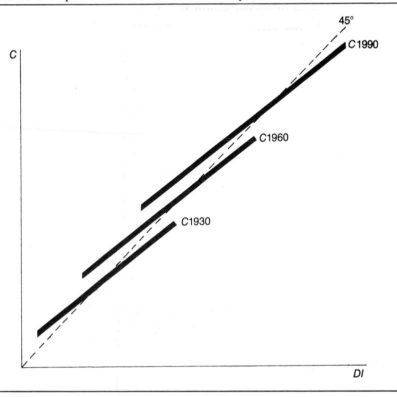

Nobel Prize in economics for this and other work in monetary theory.[1] It has come to be known as the permanent-income hypothesis. Friedman argued that the average propensity to consume out of so-called permanent income remains virtually constant across families of various income levels at a point in time and over succeeding generations of people with higher and higher incomes. This could explain, then, why the average propensity to consume in the United States has remained fairly constant despite increasing per capita incomes.

We can reconcile the apparent contradiction between the upward-sloping consumption function that implies a decreasing APC at points farther along the line and the long-run constancy of actual APC in the United States by viewing the consumption function as shifting up over time. The consumption function in the sample Keynesian model should be viewed as a short-run relationship between income and consumer spending. As long-run expected income increases, the consumption function shifts upward, as illustrated in Figure 10–2.

---

[1] Milton Friedman, *A Theory of the Consumption Function* (Princeton, N.J.; Princeton University Press, 1957).

The possibility of the economy's moving out along a given consumption function was cause for concern among a number of economists during and immediately following World War II. If consumers spent a smaller and smaller share of their incomes as their incomes increased, investment spending would have to increase in order to take up the slack, so to speak, and maintain full employment. Fortunately, their fears did not materialize; consumers show no long-run trend of "kicking" the spending habit regardless of their level of income.

As a related point, note from Table 10–1 that the 1934 APC of 0.98 was the highest of any APC since; this was in the midst of the Great Depression. It has been argued that the Great Depression was caused by an unwillingness of people to spend, that is, they saved too large a fraction of their income. This figure refutes that argument. We will have more to say about the cause of the Great Depression in later chapters.

MARGINAL PROPENSITY TO CONSUME

Marginal propensity to consume (MPC) is defined as the proportion of *extra* income spent on current consumption. For example, if your disposable income increases by a dollar and you increase your consumption by 75 cents, your MPC would be 0.75. Again, one can express this as a percentage figure by multiplying by 100. It is difficult to imagine just a one-dollar incremental increase in income. Most people enjoy something more than this when they receive a raise in pay. For this reason, economists utilize a simple formula for computing MPC that provides an average MPC over a small range of increase in income. The formula is:

$$MPC = \frac{\Delta C}{\Delta DI} = \text{Slope}$$

where the Δ symbol denotes "a change in."

Note also that MPC is equal to the slope of the consumption line. Recall from Chapter 2 that the slope of a line is determined by dividing the vertical change by the horizontal change for a given movement along the line. This is illustrated by the consumption function in Figure 10–3. In this example, the vertical change is equal to ΔC and the horizontal change is ΔDI.

PROPENSITIES TO SAVE

Having covered the propensities to consume, it is a fairly simple matter to apply these same concepts to saving. In a parallel fashion, we can talk about the average propensity to save (APS) and the marginal propensity to save (MPS). As one might expect from the preceding sections, APS is the proportion of total disposable income that is saved, and MPS is the proportion of a change in income that is saved. The formulas for computing APS and MPS are:

FIGURE 10–3   The Slope of the Consumption Function

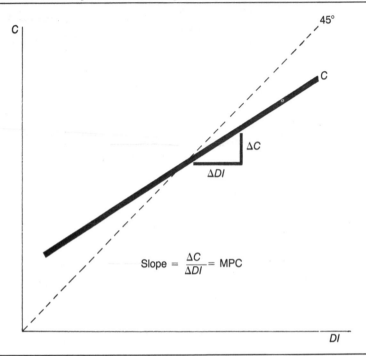

$$\text{Slope} = \frac{\Delta C}{\Delta DI} = \text{MPC}$$

$$\text{APS} = \frac{S}{DI} \qquad \text{MPS} = \frac{\Delta S}{\Delta DI} = \text{Slope}$$

The fact that people can do only two things with their disposable income, spend it or save it, means that APS and MPS bear a direct relationship to APC and MPC. The proportion that is saved (APS) plus the proportion that is spent (APC) must equal one. Moreover, the proportion of any change in income that is saved (MPS) plus the corresponding proportion that is spent (MPC) must also equal one. Thus we have:

$$\text{APC} + \text{APS} = 1 \quad \text{or} \quad 1 - \text{APC} = \text{APS}$$
$$\text{MPC} + \text{MPS} = 1 \quad \text{or} \quad 1 - \text{MPC} = \text{MPS.}$$

Also, the slope of the saving function, as in Figure 10–1*B*, is equal to the MPS.

INVESTMENT

The second major component of the simple Keynesian model is investment. We will continue to define investment as it is defined in the national-income accounts—the physical construction of buildings (including housing), machines,

FIGURE 10–4   Investment and Income

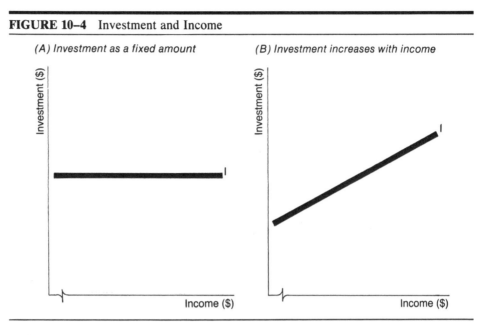

(A) Investment as a fixed amount

(B) Investment increases with income

tools, and so on, together with any change in inventories. As we will see in the next chapter, inventory change plays an important role in the model.

In the interest of preserving simplicity in developing the simple Keynesian model, we will assume that investment in the economy is a set or given amount; that is, it does not change, at least over a modest range of income. The term *autonomous investment* is often used to describe this investment figure—a figure that is assumed or imposed on the model. We can represent autonomous investment by a straight horizontal line as in Figure 10–4A. Such an investment function tells us that the level of investment remains constant over the range of income shown.

It would be more realistic to assume that investment would become a larger figure, the larger the income or output of the economy. This would be represented by the upward-sloping line in Figure 10–4B. However, in the interest of preserving the simplicity of the model, it will be constructed under the assumption of a fixed amount of investment spending. The policy implications derived from the model will not be affected by making this simplifying assumption. The main concern will be with shifts in the entire investment function and not so much with its slope. Also, to simplify the model, we will assume that saving, which provides the wherewithal to invest, is provided entirely by households.

GOVERNMENT SPENDING

The third major component of the simple Keynesian model is government spending. As pointed out in a preceding chapter, we should not think of the goods and services purchased by the government as somehow being lost to the private sector. With the exception of the goods and services necessary to run the government bureaucracy, everything the government purchases goes back to the people in the form of consumption goods, investment goods, or some combination of the two.

Again to simplify our discussion, we will assume that government spending is a fixed or set amount; that is, it does not change over a range of income or output. We know that government purchases of goods and services tend to grow with the rest of the economy. However, for relatively small changes in income or output, which we are mainly interested in, it is not too unrealistic to assume a fixed government spending figure.

Along with a fixed level of government spending, we will assume also that total taxes are a fixed or set amount; they do not change at different levels of NNP. These often are referred to as lump-sum taxes. Again it would be more realistic to allow tax receipts to increase along with NNP, as would occur under an income tax. However, this also would make the model more complex and, as we shall see later, the direction of change predicted by the model using a fixed or lump-sum tax is the same as when we use an income tax, although the magnitude of the change will be different.

In terms of a diagram, we could represent government spending in exactly the same way we represented investment in Figure 10–4A—by a straight horizontal line. Instead of drawing a separate diagram for government spending, we can visualize it to be the same as the investment diagram, only in this case the horizontal line would be labeled *G* instead of *I*.

SUMMARY

In contrast to the classical economists who took the level of employment as given and focused on prices or inflation, Keynes took prices as given and concentrated on the problem of unemployment. The heart of the simple Keynesian model is the aggregate expenditure (AE) function. It consists of consumer, investor, and government spending. Consumer spending is characterized by the consumption function which is a relationship between income and spending. In the simple model, investment and government spending are assumed to be constant at various levels of income.

YOU SHOULD KNOW

1. Who John Maynard Keynes was, and what his main concern was.

2. The basic difference between the classical economists and Keynes.

3. What the consumption function is and why is it less steeply sloped than the 45-degree line.

4. What the savings function is, and how is it related to the consumption function.

5. What the average propensity to consume is and its approximate value for the United States over the 1929–89 period.

6. Why the U.S. APC did not decrease during

the 1929–89 period despite an increase in per capita real income.

7. What marginal propensity to consume is.

8. What the propensities to save are, and how

they are related to the propensities to consume.

9. What is assumed about investment and government spending in the simple Keynesian model.

QUESTIONS

1. How did the thinking of Keynes and his followers differ from that of the classical economists with respect to the problems of unemployment?

2. What is the economic meaning of the upward-sloping consumption function that is less steeply sloped than the 45-degree line?

3. *a.* Differentiate marginal propensity to consume and average propensity to consume.
   b. Consider a family with a $20,000-per-year disposable income that receives a $1,000 increase in its income. If the family spends $800 of the extra $1,000, what is its MPC? What is the family's APC if it spends $20,000 of its $21,000 income?

4. *a.* What happens to MPC and APC as one moves up along a straight, upward-sloping consumption line?
   b. How can one reconcile these results with the fact that APC in the United States has remained relatively constant over the past half-century?

5. Is it possible for a family's spending to be greater than its disposable income? If so, can this situation be illustrated on a consumption function? Explain.

6. *a.* Show that MPC equals the slope of the consumption function.
   b. If MPC is .80, what is the slope of the saving function?

7. What are the three components or building blocks of the simple Keynesian model?

SELF-TEST

1. John Maynard Keynes was primarily concerned about the problem of:
   a. government deficits.
   b. population growth.
   c. unemployment.
   d. inflation.

2. Keynes' book, *The General Theory*, came out during:
   a. the Revolutionary War.
   b. World War I.
   c. the Great Depression.
   d. World War II.

3. Keynes argued that _____ demand may

not be large enough to take off of the market the total output of goods and services that would be produced under conditions of full employment.
   a. potential   *c.* pent-up
   b. effective   *d.* foreign

4. Keynes put less faith in _____ and more faith in _____ than the classical economists as a solution to unemployment.
   a. market forces; government action
   b. government action; market forces
   c. wage controls; market forces
   d. wage controls; government action

5. The consumption function is a relationship between:
   a. buyers and sellers.
   b. price and quantity.
   c. consumption and prices.
   d. consumption and income.

6. Keynes argued that when people enjoy an increase in their incomes, consumption expenditures increase _____ the increase in income.
   a. in proportion to
   b. less than
   c. more than

7. The 45-degree line in the simple Keynesian model has a slope of _____ .
   a. 1   c. zero
   b. −1   d. infinity

8. The implication of Keynes's argument put forth in question 6 is a consumption function that has a slope of _____ .
   a. less than one
   b. greater than one
   c. one

9. At the point where the consumption function intersects the 45-degree line, _____ equals _____ .
   a. saving; zero
   b. income; savings
   c. income; zero
   d. a and b

10. College students who spend more than their income can be represented on the Keynesian diagram as being _____ the intersection of the 45-degree line and the consumption function.
    a. at
    b. to the left of
    c. to the right of

11. Average propensity to consume is obtained by dividing _____ by _____ .
    a. GNP; C   c. DI; C
    b. C; GNP   d. C; DI

12. Along a straight-line consumption function, APC _____ as DI increases.

a. decreases
b. remains constant
c. increases

13. APC in the United States has _____ in the range of _____ over the past half-century.
    a. increased; .05 to .10
    b. remained constant; .05 to .10
    c. decreased; .95 to .90
    d. remained constant; .90 to .95

14. One way to reconcile the answers to questions 12 and 13 is to view the nation's short-run consumption function as _____ over time.
    a. shifting upward
    b. shifting downward
    c. remaining constant

15. According to Milton Friedman's permanent income hypothesis, the average propensity to consume out of permanent income _____ as income increases.
    a. increases
    b. remains constant
    c. decreases

16. Marginal propensity to consume is the _____ amount spent out of an _____ dollar of income.
    a. extra; average
    b. average; extra
    c. extra; extra
    d. average; average

17. MPC is calculated by dividing _____ by _____ .
    a. C; DI
    b. DI; C
    c. ΔC; ΔDI
    d. ΔDI; ΔC

18. The slope of the consumption function is equal to:
    a. 45 degrees.   c. APC.
    b. MPC.   d. 1/MPC.

19. MPC plus MPS equals _____ and APC plus APS equals _____ .

a. 1; −1   *c.* −1; −1

b. −1; 1   *d.* 1; 1

20. In building the simple Keynesian model, it will be assumed the investment and government spending:

a. are equal.

b. are zero.

c. remain constant at various levels of income.

d. increase as income increases.

Chapter 11

Construction and Use of the Simple Model

OVERVIEW

This chapter utilizes the three components developed in the preceding chapter as building blocks to construct the simple Keynesian model. The idea of equilibrium income is developed along with its economic rationale. The chapter concludes by showing how the simple model can explain the existence of unemployment and inflation.

THE AGGREGATE EXPENDITURE FUNCTION

We have now developed the three main components of the simple Keynesian model—consumption, investment, and government spending. The next step is to combine them into what can be called the aggregate expenditure (AE) function. The AE function gives the relationship between *actual* income and *desired* spending. A graph of the AE function shows desired spending on the vertical axis and actual income (or value of output) on the horizontal.

The AE function is constructed by adding the desired expenditures of the three groups—consumers, investors, and government—at each income level as shown in Figure 11–1.

The lowest line represents consumer spending. It tells us how much consumers *desire* to spend at each level of income. Its upward slope conveys the idea that people desire to spend more when their incomes increase. Recall that the slope of the consumption line is equal to MPC. In the current example we assume MPC = .75.

Investment spending is assumed to be $300 billion at all levels of income. Therefore, the sum of consumption and investment spending, denoted by the $C + I_n$ line, is $300 more than consumption at each level of income. Government

FIGURE 11–1   Deriving the Aggregate Expenditure (AE) Function

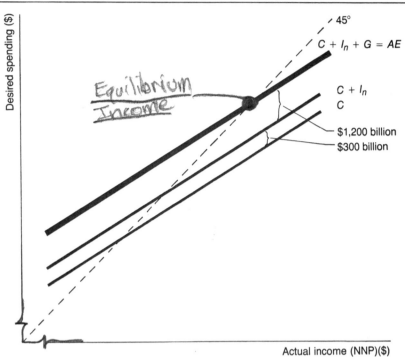

spending (federal, state, and local) is $1,200 billion in this example. The aggregate expenditure function is completed by adding the constant $1,200 billion government spending on to the $C + I_n$ line.

EQUILIBRIUM INCOME

In the simple Keynesian model, *equilibrium income* is defined as that level of income (we use NNP here) where the desired level of aggregate expenditures equals the actual income or output of the economy. Equilibrium income corresponds to the point where the aggregate expenditure function intersects the 45-degree line extending out from the origin. By definition, along the 45-degree line, actual income or output equals desired spending.

The economic rationale underlying equilibrium income is easiest to see if we choose levels of income that are not at equilibrium. Consider first the $5,200 billion level of income on Figure 11–2. At this income, the aggregate expenditure function tells us that desired spending is $5,150 billion. This means the actual output of the economy is $50 billion greater than what is being purchased. The result is an unintended increase in inventories. Therefore, business firms reduce

FIGURE 11–2   Deriving Equilibrium Income

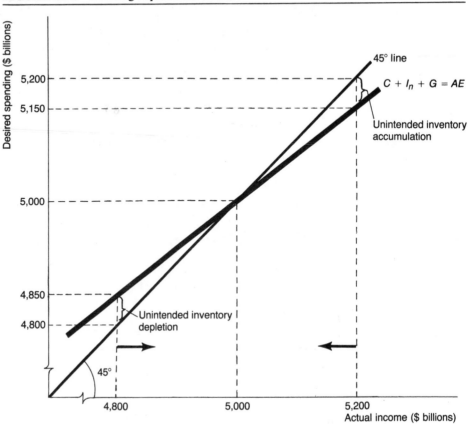

output, which in turn causes a reduction of income. Income will continue to decline as long as desired spending, as indicated by the aggregated expenditure function, is less than output.

The opposite occurs if desired spending is greater than income or output as illustrated by the $4,800 billion level on Figure 11–2. Now desired spending exceeds output, inventories decline unintentionally, and business firms increase output, which causes income to increase. Equilibrium income corresponds to the intersection of the AE function and the 45° line.

SHIFTS IN THE AGGREGATE EXPENDITURE FUNCTION

Recall that the aggregate expenditure (AE) function is made up of three components: consumption, investment, and government spending. A change in the level of any of these three components for a given level of NNP will shift the AE function up or down.

1. Consumption Shifts. From the standpoint of the long-run trend in the entire economy, we can view the consumption line as gradually and continually shifting upward over time. The permanent-income hypothesis discussed in the previous chapter provides an explanation for this long-run upward trend in consumption in relation to income. Since we are dealing with the entire economy, we would expect the growth in population also to push the aggregate consumption function to higher and higher levels. Although the continued long-run growth in consumption is important from the standpoint of maintaining a high level of aggregate demand, our major concern in the discussion to follow will be with short-term fluctuations or shifts in the consumption function.

One factor that can cause a shift in the short-run consumption function is a change in expectations of future economic conditions. For example, suppose people suddenly become pessimistic about the future, thinking they might be laid off. As a result, they might decide to tighten their belts and reduce their rate of consumption purchases. This is illustrated by consumption C_0 in Figure 11–3A. Here it is shown that people wish to reduce their consumption by $10 billion at all possible income levels, which leads to a $10 billion downward shift in the AE function. The opposite might occur if people become more optimistic about the future. An increase in consumption, as illustrated by C_2 in Figure 11–3A, would shift aggregate expenditures upward.

The expectation of the availability of goods and services in the future also can influence consumption during a particular period. For example, if people expect war to break out in the near future and as a result expect shortages to occur, some may increase their rate of purchase in order to stock up on items they anticipate will be in short supply or rationed. The periods preceding World War II and the Korean conflict provide examples of this behavior. This can be illustrated by an increase in consumption from C_1 to C_2 in Figure 11–3A. Moreover, an expectation of higher prices in the future, as commonly occurs during a war, tends to result in an increased rate of present consumption, also illustrated by C_2.

A third factor that is generally considered an important determinant of consumption is the availability of credit. As expected, this mainly affects the purchase of consumer durables such as appliances and automobiles. If loans become difficult to obtain, consumers tend to reduce their purchases of these items as illustrated by C_0 in Figure 11–3A. Conversely, if credit becomes easier to obtain, we might expect consumers to respond by stepping up their purchase of items bought on time.

A factor related to the availability of credit is the size of the interest rate, particularly the real rate of interest. An increase in the rate of interest increases the overall cost of an item purchased on time. If people respond to higher prices by reducing their purchases of these items, there will be a reduction in consumption, again as illustrated by C_0 in Figure 11–3A.

2. Investment Shifts. Because the ultimate aim of investment is to increase the future output of consumer goods and services, we would expect total investment also to exhibit a long-run upward trend in line with a growing economy. However,

FIGURE 11–3 The Effect of Changes in C, I, or G on Aggregate Expenditures

(A) *Consumption shifts*

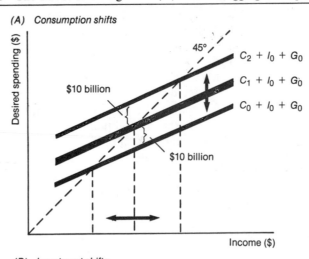

(B) *Investment shifts*

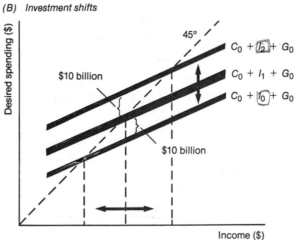

(C) *Government spending shifts*

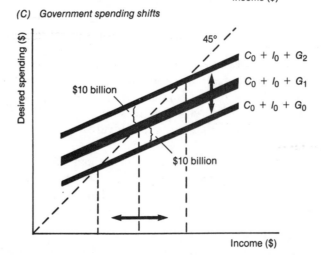

as in the case of consumption, there is also the possibility of cyclical fluctuations in investment spending by the business community.

As in the discussion of consumer spending, we would have to say that expectations by businesspeople play a key role in the determination of investment. Because investment by definition is something that pays off in the future, it is reasonable to expect that decisions to invest or not to invest depend a great deal on what investors expect the future to bring as far as business conditions are concerned. For example, if investors expect a strong future demand for consumer goods and services, that is, a high level of employment and spending, it is more likely they will decide to step up current investment spending, as illustrated by I_2 in Figure 11–3B. If they expect a period of depressed business activity and high unemployment, investors tend to reduce investment spending, as illustrated by I_0 in Figure 11–3B. In this example, we illustrate a \$10 billion change in investment spending.

Changes in the rate of interest also change the level of investment spending. Higher rates of interest increase finance costs and reduce the profitability of investment projects. Therefore, an increase in the interest rate shifts the investment expenditure line downward, other things equal. The opposite is true of a reduction in the interest rate.

3. Government Spending Shifts. Since government spending is included as a separate component of aggregate demand, any decision to change the level of government spending will change the level of aggregate demand, at least in the short run. Abrupt increases in government spending have come about mainly in wartime, as illustrated by G_2 in Figure 11–3C. Then after the end of hostilities, government spending is reduced, and G shifts downward, as shown by G_0.

In the context of the Keynesian model, the government spending component of aggregate demand takes on special significance because it can be changed by deliberate government edict to offset any changes in consumption or investment. For example, if investors become pessimistic and reduce investment by \$10 billion, the government can offset this by increasing its expenditure by \$10 billion, perhaps on new public works projects and the like. We will consider this topic in more detail in Chapter 14 on fiscal policy.

It is important to recognize that each of the above shifts has been considered in isolation of other factors. In reality, several forces can be pushing on aggregate expenditures simultaneously, some pushing it up, others down. For example, a higher rate of interest can be pushing it down, at the same time more optimistic expectations of future business conditions or expectations of inflation can be pushing it up.

THE MULTIPLIER

By now it should be clear that a shift in any one or all of the components of the aggregate expenditure function will in turn change the level of equilibrium income. An increase in C, I_n, or G, for example, increases equilibrium income, and vice versa. The next question to consider is: How much does equilibrium income change for a given change in the aggregate expenditure function? A glance at the diagrams in Figure 11–3 tells us that the change along the horizontal axis, that is, the change in equilibrium income, is greater than the vertical shift in the AE function. That this must be so is purely a phenomenon of geometry. The closer the slope of the AE function is to the slope of the 45-degree line, the greater will be the change in equilibrium income for a given shift in aggregate expenditure. It will be easier to understand this phenomenon if you draw some aggregate expenditure functions of your own, with progressively steeper slopes, and observe what happens to equilibrium income when AE is shifted by a given amount.

Recall that the upward slope of aggregate expenditure in this simple model is due entirely to the upward-sloping characteristic of the consumption function. Thus, the steeper the consumption function, the steeper is aggregate expenditure and the greater is the change in equilibrium income. Also, recall that we could have drawn the investment function with an upward slope as in Figure 10–4*B*. If we had done so, this would have added to the slope of the aggregate expenditure function (making it steeper) and caused an even greater change in equilibrium income for a given shift in aggregate expenditure.

Fortunately, there is an economic rationale for the large change in equilibrium income relative to the shift in aggregate expenditures—it is called the *multiplier effect.* The multiplier effect occurs because spending by one group is income to another group, which in turn allows the second group to increase its spending, and so on. To illustrate the multiplier, let us take as an example a $10 billion increase in government spending. This would cause a $10 billion upward shift in aggregate expenditures. The extra $10 billion spent on such things as military hardware, schools, and highways becomes extra income to the people who produce and sell these items to the government. It is reasonable to believe, therefore, that these people will spend at least a part of this extra income. The part they spend is revealed by their MPC. If MPC is 0.75, they will spend 75 cents of each extra dollar of income they receive and save the remaining 25 cents. They may buy new cars, houses, vacation trips, and other goods. In turn, the people who sell the $7.5 billion of goods and services receive a like amount as new incomes. We could expect this process to continue with round after round of new spending giving rise to new income, new income leading to new spending, and so on. The multiplier process is summarized in Table 11–1.

TABLE 11–1   Illustrating the Multiplier Process

Round	Extra Spending	Extra Income
1	$10.0 ⟶	$10.0
2	7.5 ⟵⟶	7.5
3	5.6 ⟵⟶	5.6
To infinity	$40.0	$40.0

Repeating the process round after round for an infinite number of times, the initial $10 billion increase in government spending at the maximum would give rise to a $40 billion increase in total spending in the economy (assuming MPC is 0.75). How do we know this? Surely no one would attempt to add an infinite column of numbers. Fortunately, we can use a simple mathematical formula that gives the sum of an infinite convergent series. The formula is:

$$1 + X + X^2 + X^3 + \cdots + X^n = \frac{1}{1 - X}$$

where X is less than one. If we let X equal the MPC, 0.75 in this example, you will notice that each number in the extra spending and income columns in Table 11-1 is found by multiplying the initial spending increase by the numbers in the above formula. For example, the first round is 1×10, the second 0.75×10, the third $(0.75)^2 \times 10$, and so on. Thus the total increase in spending (the sum of the columns) can be found by multiplying the sum of the infinite series times the original $10 billion increase. This can be done because the $10 billion factors out. In algebraic terms:

$$1 \times 10 + 0.75 \times 10 + (0.75)^2 \times 10 + \cdots + (0.75)^n \times 10 = \frac{1}{1 - 0.75} \times 10$$

Since $1/(1 - 0.75) = 4$, the sum of each column is $40 billion. The 4 in this example is referred to as the government spending multiplier. It is found by the formula $1/(1 - MPC)$. Hence, the closer MPC is to 1, the larger is the government spending multiplier.

Although the preceding example is given in terms of a government spending increase, the same multiplier process would occur with a government spending decrease. Only now the $10 billion decrease in government spending would cause a $40 billion decrease in total spending (at the maximum). The same multiplier process also would occur with a change in consumption or investment spending, at any given income level. Recall that changes in the willingness of consumers or businesspeople to spend also shifts the aggregate expenditure function, giving rise to the multiplier process. In Chapter 14 on fiscal policy, however, we will be primarily interested in the government spending multiplier.

UNEMPLOYMENT AND INFLATION

Before we leave the simple model, it will be useful to take a preliminary glimpse at how the model can be used to illustrate the cause of unemployment and inflation. Keynes and his followers argued that there is no reason the equilibrium level of NNP necessarily had to be equal to the level of NNP that would generate full employment at stable prices. Keynes was mostly concerned about the unemployment problem. (Remember the model was first built during the early 1930s, the years of the Great Depression.) He argued, in this case, that the economy

FIGURE 11–4   Illustrating Unemployment and Inflation by the Simple Model

(A) Unemployment

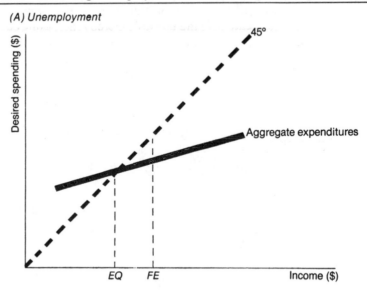

(B) Inflation

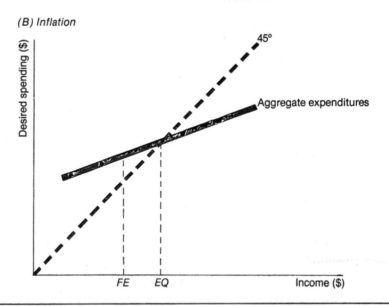

could come to rest at an equilibrium level of NNP that was less than the level necessary to generate full employment resulting in unemployment. This situation is illustrated in Figure 11–4A. The equilibrium level of NNP, denoted by *EQ*, is less than the level of NNP that would correspond to full employment, denoted by *FE*. According to this model, there is nothing in the economy that would move it to full employment. Thus, Keynes argued the government may have to take steps to shift aggregate demand upward, thereby increasing equilibrium NNP enough to make it correspond to the full-employment level. The ways in which this can be done and some of the problems involved constitute much of the material on fiscal policy and its problems in Chapters 14 and 15.

Although the simple model is not designed to deal with price changes, one can represent an inflationary situation as existing when equilibrium NNP is greater than the full-employment level. In this case, the economy moves past the full-employment level on its way to equilibrium Figure 11–4*B*. Because resources are fully employed at the full-employment level of NNP, labeled as *FE,* the increase in NNP in terms of dollars of output between *FE* and *EQ* is primarily due to the increase in prices, that is, inflation occurs. In this case, the objective of fiscal and monetary policy is to shift the AE function down until equilibrium NNP coincides with the full-employment level.

SUMMARY

The aggregate expenditure (AE) function is constructed by adding investment and government spending to the consumption function. The AE function depicts the relationship between actual income and desired spending. Equilibrium income corresponds to the intersection of the 45-degree line and the AE function. The AE function shifts up or down in response to a change in consumer, investor, or government spending. The multiplier occurs because spending by one person or group is income to someone else. Hence, there is round after round of income and spending. The spending multiplier is equal to $1/1-MPC$.

YOU SHOULD KNOW

1. What the aggregate expenditure function is, and how it is constructed.
2. The meaning of equilibrium income.
3. What happens if actual income is greater than equilibrium.
4. What happens if actual income is less than equilibrium.
5. The three sources of shifts in the aggregate expenditure function.
6. The factors that cause a shift in the consumption function.
7. The factors that cause a shift in the investment function.
8. The factors that cause a shift in the government spending function.
9. What the multiplier is, why it exists, and how to compute it.
10. How MPC is related to the multipliers.
11. How the simple Keynesian model can be used to show the existence of unemployment and inflation.

QUESTIONS

1. Construct the simple Keynesian model by the following steps:
   a. Draw and label the two axes and the 45-degree line.
   b. Draw a consumption line assuming MPC = 0.75 (do not be concerned with its level).
   c. Draw a $C + I_n$ line assuming $I_n = \$300$ billion.
   d. Draw the $C + I_n + G$ (aggregate expenditure function) assuming $G = \$1,200$ billion.

2. In the context of the simple model, what is the meaning of the aggregate expenditure function? The 45-degree line?

3. a. Define equilibrium income (NNP).
   b. Explain what happens when actual NNP is either larger or smaller than equilibrium NNP.

4. Using the Keynesian model diagram, illustrate the following:
   a. Consumers expect increased unemployment in the future.
   b. Investors become more optimistic about future business conditions.
   c. Government increases its spending because of new domestic programs.
   d. The interest rate increases.

5. It was argued that higher rates of interest reduce investment spending, causing the aggregate expenditure function to shift down and decrease equilibrium income. Yet, during the Great Depression, interest rates were low, and during more prosperous times interest rates were relatively high. Is there any way to reconcile this apparent discrepancy between theory and fact?

6. a. What is the economic rationale underlying the multiplier?
   b. If MPC is 0.80, how much does equilibrium NNP change if aggregate demand shifts up by $10 billion?

7. According to the simple Keynesian model, how could unemployment occur? Inflation?

SELF-TEST

1. The aggregate expenditure (AE) function gives the relationship between _____ income and _____ spending.
   a. desired; actual
   b. actual; desired
   c. actual; actual
   d. desired; desired

2. The AE function is obtained by adding desired _____ at various income levels.
   a. C
   b. C + I
   c. C + I + G
   d. C + I + G − S

3. If MPC is 0.75, the slope of the consumption function is _____.

   a. .75
   b. .25
   c. 1/.75
   d. 1/(1 − .75)

4. If investment spending is assumed to be $500 billion at all levels of income, the C + I line will be equal to _____ at the various income levels.
   a. $500 billion
   b. C + $500 billion
   c. C − $500 billion
   d. C/$500 billion

5. If government spending is $1,500 billion, the C + I + G or AE function equals _____ billion at various income levels if I is $500 billion.

a. $C + \$1,000$
b. $C + \$1,500$
c. $C + \$500 + \$1,500$
d. $C - \$500 - \$1,000$

6. If MPC is 0.75, the slope of the AE function is _____.
   a. .25
   b. .75
   c. 1/.75
   d. 1/(1 − .75)

7. In the simple Keynesian model, equilibrium income corresponds to the point where:
   a. consumption spending equals income.
   b. the AE function intersects the 45-degree line.
   c. the slope of the 45-degree line equals the slope of the AE function.
   d. the slope of the AE function equals one.

8. If actual income in the country exceeds equilibrium income, desired spending is _____ than actual income or output in the economy causing inventories to _____ and actual output and income to _____ .
   a. greater; increase; decrease
   b. less; decrease; increase
   c. greater; decrease; increase
   d. less; increase; decrease

9. If actual income in the country is less than equilibrium income, desired spending is _____ than actual income or output in the economy causing inventories to _____ and actual income or output to _____ .
   a. less; increase; decrease
   b. greater; decrease; decrease
   c. greater; decrease; increase
   d. less; decrease; decrease

10. If consumers become pessimistic about the future, more concerned that they might be laid off their jobs, the consumption line will shift _____ causing the AE

function to _____ and equilibrium income to _____ .
   a. upward; increase; increase
   b. upward; decrease; decrease
   c. downward; decrease; increase
   d. downward; decrease; decrease

11. Higher interest rates or an increased difficulty of obtaining credit by consumers will cause the consumption function to shift _____ causing the AE function to _____ along with equilibrium income.
   a. downward; increase
   b. upward; increase
   c. downward; decrease
   d. upward; decrease

12. If businesspeople become more optimistic about future business conditions, the investment function will shift _____ causing the AE function to _____ along with equilibrium income.
   a. downward; increase
   b. upward; increase
   c. downward; decrease
   d. upward; decrease

13. An increase in government spending on new programs or the military causes the AE function to shift _____ causing equilibrium income to _____ .
   a. downward; increase
   b. upward; increase
   c. downward; decrease
   d. upward; decrease

14. The multiplier occurs because spending by one group _____ another group.
   a. is income to
   b. is a reduction in income to
   c. is savings to
   d. has no effect on income or spending of

15. If MPC is 0.80, a $10 billion increase in spending by either consumers, investors, or the government causes equilibrium income to increase by _____ billion because of the multiplier.

a. 40   *c.* 12.5
b. 50   *d.* 10

16. Keynes argued that the high level of un-employment during the Great Depression occurred because of the _____ level of the aggregate expenditure function caus-ing equilibrium income to be _____ than the level that would generate full em-ployment.
    a. high; greater
    b. low; less
    c. high; less
    d. low; greater

17. The primary use of the simple Keynesian model is to show how _____ can occur.

    a. unemployment
    b. inflation
    c. economic growth
    d. pollution

18. An inflationary situation can be depicted by the simple Keynesian model if the AE function shifts _____ enough to cause equilibrium income to be _____ than the level of income that would generate full employment.
    a. downward; less
    b. downward; greater
    c. upward; less
    d. upward; greater

Part V

Post–Keynesian Thought

Chapter 12

The Aggregate Demand—Aggregate Supply Model

OVERVIEW

In this chapter and the next, we consider more recent developments in macroeconomic thought. The aggregate demand–aggregate supply model of this chapter evolved in the 1970s to take account of changes in the general price level (inflation). Recall that the simple Keynesian model does not explicitly show changes in the price level.

AGGREGATE DEMAND

Aggregate demand is defined as a negative relationship between the general price level as measured by a price index such as the CPI and the level of real output in the economy. The latter value is the nominal or monetary value of GNP or NNP deflated by a price index such as the CPI. Although the concept of aggregate demand is similar to market demand developed in Chapter 4, there is one important difference. With market demand, only the price of a single product is varied; all other prices are held constant. With aggregate demand, all prices change.

Similar to the market demand curve of Chapter 4, the aggregate demand curve slopes down and to the right when the price level is represented on the vertical axis and real output on the horizontal plane (Figure 12–1). When the price level is high, relative to some base year, society will demand a smaller quantity of consumption and investment goods than when the price level is relatively low. Consumption and investment goods include the goods purchased and distributed by government.

FIGURE 12–1 Aggregate Demand

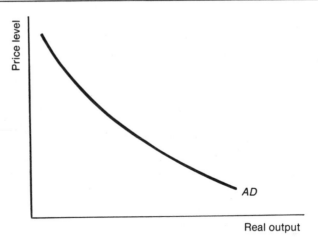

Two arguments have been used to justify the downward-sloping characteristic of aggregate demand: (1) the interest rate argument and (2) the real balance effect. According to the interest rate argument, an increase in the price level decreases the *real* value of money in the economy. For example, if the price level doubles and everything else remains unchanged, the purchasing power of the stock of money in existence is reduced by one half. In this case, it takes twice as many dollars or units of money to finance a given amount of investment or the purchase of consumer goods. The resulting "scarcity" of money causes the interest rate to increase, thereby decreasing the rate of investment and/or consumer spending. As spending is reduced, the real output of the economy declines. Conversely, at low price levels the real value of the money stock is increased. Therefore, it takes fewer units of money to finance a given expenditure. As money becomes more "plentiful" in real terms, the interest rate declines and spending is stimulated.

The real balance effect, sometimes called the Pigou Effect, after the economist who is credited with first thinking of it, also works through the purchasing power of money. When the price level rises, given the stock of money, real wealth of people declines because now each unit of money buys less. As people begin to feel poorer, they reduce their rate of purchases of goods and services, and the real quantity of output demanded declines.

The exact slope of aggregate demand depends on the responsiveness of spending to interest rate changes and to changes in the real value of the stock of money in existence. If these responses are large, the aggregate demand curve will be relatively flat, and vice versa.

The slope of the aggregate demand curve is an important consideration because the steeper the slope, the greater the effect that a policy-induced shift in aggregate demand will have on real output. Conversely, if aggregate demand is close to horizontal, a given horizontal shift will have a relatively small impact on equilibrium output. This will become more evident after developing aggregate supply and discussing the factors that can shift aggregate demand. The slope of the aggregate supply curve also is an important determinant of the impacts of demand shifts. Let us now consider aggregate supply.

SHORT–RUN AGGREGATE SUPPLY

It is necessary to divide the discussion of aggregate supply into two parts: (1) short-run aggregate supply and (2) long-run aggregate supply. *Short-run aggregate supply (SRAS)* is defined as a positive relationship between the price level and the real output of goods and services in the economy. With the price level represented on the vertical axis and real national output on the horizontal, it is hypothesized that, at least over some range, the SRAS curve will slope up and to the right (Figure 12–2). Although it has the same general shape as market supply of Chapter 4, it is different in the same sense that aggregate demand is different from market demand. With market supply, the only price that changes along the supply curve is that of the item under consideration. With aggregate supply, all prices change as one moves along the curve.

The difference between aggregate supply and the market supply discussed in Chapter 4 can be better understood by considering the economic rationale underlying its upward slope. Consider first an increase in the general price level. If the aggregate supply curve slopes up and to the right, it is an indication that the real output of goods and services increases when the price level increases. In order for this to occur, owners of productive resources, mainly labor and owners of capital, must believe that they are better off with higher prices than with lower

FIGURE 12–2   Short-Run Aggregate Supply

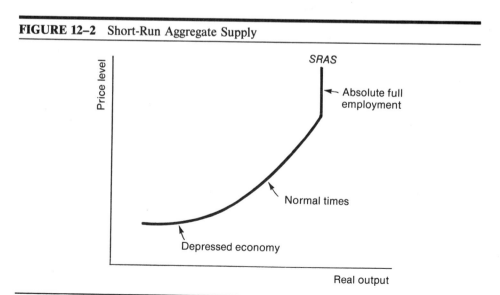

prices, or they would not offer a greater quantity of their resources on the market as the price level increased. They see their nominal wages and profits increasing but do not perceive the increase in the prices of goods and services they purchase. Hence, they become willing to supply more resources and thereby increase output. Economists refer to this behavior as a "money illusion."

The short-run aggregate supply curve is usually drawn to slope upward at an increasing rate with the lower left end rather flat and the upper right end vertical, as in Figure 12–2. This shape is intended to reflect the change from a depressed, high-unemployment economy when the price level and real output are relatively low to a situation of absolute full employment. At the lower end of the curve, a slight increase in prices is thought to bring forth a relatively large increase in output as resource owners anxiously look for an opportunity to put their unemployed resources to work. As the price level continues to increase, fewer idle resources exist, and increases in real output become more and more difficult to obtain. Finally, at some point where the curve becomes vertical, all resources are fully employed and working as hard as physically possible. At that point, no further increases in real output are possible, even at higher and higher prices.

SHORT-RUN EQUILIBRIUM

The next step is to combine aggregate demand with short-run aggregate supply and arrive at a short-run equilibrium price level and national output. Since both curves are drawn with price on the vertical axis and quantity on the horizontal, we can superimpose them on the same diagram, as in Figure 12–3.

FIGURE 12–3   Short-Run Equilibrium

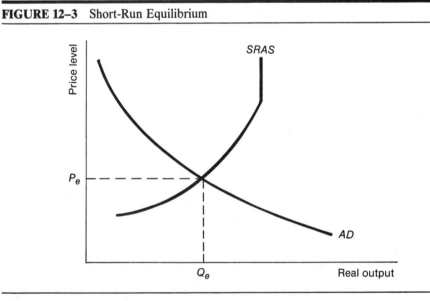

As is evident from the diagram, the equilibrium price level and quantity of real output correspond to P_e and Q_e, respectively. If the price level is above P_e, quantity demanded of goods and services is less than the quantity supplied. Hence, there will be unsold goods and the price level will decline, causing a decrease in production of goods and services. At some point when the price level declines enough, aggregate demand just equals short-run aggregate supply and equilibrium is attained. Similar reasoning is applied if the price level happens to be below equilibrium, except now aggregate demand would exceed short-run aggregate supply, a shortage of goods and services would prevail, and the price level would be forced upward, as occurs when there is a shortage in any given market.

SHIFTS IN AGGREGATE DEMAND

Once an economy establishes an equilibrium position, will it remain there for all time to come? No. The aggregate demand and short-run aggregate supply curves can be expected to shift to new positions, thereby establishing new equilibria. The growth in population, for example, can be expected to shift aggregate demand to the right. At any given price level, more people will demand more goods and services. By the same token, as the productive capacity of the economy increases due to a growth in the labor force and capital, the short-run aggregate supply will be located further to the right. (It is best to think of the short-run aggregate supply curve as existing at a particular location at a point in time rather than a gradual shifting over time because, after a period of time has elapsed, it can no longer be regarded as a short-run curve.) But this model is not intended to show the gradual

FIGURE 12–4   Shifts in Aggregate Demand

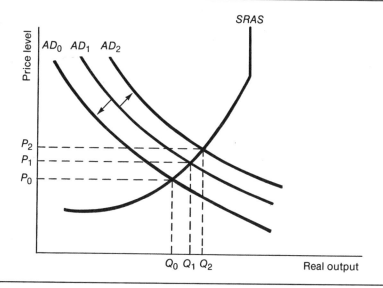

growth of the economy. Rather, it is constructed to analyze the short-run shifts in the two curves resulting from policy changes and other phenomena.

First, let us consider shifts in aggregate demand. For the most part, these shifts occur for the same reasons that caused shifts in the aggregate expenditure curve of the simple Keynesian model. For example, if consumers suddenly became pessimistic about the future and decreased their rate of spending, there would be a shift to the left as shown by the change from AD_1 to AD_0 in Figure 12–4. As another example, if the government suddenly increases its rate of spending for one reason or another, aggregate demand would increase (shift up and to the right), say from AD_1 to AD_2 in Figure 12–4. Changes in the interest rate also can be expected to shift aggregate demand with higher rates causing a decrease as consumers reduce their spending on "big-ticket" items such as cars and appliances.

Notice that a decrease in aggregate demand leads to a decrease in both real output and the price level, while an increase causes the opposite to occur.

SHIFTS IN SHORT–RUN AGGREGATE SUPPLY

When discussing the short-run aggregate supply curve, bear in mind that the time period under consideration is relatively short—too short for people to realize they are laboring under a money illusion. Thus, the normal growth of the economy resulting from a higher population and a larger amount of capital cannot be shown on this curve. The main factors shifting short-run aggregate supply are changes in physical resources. These are frequently referred to as *supply side shocks*. An example of a decrease (shift to the left) in short-run aggregate supply would be a prolonged and widespread drought that resulted in a massive crop failure (water is an important resource). Another example often used is the cut-off of oil imports from the OPEC nations in the 1970s. Again, oil is an important resource. Still another is the destruction of productive capacity through war, or some other disaster such as flood or earthquake. All of the above circumstances would cause a decrease, or shift to the left in short-run aggregate supply, as shown by the shift from $SRAS_1$ to $SRAS_0$ in Figure 12–5.

Examples of an increase, or shift to the right, of the short-run aggregate supply curve include the return to a normal situation after the above shocks have disappeared. Other examples might include the discovery of a significant new oil field, a breakthrough in technology, or a rapid increase in labor force participation. All of these examples can be illustrated by a shift from $SRAS_1$ to $SRAS_2$ in Figure 12–5.

The effects on the economy of shifts in short-run aggregate supply are similar to what would be predicted by the market demand and supply model of Chapter 4. A decrease in the $SRAS$ curve causes an increase in the price level and a decrease in the level of output in the economy. Conversely, an increase, or shift to the right of the curve, causes the equilibrium level of prices to decline and output to increase.

FIGURE 12–5   Shifts in Short-Run Aggregate Supply

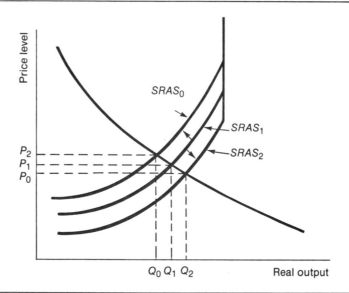

LONG-RUN AGGREGATE SUPPLY

Recall that the main assumption underlying the short-run aggregate supply curve is the presence of money illusion. As prices and wages increase, people at first believe they are better off because they see their wages increasing but do not take into account that the prices of the goods and services they purchase also increase. The long-run aggregate supply is defined as the relationship between the price level and real output when there is no money illusion. The length of time it takes to go from a short-run to a long-run aggregate supply, or even if there is such a thing as a money illusion, is not universally agreed upon. Some economists think people are not well-informed about the relationship between resource and product prices. If so, the length of time it takes to go from the short-run to the long-run aggregate supply is relatively long, say several years. The opposite is true if people are well-informed about the relationship between resource and product prices. In this case, the long run can occur a short time after a shift in aggregate demand. Other economists argue that the long run can occur almost simultaneously with the shift in aggregate demand.

The shape of the long-run aggregate supply curve can best be determined by drawing it on a diagram, as in Figure 12–6. Suppose we begin at the short-run equilibrium denoted by point a as determined by AD_0 and $SRAS_2$. Also suppose that the corresponding level of real output, Q_0, is less than the level that would generate full employment. In an attempt to stimulate the economy, the govern-

---

FIGURE 12–6 Derivation of Long-Run Aggregate Supply (*LRAS*)

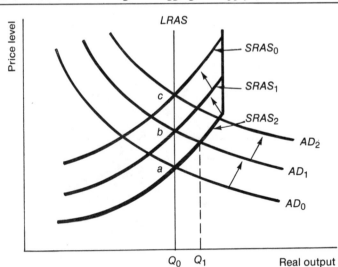

ment shifts aggregate demand to the right by a spending increase or a tax cut. In the short run, when people are reacting to a money illusion, they increase real output to Q_1. But now in the long run, when the money illusion no longer exists, they will not produce any more under a higher price level than under a lower one. This means the increase in the price level causes short-run aggregate supply to shift to the left enough to intersect AD_1 at the same level as the original output, Q_0. This is denoted by point *b* in Figure 12–6. The same process could be repeated where aggregate demand is shifted to the right again, say to AD_2. The higher level of prices coupled with an absence of a money illusion causes the short-run aggregate supply to shift to $SRAS_0$, and a new equilibrium point is reached at *c*. If we connect points *a, b,* and *c*, we obtain a vertical line that is the long-run aggregate supply curve. Thus, the long-run aggregate supply curve, which is the supply curve without the assumption of a money illusion, is a vertical line.

Notice that a vertical long-run aggregate supply implies that a shift in aggregate demand will not affect the real output of the country. This has rather important implications for the ability of the government to influence real output and employment in the economy through fiscal and monetary policies, as will be discussed in later chapters.

SHIFTS IN LONG–RUN AGGREGATE SUPPLY

As its name implies, the long-run aggregate supply is a long-run concept. There-fore, as the productive capacity of the economy increases due to population growth and the increase in capital resources, the long-run aggregate supply curve

FIGURE 12–7   Shifts in Long-Run Aggregate Supply

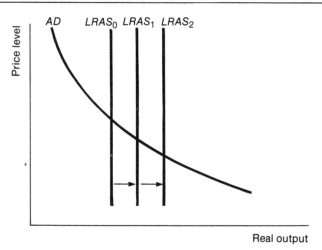

will gradually shift to the right, as shown in Figure 12–7. This does not mean that the price level will steadily decline. As the population and per capita income increase, aggregate demand also will increase or shift to the right. (To focus on aggregate supply, shifts in aggregate demand are not shown in Figure 12–7.)

One should not conclude from the preceding discussion that shifts in long-run aggregate supply occur naturally and are out of society's control. Government policies such as those that stimulate investment or new technology cause long-run aggregate supply to shift to the right more rapidly than policies that do not. It is important that the long-run aggregate supply shift to the right at least as rapidly as population grows. Otherwise the economy will be sluggish and suffer from unemployment and rising prices.

UNEMPLOYMENT AND INFLATION

The main reason for developing the aggregate demand–aggregate supply model is to show the conditions that can cause unemployment or inflation, and what can be done to alleviate these problems. Suppose full employment without inflation can be attained at a level of real output corresponding to Q_1 in Figure 12–8. If the economy is at an equilibrium real output that is less than Q_1, say Q_0, unemployment will be a problem. This could occur if aggregate demand is AD_0 and short-run aggregate supply, SRAS. In the short run, full employment can be obtained by shifting aggregate demand to AD_1. (We consider only short-run changes here and therefore omit consideration of long-run aggregate supply.)

If equilibrium output exceeds the level that corresponds to full employment, such as would occur at the intersection of AD_2 and *SRAS*, inflation will be a

FIGURE 12–8   Illustrating the Problems of Unemployment and Inflation with the
Aggregate Demand–Aggregate Supply Model

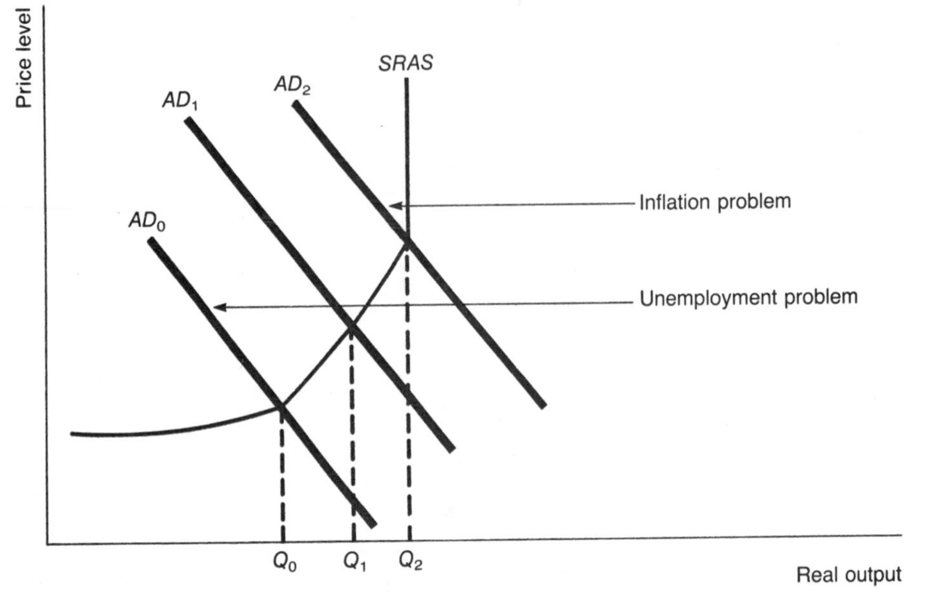

problem. The inflationary pressure can be relieved if aggregate demand can be
decreased from AD_2 to AD_1. Much of the discussion in the policy chapters centers
on attempts to maintain full employment without inflation.

RELATIONSHIP TO THE KEYNESIAN MODEL

It will be helpful at this point to summarize the similarities and differences
between the Keynesian model discussed in Chapters 10 and 11 and this model.
The same factors that shift the aggregate expenditure function in the Keynesian
model shift the aggregate demand curve in this model, and in the same direction.
In fact, before the aggregate demand–aggregate supply model was conceived, the
aggregate expenditure function in the Keynesian model was called *aggregate
demand.* Now to avoid confusion, it is called the *aggregate expenditure function.*
   If the short-run aggregate supply curve were a horizontal line, a given increase
in government spending would increase real output by the same amount in both
models. The same is true for the other factors that can shift the Keynesian
aggregate expenditure function, such as a change in interest rates or a change in
spending by investors and consumers.
   The fact that this model contains an aggregate supply line and that it is not
horizontal makes the two models different. If the short-run aggregate supply curve

is upward sloping, an increase (shift to the right) in aggregate demand results in an increase in both real output and the price level. In other words, part of the effect of an increase in aggregate demand shows up as an increase in real output and part as an increase in prices. In this case, a given increase in government spending does not increase real output as much as predicted by the Keynesian model. In the case of the vertical long-run aggregate supply, an increase in aggregate demand causes only a price increase and no increase in real output. Here the model departs even more from the Keynesian theory.

The ability of this model to show the effects of supply-side changes also adds to its flexibility over the Keynesian model. In fact, one of the main reasons for developing this model was to show why the supply-side shock brought on by the cutting-off of oil supplies from the Middle East during the mid-1970s caused higher prices and a decrease in real output. The Keynesian model could not show this. During the inflationary times of the 1970s, it became clear that a more complete model was needed; one that could show price-level changes as well as changes in real output. Recall that in the Keynesian model, the price level is not explicitly shown.

SUMMARY

Aggregate demand is defined as a negative relationship between the price level and real output. It is hypothesized that people will buy less when the price level is high than when it is low because high prices result in higher interest rates, and/or because high prices depreciate the value of money, making people feel poorer— the Pigou Effect. The upward-sloping aggregate supply curve requires the assumption of a money illusion whereby resource owners notice the increase in their nominal incomes because of higher prices but do not notice the increase in their cost of living. The long-run aggregate supply drops the assumption of a money illusion and is a vertical line, meaning the level of real output of the country does not depend on the price level. Shifts in aggregate demand stem from the same factors that shift the aggregate expenditure function of the simple Keynesian model. Shifts in aggregate supply originate from changes in the stock of resources available to society.

YOU SHOULD KNOW

1. What is aggregate demand.

2. The two arguments as to why aggregate demand slopes down.

3. What short-run aggregate supply is.

4. The assumption required to obtain an upward-sloping, short-run aggregate supply curve.

5. The meaning of short-run equilibrium income.

6. The factors that cause shifts in aggregate demand.

7. The factors that cause shifts in short-run aggregate supply.

8. What long-run aggregate supply is, and how it is derived.

9. The shape of long-run aggregate supply.
10. The factors that shift long-run aggregate supply.
11. How the aggregate demand–short-run aggregate supply model can be used to represent an unemployment or an inflation problem.
12. The similarities and differences between the simple Keynesian model and the aggregate demand–aggregate supply model.

QUESTIONS

1. *a.* What is aggregate demand?
   b. Why is it thought to slope down and to the right?
2. *a.* What is short-run aggregate supply?
   b. What assumption is necessary to obtain an upward-sloping, short-run aggregate supply curve? Explain.
3. Using the aggregate demand and short-run aggregate supply model, show the effect of an oil embargo on the price level and the quantity of real output. What would such a phenomenon be called?
4. *a.* Derive long-run aggregate supply.
   b. What assumption is required for short-run aggregate supply that is not required for long-run supply?
5. In the short run, what effect does an increase in aggregate demand have on the economy? In the long run?
6. Illustrate how unemployment and inflation could occur using the aggregate demand–aggregate supply model.
7. What are the similarities and differences between the simple Keynesian model and the aggregate demand–aggregate supply model?

SELF-TEST

1. Aggregate demand is defined as a _____ relationship between the price level and _____ .
   a. positive; spending
   b. positive; real output
   c. negative; spending
   d. negative; real output
2. Aggregate demand differs from market demand of Chapter 4 in that:
   a. the price level is held constant.
   b. all prices change.
   c. only one price is assumed to change.
   d. spending rather than quantity is shown on the horizontal axis.
3. According to the downward-sloping aggregate demand curve, a greater amount of goods and services is demanded when:
   a. inflation is present.
   b. inflation is absent.
   c. the price level is high than when it is low.
   d. the price level is low than when it is high.
4. According to the interest rate argument, an increase in the price level decreases the purchasing power of money. As more nominal dollars are demanded, interest rates _____ and the quantity of goods and services demanded _____ .
   a. increase; increases
   b. increase; decreases
   c. decrease; increases
   d. decrease; decreases
5. According to the real balance, or Pigou

Effect, an increase in the price level causes the purchasing power of money to _____ . This makes people feel _____ so they buy _____ .

a. decrease; poorer; less
b. increase; richer; more
c. decrease; richer; more
d. increase; poorer; less

6. Short-run aggregate supply is a _____ relationship between _____ and _____ .

a. negative; the price level; real output
b. positive; the rate of inflation; spending
c. negative; the rate of inflation; spending
d. positive; the price level; real output

7. Short-run aggregate supply implies that producers will place a larger quantity of goods and services on the market when:

a. inflation is present.
b. inflation is absent.
c. the price level is high than when it is low.
d. the price level is low than when it is high.

8. The upward-sloping characteristic of short-run aggregate supply suggests that producers place a _____ amount of goods on the market when the price level is high than when it is low. Such behavior implies a _____ .

a. larger; money illusion
b. larger; Pigou Effect
c. smaller; money illusion
d. smaller; Pigou Effect

9. If people have a money illusion, they _____ an increase in their incomes _____ the increase in their cost of living.

a. do not notice; and do not notice
b. notice; but do not notice
c. do not notice; but do notice
d. notice; and notice

10. The SRAS curve becomes steeper as the economy moves toward:

a. a recession.
b. a depression.
c. inflation.
d. absolute full employment.

11. In the aggregate demand (AD)–short-run aggregate supply (SRAS) model, the equilibrium price level and real output:

a. are at a maximum.
b. are at a minimum.
c. correspond to the intersection of SRAS and the vertical axis.
d. correspond to the intersection of SRAS and AD.

12. The AD-SRAS model tells us _____ , which the simple Keynesian model does not.

a. the level of equilibrium output
b. the price level
c. how unemployment can occur
d. how inflation can occur

13. If consumers and/or investors become more optimistic about the future, aggregate demand _____ causing the equilibrium price level to _____ and real output to _____ .

a. increases; increase; decrease
b. increases; increase; increase
c. decreases; decrease; decrease
d. decreases; decrease; increase

14. The Arab oil embargo of the 1970s has come to be known as a _____ , causing the nation's price level to _____ and real output to _____ .

a. supply-side shock; decrease; increase
b. supply-side shock; increase; decrease
c. demand-side shock; decrease; increase
d. demand-side shock; increase; decrease

15. *Long-run aggregate supply* is defined as the relationship between the price level and real output when there:

a. is no money illusion.
b. is a money illusion.
c. is no Pigou Effect.
d. is a Pigou Effect.

16. The time it takes to go from short-run aggregate supply to long-run aggregate supply is:
    a. one month.
    b. one year.
    c. 10 years.
    d. not universally agreed upon.

17. When there is an increase in aggregate demand, real output _____ when there is a money illusion. When the money illusion disappears, real output:
    a. increases; increases even more.
    b. increases; returns to its original level.
    c. decreases; decreases even more.
    d. decreases; returns to its original level.

18. The absence of a money illusion implies that _____ is a _____ line.
    a. SRAS; vertical
    b. LRAS; vertical
    c. SRAS; horizontal
    d. LRAS; horizontal

19. According to the aggregate demand–aggregate supply model, unemployment will be a problem if equilibrium real output is _____ than the output that corresponds to full employment output. Conversely, inflation will be a problem if equilibrium real output is _____ than the full employment level.
    a. less; greater
    b. greater; less
    c. less; less
    d. greater; greater

20. The aggregate demand–aggregate supply model shows _____ , which the Keynesian model does not.
    a. the price level
    b. the effect of aggregate supply on the size of the government spending multiplier
    c. the effect of shifts in aggregate supply
    d. all of the above

Chapter 13

Rational Expectations

OVERVIEW

During the mid- to late 1970s, a new problem appeared on the macroeconomic scene—the simultaneous existence of unemployment and inflation. Economists labeled this problem *stagflation*. Efforts to understand this problem led to a school of thought called the *rational expectations hypothesis*.

INTRODUCTION

The core of the rational expectations idea is that people try to maximize their utility, that is, act rationally, given the information at their disposal. The rational expectations hypothesis does not say that the information available to people at any given time is perfect in terms of being accurate or complete. No human being has perfect foresight. But the theory does argue that people learn from their mistakes and, when new information becomes available, they modify their behavior in order to better their lot in life. In and of itself, the idea of rational behavior is not a new or startling concept in economics. A large part of the body of economic theory is built on this foundation. The theory of rational expectations extends the basis for rational behavior to include expectations of future conditions as well as knowledge of current conditions.

The idea of rational expectations was first put forth by economist John Muth in 1961.[1] Muth's early work dealt mainly with the effect of expectations on the behavior of consumers and producers in markets—market demand and supply. Muth's idea of rational expectations lay dormant for nearly 10 years. While the

---

[1] John F. Muth, "Rational Expectations and the Theory of Price Movements," *Econometrica* 29 (July 1961), pp. 315–35.

idea is conceptually appealing, mathematically and statistically it is a rather complex theory. It was not until the idea was applied to the problem of macroeconomic policy that it finally took root in the economics profession.[2]

FORMATION OF EXPECTATIONS

According to established economic theory, in making economic decisions people utilize information on current economic conditions and on expected future conditions. This idea was first encountered in Chapter 4. Recall that one of the five demand shifters indicated that the current demand for a good or service will depend in part on the expectations of consumers regarding future prices and incomes. For example, if consumers expect the future price of a good to be higher than the current price, many will likely increase their current demand in order to take advantage of the better buy at the present. To believe that people would not do so would be irrational, because one would thus assume that people do not desire to obtain the most for their money.

Probing a bit deeper into the process, one might ask, How do consumers form their expectations? In part, expectations of future conditions may be formed from trends in the recent past. If the price of an item has been increasing for several months and there is no reason to expect a reversal of the trend, consumers may expect the trend to continue, at least for a short period. Of course, the same expectation can be formed from just the opposite trend. If the price of an item has been declining for several months and consumers observe that it is much lower than normal, they may expect the trend to reverse and the price to rise in the near future. Thus, it is not always correct to assume that past trends will continue. Indeed, if consumers observe that the price of an item has been stable for an extended period, they may use this information to form an expectation of a rising price in the future. This situation might occur if other prices have been rising while the price of the item in question has remained constant.

In addition to past trends, expectations of future prices will be formed on the basis of information that becomes available to people at the present. To continue the demand example, people are likely to expect higher future prices of a good if its supply is interrupted. For example, a war in the Middle East that disrupts petroleum shipments will almost certainly lead to higher expected prices of petroleum products, and the expectation will in all probability turn out to be correct. Other information, such as government or industry reports, also will

---

[2] A collection of papers on rational expectations appears in Robert E. Lucas, Jr., and Thomas J. Sargent, eds., *Rational Expectations and Economic Practice,* vols. 1 and 2 (Minneapolis: University of Minnesota Press, 1981). The reader is warned that an understanding of these papers requires a high level of understanding of economics, mathematics, and statistics. For a less technical paper on rational expectations, see Mark H. Wiles, "The Future of Monetary Policy: The Rational Expectations Perspective," *Quarterly Review,* Federal Reserve Bank of Minneapolis 4, no. 2 (Spring 1980), pp. 1–7.

influence expectations. The U.S. Department of Agriculture, for example, periodically issues crop and livestock reports that provide information on production and stocks of agricultural commodities. A report that shows an abnormally small crop or poor yield is likely to cause an increase in expected future prices of the item.

People also learn from past mistakes. For example, suppose the teacher of one of your classes habitually shows up 10 minutes late. The first week or two you may arrive on time thinking the class will start on time. But as you learn that the class actually begins 10 minutes after the scheduled time, you also start to arrive a little late so as to avoid wasting this 10 minutes waiting for the teacher. In other words, at the beginning of the term you made the mistake of arriving for class on time. Then you learned from your mistake to arrive closer to the actual starting time.

THE PHILLIPS CURVE

In order to see more clearly how rational expectations applies to macro-economic policy, it is necessary to introduce at this point the relationship between unemployment and inflation that has come to be known as the Phillips curve. A. W. Phillips, an English economist, observed in the 1950s that in the United Kingdom during the 1864–1957 period, the annual rate of change of money wage rates was inversely correlated with the level of unemployment.[3] In other words, during the years when money wages were rising relatively fast, the level of unemployment was comparatively low, and vice versa. Professor Phillips hypothesized that when the demand for labor is high and relatively few people are unemployed, employers will bid wage rates up in their attempt to hire more workers. On the other hand, he argued, when business is slow and the demand for labor is declining, money wage rates will rise little if at all. Phillips also argued that workers and unions will be reluctant to take wage cuts during times of depressed business activity. Consequently, employers have little choice but to lay off workers during these periods, resulting in relatively high rates of unemployment. Because of the alleged stickiness of wages when the demand for labor is declining, Phillips postulated that the relationship between rates of change of money wages and unemployment would be curvilinear when shown on a diagram. In other words, when the labor market is depressed, a small reduction in the rate of change of money wages would be associated with a relatively large increase in unemployment. The kind of relationship Phillips had in mind is depicted by Figure 13–1.

In the years following the publication of Phillips's article, economists modified the Phillips curve slightly by substituting the rate of change of prices, that is, the

---

[3] A. W. Phillips, "The Relation between Unemployment and the Rate of Change of Money Wage Rates," *Economica* 25 (November 1958), pp. 283–300.

inflation rate, for the rate of change of money wage rates. Because the two variables are highly correlated, the basic shape of the curve remains about the same as that shown by Figure 13–1. Now when economists speak of the Phillips curve, they invariably refer to the inflation-unemployment relationship.[4]

During the late 1960s and 1970s, the Phillips curve was used a great deal by economists to show the trade-off between inflation and unemployment. According to the Phillips curve, if a nation was willing to accept some inflation, it could keep its unemployment rate low. On the other hand, if stable prices are of a high priority, a country must be willing to live with higher unemployment.

The simultaneous growth of both unemployment and inflation during the 1970s in the United States as well as in many other countries began to cast doubt on the validity of the Phillips curve. The relationship between the rates of inflation and unemployment for the United States over the 1947–89 period is shown in Figure 13–2. Notice that it is possible to trace a line resembling a Phillips curve from the observations of the 1950s and 1960s. No doubt these observations gave economists confidence in the stability of the Phillips curve. But as the nation moved into the 1970s, the relationship began to break down. If one takes a little artistic license, it is possible to represent the observations from the 1970s and 1980s as being along a number of higher Phillips curves. During the 1970s, there were many attempts to rationalize the apparent upward shift of the Phillips curve. Reasons such as the Arab oil embargo and poor crop years in the United States and Soviet Union were given for the unusual location of the Phillips curve during the early to mid-1970s. But as these conditions disappeared in the late 1970s and the Phillips curve did not shift down to its original location, more and more economists came

FIGURE 13–1 The Original Phillips Curve

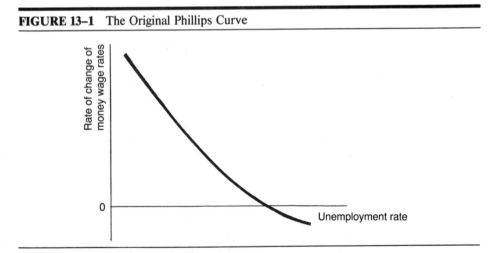

[4] Actually this relationship was first observed in 1926 by Irving Fisher. See Irving Fisher, "A Statistical Relation between Unemployment and Price Changes," *International Labor Review* (June 1926), reprinted in *Journal of Political Economy* 81, no. 2 (March–April 1973), pp. 496–502.

FIGURE 13–2   Relationship between Annual Percentage Change in the Consumer
Price Index and the Rate of Unemployment, United States, 1947–1989

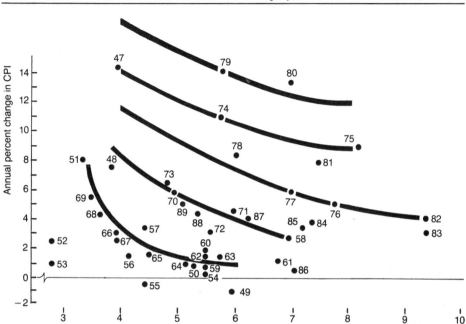

to believe that the Phillips curve is not a stable relationship between inflation and
unemployment, as originally believed. Some economists never believed the
Phillips curve represented a stable relationship, at least in the long run. This takes
us to the "natural rate hypothesis."

THE NATURAL RATE HYPOTHESIS

Professor Milton Friedman in his presidential address to the American Economic
Association in December 1967 predicted that expansionary monetary policy could
have only a temporary effect on unemployment, not a permanent effect.[5] Friedman argued that there is a "natural rate of unemployment" to which the economy
will always move in the absence of government policies that either stimulate or
dampen economic activity. This argument has come to be known as the *natural
rate hypothesis*. Friedman pointed out that the natural rate is not a fixed number
for all times or all countries. High levels of legislated minimum wages, unem-

---

[5] Milton Friedman, "The Role of Monetary Policy," *American Economic Review* 58 (March 1968),
pp. 1–17.

ployment compensation and welfare programs, and strong unions, for example, will give rise to a higher natural rate of unemployment than in their absence.

Friedman's argument for the temporary effect of monetary policy on unemployment was based on expectations. To begin, suppose the government attempts to stimulate the economy by increasing the rate of growth of the money supply. The initial effect will be to increase money incomes and spending, with most of the initial effect on real output rather than prices. Then, as the unexpected increase in demand is felt in the market, the prices of goods and services begin to rise. To employers this means that real wages paid to employees begin to fall because, as Friedman argued, the prices of goods sold increase initially more than wages do. This improves the net earnings of business firms and provides an incentive for them to hire more workers, thereby reducing unemployment. However, it will not take long before employees catch on that the prices of things they buy have gone up more than their wages. Consequently, employees and their union representatives will press employers for real wage increases in order to regain at least what they have lost. However, when real wages increase, most likely after increased strike activity, and business earnings are reduced, unemployment increases back to where it was before the stimulus was put into effect.

The opposite process takes place if the government attempts to reduce inflation by decreasing the rate of growth of the money supply. Now there is a decrease in the growth of demand for goods and services, resulting in a reduction in the prices of many items. Since money wages are not likely to decline immediately, real wages paid to employees rise, causing reduced profits to business and a reduction in employment, that is, increased unemployment. The fact that businesses are likely to experience increased inventories of unsold goods at this time also will result in increased layoffs and more unemployment. As unemployment continues and wage demands soften, real wages decline back to their original levels, thereby helping to restore profits and stimulating employment.

One of the main points of Friedman's argument is that the government cannot permanently affect the level of unemployment. If it wants to reduce unemployment, for example, over a long period of time, the government will have to stimulate the economy more and more in order to prevent it from slipping back to its natural rate of unemployment. In order to maintain a low level of unemployment, the government will have to accelerate the rate of inflation to higher and higher levels. At some point, of course, inflation becomes intolerable, and the expansionary policy is abandoned.

THE LONG-RUN PHILLIPS CURVE

Friedman's argument about the eventual return of the economy to its so-called natural rate of unemployment led to the construction of the long-run Phillips curve. The long-run Phillips curve is a vertical line extending up from a point on the horizontal axis that corresponds to the natural rate of unemployment. In deriving this curve, it will help to refer to Figure 13–3. In the long-run Phillips

FIGURE 13–3   Derivation of the Long-Run Phillips Curve

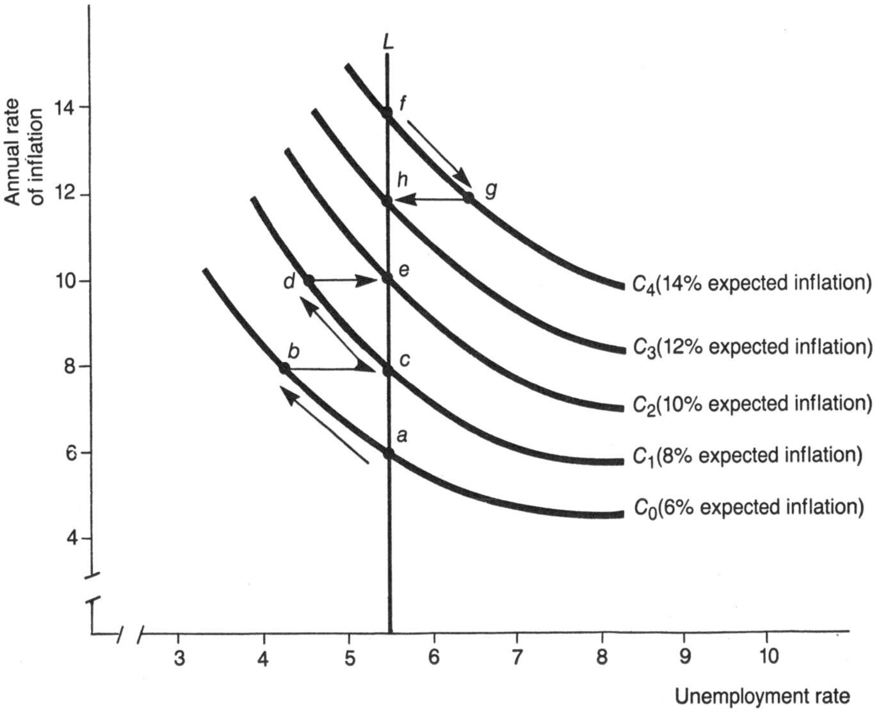

curve diagram, there can be a large number of individual short-run curves, each corresponding to a certain expected rate of inflation. To keep the example manageable, only five inflation rates are considered—6, 8, 10, 12, and 14 percent. The natural rate of unemployment in this example is taken to be 5.5 percent.

To begin the derivation of the long-run Phillips curve (L), let us assume that the current level of unemployment is 5.5 percent and that the government wishes to reduce it to a lower figure. Also assume that the current rate of inflation is 6 percent, which places the country at point *a* on Figure 13–3. The government now, in an attempt to stimulate the economy, increases the rate of growth of the money supply. This causes an unexpected increase in prices for goods and services, lower real wages, and reduced unemployment. Thus, the economy moves up along curve C_0 from point *a* toward point *b*. Now let us suppose that the government, seeing the reduction in unemployment, stabilizes the growth of the money supply, causing the rate of inflation to stabilize at 8 percent per year. The economy then comes to rest at point *b*.

Wage earners and unions now observe that prices of goods and services have increased faster than their wages. Consequently they press employers, under threat of strike, to increase wages faster than the inflation rate in order to catch up. As real wages increase, unemployment increases, and the economy moves from point *b* toward point *c*. As people come to expect the 8 percent rate of inflation, the short-run Phillips curve shifts from C_0 to C_1. The government can achieve another temporary reduction in unemployment if it causes another unexpected spurt in the rate of inflation, say to 10 percent per year. Now the economy moves from point *c* to point *d* and then back to *e* as real wages catch up and people come to expect the new higher rate of inflation (10 percent). The short-run Phillips curve will now be at C_2. Similar expansionist policies would move the economy up to C_3 and C_4 (12 and 14 percent expected inflation rates).

At some point, it is likely that society will begin to view inflation as the overriding problem and call on the government to take steps to reduce it. As explained earlier, a reduction in the rate of growth of the money supply causes a reduction in the growth of the demand for goods and services, relative price reductions, increased inventories, higher real wages, and higher unemployment. In terms of Figure 13–3, this corresponds to a movement from point *f* to point *g* if the inflation rate is 14 percent. If the government, seeing the increased level of unemployment, backs off on its restrictive monetary policy so that the rate of inflation stabilizes at 12 percent, unions and employees will soften their wage demands, real wages will decrease to their former level, and unemployment will ease back down toward its natural rate. As people come to expect a 12 percent inflation rate, the short-run Phillips curve shifts down to C_4 and C_3, and the economy comes to rest at point *h*. Further contractions will shift the economy down to still lower short-run curves.

If one were to repeat the expansion and contraction process over and over, and the number of resting points, such as *a, c, e, f,* and *h* increased, it would become evident that they traced out a vertical line extending upward from the natural rate of unemployment on the horizontal axis. This line is called the long-run Phillips curve because it represents points where the economy comes to rest after its long-run adjustment.

Notice that, according to the natural rate hypothesis, the level of unemployment in the economy depends not on the rate of inflation, but rather on *changes* in the rate of inflation. Thus, it is possible for an economy to experience high rates of unemployment even though it has a high rate of inflation, if the government has recently taken steps to reduce the inflation rate. This situation depicts the U.S. economy in the early 1980s and also characterizes many of the less developed countries. By the same token, an economy can enjoy low rates of inflation and low unemployment at the same time once it has stabilized the price level, as existed in the late 1980s.

Although the natural rate hypothesis admits to a trade-off between unemployment and inflation in the short run, in the long run there is no trade-off. In a sense, this is a more optimistic view of the economy than was implied by the original Phillips curve, which led economists to believe that only one of the twin goals of full employment and stable prices was possible at a time. In another sense, it is more pessimistic because it implies government policy cannot have a lasting effect on employment.

THE RATIONAL EXPECTATIONS ARGUMENT

By and large the rational expectations hypothesis as it applies to macroeconomic policy has grown out of the two articles mentioned earlier, by John Muth and Milton Friedman. Muth's rational expectations idea has been brought to bear on Friedman's natural rate hypothesis. Much of the work on rational expectations has been to integrate the two ideas, give them a rigorous analytical framework, and push them to their logical conclusions. If one were to represent the rational expectations idea on a diagram, the long-run Phillips curve derivation presented in Figure 13–3, in reference to the natural rate hypothesis, probably is the easiest to work with. While there is a subtle difference between the natural rate and the rational expectations explanations of how business and labor react to changes in government policy, the general outcome is the same for both.

In the rational expectations framework, the availability of information and the ability of decision makers to acquire new information play central roles. Let us begin once again at point a in Figure 13–3. In an attempt to reduce unemployment, the government stimulates the economy, say by increasing the rate of growth of the money supply. Prices start to rise. According to the rational expectations hypothesis, business firms have better information on prices in their own industry than on the general level of prices. They mistakenly interpret the increase in prices they observe as coming from an increase in demand for their specific products. Consequently, firms hire more employees in an effort to increase output, and in the process they reduce unemployment. At first, employees also mistake the price increases as being specific to their own industries and willingly take job offers thinking that the increase in money wages is an increase in real wages. Thus, the economy moves upward on the short-run Phillips curve C_0 from point a to point b. But soon business and labor discover that the increase in prices and wages is general to most industries. Business firms find they are no better off than before, because their costs have risen. Labor discovers the purchasing power of wages declining and presses for wage increases sufficient to at least offset the increase in the general level of prices. When the dust settles, both business and labor find that they are no better off than they were originally at point a. Thus, the economy moves from point b to point c. The only thing that has changed is the inflation rate, which is now higher because of the government attempt to stimulate the economy.

According to the rational expectations argument, the next time the government attempts to reduce unemployment, there is less chance to fool employers and employees into thinking the price increases are specific to their industry. Now people will keep an eye on prices and costs in the general economy. If business firms come to expect higher costs along with higher prices of their products, they are not so likely to increase production, as occurred along the short-run curve C_0. Similarly, employees are not likely to be so willing to increase work if they expect their real wages to decrease rather than increase. And labor unions are likely to become more militant in their wage demands in order to keep their members from falling behind, as occurred in the initial attempt to stimulate the economy.

Advocates of the rational expectations framework argue that after repeated attempts to stimulate the economy, people catch on to the policy and come to expect inflationary pressure. This in turn causes the short-run Phillips curve to shift upward more and more quickly so that, after a time, most of the impact is on prices rather than real output.

After repeated attempts to stimulate the economy, the government at some point is likely to change its priority to fighting inflation rather than unemployment. However, if business and labor come to expect inflation, they will build this expectation into their pricing policies and contractual arrangements. Business firms will continue to increase the list prices of their products to keep pace with expected inflation. But if the rate of growth of the money supply is reduced, the growth of demand for goods and services also will be reduced. As a result, there will be increased inventories of unsold goods, and some goods will have to be sold at prices lower than expected. In turn, profits will decline, output will fall, and layoffs will occur. This undesirable outcome is magnified in the labor market. Unions, becoming accustomed to higher and higher rates of inflation, press for continued wage increases to keep pace with inflation. Because of the unexpected decline in the growth of the money supply, growth in demand for goods and services will slow, as will the rate of increase of the price level. Consequently, real wages will increase, business will suffer reduced profits (or larger losses), and unemployment will grow. It may take many months for expectations to be revised to take account of the new anti-inflationary policy of the government.

Once an inflationary psychology has built up, it becomes very difficult to bring inflation under control without causing unemployment. Advocates of the rational expectations hypothesis argue, however, that inflation can be brought under control without causing high unemployment if the government announces in advance its policy of reducing the growth of the money supply so that people will not be taken by surprise. They point to the success of Germany in the 1920s in bringing its hyperinflation under control without causing widespread unemployment. The German government simply announced what it was going to do and did it—that is, it scrapped the old money and started over with a new monetary standard. In the German case, the people appeared to change their inflationary expectations quickly because something had to be done and they had no reason to believe the government would not do what it said. In the United States, however, during the late 1960s and 1970s, the government probably made hundreds of announcements that inflation would be brought under control but did not follow through on any of them. Consequently, people became skeptical that the government would in fact do what it said. When inflation finally was brought under control in the early 1980s, it came as a surprise to most people.

It is interesting to note that, according to the rational expectations hypothesis, the government must fool the people about its policy intentions in order to reduce unemployment even temporarily. But in order to stop inflation without causing widespread unemployment, the government must announce its intentions in advance and convince people that it will do what it says.

POLICY IMPLICATIONS

The policy implications of rational expectations represent a radical departure from those implied by the Keynesian and aggregate demand–aggregate supply models. According to these models, the government can have a more prolonged impact on unemployment by shifting aggregate expenditure or aggregate demand, particularly if the vertical long-run supply takes a relatively long time to occur. In contrast, the rational expectations argument implies that the government cannot have a lasting impact on the level of unemployment.

Understandably, the appearance of rational expectations has evoked considerable controversy among economists. Those who believe the Keynesian and aggregate demand–short run aggregate supply models are accurate representations of the economy tend to think that government can have a significant and lasting impact on reducing unemployment. On the other hand, the rational expectations advocates are less convinced that activist government policy is in the best interest of the economy, fearing that such policy can cause inflation. The rational expectations school of thought has been called the *new classical economics*. Recall that the classical economists also advocated a minimum of government intervention.

SUMMARY

The basic premise of the rational expectations hypothesis is that people try to maximize their utility or welfare given the information at their disposal. The original Phillips curve depicted the rate of change of wage rates and the unemployment rate. The more recent formulation shows the negative relationship between inflation and unemployment. At first, economists thought there was a single Phillips curve for a country. Now there appears to be some agreement that there are many short-run Phillips curves, each corresponding to an expected rate of inflation. According to the natural rate hypothesis, an attempt by government to reduce unemployment by stimulating the economy can at best have a temporary effect if prices of goods and services increase before wages. But in the long run, the economy will eventually come to rest on a vertical long-run Phillips curve extending up from the natural rate of unemployment. According to the rational expectations argument, the government may achieve a temporary decrease in unemployment by stimulating the economy if people believe the price increase is specific to their own industry. But in the long run, the economy will come back to its natural rate of unemployment. The implication of the natural rate and rational expectations hypotheses is that the government cannot permanently reduce unemployment below its natural rate.

YOU SHOULD KNOW

1. The basic assumption underlying the rational expectations hypothesis.
2. How people form expectations.
3. The original Phillips curve and the more recent formulation.
4. What is the natural rate hypothesis.
5. How to derive the long-run Phillips curve.
6. The subtle difference between the rational expectations and the natural rate hypothesis.
7. The policy implications of the natural rate and rational expectations hypotheses.

QUESTIONS

1. How do people form expectations of future events?
2. What is shown by the original Phillips curve? How does it differ from the more recent formulation?
3. *a.* What is the natural rate hypothesis? What is its underlying rationale?
   b. Using the natural rate hypothesis, derive the long-run Phillips curve from several short-run Phillips curves.
4. According to the natural rate hypothesis, is it possible for a country to experience a high rate of inflation and high unemployment at the same time? Explain. How about low inflation and low unemployment?
5. How does the rational expectations differ from the natural rate hypothesis in regard to its underlying rationale?
6. *a.* According to the rational expectations hypothesis, when does the government have to fool the people in order to carry out its policy objectives? Explain.
   b. According to the rational expectations hypothesis, when does the government have to convince the people it will do what it says in order to carry out its policy objectives? Explain.
7. Why is the rational expectations hypothesis sometimes called the *new classical economics*?

SELF-TEST

1. The problem that appeared during the 1970s that led economists in search of a new theory of the macroeconomy was:
   a. inflation.   *c.* unemployment.
   b. the Vietnam War.   *d.* stagflation.
2. Expectations are formed by:
   a. recent trends.   *c.* past mistakes
   b. new information.   *d.* all of the above.
3. The rational expectations hypothesis assumes that people:
   a. have a money illusion.
   b. have perfect information.
   c. have perfect foresight about the future.
   d. act rationally, that is, attempt to maximize their well-being given the information and resources at their disposal.

4. The original Phillips curve depicted the relationship between _____ and _____ .
   a. wage rates; unemployment
   b. wage rates; inflation
   c. rate of change of wage rates; unemployment
   d. rate of change of wage rates; inflation

5. The more recent formulation of the Phillips curve refers to the relationship between _____ and _____ .
   a. inflation; unemployment
   b. the price level; unemployment
   c. inflation; rate of change of wage rates
   d. the price level; wage rates

6. If there is one Phillips curve for an economy, the implication is that if low unemployment is desired, there must be a _____ rate of inflation or if stable prices are desired, there must be a _____ rate of unemployment.
   a. low; low   c. low; high
   b. high; high   d. high; low

7. Originally, most economists thought there _____ Phillips curve(s). The experience gained during the 1970s convinced most economists that there _____ short-run Phillips curve(s).
   a. were many; is one
   b. was one; are many
   c. were many; are many
   d. was one; is one

8. Friedman argued that there is a _____ rate of _____ to which the economy will move in the absence of government policies that neither dampen nor stimulate economic activity.
   a. zero; unemployment
   b. natural; unemployment
   c. zero; inflation
   d. natural; inflation

9. According to the natural rate hypothesis, an attempt by the government to reduce unemployment by stimulating the economy will lead to a _____ reduction in unemployment because _____ increase before _____ , leading to a(n) _____ in real wages.
   a. permanent; prices; wages; decrease
   b. temporary; prices; wages; decrease
   c. permanent; wages; prices; increase
   d. temporary; wages; prices; increase

10. According to the natural rate hypothesis, an attempt by government to reduce inflation by dampening economic activity causes real wages to _____ thereby _____ unemployment.
    a. increase; increasing
    b. decrease; increasing
    c. decrease; decreasing
    d. increase; decreasing

11. The implication of the natural rate hypothesis is that the government cannot _____ alter the rate of _____ in the economy.
    a. temporarily; unemployment
    b. temporarily; inflation
    c. permanently; unemployment
    d. permanently; inflation

12. In deriving the long-run Phillips curve, each short-run Phillips curve corresponds to an _____ rate of _____ .
    a. expected; unemployment
    b. actual; unemployment
    c. expected; inflation
    d. actual; inflation

13. The long-run Phillips curve is a _____ line extending up (out) from the natural rate of _____ .
    a. vertical; unemployment
    b. horizontal; unemployment
    c. vertical; inflation
    d. horizontal; inflation

14. According to the long-run Phillips curve diagram, if an economy is experiencing a high rate of inflation, a movement down along a relatively high short-run Phillips curve implies that the economy _____

experience high inflation along with high unemployment. In the long run as the expected rate of inflation declines, the unemployment rate _____ settle in at a low level.

a. can; can
c. can; cannot
b. cannot; can
d. cannot; cannot

15. According to the rational expectations argument, an attempt by the government to stimulate the economy can _____ reduce the level of unemployment because:

a. temporarily; prices increase before wages increase.
b. temporarily; people think at first the price increase is specific to their own industries.
c. permanently; prices increase before wages increase.
d. permanently; people think at first the price increase is specific to their own industries.

16. After repeated attempts to stimulate the economy, the rational expectations argument implies that the government can only:

a. cause unemployment.
b. cause inflation.
c. increase taxes.
d. increase its spending.

17. The rational expectations hypothesis implies that if the government wishes to reduce unemployment, it must:

a. not stimulate economic activity.
b. inform the people of its policy intentions.
c. surprise the people by its actions.
d. increase unemployment compensation.

18. The rational expectations hypothesis implies that if the government wishes to reduce inflation without causing higher unemployment, it must:

a. not dampen economic activity.
b. inform the people of its policy intentions.
c. surprise the people by its actions.
d. increase unemployment compensation.

19. In contrast to the simple Keynesian model, which provides the rationale for a(n) _____ role of government in the economy, the rational expectations hypothesis suggests that the government should intervene _____ .

a. passive; more
b. active; even more
c. passive; even less
d. active; less

Part VI

Fiscal Policy and Problems

Chapter 14

Fiscal Policy

OVERVIEW

The objective of this chapter is to show how government can alter the level of economic activity by its taxing and spending powers. The impact of spending and tax changes is discussed in the context of the Keynesian, aggregate demand–aggregate supply, and rational expectations models. Most of the discussion will center on the simple Keynesian model.

FISCAL POLICY DEFINED

Although *fiscal policy* has become something of a household phrase, it will be useful nevertheless to define its meaning in rather precise terms. We will define *fiscal policy* as the attempt by government to promote full employment without inflation through its spending and taxing powers. Throughout this chapter, then, we will be primarily interested in the effects of government spending and taxation on the level of output and employment in the economy.

EVOLUTION OF FISCAL POLICY IN THE UNITED STATES

The deliberate attempt by government to promote full employment by its spending and taxing powers began during the early years of the Franklin Delano Roosevelt administration, as evidenced by the creation of the public works programs instituted to create jobs and stimulate economic activity.

Yet a close reading of the record reveals that the idea still had a long way to go.[1] Although President Roosevelt endorsed the public works programs, he was not

---

[1] Herbert Stein, *The Fiscal Revolution in America* (Chicago: University of Chicago Press, 1969) gives a comprehensive review of the development of fiscal policy.

entirely convinced that a big public spending program was the answer to the country's unemployment problem. For example, on seeing a list of projects under a $5 billion spending program, President Roosevelt proceeded to rip the list to pieces in the presence of his cabinet, indicating that many of the projects were impractical or useless.[2] Roosevelt agreed in May 1933 to a $3.3 billion spending program as a compromise between the $5 billion proposal and the $1 to $1.5 billion suggested by him.

It is also interesting to note that President Roosevelt appeared quite concerned about balancing the budget at that time. To meet the growing federal deficit, Roosevelt asked for and received tax increases in 1935 and 1936. Granted, the 1935 tax increase was directed mainly at high-income persons and large corporations in an attempt to reduce the concentration of wealth; but the 1936 increase was more clearly sold on the basis of raising additional revenue.

It is not likely that we would see a tax increase today if the unemployment rate were 15 to 20 percent as it was in the mid-1930s. Of course, this is not to say that Roosevelt would have adhered to the same policy today had he been able to benefit from the 50 years of hindsight available to us. We have learned a great deal during the past half-century about how the economy operates, but, as will become evident, we still have a lot to learn.

The passage of the Employment Act of 1946 represents another significant milestone toward the establishment of a deliberate and conscious set of spending and taxing policies aimed at promoting full employment without inflation. In this act, Congress declared that it was the responsibility of the federal government to promote the maximum employment, production, and purchasing power of the economy. The act also established a Council of Economic Advisors to assist the president on economic policy and a joint Economic Committee of Congress to investigate economic problems of national interest.

BUILT–IN STABILIZERS

Before discussing the deliberate changes in taxes and spending that can be undertaken by the government to promote full employment without inflation, it is necessary to call attention to fiscal policy measures that have been built into our economic system. These policies specify that government spending or tax changes will take place automatically in response to upturns or downturns in economic activity.

Two important automatic spending measures are unemployment compensation and the various welfare programs. Although these programs probably were put into effect to redistribute income, they also reduce the severity of economic fluctuations in the economy. For example, as unemployment rises and family incomes fall, the influx of money through unemployment compensation prevents a

---

[2] Ibid., p. 53.

more drastic decline in economic activity. Then, as the economy recovers and people return to their jobs, a reduction in unemployment compensation helps to hold down inflationary pressure in the future period. Thus, unemployment compensation is in effect an automatic or built-in stabilizer for the economy. Welfare programs have a similar effect of injecting more money when more people are out of work and incomes are down.

The progressive income tax, which is another device for redistributing income, also has a stabilizing effect on the economy. A *progressive income tax* taxes high-income people at higher *rates* than low-income people. In times of inflation, for example, more people are pushed into higher tax brackets. Consequently, more money is pulled out of the economy than would occur with a proportional tax, and as a result there is less inflationary pressure than there would otherwise be. The opposite occurs during recessions, when people with reduced incomes are taxed at lower rates, thus leaving them more money to spend than if they were taxed at higher rates. We can say, therefore, that the progressive income tax is a built-in stabilizer because it pulls proportionately more purchasing power out of the economy during inflationary times and leaves proportionately more in during recessions. Granted, inflation and recessions still occur, but they should not be as severe as they would be without the built-in stabilizers.

Built-in, or automatic, stabilizers often are referred to as *nondiscretionary fiscal policy* because they operate without specific congressional edict. The built-in stabilizers were originally created by an act of Congress, but once they have been instituted, Congress does not have to pass further legislation in order for them to operate.

Most of our discussion in this chapter will dwell on so-called *discretionary fiscal policy*. Here we have in mind tax or spending policies designed to deal with specific problems during specific periods. The 1982 income tax cut is an example of such a policy. By cutting taxes, the government allowed the people to keep a little more money that they could spend in order to stimulate economic activity and reduce unemployment. Other examples of discretionary fiscal policies include the public works projects of the 1930s and the start of the superhighway construction program of the late 1950s. Both of these policies were aimed at stimulating business activity so as to reduce unemployment during these periods, although the highway program was sold in part by citing its military significance.

FISCAL POLICY IN THE CONTEXT OF THE SIMPLE KEYNESIAN MODEL

In discussing the simple Keynesian model in Chapter 11, it was noted that the equilibrium level of NNP may not coincide with full-employment NNP. If equilibrium occurs at a lower level of NNP than is necessary for full employment, unemployment will develop. Conversely, if equilibrium NNP is greater than the level that corresponds to full employment, inflation will appear.

Let us first consider the problem of unemployment as illustrated by Figure 14–1*A*. Suppose that equilibrium NNP is $5,000 billion, but in order for the

FIGURE 14–1 Fiscal Policy in the Context of the Simple Keynesian Model

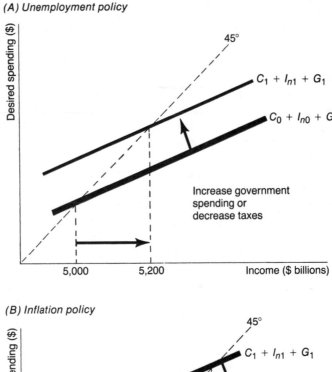

(A) Unemployment policy

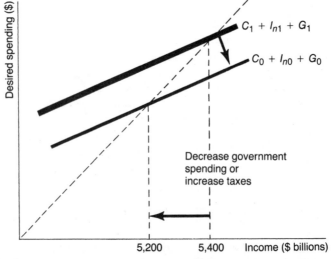

(B) Inflation policy

economy to be at full employment a $5,200 billion NNP is required.[3] The object of fiscal policy, then, is to shift the aggregate expenditure function upward so that equilibrium NNP coincides with full-employment NNP. In this example, the gap

---

[3] Full employment in this case is taken to mean 5 to 6 percent frictional unemployment.

between equilibrium and full-employment NNP is $200 billion. In order to increase (shift up) aggregate expenditures, the government should increase its spending, decrease taxes, or undertake some combination of the two. If we know how much NNP has to be increased to reach full employment, the simple model can even tell us how much government spending has to be increased or taxes reduced.

GOVERNMENT SPENDING MULTIPLIER

Recall from the discussion of the multiplier in Chapter 11 that a dollar of new or additional spending will bring forth several additional dollars of spending in the economy. This occurs because spending by one person is income to another, and when people receive income they generally spend part of it. Also recall that the fraction of additional dollars of income that is spent is referred to as the marginal propensity to consume (MPC). In the discussion of the multiplier, we saw that the government spending multiplier is equal to $1/(1 - \text{MPC})$. Thus, if MPC is 0.75, an additional dollar of new government spending ultimately will bring forth $4 of new spending in the economy, that is, $1/(1 - 0.75) = 4$.

With the multiplier in mind, it is an easy step to stipulate how much government spending should be increased to bring the economy from the $5,000 billion level of NNP to the $5,200 billion full-employment level. If each additional dollar of government spending brings forth $4 of new spending in total, the $200 billion increase in NNP can be obtained by a $50 billion increase in government spending. A convenient formula for determining how much government spending has to be increased in order to restore full employment is:

$$\frac{\text{Gap}}{M_g} = \Delta G$$

where the gap is the *difference* between the actual equilibrium NNP and the equilibrium NNP that corresponds to full employment ($200 billion in this case), M_g is the government spending multiplier (4 in this example), and ΔG is the required change in government spending. In this example, a $50 billion increase would shift aggregate demand up enough to push equilibrium NNP ahead by $200 billion, and in so doing restore full employment without inflation.

TAX MULTIPLIER

Offhand one might conclude that the unemployment problem in the preceding example could be taken care of by a decrease in taxes of $50 billion. But this is not correct. A $1 billion tax decrease will not have as large an impact on NNP as a comparable increase in government spending. In other words, a $1 billion tax decrease will not shift the aggregate expenditure function up by a full $1 billion, as is the case with a $1 billion government spending increase. Why? To answer this

TABLE 14–1   Comparing the Multiplier Process of a Government Spending Change
with a Tax Change

	$1 Billion Increase in Government Spending	*$1 Billion Decrease in Taxes*
Round 1	$1 billion	$0.75 billion
Round 2	0.75	0.56
Round 3	0.56	0.42
.	.	.
.	.	.
To infinity	.	.
	$4 billion	$3 billion

question, it is first necessary to understand that people do not increase their spending by the full amount of a tax cut. The MPC tells us that. For example, if the government reduces taxes by $1 billion, the people will have an additional $1 billion that can be considered as additional disposable income. But it is not likely they will spend the entire $1 billion; they will spend part and save part. If their MPC is 0.75, the people will spend $0.75 billion and save the remaining $0.25 billion. Thus, a tax decrease of $1 billion will shift the aggregate expenditure function upward by only $0.75 billion if the MPC is 0.75.

The fact that people increase their saving as well as their spending in response to a tax cut is the reason the tax multiplier is less than the government spending multiplier. With just a little extra effort, we can determine how much less the tax multiplier will be. Perhaps the easiest way to approach this is to compare the multiplier process of a government spending change with a comparable tax change. In Table 14–1, we compare the first three rounds of the multiplier process for a $1 billion government spending increase with that of a $1 billion tax decrease. Notice that on the first round in the government spending column, the entire $1 billion is spent. But in the tax column, the first round shows only $0.75 billion being spent. The remaining $0.25 billion is saved. In all subsequent rounds, the numbers in the tax column are progressively smaller.

Using the multiplier formula developed in Chapter 11, we see that the total increase in spending in the economy will increase by $4 billion because of the $1 billion initial increase in government spending. However, in the case of the $1 billion tax decrease, total spending increases by only $3 billion. Hence, the government spending multiplier is 4 in this case, and the tax multiplier is 3, or one less. Under the assumptions of the simple model, the tax multiplier always will be one less than the government spending multiplier for a lump-sum tax. If we let MPC be 0.80, for example, M_g would be 5 and M_t (the tax multiplier) would be 4. The fact that the tax multiplier is one less than the government spending multiplier can be proven algebraically, but this is best left to an intermediate-level macro course.

Now that we know that the tax multiplier is always one less than the government spending multiplier, we can modify the formula we developed in regard to a government spending change so it can be used also to predict a tax change. Now we have:

$$\frac{\text{Gap}}{M_t} = \Delta T$$

where again the gap is the difference between actual equilibrium NNP and full-employment equilibrium, M_t is the tax multiplier, and ΔT is the required decrease in taxes to restore full employment without inflation.

In the context of the preceding example, the $200 billion gap divided by the tax multiplier of 3 (assuming MPC is 0.75) tells us that taxes should be decreased by $66.7 billion.

Although the discussion in this section has been couched in terms of an unemployment problem, the same procedure can be used to deal with an inflation problem, as illustrated by Figure 14–1B. In this example, the aggregate expenditure function intersects the 45-degree line at a level of NNP that is $200 billion greater than full employment. As the economy moves past the $5,200 billion full-employment level, the increase in NNP is due largely to an increase in the price level. In other words, inflation occurs. The objective of an anti-inflationary fiscal policy is to shift aggregate expenditure down by a government spending decrease, a tax increase, or some combination of the two. The same formulas that are utilized to specify the appropriate government spending or tax changes in the unemployment situation can be used to specify the required government spending decrease or tax increase for the inflation problem. In this case, the $200 billion decrease in equilibrium NNP can be accomplished by either a $50 billion spending decrease or a $66.7 billion tax increase.

BALANCED–BUDGET MULTIPLIER

An interesting implication of the government spending multiplier being one greater than the lump-sum tax multiplier is that equilibrium NNP can be increased even if taxes are increased to pay for the added government spending in the case of an unemployment problem. For example, suppose the government increases its spending by $1 billion and at the same time increases taxes by $1 billion so as to maintain a balanced budget. If the MPC is 0.75, the government spending multiplier tells us that the government spending increase by itself will increase equilibrium NNP by $4 billion. But because M_t is one less than M_g (three in this example), the tax increase will reduce equilibrium NNP by $3 billion. Viewing this process as a sequence, the $1 billion government spending increase pushes NNP up by $4 billion, but the tax increase pulls it back by $3 billion, leaving a $1 billion net increase.

If we had increased government spending and taxes by $10 billion, the net increase in NNP would have been $10 billion. Moreover, this would be true regardless of the size of the MPC. It will be helpful to prove this to yourself by choosing different changes in *G* and *T* and working out the outcomes under different values of MPC. You will find that the value of MPC does not alter the fact that comparable changes in *G* and *T* always change equilibrium NNP by this exact same amount. Economists refer to this phenomenon as the *balanced-budget multiplier*. The value of this multiplier is one, because equilibrium NNP changes by one times the initial change in *G* and *T*.

FISCAL POLICY IN THE CONTEXT OF THE AGGREGATE DEMAND–AGGREGATE SUPPLY MODEL

Fiscal policy prescribed by the aggregate demand–short-run aggregate supply model is similar to that prescribed by the simple Keynesian model. In the event of unemployment, a government spending increase, a tax decrease, or some combination of the two will shift aggregate demand to the right. In the context of Figure 14–2, aggregate demand shifts from AD_0 to AD_1 resulting in a new equilibrium at Q_1.

FIGURE 14–2   Fiscal Policy in the Context of the Aggregate Demand–Aggregate Supply Model

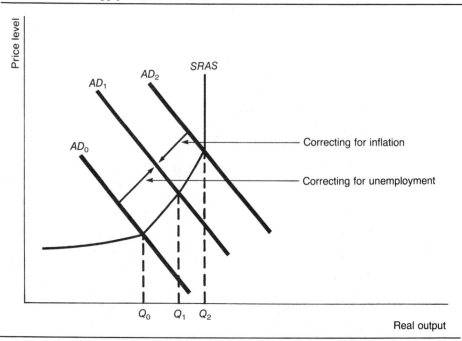

One difference between this and the Keynesian model is that the multiplier is not so easily predicted. If short-run aggregate supply is horizontal, the change in real output will equal the change that would be obtained by the Keynesian model. But if *SRAS* is upward-sloping, the change in real output will be less than that predicted by the Keynesian model. In the extreme case of a vertical *SRAS,* an increase in aggregate demand will not change real output, resulting only in an increase in the price level.

An inflation problem could be dealt with by a decrease in government spending, an increase in taxes, or some combination of the two. Bear in mind, though, that the vertical axis on the aggregate demand–aggregate supply model shows the price level rather than the rate of inflation. Rarely has the absolute level of prices declined. The last time the United States experienced such a phenomenon for any length of time was in the early 1930s during the Great Depression. Thus, the aggregate demand–aggregate supply model (short run or long run) does not yield very reasonable results when applied to an inflation problem.

FISCAL POLICY IN THE CONTEXT OF RATIONAL EXPECTATIONS

Consider first an unemployment problem. As explained earlier, the Keynesian model would call for a tax decrease and/or a government spending increase. According to the rational expectations hypothesis, such policy will reduce unemployment only if its full effects on the economy are unexpected by the people. If the government announces a tax decrease or government spending increase, labor unions are likely to press for higher wages because of their concern that the added stimulus to the economy will be inflationary. The higher wage demands will in turn offset the possible employment-increasing effects of the fiscal policy.

The rational expectations people maintain that fiscal policy such as tax cuts or government spending increases may have a short-term effect on reducing unemployment provided business and labor are not aware of the inflationary tendencies of fiscal policy implemented to stimulate the economy. But after one or two attempts to reduce unemployment by such policy, people learn of its side effects and take action immediately to protect themselves against the expected future inflation and in so doing nullify even the short-term employment-increasing effects.

In the context of the long-run Phillips curve diagrams presented in Chapter 13, the initial effect of the unexpected stimulus is to move the economy up along a short-run Phillips curve, reducing the level of unemployment but increasing the inflation rate. Then, as people come to expect a higher inflation rate and as wages catch up to prices, unemployment increases, and the economy moves back to a point on the long-run Phillips curve. As repeated attempts to stimulate the economy become better known to the people and are expected, the leftward movement along a short-run Phillips curve becomes smaller and smaller before the curve itself shifts up to higher expected inflation levels. When this happens, the main impact of attempts to stimulate the economy will, according to the rational expectations hypothesis, be higher rates of inflation rather than reductions in unemployment.

SUMMARY

Fiscal policy is the attempt by government to maintain full employment and stable prices through its taxing and spending powers. It was first tried in the United States during the Franklin Delano Roosevelt administration in an attempt to stimulate the economy during the Great Depression of the 1930s. Nondiscretionary fiscal policy works automatically to smooth out the ups and downs of the economy. Examples of nondiscretionary fiscal policy include unemployment compensation, welfare programs, and the progressive income tax. Discretionary fiscal policy requires specific action by Congress and the president. According to the simple Keynesian model, an unemployment or inflation problem can be solved by government spending and/or tax changes. These changes are determined by dividing the gap between equilibrium income and full-employment income by the appropriate multiplier. Similar policy recommendations flow from the aggregate demand–aggregate supply short-run model, although the government spending and tax changes cannot be exactly specified unless the slope of the aggregate supply curve is known. The rational expectations hypothesis suggests a less activist role for government than the preceding models.

YOU SHOULD KNOW

1. The definition of *fiscal policy*.
2. When fiscal policy was first used in the United States.
3. The main built-in stabilizers.
4. How to use the multipliers to compute the necessary change in government spending to combat an unemployment or inflation problem.
5. How to compute the tax multiplier, and why it is less than the government-spending multiplier.
6. How to compute the balanced-budget multiplier.
7. How to use the aggregate demand–short-run aggregate supply model to prescribe fiscal policy.
8. What the rational expectations hypothesis implies about the likely success of fiscal policy.

QUESTIONS

1. What are the main built-in stabilizers, and how do they operate?
2. *a*. According to the simple Keynesian model, how much would government spending have to be increased if actual equilibrium NNP is $50 billion less than

the NNP that would generate full employment? (Assume MPC is 0.80.)

b. How much would taxes have to be decreased under the same conditions as stipulated in part a above?

c. How much would government spending and taxes have to increase to achieve full employment under the conditions stipulated in part a above? Would your answer be different if MPC = 0.75? Explain.

3. a. Why is the tax multiplier less than the government-spending multiplier?

b. Why is the balanced-budget multiplier equal to one?

4. a. What condition is required for the multipliers in the aggregate demand–aggregate supply model to be the same as those of the Keynesian model?

b. Under what condition will they differ?

5. What is the effect on the price level of a decrease in aggregate demand? Is this realistic? When did the U.S. price level last decline for a prolonged period?

6. a. What does the aggregate demand–aggregate supply model show that the Keynesian model does not?

b. Are the spending multipliers larger or smaller in the aggregate demand–aggregate supply model than in the Keynesian model? Explain.

c. Does the slope of the aggregate supply function have any bearing on the size of the multiplier in the aggregate demand–aggregate supply model? Explain.

7. According to the rational expectations hypothesis, what conditions are required for the success of fiscal policy implemented to reduce unemployment?

8. Contrast the Keynesian view of using fiscal policy to mitigate the problems of unemployment with the rational expectations theory.

SELF-TEST

1. Fiscal policy refers to attempts by government to maintain full employment and stable prices through its _____ powers.
   a. military
   b. spending
   c. taxing
   (d.) b and c

2. The use of fiscal policy to influence the level of economic activity began in the United States during the _____ administration coinciding with _____ .
   a. Roosevelt; World War I
   b. Hoover; the Great Depression
   (c.) Roosevelt; the Great Depression
   d. Truman; the post-World War II recession

3. Which of the following would be classified as built-in stabilizers, or nondiscretionary fiscal policy?
   a. Unemployment compensation
   b. Welfare programs
   c. Progressive income tax
   (d.) All of the above

4. Which of the following would be classified as discretionary fiscal policy?
   a. Welfare programs
   b. Progressive income tax
   (c.) Reagan administration tax cut
   d. Unemployment compensation

5. In the 1990s, an unemployment problem will exist if the unemployment rate exceeds:
   a. zero.
   (c.) 5 to 6 percent.
   b. 3 to 4 percent.
   d. 8 to 10 percent.

6. In the context of the simple Keynesian model, an unemployment problem will exist if equilibrium income is _____ than _____ income.
   a. less; equilibrium
   (b.) less; full-employment

c. greater; equilibrium

d. greater; full-employment

7. In the context of the simple Keynesian model, an inflation problem will exist if equilibrium income is _____ than _____ income.

   a. less; equilibrium

   b. less; full-employment

   c. greater; equilibrium

   d. greater; full-employment

8. According to the simple Keynesian model, a gap of $100 billion between equilibrium income and full employment that causes an unemployment problem can be erased by a government spending increase of $ _____ billion. (Assume MPC is 0.80.)

   a. 100   *c.* 20

   b. 80   *d.* 12.5

9. According to the simple Keynesian model, an inflation problem caused by a $75 billion excess of actual income over full-employment income can be erased by a $ _____ billion decrease in government spending. (Assume MPC is 0.75).

   a. 75   *c.* 25

   b. 100   *d.* 18 3/4

10. In the simple Keynesian model with lump-sum taxes and autonomous investment and government spending, the tax multiplier is _____ .

    a. zero

    b. one

    c. one greater than the government-spending multiplier

    d. one less than the government-spending multiplier

11. The tax multiplier is _____ than the government-spending multiplier because part of the increase in disposable income obtained through a tax cut is:

    a. less; saved.

    b. less; spent on consumer durables.

c. greater; saved.

d. greater; spent on consumer durables.

12. In the situation described by question 8, how much would taxes have to be decreased?

    a. $25 billion

    b. $33 1/3 billion

    c. $100 billion

    d. $133 1/3 billion

13. In the situation described by question 9, how much would taxes have to be increased?

    a. $75 billion

    b. $25 billion

    c. $133 1/3 billion

    d. $18 3/4 billion

14. Because the government-spending multiplier is _____ the tax multiplier, the balanced budget multiplier must be _____ .

    a. one less than; one

    b. one greater than; one

    c. one less than; zero

    d. one greater than; zero

15. If the government wished to maintain a balanced budget in the situation described in question 8, it should increase its spending and taxes by $ _____ billion.

    a. 100   *c.* 25

    b. 400   *d.* 20

16. In the context of the aggregate demand–short-run aggregate supply model, an increase in government spending or a decrease in taxes in response to an unemployment problem will _____ price level and _____ real output.

    a. maintain the same; increase

    b. increase the; increase

    c. increase the; maintain the same

    d. maintain the same; maintain the same

17. In the situation described in question 16, the steeper the short-run aggregate supply curve, the _____ the increase in the price level and the _____ the increase in real output.

a. larger; smaller
b. larger; larger
c. smaller; smaller
d. smaller; larger

18. The last time the United States experienced a significant decrease in the price level was during:
    a. the Great Depression.
    b. World War II.
    c. the immediate post-World War II years.
    d. the early 1980s.

19. The rational expectations hypothesis implies that the government has _____

control over _____ than is implied by the simple Keynesian model.
a. less; inflation
b. more; inflation
c. less; unemployment
d. more; unemployment

20. According to the rational expectations hypothesis, in order for the government to _____ reduce unemployment, it must _____ the people of (with) its actions.
    a. permanently; inform
    b. permanently; surprise
    c. temporarily; inform
    d. temporarily; surprise

Chapter 15

Problems of Fiscal Policy

OVERVIEW

Although the United States and other market economies of the world have not experienced in the last half-century anything as severe as the Great Depression, people still regard unemployment and inflation as potentially serious problems. This tells us that the use of fiscal policy to deal with those problems is perhaps more complicated than the discussion in the preceding chapter may have implied. In this chapter, we will look at some of these problems.

FINANCING PROBLEMS

It used to be argued that the money to finance increased spending or reduced taxes would be collected as increased taxes during inflationary times, when it was presumed that the government would run a surplus. Yet the record reveals that between 1929 and 1989 the federal government incurred deficits—that is, spent more than it took in—in 51 out of those 61 years. Moreover, the average annual deficit was more than three times larger than the average annual surplus. Thus, the chance of the government having money on hand to deal with an unemployment problem is not very good. The government could increase taxes if it wished to increase spending, but this would just reduce private spending even more. Also, a tax increase during a time of high unemployment is not likely to be politically feasible. Thus, it is likely that during a time of unemployment the government will not have extra money on hand if it wishes to increase spending or cut taxes. What can it do then? Most likely it will spend more than it takes in as taxes, that is, incur a deficit.

The federal government finances deficits by selling government bonds. The money it receives from the sale of the bonds is then used to make up the difference between what is taken in by tax revenue and what is spent. The impact of selling bonds depends in part on who buys them. There are three important buyers: (1) U.S. citizens, (2) foreign buyers, and (3) the Federal Reserve bank.

The sale of bonds to U.S. citizens can be a problem if the money used to purchase the bonds would have been used instead to finance private investment and consumer spending. In order to sell bonds, the government may have to offer higher interest rates. If so, private borrowers in order to compete for these funds also have to pay higher rates of interest. This makes investment less profitable and consumer durables more expensive, thereby reducing private spending in these areas. This phenomenon has come to be known as *crowding out*—federal borrowing crowding out private borrowing.

The sale of bonds to foreign buyers also can result in a reduced level of domestic spending if interest rates are increased to provide an incentive for these buyers to purchase the bonds. In addition, the sale of bonds to foreign buyers can result in an increase in the price of the dollar in terms of foreign currencies. In order for foreign buyers to purchase U.S. governmental bonds, they must first buy U.S. dollars. The increased demand for dollars increases their price in terms of foreign currencies. The problem here is that the stronger dollar makes U.S. goods more expensive in the world market, causing a decrease in exports and increased unemployment and financial difficulties for export-oriented industries. Also, the stronger dollar reduces the price of foreign-made products relative to domestic goods, which in turn increases imports. This makes it more difficult for U.S. firms to compete with foreign producers. (These changes are discussed in greater detail in Chapter 24 on exchange rates.)

If the government bonds are sold to the Federal Reserve bank, there is a danger that the nation's money supply will be increased, causing inflation. To see how this might occur, be aware that when the U.S. Treasury receives payment for the bonds it issues, the Federal Reserve credits (adds) the corresponding amount to the Treasury's checking account at the Federal Reserve. The Treasury can then write checks on the added numbers in its account. The new numbers in the Treasury's checking account are equivalent to the new $10 or $20 bills in buying goods and services. The practice has been called *monetizing the debt* or *printing money* to finance deficits. (This phenomenon will be described in greater detail in Chapter 20, ''Problems of Monetary Policy.'')

TIMING PROBLEMS

In order for fiscal policy to have its desired effect to combat either inflation or unemployment, the impact of policy action must come at the correct time. In order to obtain the desired effect of fiscal policy, two timing problems must be overcome. The first is the problem of when to undertake needed changes in government spending and taxation in order to stabilize the economy. The second is the lag between the decision to undertake spending or tax changes and the effects of such changes on the economy.

The first problem is really a matter of identifying when the economy is headed for a recession or a round of inflation. This problem exists because the economy tends to fluctuate from year to year in a rather uneven and unpredictable fashion.

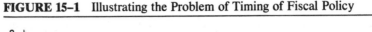

FIGURE 15-1   Illustrating the Problem of Timing of Fiscal Policy

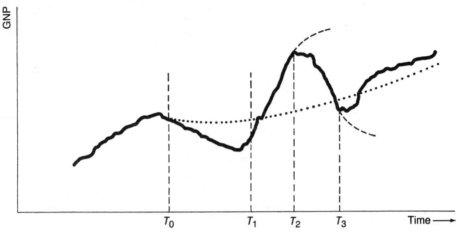

The difficulty, then, is to decide whether an upturn or downturn is just a minor fluctuation or whether it is the beginning of something big. If the government takes rather drastic measures to curb a recession, for example, at the hint of a slight downturn in economic activity, the result might well be a forthcoming inflationary spiral. Theoretically, then, the government should take antirecessionary measures (a spending increase or a tax cut) when the economy is just beginning to enter a downturn in economic activity, as illustrated by time T_0 in Figure 15-1. By the same token, anti-inflationary measures should be reserved for a time such as T_1. The object is to smooth out the booms and busts, as shown by the dotted line starting at T_0 in Figure 15-1.

If the government is successful in identifying critical turning points in the economy, such as T_0 and T_1, there is still the question of doing something soon enough to have the desired effect. Suppose, for example, that the time span between T_0 and T_1 is three years. If it takes the government two years to push a tax cut through Congress or to decide on new government projects, the actual effect may be just the opposite of what is desired. If the antirecessionary measures do not begin to be felt until around T_1, the result may well be to stimulate the economy in the forthcoming boom period following T_1. As a result, the inflation following T_1 could be even worse than it would have been had no action been taken. This is illustrated by the dashed line beginning at T_2. Also, it is not very feasible to shut down government projects that have been initiated during a recession even when an inflationary period looms on the horizon. Hence, these additional projects accentuate the forthcoming inflation.

The same problems of timing and effect confront the government when inflation threatens, such as at T_1. Again a tax increase or a spending reduction may require one or two years to pass Congress (especially if there is an upcoming election). As a result, the anti-inflationary policy may become a prorecessionary policy and pull the economy into a more severe state of unemployment, as illustrated by the downward-sloping dashed line beginning at T_3.

There is also the problem of predicting when actual government spending or tax changes will have their major effect on the economy. We have implicitly assumed in our previous discussion that the desired effect of policy takes place immediately after action is taken. But this need not be the case. The major problem is that relatively little is known about the duration of lags between government action and its effect. Indeed, the lag may change from one period to the next.

ADJUSTMENT PROBLEMS

The underlying reasons for the increase in unemployment when attempts are made to reduce inflation are still not well understood, although one can think of some reasonable, albeit tentative, explanations for this phenomenon. Consider first a decrease in government spending. People who had been producing goods and services purchased by the government suddenly find that their market has dried up. If these people are working for private firms, their employers have little choice but to lay them off unless new markets can be found immediately, which is not likely. The problem is likely to be most noticeable when firms lose military contracts. Because of the specialized nature of these goods, it takes time for such firms to retool to produce for the nonmilitary market. Indeed, just a change in the *kind* of government spending can be expected to have a similar effect because of the time it takes people to find new jobs in expanding industries. When the affected people are employed directly by the government, a similar adjustment must be made. Again there is a period of increased unemployment until they can find new jobs. The release of military personnel after a war or military buildup accentuates this problem.

An increase in taxes can be expected to have a similar effect. If people have less money to spend, it is likely they will reduce spending on consumption and investment goods. Again, the people who had been producing these goods will be laid off, resulting in increased unemployment.

In addition, one should recognize the likelihood of a multiplier effect. The initial people laid off because of a decrease in government spending or increase in taxes will decrease their spending. As a result, people who had been supplying these goods will find their jobs in jeopardy. This does not mean, of course, that people who become unemployed because of a decrease in government spending or increase in taxes will be unemployed permanently. The unemployment occurs because of the time it takes to find jobs in other occupations or localities. In order for these people to find new jobs they may have to accept a relative decline in their wages, which is not easy to take, especially when taxes have increased.

Not only will attempts to reduce inflation by a reduction in government spending or increase in taxes be likely to increase unemployment, but it is also virtually certain that inflation will not stop abruptly. It is more likely that inflation will continue for many months or even years, although it is likely to continue at a decreasing rate. The reason inflation persists is likely to be the result of expectations. During inflation, people come to expect a continuing increase in the price level. As a result, wages and other contracts will reflect inflationary expectations. For example, if prices have been rising at 10 percent per year, wage contracts will build in a 10 percent per year increase just to maintain the purchasing power of employee salaries. The same is true of contracts to supply raw materials or finished goods. With the increase in the unemployment rate and a falling off of demand for certain goods and services stemming from anti-inflationary fiscal policy, there will be a "softness" in the markets for labor and goods. Therefore, new contracts will reflect this softness and stipulate a smaller growth in wages and prices. But it may take several years to bring wage and price increases down to a noninflationary level.

During contract renegotiations, it also is possible, indeed likely, for wages and prices to be thrown out of balance. If the rate of growth of prices, for example, becomes lower than the growth in wages, real wages will increase, thus lowering profits and causing firms to reduce their output of unprofitable goods. As a result, more unemployment is experienced. On the other hand, if the rate of growth of wages is lower than the growth in prices, we are likely to observe a period of increased strike activity. The imbalance between wages and prices basically is due to an inability to accurately forecast future inflation. This problem can exist even in the absence of an anti-inflationary fiscal policy. One thing is certain, the adjustments in the economy to both inflation and anti-inflationary fiscal policies are very complex. We still have a lot to learn about this process. The main point of this section is that we should expect to experience both unemployment and inflation for a time after attempts are made to control inflation through fiscal policy. This is not to say that the country should abandon anti-inflation policies, but it would be better not to have started the inflation in the first place. Similar adjustment problems occur when monetary policy is used to reduce inflation, as will be pointed out in Chapter 20.

POLITICAL PROBLEMS

By now it probably has become apparent that carrying out a successful fiscal policy requires that some rather complicated economic problems be overcome, including financing, timing, and adjustment problems. It should also be kept in mind that discretionary fiscal policy requires action by Congress and the executive branch of the federal government. Before such action can be undertaken, there must be agreement regarding the kind of fiscal policy to be undertaken, how strong it should be, whom it should affect, and when it should be undertaken. Considering the differences in viewpoints between liberals and conservatives, it should come as no surprise that obtaining such widespread agreement poses some rather formidable political problems.

As mentioned in Chapter 1, liberals tend to favor or at least more readily accept increased government spending on goods and services while conservatives prefer a lesser role for government. Thus, during a time of increased unemployment, we would expect liberals to favor increased government spending and conservatives to argue for a tax reduction. This difference in philosophy became quite apparent during the late 1970s in the debate over the Kemp-Roth bill. Conservative lawmakers supported the bill, which proposed a significant reduction in federal income taxes, while their liberal counterparts opposed it, arguing that it would cause inflation or cut deep into government spending and services.

Assuming agreement can be reached on the appropriate spending increase or tax cut (in the case of increased unemployment), further decisions have to be made on where the additional spending should take place or whose taxes should be reduced. Most senators and members of Congress, regardless of political affiliation, like to obtain a "fair share" of any increase in government spending for their area or constituents. Understandably, this creates conflict, since the amount of any needed spending increase is not likely to be great enough to be spread across the entire nation.

In regard to a tax decrease, disagreement is likely to arise on who should obtain a tax break and the kind of taxes to be reduced. For example, should we have a proportionate, across-the-board tax decrease, or a tax reduction for only certain income levels, such as low-income people? Or should business firms be given a tax cut, say in the form of accelerated depreciation or investment credits, to stimulate economic activity? It is not likely that liberals and conservatives will readily agree on the answers to these questions.

The political controversy generated by a proposed government spending decrease or tax increase (as would be appropriate during inflation) is likely to be even more intense. Even if there is general agreement on the need for a spending decrease, few senators or members of Congress are going to welcome it for their states or regions, particularly before an election. People whose jobs depend on government spending, or who benefit in some way from this spending, can be very vocal in their opposition to spending cuts. At any rate, it is becoming apparent that it is a good deal easier for government to increase spending than to decrease it.

A proposed tax increase involves similar problems. With the cost of living rising, probably more rapidly than wages during the early stages of inflation, few lawmakers are likely to push for higher taxes and further reduce the real take-home pay of workers. This is particularly true in a period immediately preceding an election. Some people have advocated giving the president power to vary income tax rates, within limits, in order to obtain more flexibility and more prompt action. However, it does not appear that Congress will soon buy such a proposal.

THE NATIONAL DEBT

A discussion of fiscal policy would not be complete without a consideration of the national debt. Although state and local governments also borrow, we will define the national debt here as debt owed by the federal government. The national debt was incurred because of government deficits. When the government wishes to

TABLE 15–1   National Debt, 1929–1989 (constant 1989 dollars)

Year	Total ($ billions)	Per Capita ($)	Percent of GNP
1929	121	980	16
1934	276	2,172	46
1939	380	2,895	47
1944	1,471	10,634	101
1949	1,111	7,441	85
1954	1,055	6,474	63
1959	1,019	5,731	51
1964	1,072	5,589	43
1969	1,061	5,235	34
1974	1,218	5,747	34
1979	1,420	6,438	35
1984	1,881	7,952	43
1989	2,866	11,520	55

Source: *Economic Report of the President*, 1976, p. 195, and 1990, p. 383.

spend more than it takes in through taxes, it must borrow by selling government bonds to the general public, to foreign investors, and to the Federal Reserve. Thus, the magnitude of the national debt is measured by the amount of federal government bonds outstanding.

As shown by Table 15–1, the U.S. national debt amounted to $2,866 billion in 1989. The most rapid increase in the national debt occurred during World War II, when the government issued large numbers of bonds to pay for military expenditures. In constant 1989 dollars, the total national debt remained relatively stable during the 1950s and 1960s. However, between 1969 and 1989 the total national debt more than doubled in real terms. By 1989, the per capita debt in real terms exceeded the 1944 figure, which had been the all-time high.

In recent years, many people have expressed concern about the size of the national debt. We hear phrases such as "the country going broke" or "fiscal irresponsibility" in regard to the growing size of the national debt.

Is the national debt really something to be concerned about? It used to be argued that when government bonds were sold primarily to U.S. citizens the national debt is debt the government owes to the people. However, because the people "own" the government, it is debt that the people owe to themselves. If the government decided to pay off, say, $100 billion of the national debt, it would increase taxes by $100 billion and immediately pay this amount back to the people. As you can see, this $100 billion payment would not make the nation any "poorer" because the people would still have the $100 billion. Granted, there may be a redistribution of wealth toward former bondholders, but the total wealth of the nation would remain unchanged. Of course, it is not likely the government ever would want to pay off such a large amount of the debt in a short time, because such action likely would have a destabilizing effect on the economy.

During the early 1980s, the increase in real interest rates attracted foreign buyers of U.S. government bonds. In this case, the national debt takes on more of the characteristics of private debt in that paying off the debt removes real wealth from the economy. True, when the debt was incurred, that is, when the bonds were sold, real wealth was transferred into the economy from other countries. Consequently, paying off the debt cancels out the wealth obtained when the debt was incurred. On the other hand, interest payments on the bonds represent a net transfer of wealth out of the country.

Regardless of whether the government bonds are sold to U.S. citizens or to foreign buyers, it is important to recognize that tax money must be raised to pay off the debt. Unless people are informed about their tax liabilities, they may be unpleasantly surprised to see their taxes increasing in order to pay off debt without receiving any increase in the level of public goods or services. In 1989, interest payments on the national debt amounted to over 15 percent of all federal government expenditures. Also, high rates of taxation could in turn reduce the incentives of taxpayers to work and invest and as a result reduce the real output of the economy. In this sense, an excessively heavy burden of national debt could drag the economy down to a lower standard of living.

Should this phenomenon become a recognizable problem, the government would be increasingly tempted to print money to finance the deficit, thereby inflating the economy and in so doing reduce the debt in real terms. If the price level should double, for example, the real value of previously sold government bonds outstanding would decline by one half. The losers in this process would be the people or institutions that owned these bonds. In effect, they would be paying off this portion of the national debt.

SUMMARY

The government incurs a deficit when it spends more than it takes in as taxes and fees. Federal deficits are financed by selling bonds to U.S. citizens, foreign buyers, or the Federal Reserve bank. Selling bonds to U.S. citizens results in crowding out of private borrowers who have to pay higher interest rates to raise funds. This decreases consumer and investment spending. Selling bonds to foreign buyers increases the demand for dollars and the price of dollars in the foreign exchange market, which in turn decreases exports and increases imports. Selling bonds to the Federal Reserve amounts to printing money, which in turn causes inflation. Fiscal policy implemented at the wrong time can worsen unemployment and inflation problems. Attempts to reduce inflation by fiscal policy can be expected to increase unemployment. Liberals and conservatives tend to disagree on the appropriate fiscal policy. During a period of unemployment, liberals tend to favor a government spending increase while conservatives would rather see a tax cut. The national debt increased substantially from the mid-1970s to the late 1980s, and in 1989 it was the highest in real terms (per capita and total) of any time in U.S. history.

YOU SHOULD KNOW

1. How the federal government finances deficits.
2. The three groups of buyers of government bonds, and the problems associated with selling bonds to each.
3. The meaning of *printing money* to finance deficits, and the likely outcome of this practice.
4. Why the correct timing of fiscal policy is crucial, and why timing is a problem.
5. Why attempts to reduce inflation tend to cause an increase in unemployment.
6. The kind of fiscal policy likely to be favored by liberals and the kind preferred by conservatives.
7. How the national debt was incurred, and how it compares now in real terms with times past.
8. Why it was argued that paying off the debt would not make the nation poorer.
9. Why the above argument may no longer be valid.
10. What happened to the national debt per capita and as a percent of GNP during the 1970s and 1980s.

QUESTIONS

1. *a.* List the three main buyers of government bonds in years when the federal government increases deficits.
   b. What are the consequences of selling bonds to each?
2. *a.* What is meant by the term *printing money* to finance the deficit?
   b. Does printing money increase the national debt?
3. How can bad timing further destabilize the economy?
4. It has been argued that "inflation contains the seeds of unemployment." In what way might this be a valid argument?

5. *a.* In a time of unemployment, how would you expect liberals and conservatives to differ in regard to the desired fiscal policy? How about a time of inflation?
   b. How does the actual fiscal policy adopted depend on the proximity of elections?
6. *a.* What is the national debt? How was it incurred?
   b. It has been argued that paying off the national debt does not reduce the wealth of the country. How might this be true?
   c. How might the argument in part *b* above not be true?

SELF-TEST

1. During the vast majority of the years from 1929 to the present, the federal government ran a _____ .

   a. surplus
   b. balanced budget
   c. deficit

2. The federal government finances deficits by:
   a. buying bonds.
   b. selling bonds.
   c. counterfeiting money.
   d. raising taxes.

3. The "crowding out" phenomenon is most likely to occur if the government sells bonds to:
   a. U.S. citizens.
   b. foreign buyers.
   c. the Federal Reserve bank.

4. Crowding out occurs because of _____ interest rates, which _____ private spending.
   a. higher; decreases
   b. higher; increases
   c. lower; decreases
   d. lower; increases

5. The sale of bonds to foreign buyers can _____ domestic investment spending because the stronger dollar makes U.S. exports _____ expensive to foreign buyers and foreign imports _____ expensive to U.S. buyers.
   a. decrease; more; less
   b. decrease; less; more
   c. increase; more; less
   d. increase; less; more

6. The term *printing money* describes:
   a. counterfeiting.
   b. sale of bonds to U.S. citizens.
   c. sale of bonds to foreign buyers.
   d. sale of bonds to the Federal Reserve.

7. The most likely outcome of printing money to finance deficits is:
   a. legal difficulties.
   b. unemployment.
   c. inflation.
   d. a run on banks.

8. Identifying when to undertake fiscal policy can be a problem because:
   a. of a lack of good data on unemployment rates.
   b. of temporary month-to-month fluctua-

tions in economic activity.
   c. of long-term business cycles.
   d. liberals and conservatives disagree on the most appropriate policy.

9. Bad timing of fiscal policy:
   a. at worst will do no harm.
   b. can destabilize the economy.
   c. will decrease unemployment but leave inflation unchecked.
   d. will decrease inflation but leave unemployment unchecked.

10. Attempts to reduce inflation by decreasing government spending have _____ unemployment.
    a. decreased
    b. not affected
    c. increased

11. Higher levels of unemployment that occur after a(n) _____ in government spending result from some workers having to:
    a. decrease; find different jobs.
    b. increase; find different jobs.
    c. decrease; work more overtime.
    d. increase; work more overtime.

12. An attempt to bring inflation under control by decreasing government spending or increasing taxes results in a situation where there is for a time _____ inflation and _____ unemployment.
    a. high; low   c. high; high
    b. low; high   d. low; low

13. During a time of unemployment, liberals favor _____ while conservatives prefer a _____ .
    a. tax increase; government spending decrease
    b. government spending decrease; tax increase
    c. tax decrease; government spending increase
    d. government spending increase; tax decrease

14. The national debt is measured by:
    a. the Treasury's checking account balance at the Federal Reserve.

b. the value of government bonds sold during a given year.

c. the value of government bonds outstanding.

d. the loans taken out by the Treasury from the Federal Reserve bank.

15. In 1989, per capita national debt in the United States was about _____ . This was the highest it has been:

a. $2,500; since World War II.

b. $11,500; since World War II.

c. $2,500; in history.

d. $11,500; in history.

14,000

16. From 1979 to 1989, the national debt as a percent of GNP _____ from _____ percent to _____ percent.

a. increased; 35; 55

b. increased; 25; 35

c. decreased; 55; 35

d. decreased; 35; 25

17. It used to be argued that paying off the national debt would:

a. make the country poorer.

b. make the country richer.

c. push the country into bankruptcy.

d. make the country neither richer nor poorer.

18. As the national debt increases, the government may be tempted to _____ money, thereby causing _____ and a(n) _____ in the real value of bonds outstanding.

a. print; inflation; decrease

b. destroy; inflation; decrease

c. print; unemployment; increase

d. destroy; unemployment; increase

Chapter 16

Taxes

OVERVIEW

Taxation has been described as the art of fleecing the goose with the least amount of squawking. In market economies, every government must rely on taxes to finance all or part of its cost of operation and spending. This chapter provides some insights into the principles underlying a country's tax system, how taxes affect economic activity, and the sources and uses of tax monies in the United States.

PRINCIPLES OF TAXATION

In adopting various taxes, most societies have attempted to follow certain guidelines or principles to make taxes as fair as possible. Two widely used principles are (1) ability to pay and (2) benefits received.

A. Ability to Pay

There seems to be consensus that people with high incomes should pay more taxes per person than their poorer counterparts. The question is, how much more? If the taxes paid increase in proportion to the increase in income, the tax system is called *proportional*. This is easiest to see with an income tax. The $100,000-per-year-income person will pay 10 times more in taxes than the person with $10,000 per year income.

Most societies that employ an income tax go beyond a proportionate or "flat-rate" tax where everyone regardless of income pays the same tax rate. Income taxes tend to be progressive in nature. A *progressive tax* is one where the proportion of income paid as taxes increases as income increases. Generally, this is accomplished by increasing the tax rate on the marginal or extra dollar earned. The rate at which additional income is taxed is called the *marginal tax rate*. Progressive income taxes have increasing marginal tax rates. An example of a progressive income tax with increasing marginal tax rates is given below.

Income Level ($1,000)	Marginal Tax Rate (%)
0–5	0
5–10	10
10–20	15
20–30	20
30–50	25
50–75	30
75 and over	35

A person with a $20,000 per year income, for example, pays zero tax on the first $5,000 of income, 10 percent on the next $5,000, and 15 percent on the last $10,000 for a total of $2,000 of taxes. In this case, the proportion of income paid as taxes is 0.10, or 10 percent. If the person's income goes up to $30,000, the last $10,000 is taxed at 20 percent, according to the tax schedule presented above. Now the person's total bill is $4,000—the $2,000 on the first $20,000 of income and the $2,000 on the last $10,000. Hence, the overall proportion of income paid as taxes with $30,000 income is 0.133 or 13.3 percent.

It is possible to achieve a mild progressivity of the tax system by a flat-rate tax schedule if the lowest level of income is not taxed. In the preceding example, the first $5,000 earned is not subject to tax. Consider an example where all income except the first $5,000 is taxed at 10 percent. A $10,000 income is, therefore, subject to $500 in taxes, or 5 percent. A $20,000-income person pays $1,500 in taxes, or 7.5 percent. In order to have a strictly proportional tax system, all income must be taxed at the same rate.

A *regressive tax* is one where the proportion of income paid as taxes decreases as income increases. It is not likely that a government would deliberately make an income tax regressive by decreasing the tax rates at higher income levels. However, it is common for sales or excise taxes to be regressive because low-income people tend to spend a larger share of their income on the taxed goods and services than those with higher incomes. The exemption of food, clothing, and other necessities from sales taxes in many states is an attempt to reduce their regressivity. Social security taxes in the United States also are regressive because after the maximum tax is paid by an individual, additional income is not taxed. Hence, the overall proportion of income paid as social security taxes decreases as income above the cut-off point increases.

B. Benefits Received

A second principle on which to base a tax system is benefits received from the government; the greater the benefits, the higher the tax. However, for many public goods, it is difficult to tie tax payments to specific benefits. For example, it might be argued that expenditures on national defense, police, and fire protection benefit people equally because everyone's life and liberty are protected. On the other hand, high-income people tend to have more property that receives protection, implying they should pay higher taxes.

The benefits-received principle is more clearly applied to the purchase of goods and services supplied by government such as auto licenses, excise taxes on gasoline, highway tolls, parking fees in publicly owned lots or garages, tuition at public universities, and entrance fees to national parks or public recreation areas. In these cases, it is easier to tie the taxes to benefits received.

It is common for governments to use both the ability-to-pay and benefits-received principles in deciding the tax structure. Fees for the use of certain public goods or services may be set below cost so low-income people can afford their use with the difference made up by taxes based on ability to pay. Tuition fees at publicly supported colleges and universities are good examples of this arrangement. On the average, these fees cover a third or less of the cost of operating these institutions. The remainder is made up by taxes imposed on the general public.

PROGRESSIVE TAXATION

Recall from the preceding section that a progressive tax is one where the proportion of income paid as taxes increases with increasing income. It will be useful to explore more fully the perceived justifications for this kind of tax, beyond the ability to pay.[1] The willingness of society to levy progressive taxes implies that high-income people receive less utility from an extra dollar of income than those with low incomes. And closely related to this idea is the implicit assumption that as a person's income increases, the extra utility or satisfaction obtained from an extra dollar becomes less and less. If these two propositions are valid, then high-income people do not necessarily sacrifice more utility by paying a higher proportion of their income as taxes than low-income people. In effect, they say that the rich can pay proportionally more of their income in taxes than the poor without sacrificing more utility because an extra dollar isn't worth as much to the rich as to the poor.

While this assertion may strike most people as reasonable, it may come as a surprise to learn that economists have not been able to prove it is true. In other words, they have not been able to prove the existence of *diminishing marginal utility of money*—the idea that the added satisfaction obtained from additional income on wealth becomes less and less. Nor have they been able to prove that rich people receive less satisfaction from an extra dollar than poor people. Of course, just because something cannot be proved does not mean it is false. In setting up their tax systems, most societies proceed as if the two propositions are true.

Even if it could be proved that diminishing marginal utility of money does not exist and a rich person receives as much satisfaction from an extra dollar as a poor

---

[1] For further discussion on this topic, see Walter J. Blum and Harry Kalven, Jr., *The Uneasy Case for Progressive Taxation* (Chicago: University of Chicago Press, 1963).

person, societies may still opt for progressive taxation. For one thing, there is the humanitarian motive of using the tax money paid by the rich to help low-income people obtain more of the basic necessities of life such as education, food, housing, and medical care. There also may be the perception that societies characterized by extreme inequality of income and wealth may not be stable, more prone to civil unrest or even overthrow of the government. This situation hurts rich and poor alike.

TAXES AND RESOURCE ALLOCATION

It should be clear at this point that taxes can and probably do alter the distribution of income and wealth within a country. Progressive taxes should make the distribution of income more equal than a proportional or regressive tax system.

Taxes also can alter the allocation of resources in an economy by influencing the relative prices of the resources and of the goods they produce. A tax on a good or a resource (labor, capital, energy, or raw materials) increases the price paid for the item and lowers the net after-tax price received. How this occurs is more fully explained in Chapter 13 of the companion micro text, but an intuitive explanation will be useful here. Consider as an example a sales tax of 6 percent on a good. When the consumer purchases the item, the seller adds 6 percent to the before-tax price. Thus, it is easy to see why the tax increases the price paid. But why does it lower the net after-tax price received? Because the price paid is higher with the tax, the quality of the item demanded is reduced. A reduction in sales reduces profits. To minimize this loss, the seller finds it more profitable to reduce the net after-tax price than to keep it high and suffer an even greater reduction in sales. Thus, the price to the buyer increases by something less than 6 percent (in this example). And the net after-tax price received by the seller decreases by the difference between the increase in selling price and the amount of the tax. In this case, both buyer and seller share the burden of the tax.

Taxes can influence the mix of goods and services produced in an economy by changing the relative prices paid and received. If a relatively high tax is levied on an item, its selling price will increase relative to other goods, which in turn discourages both its consumption and production. How much quantity is reduced depends on the responsiveness of consumers to a change in the price of the items. If consumers are relatively responsive to a tax-induced price increase, quantity will decline more than if consumers are less responsive.

The logical question to ask at this point is, so what? Why be concerned that taxes can change the output mix in the economy? As explained in Chapter 13 of the companion micro text, a tax-induced change in the output mix from that which would prevail without the distortions results in a deadweight loss and reduces the total value of output and welfare of society. This occurs because resources are diverted into the production of goods less heavily taxed, which at the margin yield less satisfaction to consumers than the taxed items. Thus, there is a decrease in the consumption of goods that have a relatively high value at the margin, and an increase in the consumption of goods less heavily taxed but yielding less utility. This situation will prevail if different items are taxed at different rates or if some items are taxed and others are not.

A similar result occurs if resources or inputs are taxed at different rates or if some are taxed and others not. The taxed items become more expensive to buyers and less profitable to sellers. As a result, there is an incentive to use less of the more highly taxed inputs. In turn, productivity declines and costs increase, especially for goods that would ordinarily use relatively large amounts of the taxed inputs.

The preceding discussion may give the impression that taxes on goods or resources are bad, reducing the welfare of society. But this is not always the case. If the production or consumption of a good causes undesirable side effects such as pollution, health, or safety problems, a tax on the good or resources used to produce it will increase the welfare of society. This will occur if producers do not take into account the pollution, or if consumers fail to heed the long-term health or safety effects such as occurs from the use of tobacco and alcohol. Taxes reduce the production and consumption of these goods from what they would otherwise be, thereby reducing pollution and/or health and safety problems.

SUPPLY-SIDE ECONOMICS AND THE LAFFER CURVE

In the discussion of fiscal policy, it was implicitly assumed that an increase in tax rates resulted in an increase in tax revenue received by the government, and vice versa. This assumption has been questioned by a school of thought that has come to be known as supply-side economics. Economists who adhere to this view argue that in each country there is a tax rate that maximizes tax revenue. In other words, as the rate of taxation increases from a low level, tax revenue received from the tax also increases. However, as the tax rate is increased to higher and higher levels, the tax revenue reaches a maximum and then begins to decrease.

This hypothesized relationship between tax rates and tax revenues is commonly referred to as the *Laffer curve* after the economist who popularized it. The Laffer curve traces the relationship between tax rates and tax revenue. It is generally drawn as a backward-bending line as shown in Figure 16–1. At the relatively low tax rate T_1, tax revenue also is relatively small, R_1. As the tax rate increases, revenue continues to increase and reaches a maximum at R_2 at the tax rate T_2. As the tax rate increases above T_2, tax revenue declines.

The economic rationale underlying this relationship put forth by the supply-side economists is that beyond some point, high taxes dampen economic activity and place a premium on tax avoidance. Supply siders say that if entrepreneurs and investors must pay a large part of their earnings as taxes, they will not take risks to start new firms or introduce new products. As tax rates continue to increase, supply siders also argue that it becomes more profitable for businesspeople to turn their talents to avoiding taxes rather than producing. As a result, the tax revenue received by the government can decline as tax rates increase. By the same token, if the tax rate is above T_2 in Figure 16–1, reducing the rate will increase tax revenue.

FIGURE 16–1 The Laffer Curve

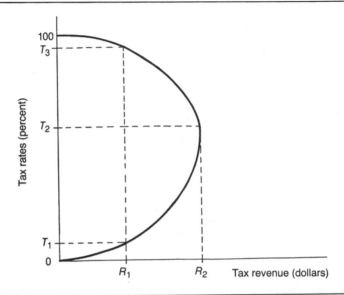

The possibility of increasing tax revenue by lower tax rates together with the objectives of increasing economic growth and reducing unemployment prompted the Reagan administration to push tax cuts through Congress in the early 1980s. Although the rate of economic growth picked up in the mid-1980s and unemployment declined, huge deficits continued to pile up during this time. No one knows for sure if deficits would have been smaller had tax rates not decreased. However, the decrease of personal and corporate income tax revenue as a percent of GNP during the early to mid-1980s suggests that tax revenue would have been higher had tax rates not been cut.

In general, supply-side advocates are not convinced that an active pursuit of fiscal policy to counteract cyclical fluctuations in economic activity is the best thing for the economy. They fear that such policy will lead to repeated bouts of inflation and then increased unemployment when the government attempts to bring inflation under control. Supply siders maintain that stable and low levels of government spending and tax rates will result in higher levels of economic growth and less unemployment in the long run. As their name implies, supply siders argue that a low rate of taxation results in a more rapid shift to the right of long-run aggregate supply, which in turn promotes full employment in the economy.

TAXES AND INVESTMENT

Supply-side advocates mentioned in the preceding section have expressed concern that high taxes can reduce investment and consequently dampen economic growth and job creation. This can occur for two reasons: (1) high taxes on high-income people reduce the savings available to undertake investment, and (2) high taxes can discourage investment in new or risky ventures.

Recall from earlier discussion that investment can occur only if there is saving. If all income were spent on consumer goods, no resources would be available to carry on investment. Thus, saving provides the wherewithal to invest. As shown in Table 16–1, high-income people have a higher rate of saving than those with low incomes. In fact, people in the lowest-income group spend more than they earn, that is, saving is negative. A progressive income tax removes a larger share of the income from the higher-income groups than of those with low income, thereby reducing the amount of money available for investment purposes.

In large part, the motivation for reducing marginal tax rates by the Reagan administration was to increase the rate of saving and investment in the United States. The rate of investment in the United States has been among the lowest of the major industrial nations, just over half the rate in Japan (Table 16–2). It appears, however, that the reduction in tax rates during the early 1980s did not

TABLE 16–1 Income and the Savings Rate, 1972–73

Pretax Income Level	Percent Saved
Less than $3,000	−96
$7,000–$7,999	3
$12,000–$14,999	18
$20,000–$24,999	29
$25,000 and over	43

Source: Bureau of Labor Statistics, *Handbook of Labor Statistics* (Washington, D.C.: U.S. Department of Labor, December 1980), pp. 369–74.

TABLE 16–2 Gross Investment as a Percent of GNP, 1965 and 1987

Country	1965	1987
Japan	27	30
West Germany	18	20
Canada	26	21
France	26	20
Italy	23	21
United Kingdom	21	18
United States	17	16

Source: *World Development Report* (Washington, D.C.: World Bank, 1989), p. 181.

have the desired impact on investment. As shown in Table 16–2, the share of gross investment in GNP decreased slightly between 1965 and 1987.

The argument for reducing tax rates on high-income people to stimulate saving and investment assumes that the tax funds will be used for public consumption rather than for public investment such as the construction of infrastructures or to finance education and research. If the taxes are used for these purposes, total investment (private plus public) need not be smaller with the higher taxes. The use of taxes to finance public investment has been called *forced saving*. Of course, if the extra taxes are spent on noninvestment goods and services such as the military or transfer payments, then total investment will be smaller with higher taxes.

The second reason supply siders have expressed concern over the level of taxation in the United States is the effect of taxes on the willingness to bear risk. They point out that over three quarters of the new jobs created in the United States during the 1970s and 1980s came from small, newly established firms. Establishing a new firm or venture entails risk—the possibility that the business can fail. If marginal tax rates are relatively high, the chances of striking it rich are reduced even if the business succeeds. If the business succeeds, the government shares in the profits, but if the business fails, the entrepreneurs and/or outside investors bear the loss alone, unless it can be written off against other income.

DOUBLE TAXATION

The income tax is viewed by many economists as one of the more neutral taxes from the standpoint of not distorting the allocation of resources in the economy. At least it has the potential of being neutral. The U.S. income tax law has certain provisions, however, that discourage investments in some areas while encouraging it in others. One such provision is the double taxation of dividend income from corporate stocks. Because of the corporation income tax, corporations must pay an income tax on the earnings of equity capital (capital financed by the sale of stock). Then, after the dividends are paid back to stockholders, the stockholders pay a tax on this money a second time via the personal income tax. The net effect of this double taxation is to discourage saving by individuals and investment in the corporate sector of the economy.

On the other hand, interest income earned from the ownership of municipal bonds is not subject anywhere to federal income taxation. And if the bond purchasers reside in the state where the money is used, they are also exempt from state income taxes. As one might expect, the favorable tax treatment of municipal bond interest pulls more resources into urban and municipal facilities than if all sources of income were taxed equally. Municipal bonds have been quite attractive to higher-income people in the upper tax brackets. This is not to say that investing in cities is undesirable. The only implication is that the double taxation of corporate stock dividends and the escape from taxation of interest income of municipal bonds can be expected to cause underinvestment in the private sector and overinvestment in the public sector. In this case, the income tax also distorts the allocation of the country's resources.

VALUE-ADDED TAX (VAT)

One of the newer forms of taxes that is not used in the United States but is used in Western Europe is the value-added tax (VAT). As its name implies, this is a tax on the value added by business firms. Recall that value added is the difference between the sales of a firm and its purchases from other firms of such things as unfinished goods, raw materials, and energy. The value added of a firm is the earnings of the capital and labor employed by the firm. Although a value-added tax is collected from business firms, buyers of goods and services in large part pay the tax in the form of higher prices for the things they buy, although as with the sales tax, the net after tax received by producers also can be lower.

Several advantages can be cited in favor of the value-added tax. First, if all industries are taxed equally, it could be relatively neutral in its effect on the nation's allocation of resources. However, similar to sales taxes, there likely would be a temptation to tax some industries at higher rates and exclude others. Second, the value-added tax has an element of simplicity. Complicated rules on depreciation of capital, what can be deducted and what cannot, and tax shelters could be eliminated. The third and probably main advantage is that a value-added tax should encourage saving because the income from saving would not be subject to double taxation as with the corporate and personal income taxes. Also, a VAT gives people more discretion on the decision to spend or save. With the income tax, people have no choice but to pay the tax before they can decide how much to spend or save. A person can avoid or at least postpone paying a VAT by not spending, that is, by saving.

Probably the main disadvantage of the VAT is its element of regressivity. Similar to a sales tax, people who spend the greatest share of their income pay a larger proportion of their income as a VAT. Since these people tend to have lower incomes, the VAT would be regressive. However, this disadvantage could be overcome by giving VAT rebates to low-income people.

A value-added tax, like the income tax, also penalizes firms for being productive. An efficient firm that has high value-added-per-dollar sales will pay more taxes per dollar of sales than another less-efficient firm of the same size. Also, like the income tax, the government shares in the profits of the firm but does not share in the risk of a loss. In fact, a firm may have to pay a value-added tax even though it incurred a loss. Value added can be positive even when a loss is incurred because the costs of labor and capital are not subtracted when computing value added.

SOURCES AND USES OF TAX RECEIPTS

This section provides an overview of the sources and uses of tax funds for both the federal government and state and local governments. The figures are for 1989.

As shown in Table 16–3, personal income taxes accounted for the largest share of federal government revenue (45 percent), and social security taxes were a close second (36 percent). On the expenditures side, health, education, and welfare accounted for 27 percent of all federal outlays. Another 27 percent was spent on the

TABLE 16–3   Federal Government Receipts and Expenditures, 1989

Receipts	$ Billion	Percent
Personal income taxes	$445.7	45
Corporate income taxes	103.6	11
Social security taxes	359.4	36
Other taxes and fees	82.0	8
Total	990.7	100
Expenditures		
Health, education, and welfare	306.1	27
Military	303.6	27
Social security	232.5	20
Interest	169.1	15
Other	131.3	11
Total	$1,142.6	100

Source: *Economic Report of the President*, 1990, p. 385.

TABLE 16–4   State and Local Government Receipts and Expenditures, 1987–88

Receipts	$ Billion	Percent
Property taxes	$132.2	18
Sales taxes	156.3	22
Personal income taxes	88.3	12
Corporate income taxes	23.7	3
Federal government grants	117.6	16
Other	209.0	29
Total	727.1	100
Expenditures		
Education	242.7	34
Highways	55.6	8
Public welfare	89.1	13
Other	317.5	45
Total	704.9	100

Source: *Economic Report of the President*, 1990, p. 391.

military. Notice that social security outlays in 1989 were over $126 billion less than social security taxes. The intention is to build up the social security trust fund in anticipation of higher outlays in the 21st century. Notice also that total federal expenditures exceeded total receipts by over $150 billion in 1989—the 1989 federal addition to the national debt. Interest payment on the debt was $169 billion in 1989, up 88 percent in real terms from 1979.

As indicated by Table 16–4, sales taxes make up the largest single revenue source for state and local governments, with property taxes a close second. Unlike the federal government, receipts of the state and local governments exceeded expenditures. Most of these governments are required to operate with a balanced budget over the long run. The largest single use of state and local taxes is for education, with public welfare and highways a distant second and third, respectively.

SUMMARY

Most taxes are based on two priniciples of taxation: ability to pay and benefits received. Under a proportional or flat-rate income tax, the tax rate is constant across income groups. Virtually all income taxes throughout the world are progressive, where the marginal tax rate increases at higher-income levels. With a progressive tax, the proportion of income paid as taxes increases as income increases. Progressive taxes are at least in part based on the belief that the marginal utility of money decreases as income increases. Taxes can and do distort the nation's allocation of resources by affecting prices paid and received. Supply-side advocates favor low tax rates in order to encourage saving and stimulate investment. Under the U.S. income tax, stock dividends are taxed twice. The value-added tax is attracting some interest in the United States because it does not discourage saving. The United States has the lowest saving and investment rates among the industrialized countries. At the federal level, personal income taxes constitute the largest single source of revenue. The largest single expenditure category is health, education, and welfare, with the military a close second. At the state and local level, property taxes are the largest revenue source, and education is the largest use category.

YOU SHOULD KNOW

1. The two principles of taxation.
2. What a progressive tax is.
3. What the marginal tax rate is.
4. What a regressive tax is.
5. What the diminishing marginal utility of money is, and how it is used to justify progressive taxation.
6. How taxes can alter resource allocation.
7. How sales taxes affect prices paid and prices received.

8. How unequal rates of taxation on goods can decrease the value of output to society.

9. What the Laffer curve is, and what school of thought it is associated with.

10. When an increase in tax rates would result in a decrease in tax revenue.

11. Why high taxes may dampen saving and investment.

12. What income is subject to double taxation.

13. What a value-added tax is, and what its main advantages and disadvantages are in comparison to an income tax.

14. What the major sources and uses of tax funds of the state and local, and federal governments are.

QUESTIONS

1. What are the two guidelines that most societies use in establishing their tax system?

2. *a.* Why is a general sales tax thought to be regressive?
   b. Is it possible to make a sales tax progressive? Explain.
   c. What is the drawback of making a sales tax progressive?

3. What are the two propositions on which a progressive tax system is based?

4. Is it possible to make a flat-rate tax progressive?

5. *a.* How do sales taxes influence a nation's allocation of resources?

   b. How do income taxes influence the level of a nation's investment?

6. *a.* What is the Laffer curve and what is its underlying economic rationale?
   b. According to the Laffer curve, is it possible for a government to increase tax revenue by decreasing tax rates? Explain.

7. *a.* What are the main advantages and disadvantages of a value-added tax?
   b. Which would you prefer, an income tax or a value-added tax? Why?

8. Compare and contrast federal government tax revenues and expenditures with those of state and local governments.

SELF TEST

1. The two widely used principles of taxation are:
   a. ability to pay and what the "traffic will bear."
   b. benefits received and what the "traffic will bear."
   c. ability to pay and benefits received.
   d. income and sales taxes.

2. With a progressive income tax, the tax rate on an extra dollar of income _____ as income increases. This means that high-income people pay a _____ share of their income as taxes than those with lower incomes.
   a. increases; larger
   b. increases; smaller
   c. decreases; larger
   d. decreases; smaller

3. Under a proportional or flat-rate income tax, a person with $100,000 per year income will pay _____ as a person with an income of $10,000 per year.
   a. the same total tax
   b. 10 times as much in taxes

c. 1/10th of the tax

d. 100 times as much in taxes

4 Under a regressive tax:

   a. low-income people pay a larger proportion of their income as taxes than high-income people.

   b. low-income people pay more total taxes than those with high incomes.

   c. high- and low-income people pay the same percent of their income as taxes.

   d. *a* and *b.*

5. Sales taxes are thought to be _____ because low-income people spend a _____ share of their income than those with higher incomes.

   a. progressive; smaller

   b. progressive; larger

   c. regressive; smaller

   d. regressive; larger

6. _____ is a tax based on benefits received.

   a. Income tax

   b. Sales tax

   c. Excise tax on gasoline

   d. Property tax

7. Diminishing marginal utility of money _____ be proved. It is used to justify _____ .

   a. can; progressive taxes

   b. cannot; progressive taxes

   c. can; regressive taxes

   d. cannot; regressive taxes

8. It is commonly thought that a higher-income person sacrifices less by paying an extra dollar of tax than a person with a low income. This implies:

   a. increasing marginal utility of money.

   b. diminishing marginal utility of money.

   c. that high-income people save a larger share of their income.

   d. that high-income people save a smaller share of their income.

9. A progressive tax system should make the distribution of income _____ equal and

_____ the humanitarian motives of society.

   a. less; serve

   b. more; go against

   c. less; go against

   d. more; serve

10. Sales taxes tend to _____ the prices paid by consumers and _____ the net after-tax price received by sellers.

   a. increase; leave unchanged

   b. increase; decrease

   c. leave unchanged; increase

   d. leave unchanged; decrease

11. A tax on a good or service _____ its price and _____ its use.

   a. increases; increases

   b. decreases; increases

   c. increases; decreases

   d. decreases; decreases

12. A tax on a resource or input _____ its price and _____ its use.

   a. increases; increases

   b. decreases; increases

   c. increases; decreases

   d. decreases; decreases

13. The levy of different tax rates on products or resources _____ the value of output to society because resources are pushed into _____ value uses.

   a. increases; higher

   b. increases; lower

   c. decreases; higher

   d. decreases; lower

14. The phenomenon described in question 13 above is known as:

   a. deadweight loss.

   b. diminishing marginal utility of money.

   c. ability-to-pay principles of taxation.

   d. benefits-received principle of taxation.

15. Advocates of supply-side economics argue that a tax rate increase _____ tax revenue.

   a. must increase

   b. may increase

    c. may decrease

    d. *b* and *c*

16. The Laffer curve is a:

    a. famous pitch thrown by a relief pitcher for the Minnesota Twins during the 1987 World Series.

    b. a relationship between tax rates and tax revenues.

    c. a relationship between unemployment and inflation.

    d. a relationship between tax rates and unemployment.

17. The economic rationale underlying the backward bending portion of the Laffer curve: As tax rates increase, people _____ .

    a. save less

    b. turn their energies to tax avoidance rather than productive activity

    c. flee the country

    d. turn their energies to productive rather than leisure activities in order to make up for the income they have lost

18. One of the arguments put forth by supply-side advocates for lowering upper-level tax rates was that high-income people save _____ than those with low incomes. Lower tax rates were seen as a way of increasing _____ as a percent of GNP.

    a. less; investment

    b. more; investment

    c. less; consumption

    d. more; consumption

19. As a percent of GNP, gross investment in the United States is _____ than in the other industrialized nations and _____ from 1965 to 1987.

    a. smaller; decreased

    b. smaller; increased

    c. larger; decreased

    d. larger; increased

20. Which of the following income is taxed twice?

    a. Interest on corporate bonds

    b. Interest on government bonds

    c. Earnings on corporate equity capital (dividends)

    d. Earnings on corporate debt capital (interest)

21. A value-added tax is collected from _____ . Compared to an income tax, it is thought to _____ saving.

    a. consumers; discourage

    b. business firms; discourage

    c. consumers; encourage

    d. business firms; encourage

22. The federal government receives the greatest share of its revenue from _____ taxes, and its largest expenditure category is _____ .

    a. sales; the military

    b. income; the military

    c. sales; health, education, and welfare

    d. income; health, education, and welfare

23. The largest single source of income for state and local governments is _____ . The largest single expenditure category for state and local governments is _____ .

    a. personal income taxes; public welfare

    b. personal income taxes; education

    c. sales taxes; public welfare

    d. sales taxes; education

Part VII

Money and Banking

Chapter 17

Money and the New Quantity Theory

OVERVIEW

In the next four chapters, attention is directed at money, banking, monetary policy, and problems. After discussing the characteristics and functions of money, this chapter extends the original quantity theory of money by considering the factors that can change velocity.

CHARACTERISTICS OF MONEY

Perhaps the first thought that comes to our mind when we consider money is the image of currency and coins in our billfolds or purses. Further reflection might bring to mind the money in our checking and savings accounts at the bank. From our knowledge of history, we know that people have utilized a variety of objects as money. What was used depended mainly on the resources and technology available at the time. Primitive tribes that "lived off the land" generally utilized certain bones of agreed-upon animals, stones, beads, or other objects that were not overly abundant in nature.

With the coming of animal domestication and agriculture, we read of animals such as cattle or goats, or crops such as wheat, being used as money. Then the precious metals, particularly gold and silver, came into use as money. These examples by no means exhaust the list. It is interesting to note, for example, that even cigarettes were used as money in some prisoner-of-war camps during World War II.[1]

---

[1] For an interesting article on the use of cigarettes as money in a World War II P.O.W. camp, see R. A. Radford, "The Economic Organization of a P.O.W. Camp," *Economica* 12 (November 1945), pp. 189–201. Note how prices varied directly with the supply of cigarettes.

One desirable characteristic of money is that it be made out of material that is relatively cheap to produce. The more resources a society must employ to produce money, the less there are available to produce the real goods and services that sustain life and make it more interesting and enjoyable. For example, if the people of the world insisted on using a costly material such as gold as the only legal form of money, a significant share of the world's population might find it individually profitable to spend their time and effort producing money, that is, mining. But from society's standpoint, the efforts of these people would be for naught. The world would lose the goods and services that these people and their capital resources could have produced instead.

Considering the relatively high cost of mining and processing gold or any other metal for money, it is fortunate that paper money has come into such widespread use. The cost in terms of resources used for the paper and printing may add up to only a few dollars for millions of dollars produced. If a society decided that the face value of its money should be equal to its value as a commodity, then producers of the money (for example, miners) would have an incentive to spend up to a dollar's worth of resources to obtain an extra dollar of the money. Granted, the main motivation for adopting paper money probably came more from a desire for greater convenience than to reduce costs to society.

Going further, modern societies have devised other ways to cheapen the resource cost of money and increase its convenience. Checking account money is a good example, although the coming of checking accounts probably was motivated more by the increased convenience to the individual than by a decreased resource cost to society. As a result of a desire for still greater convenience, money as we know it today may someday become obsolete. We will return to this topic in a following section.

Another desirable characteristic of money is that it be reasonably durable, yet easy to carry around. No material is perfect in this regard. Cast iron may be durable, but it makes for a weighty change purse. Gold fares rather badly on both counts. Being a rather soft metal, it is not extremely durable, and the fact that it is a metal makes it heavy to carry around. In this regard, paper would have to rank ahead of gold as a desirable form of money.

Although money should be cheap and easy to manufacture, it should at the same time be very difficult to duplicate or counterfeit. Gold ranks high on this point, which probably explains its popularity in medieval times. Yet, when gold coins came into use, the possibility of "sweating" was introduced. People soon found that small particles of gold could be removed from gold coins simply by shaking them in a bag. And by melting the particles together, one might obtain, for example, 51 coins from a bag of 50. This same problem occurred in prisoner-of-war camps where cigarettes were used as money. Here the men found that by rolling a cigarette between thumb and forefinger some tobacco could be extracted without noticeably altering the form of it. Thus, some could smoke their money and have it too.

FUNCTIONS OF MONEY

The fact that money has existed as long as human beings have populated the earth ought to tell us that money is useful. The word *useful* in this case does not refer to the goods and services that money "buys." Rather it refers to the fundamental reasons for a society to utilize something called money. Money is useful for three basic reasons: It serves as (1) a medium of exchange, (2) a standard or measure of value, and (3) a store of value.

Regarding the first use, if it were not for the concept of money, we would have to operate under a barter system. In other words, each person would have to exchange the goods or services he or she produces directly with another person for the goods or services desired. A little reflection will impress upon us how incredibly inefficient a barter system would be. For example, an economics professor would have to exchange lectures for food, clothing, and other goods and services—not a very easy task if owners of food or clothing did not want to listen to economics lectures. The example becomes even more absurd when we consider what the producers of jetliners or guided missiles would exchange for the things they desire. The lesson is clear: Were it not for money, people would have to spend much of their time shopping rather than producing, and as a result society's output would be reduced drastically. Thus, if money did not exist, someone would have to invent it.

Money is useful also to measure the value or price of things. With a barter economy, we would have to remember the price of each good or service in terms of every other good or service. For example, one economics textbook might be exchanged for a pair of gloves, three textbooks for a pair of shoes, and so on. Thus, each good or service would have thousands of prices, the amount of every other good or service that is worth the same as the good or service in question. It does not take long to realize that even in a relatively primitive society, the task of determining prices would be next to impossible without a common denominator—money. With money, each good or service has only one price, its price in terms of the monetary unit.

Most people like to put away part of the fruits of their labor for future use. Thus, money is useful as a store of value. Without money we would have to save material objects. But what would these objects be? Obviously they could not be things that deteriorated or depreciated with time, or else time would erase our savings. Also, they should not be items that are costly to guard and store, or else a major part of our efforts would be devoted to guarding our savings rather than producing and enjoying life. Money is a convenient object to save; it does not deteriorate with reasonable care, and it is relatively costless to store.

WHAT GIVES MONEY PURCHASING POWER?

We know that paper money and coins are worth only a small fraction of their face value as a commodity. A $10 bill, for instance, is worth only a fraction of a cent in the used-paper market. But at a store it can be exchanged for a good deal more than that, even at today's inflated prices. The same is true of coins.

In fact, it would not be desirable for the commodity value of money to approach or exceed its face value. This happened in the early 1960s with respect to silver nickels. Higher silver prices drove their price up in the market until the value of the metal in a nickel coin was about seven cents. It soon became apparent to some enterprising people that a profit could be earned by melting nickels and selling the metal in the market, perhaps even back to the government. Thus, money that is worth more than its face value tends to disappear from circulation.

Also, as mentioned earlier, if the commodity value of money approaches its face value, it is an indication that the money is far too costly to produce. If a nickel is worth seven cents, this is an indication that society is devoting seven cents worth of resources to produce each nickel—not a very good buy for society.

But we are still faced with the question, Why can paper money, which has virtually no value in itself, be used to purchase valuable goods and services? We might be tempted to say that the gold in Fort Knox provides a backing and hence a value to our paper money. Before the price of gold was allowed to rise in the 1970s, each dollar outstanding was backed by just a little over one cent of gold. Indeed, if all the gold in Fort Knox were to disappear, and no one knew about it, paper money would no doubt go on being used just as before.

It might be argued that confidence in the government that issued the money gives paper money value. But one can find instances in history where governments have disappeared, yet their money continued to be used and retained its value. For example, the money issued by the old czarist government in Russia continued to be used by the Russian people long after this government disappeared. Moreover, the old czarist money retained its value while the money issued by the new Communist government lost value.

The real reason paper money has value is because people *accept* it as having value. You accept paper money in payment because you know that other people will accept this money when you wish to buy something. Thus, it is the acceptance of paper money by both buyers and sellers of goods and services that gives value to this money. If for some reason a sizable fraction of people decided they would no longer accept paper money as payment, it soon would go out of circulation. However, it would have to be replaced by something else, since a modern economy really could not function without some form of money.

A CASHLESS SOCIETY

As noted, money has taken many different forms throughout history. Even within fairly recent times, we have seen a gradual transition from the use of currency to demand deposits, or checking account money. And within recent years, the credit card has become a convenient tool for making small purchases. However, the use of credit cards does not rule out the use of checks or currency. It is just a means of paying for several purchases with one check or cash payment.

A truly cashless society would be one step removed from the credit card society of today. Each person might have to present the equivalent of a credit card or some form of identification when making a purchase. But instead of billing the customer later, the procedure would be to deduct the amount of the purchase from the buyer's bank account at the moment of purchase. In this situation, there would be little need to carry cash or to have a checking account. Bills would be paid by a simple subtraction of numbers. Similarly, people would receive their income when employers or buyers credited or added the appropriate amount to a person's account.

Although such a procedure would characterize a cashless society, it would not imply a moneyless society. The numbers that would be added to or subtracted from accounts would still be given in terms of dollars. But the dollars would not be green pieces of paper or coins. Instead, they would be just numbers in people's accounts, and these accounts would be found in the memory cores of computers utilized by financial institutions. Thus, the concept of money would still be used, although its form would change from tangible objects, that is, paper and metal, to intangible numbers in people's accounts.

Whether we will experience a cashless society in our lifetime will depend on the cost and convenience of such a monetary system. If some technical problems can be solved, and if people accept it, we may see a gradual transition to this kind of monetary system. The reason for this change is really no different from that for changes in the past. The printing press made it possible for paper money to come into existence. A highly organized and coordinated banking system makes checking account money possible. And the computer may bring forth a cashless society. Of course, the use of coins and currency may still prove to be the best way to handle small, day-to-day purchases made through vending machines, at lunch counters, and so on.

BENEFITS OF HOLDING MONEY

As mentioned in Chapter 9, probably the most serious limitation of the quantity equation of exchange utilized by the classical economists to predict price and output changes from changes in the quantity of money is the necessity of assuming a constant velocity. In the post-World War II years, considerable work was done to better understand why velocity might change and to predict such changes. The outcome of this work is sometimes called the *new quantity theory of money,* as opposed to the old quantity theory, which assumed velocity to be a constant.[2]

In order to understand why velocity may change from one year to the next, it is necessary to understand why people hold part of their assets or wealth in the form of money. Each person's assets or wealth can be divided into two categories:

---

[2] See Milton Friedman, "The Quantity Theory of Money: A Restatement," in *Studies in the Quantity Theory of Money,* ed. Milton Friedman (Chicago: University of Chicago Press, 1956).

monetary assets (money) and nonmonetary assets. The latter includes securities, such as stocks and bonds, as well as all personal property, such as real estate, cars, clothes, appliances, and books. From personal experience we know that every person owns some of both kinds of assets. There may be a few unusual people who have most of their assets in the form of money and a few of the opposite kind who own mostly nonmonetary assets, but most of us fall somewhere between these two extremes. The question is: Why do we hold part of our wealth as money but nowhere near all of our wealth as money? The answer is to be found in the relationship of the benefits of holding money and the cost of holding money.

The benefits of holding money can be summarized by two words: convenience and security. Because most people make purchases on a continuing basis while getting paid only periodically, it is more convenient to hold a certain amount of money to make these purchases than to sell off assets whenever a purchase is to be made. For example, it would be very inconvenient for people to sell nonmonetary assets every time they wished to buy lunch, gas for their car, movie tickets, or the many small purchases people make each week. Nor would it be very convenient for people to make all their purchases at one time, say right after payday. Instead, most of us prefer to spread our purchases out over a period of time, and as a result we need to hold some money in order to make these purchases.

As mentioned, a second major benefit of holding money is that it provides security. We never know, for example, when a sudden toothache will necessitate an unplanned trip to the dentist or a flat tire on the car will require an unforeseen purchase at a service station. Hence, most of us like to have a few dollars available to avoid financial embarrassment in case of unforeseen situations. Also, it is desirable to have some money on hand to take advantage of exceptional bargains. If we knew in advance just how much we would spend in the coming year, we would not have to hold as much in reserve.

Business firms also hold a certain amount of money in the form of either cash in their vaults or deposits in banks. From the standpoint of business firms, money can be looked upon as a factor of production that saves on other services, particularly labor. For example, without a cash reserve, each payday someone in each firm would have to take the time to sell enough of the firm's assets, such as stocks or bonds, in order to acquire the necessary cash to pay its employees. Thus, holding part of the firm's assets in cash or money also proves convenient for the business firm and increases its productivity. Also, firms, like individuals, may desire to have ready cash available either as a reserve against contingencies or to take advantage of exceptional bargains that come along.

COST OF HOLDING MONEY

Although most people prefer to hold a part of their assets in the form of money, no one would want to hold all of his or her assets in this form. If an individual did, the person would not have any clothes to wear, no personal belongings, house, car, and so on. It soon becomes evident that holding all of one's wealth in the form of money is not desirable. Thus, all people must decide what part of their wealth, or income equivalent, they will hold as money and what part they will hold as so-called earning assets, such as securities (stocks and bonds), or directly usable items, such as house, car, appliances, and personal belongings. In making this decision, a person must balance the benefits of holding money (convenience and security) against the cost of holding money. An individual will choose to hold a greater proportion of his or her wealth in the form of money only if the added return outweighs the cost. In the previous section, we considered the benefits of holding assets in the form of money; in this section, we consider the cost.

Offhand one might say that the cost of holding money is negligible because banks are willing to guard money for free and, in the case of savings accounts, even pay people for the privilege of providing the storage service. But the cost of holding assets in the form of money is not the storage cost. Rather it is the *opportunity cost*—what the money could earn if it were converted into so-called earning assets, such as stocks and bonds, real estate, machines, or the value of the services obtained from consumer durables and other personal belongings. The returns from stocks and bonds can be easily measured in terms of dividends and interest. The returns become somewhat more difficult to measure for physical assets, such as real estate and machines, although most owners of such assets probably have some idea of the rate of return on their investment. It is still more difficult to measure the returns on consumer durables and personal belongings, such as house, appliances, car, clothes, and shoes. Although most people probably do not bother to convert the value of the services provided by consumer durables or personal belongings into a monetary value, they still are likely to have a fairly good idea of how useful such assets are in providing services. For example, we may infer that the transportation service provided by the car is more valuable to car owners than the convenience and security provided by the same amount of money; otherwise, they would not have decided to own the car as opposed to holding money.

Because of the difficulty of measuring the value of the services provided by real assets, the cost of holding money has commonly been approximated by the interest return on securities, such as stocks and bonds. The higher the interest return on securities, the higher is the cost of holding money. If one includes savings accounts as part of money (the broad definition), this part of a person's monetary assets also earns interest. Hence, the net cost of holding money in this form is the difference (if any) between the interest (or dividend) return on securities and the interest earned by money in a savings account.

The existence of inflation also has a bearing on the cost of holding money. As explained in Chapter 6, inflation depreciates the value of money. Hence, inflation makes it more costly to hold money in relation to other assets that increase in value with the price level, such as real estate. During inflation, the nominal rate of interest on securities is likely to rise, so part of the cost of inflation is already taken into account by the higher interest rate. However, usury laws and the uncertainties over what the actual rate of inflation will turn out to be during any given year may keep the interest rate from increasing by the full extent of the rate of inflation, at least in its early stages.

THE PROPORTION OF INCOME HELD AS MONEY

Every person who earns an income or owns some assets must continually weigh the benefits of holding money against the cost of holding money. If the benefits outweigh the costs, it behooves a person to convert a bit more of his or her assets to money and a little less to nonmonetary forms. Moreover, each payday a decision must be made regarding how much of a person's paycheck will remain in the form of money and how much will be converted to other assets. Some assets, such as groceries, gasoline, and movie tickets, are used up in a relatively short time, while others, such as car, clothes, real estate, and stocks and bonds, may be around for years or even a lifetime.

A useful number to compute is the equivalent proportion of annual income held as money. For example, if you earn a $20,000-per-year income and you own $10,000 of money ($M_2$), then you hold the equivalent of half of your annual income as money. It turns out that in deriving the quantity equation of exchange we in effect computed the reciprocal of the proportion of annual income held as money. Recall that the quantity equation of exchange is:

$$M \times V = P \times Q$$

If we divide both sides of this equation by V, we obtain:

$$M = \frac{1}{V} \times P \times Q$$

A commonly used symbol for $(1/V)$ is K. Substituting K for $(1/V)$, we have:

$$M = K \times P \times Q$$

Notice that K is the equivalent proportion of income held as money. For example, if $P \times Q$ for the country is $2,000 billion and M is $1,000 billion, then K is 0.5, or half. This says people are holding the equivalent of half of their annual income as money. Notice also that V is equal to 2 in this example. The K value also can be computed for an individual. What proportion of your annual gross (before-tax) income do you hold in the form of money on the average? For the nation as a whole, it is about 0.67 when using the broad definition of money (M_2). If we can determine what causes people to change the proportion of income held as money, then we have at the same time identified the factors that can change the velocity of money, because velocity is just the reciprocal of K.

FACTORS AFFECTING THE PROPORTION OF INCOME HELD AS MONEY

As stated earlier, people hold money because of the benefits of holding money. They do not as a rule hold all of their assets as money, however, because of the cost of holding money, namely the income or services that must be given up by not owning so-called earning or nonmonetary assets. It seems reasonable, therefore, that if the cost of holding money changes in relation to the benefits derived from holding money, then people may change the proportion of their income held as money—the K value. Two major factors are considered important in explaining why people may change the proportion of their income held as money.

1. Interest Rate Changes. As mentioned, the cost of holding money is approximated by the interest return on earning assets, such as stocks and bonds. If the interest (or dividend) return on stocks and bonds increases, for example, then the cost of holding assets in the form of money will increase. In other words, by holding money, a person will be giving up more income from nonmonetary assets when their interest return is high than when the return is low. If the cost of holding money goes up because of an increase in the interest return on earning assets, then people may decide to hold a smaller proportion of their income as money. This means that K would decrease and V increase.

Just how responsive people are to interest rate changes in deciding how much money they desire to hold is an unsettled issue among economists. Some economists argue that people do not change the amount of money they desire to hold very much when the interest rate changes, whereas others believe people are relatively responsive to this factor. This issue turns out to be rather important because if people are not responsive to interest rate changes, then changes in the money supply that may cause interest rates to change will not have much effect on K or V. This means that the quantity equation of exchange will be an accurate predictor of what happens to $P \times Q$ when there are changes in M. We will come back to this point in Chapter 19 on monetary policy.

2. Changes in Expectations of Future Unemployment and Inflation. No one knows the future with certainty, but most people probably have some expectation of what the future may bring at least in regard to unemployment, and inflation. For example, if people expect an increase in unemployment, it is reasonable to believe that at least some will attempt to build up their monetary holdings in order to have something in reserve when times become hard. This in turn means that an expectation of higher unemployment in the future should cause K to increase and V to decrease. The opposite may occur if people come to expect a higher rate of inflation in the future. As explained in Chapter 6, money is not a desirable asset to own during inflation because inflation reduces the purchasing power of money. We might expect, therefore, that people will try to reduce the proportion of income held as money during a time when inflation threatens. As a result, K would decrease and V increase.

The preceding discussion is summarized in the following table:

Conditions	V	K
Increase in interest rate	Increase	Decrease
Expected increase in unemployment	Decrease	Increase
Expected increase in inflation	Increase	Decrease

It is interesting to note that the expectation of an increase in unemployment rates, which may cause a *decrease* in V, by itself is enough to cause an *increase* in actual unemployment. If M is constant, $P \times Q$ must decline if V declines. In the case of an expectation of inflation, the resulting *increase* in V is enough to cause an *increase* in $P \times Q$, with most of the increase coming in P if the nation is at or near full employment. These changes in expectations cause even more severe unemployment or inflation problems than would be caused by a change in M alone, say through government policy. For example, when M declined during the Great Depression, $P \times Q$ declined by an even greater proportion because of the expectation of higher unemployment and the resulting decrease in V. Similarly, during high rates of inflation, the price level generally increases more than the increase in M because of the increase in V. However, during the 1970s, there was no significant upward trend of V in the United States despite inflation. In 1983, there was a slight decrease in the U.S. velocity. This is consistent with the new quantity theory; as people became more concerned about unemployment, they attempted to increase their monetary assets, leading to a decrease in V and an increase in K. In countries that have experienced really high rates of inflation, say 100 to 500 percent per year, it has been common to observe an increase in V, which pushes prices up more than in proportion to the increase in M, at least in the early stages of inflation.

HOW MONEY AFFECTS THE ECONOMY IN THE CONTEXT OF THE NEW QUANTITY THEORY

From our knowledge of the quantity equation of exchange, it is evident that a change in M must change $P \times Q$ in the same direction, providing V does not change in the opposite direction; this is a mathematical necessity. It is important also to understand the economic logic underlying this phenomenon.

Suppose we begin at an equilibrium position where people are holding the amount of money they desire to hold. For example, if people desire to hold half of their annual income in the form of money ($K = 0.5$) and the actual amount of M in existence is $1,000 billion, then income, or $P \times Q$, will be $2,000 billion.

Now let us suppose that the government for one reason or another increases the actual quantity of money by $100 billion. Remember that every dollar in existence must always be held or owned by somebody. If income is $2,000 billion and people continue to desire to hold the equivalent of half of their annual income in the form of money, it follows that because of the $100 billion increase in the quantity of money, some people must be holding more money than they desire to hold at this level of income. In other words, the increase in the quantity of money causes an imbalance between the *desired* holdings of money and the *actual* amount of money in existence.

What can people do to make the desired K equal to actual K? One thing they can do is to try to convert this "excess" money into securities, such as stocks and bonds. The increased demand for stocks and bonds will cause an increase in their prices, but the increase in the prices of stocks and bonds will cause a decrease in their interest rate. The relationship between the price of a security and its interest return is easiest to see for a bond. A bond that carries a face value of, say, $100 while stipulating a 10 percent rate of interest return always pays $10 per year to the owner regardless of the actual selling price of the bond. (Bonds can sell for a premium over the face value or at a discount below the face value.) If the market price of the bond is bid up to $200, then its interest return is reduced to 5 percent ($10/$200).

However, before securities prices and interest rates change very much, it is expected that people will buy other assets, such as real estate, automobiles, appliances, gold, education, medical care, and travel experiences. As the interest return on securities declines, these other assets become more attractive. Therefore, it does not take much of a decrease in the interest return on securities for people to start to increase their purchases of other assets.

Notice, however, that the increased rate of purchases of the other assets mentioned previously increases $P \times Q$ for the economy. In other words, as people come into the market to buy additional goods and services, the prices and/or quantities of these items increase, thereby increasing $P \times Q$. If people still desire to hold the equivalent of half of their annual income in the form of money, then $P \times Q$ will increase until people are able to reestablish their equilibrium. In the example given, $P \times Q$ would increase to $2,200 billion because of the increase in M to $1,100 billion, thereby reestablishing their desired K of 0.5. It is not possible to say how much of the increase in $P \times Q$ comes in the form of increased prices and how much in the form of larger real output (Q). If the economy is at or near full employment, most of the increase will be in P. If there is unemployment or idle resources, both P and Q probably will increase, but there is no way of telling how much each will change. The only thing we can say for sure is that $P \times Q$ will increase by $200 billion up to the $2,200 billion level. The preceding discussion can be summarized by the following chain of causation:

Increase $M \rightarrow$ Increase in actual K over desired $K \rightarrow$ Increase in demand for and price of securities $\rightarrow$ Decrease in interest rate $\rightarrow$ Increase in purchase of other assets $\rightarrow$ Increase in $P \times Q \rightarrow$ Return to equilibrium of actual K with desired K

The opposite results occur when M is decreased. You might try to reason out this process on your own.

It is possible for people to change their desired level of K. In this case, $P \times Q$ can change without a change in M. For example, if people expect an increase in unemployment, they may try to increase their holdings of money in order to have something in reserve. However, if the government does not increase the actual amount of money in the economy, all people cannot increase their holdings of money. If one person succeeds in holding more money, someone else must end up holding less. What happens in this case is that $P \times Q$ decreases as people reduce their rate of purchases of goods and services in an attempt to increase their monetary assets. Eventually $P \times Q$ decreases enough to increase the actual K up to the higher desired K level. As mentioned in the preceding section, such a phenomenon is most likely to occur when M itself is reduced, as in the Great Depression. Conversely, K is most likely to decrease (V increase) during extreme inflationary times as people try to get rid of money due to its decrease in value. However, in this case, if one person succeeds in converting money to non-monetary assets, someone else ends up holding more money. But people still can decrease K by spending money more rapidly (increase V), thereby increasing $P \times Q$. Therefore, a change in M is most likely to result in a change in K in the opposite direction, thereby accentuating the unemployment or inflation problem brought on by the initial change in M. Or one could say that a change in M is most likely to cause a change in V of the same direction, thereby accentuating the impact of the initial change in M. The relationship between changes in M and changes in the desired K is summarized below:

Increase $M \rightarrow$ Increase inflation $\rightarrow$ Increase in cost of holding
money $\rightarrow$ Decrease in desired $K \rightarrow$ Increase in $P \times Q \rightarrow$ Still more inflation

Decrease $M \rightarrow$ Increase unemployment $\rightarrow$ Increase in desired
$K \rightarrow$ Decrease in $P \times Q \rightarrow$ Still more unemployment

SUMMARY

Paper is a desirable form of money because it is inexpensive to produce, reasonably durable, and easy to carry. Money is used as (1) a medium of exchange, (2) a standard of value, and (3) a store of value. Paper money has value because people accept it as having value. Although every society always will use money, there is a trend in developed countries toward cashless societies where money becomes numbers in people's accounts. The benefits of holding money are the convenience and security it affords. The cost of holding money is its opportunity cost. The quantity equation of exchange, $M \times V = P \times Q$, can be rewritten as $M = K \times P \times Q$ where K is $1/V$. K is the equivalent proportion of income held as money. The new quantity theory attempts to explain changes in V by changes in K. The main factors affecting K are changes in the interest rate and changes in expectations of future unemployment and inflation. An increase in M

brings forth an increase in $P \times Q$ because it causes actual K to exceed desired K. As people try to bring actual K down to desired K, they spend more, which increases $P \times Q$ and reestablishes equilibrium. The same process occurs if people change their desired K.

YOU SHOULD KNOW

1. What the desirable characteristics of money are.
2. What the three functions of money are.
3. What gives money purchasing power.
4. Why a cashless society would not be a moneyless society.
5. How the new quantity theory differs from the old quantity theory.
6. What the two major benefits of holding money are.
7. What the cost of holding money is.
8. How the proportion of income held as money, the K value, is related to velocity of money.
9. The two main factors that could change the proportion of income held as money.
10. How money affects the economy in the context of the new quantity theory.
11. What happens in the economy when the government increases (decreases) the quantity of money.
12. What happens in the economy when people increase (decrease) their desired K.
13. Why prices increase more than the increase in the quantity of money during the early stages of inflation.
14. Why $P \times Q$ decreases more than the decrease in the quantity of money during a depression.

QUESTIONS

1. If money did not exist:
   a. how would people pay for their purchases?
   b. how would prices be quoted?
   c. how would people save?

2. a. Why is a $20 bill, which is worth a fraction of a cent on the used-paper market, worth so much more as money?
   b. If people were free to print their own money on paper, would paper money have any value? Explain.

3. a. Why do people hold part of their wealth in the form of money?
   b. Why don't people hold all their wealth in the form of money?

4. a. How is the proportion of income held as money (the K value) related to the velocity of money?
   b. What factors may cause people to change the proportion of their income held as money?

5. According to the new quantity theory, why does an increase in M cause an increase in $P \times Q$?

6. According to the new quantity theory, how do people achieve an equilibrium if they happen to be holding more money than they desire to hold? Less than they desire to hold?

7. a. During extreme inflation, it has been observed that P increases more than the increase in M. Is this consistent with the new quantity theory? Explain.
   b. During the Great Depression, $P \times Q$ decreased in proportion to the decrease in M. Was this phenomenon consistent with the new quantity theory? Explain.

SELF-TEST

1. Which of the following have at one time in history been used as money?
   a. animals
   b. stones
   c. cigarettes
   d. all of the above

2. The use of paper as money _____ its cost to society and makes it _____ to carry around in comparison to gold.
   a. decreases; harder
   b. increases; easier
   c. decreases; easier
   d. increases; harder

3. The use of money as a medium of exchange eliminates the need for _____ and facilitates exchange transactions.
   a. barter
   b. prices
   c. saving
   d. a central bank

4. The use of money as a standard of value _____ the number of prices in the economy.
   a. increases
   b. decreases
   c. decreases to zero
   d. decreases to one

5. The use of money as a store of value reduces the cost of _____ .
   a. spending
   b. producing
   c. pricing
   d. saving

6. Paper money has value because:
   a. the government says it does.
   b. people accept it as having value.
   c. it is backed dollar for dollar by gold or silver.
   d. the ink is very expensive.

7. The use of credit cards and electronic transfer of funds between accounts in financial institutions implies a movement toward a _____ society.
   a. moneyless
   b. cashless
   c. paperless
   d. goldless

8. As opposed to the original quantity theory put forth by the classical economists, the new quantity theory is an attempt to explain and predict changes in _____ .
   a. money
   b. real output
   c. velocity
   d. prices

9. The benefits of holding money are:
   a. profit and loss.
   b. cost and returns.
   c. convenience and security.
   d. income and wealth.

10. The cost of holding money is:
    a. interest received on money market funds.
    b. service charge on checking accounts.
    c. opportunity cost of not owning non-monetary assets.
    d. safety deposit box rental.

11. Because of the difficulty of measuring the monetary return from personal assets such as house and car, the opportunity cost of holding money is approximated by:
    a. the interest return on stocks and bonds.
    b. the interest paid on personal loans.
    c. automobile rental.
    d. house rents.

12. Dividing both sides of the quantity equation of exchange by V equals _____ where K is _____ .
    a. $M = 1/K \times P \times Q; V$
    b. $K = M \times P \times Q; 1/V$
    c. $M = K \times P \times Q; 1/V$
    d. $K = M \times P \times Q; V$

13. In the equation for the correct answer to question 12 above, K is:
    a. the same as velocity.
    b. the equivalent proportion of annual income held as money.
    c. the equivalent proportion of total assets held as money.

d. the equivalent proportion of annual income held as total assets—monetary and nonmonetary.

14. The new quantity theory, by attempting to explain and predict changes in K, attempts to explain changes in ___ because V and K move in ___ direction(s).
    a. V; the same
    b. M; the same
    c. V; opposite
    d. M; opposite

15. Higher rates of interest earned on stocks and bonds (securities) ___ the opportunity cost of holding money, which in turn causes K to ___ and V to ___ .
    a. increase; decrease; increase
    b. increase; increase; decrease
    c. decrease; decrease; increase
    d. decrease; increase; decrease

16. If people expect unemployment to increase, they can be expected to attempt to ___ their monetary assets, which in turn will cause K to ___ and V to ___ .
    a. decrease; increase; decrease
    b. decrease; decrease; increase
    c. increase; increase; decrease
    d. increase; decrease; increase

17. If people expect inflation to increase in the near future, they can be expected to ___ their monetary assets, which in turn will cause K to ___ and V to ___ .
    a. decrease; increase; decrease
    b. decrease; decrease; increase
    c. increase; increase; decrease
    d. increase; decrease; increase

18. According to the new quantity theory, an increase in M causes actual K to be ___ than desired K, assuming people were in equilibrium before the increase. In an attempt to return to equilibrium, people spend ___ causing $P \times Q$ to ___ .
    a. less; less; decrease
    b. less; more; increase
    c. greater; less; decrease
    d. greater; more; increase

19. According to the new quantity theory, the expectation of higher rates of prolonged unemployment in the future causes actual K to be ___ than desired K. In an attempt to return to equilibrium, people spend ___ causing $P \times Q$ to ___ .
    a. less; less; decrease
    b. less; more; increase
    c. greater; less; decrease
    d. greater; more; increase

Chapter 18

Commercial Banking and the Federal Reserve System

OVERVIEW

We now turn our attention from money to the industry most directly involved with this commodity: the banking system. In this chapter, we will present a brief description of the banking system in the United States, including both commercial banks and the Federal Reserve System. Particular attention is given to the transactions that take place in commercial banks. We will see how one of these transactions results in the creation of money. In studying bank transactions, it is necessary to utilize the balance sheet. So before undertaking a study of banking, let us review this important accounting tool.

THE BALANCE SHEET

A balance sheet itemizes the assets, liabilities, and net worth of a person, firm, or institution as of a particular point in time. *Assets* are defined as anything of value. A person's assets typically include clothes, car, real estate, appliances, cash, stocks, and bonds. A business firm's assets include mainly the real estate and capital equipment the firm has under its control, together with its monetary assets, such as cash and bank deposits. A commercial bank's assets include many of the same items found in an ordinary business firm. There are some special items among a bank's assets, however, that will come to our attention later.

We should be aware, though, that the asset value of a particular item does not tell us anything about who has ultimate claim on the item. For example, if you "own" a $4,000 automobile but have $2,000 yet to pay on it, you have a $2,000 claim on the auto and the lender has a $2,000 claim. The balance sheet would carry the auto as a $4,000 asset regardless of how much you still owed on it. For this reason, it is necessary to know the amount of liabilities and net worth also.

The *liability* figures in a balance sheet indicate the amount owed to creditors. Sometimes the balance sheet will separate short-term from long-term liabilities to indicate how soon the debts have to be paid. For our purposes, it will be sufficient to know just that liabilities are debts that will have to be paid sometime in the future. *Net worth* represents the assets owned free and clear by the individuals controlling the assets. Essentially, we can view liabilities as the creditors' claim to the assets in a balance sheet and net worth as the owners' claim to these assets.

As its name implies, the balance sheet must always balance; that is, the total value of assets must always equal the total claim on these assets. We are assured that assets always equal liabilities plus net worth because the net worth figure is obtained as a residual by subtracting liabilities from assets. These relationships are summarized below:

$$Assets = Liabilities + Net\ worth$$
$$Net\ worth = Assets - Liabilities$$

A convenient method of presenting the balance sheet is in the form of a T-account. With this format, assets are listed on the left side of the vertical line and liabilities and net worth on the right side. The following example illustrates the format of a T-account balance sheet and some typical entries for a college student. Notice that the balance sheet is drawn up at a particular point in time. Typically, business firms or institutions compute their balances at the end of the calendar year or fiscal year. The asset figures should reflect the current market value of the items listed, $6,000 in this example. The unpaid balances of two loans outstanding represent the liabilities of the student, $2,000 in this example. The $4,000 net worth figure is found by subtracting the $2,000 in liabilities from the $6,000 assets total.

Balance Sheet of a College Student as of a Point in Time

Assets		*Liabilities + Net Worth*	
Automobile	4,000	Bank loan	1,200
Computer	400	Loan from parents	800
Clothes	1,600	Net worth	4,000
	6,000		6,000

We will return to the balance sheet in the discussion of commercial bank transactions.

EVOLUTION OF BANKING

To the average person, banking is a rather mysterious business. Other than bank employees, relatively few people have an opportunity to see firsthand how banks operate. In the remainder of this chapter, we will take a figurative look behind the teller's window in order to better understand banking operations. It will be helpful to begin the discussion with the earliest and simplest kind of banker—the ancient goldsmith. By so doing, we will be able to see more clearly why banks came into existence and obtain a better understanding of what banks do. Understandably, banking was a good deal simpler in those early days. In this section we will use present-day terminology, recognizing that names and words that describe banking activities are different now than in ancient times.

During the early period of civilization, gold and silver were the predominant forms of money. Those who were fortunate enough to accumulate a sizable amount of these metals were confronted with the problem of keeping it safe from those who were bent on redistributing the wealth of the land—that is, thieves and robbers. It should not be surprising then that the ancient goldsmith emerged as the person best able to store money for safekeeping. Since the basic raw material used in his business had to be closely guarded anyway, the goldsmith no doubt found it profitable to take in other people's gold for safekeeping in return for a fee. Of course, at the time of deposit, the customer had to be given a receipt indicating the date and amount of deposit. Understandably, this receipt had to be presented when the depositor wished to reclaim the gold.

In providing a storage service, the goldsmith's place of business became, in effect, a warehouse for gold. It also became the forerunner of the modern bank. The goldsmith accepted deposits of money and paid them out again on demand. This describes in large part the activities of a modern bank. However, present-day banks also make loans. Let us see how this activity might have emerged.

It probably did not take long for the more perceptive goldsmiths to discover that during any one day the gold withdrawn was in large part offset by the gold deposited. During some days, withdrawals may have exceeded deposits by a small amount, or vice versa, but on any given day, the goldsmith was not likely to have all his gold withdrawn, unless his reputation suddenly became suspect. We know, too, that gold is a completely homogeneous commodity: that is, an ounce of gold is the same no matter who deposits it. Hence, the actual gold that was withdrawn during any one day probably was the same gold that had come in through deposits on that very day or the day before. Because gold is homogeneous, there was no need for the goldsmith to dig to the bottom or to the back of his vault to locate gold deposited months or years before. At any rate, the perceptive goldsmith undoubtedly noticed that a relatively large share of his gold deposits was lying in the vault gathering dust.

Let us say, for example, that only about 20 percent of his gold was actively used to pay withdrawals on days when deposits were unusually low. For all practical purposes, the remaining 80 percent of the gold was never used. In fact, it no doubt was considered a hindrance, since it required more space and provided a greater temptation for would-be robbers.

There always have been people in need of loans for various purposes. Without people or institutions that specialized in making loans, borrowers had to prevail upon friends or relatives. For the poor who had only poor friends or relatives, there was little chance of obtaining credit. It took people awhile to get used to the idea of paying interest, however. And without interest to compensate for waiting and for the risk involved, there is not much incentive to lend money.

Once the payment of interest, in one form or another, became socially acceptable, the goldsmiths discovered a grand opportunity to benefit both themselves and their customers. By lending out some of the unused gold, they provided a source of credit for people who wanted to make a fairly large purchase, such as a business, a cart, or an animal. These people were helped because the loans enabled them to purchase resources that increased their earning power and standard of living, just as is true today. The goldsmith benefited because of the interest income he earned from the loans. Finally, his depositors benefited because they could now be paid for depositing gold rather than having to pay for the storage service.

So far we have followed the evolution of banking through two steps. First, institutions evolved to satisfy the demand for storage services by people who had accumulated money. Second, these institutions, goldsmiths in the main, discovered that daily deposits and withdrawals normally came close to canceling each other out. Thus, goldsmiths could lend out part of their deposits, keeping only a part on reserve. Today we refer to this procedure as *fractional reserve banking*.

An additional step toward banking as we know it today was taken when depositors began to use their deposit receipts as money. It is fairly easy to see how this practice came into being. Visualize yourself as living in that time with, say, $500 of gold on deposit at the local goldsmith. Suppose you decided to trade in your old chariot for the latest model. Suppose also that the new chariot cost you $500 in gold plus your trade-in. You could, of course, make a trip to the goldsmith to draw out your $500 in gold. But the chariot dealer would just have to return to the goldsmith the same day with the same gold for redeposit. Both you and the chariot dealer could save a trip to the goldsmith if you just endorsed your deposit receipt over to the chariot dealer, instructing the goldsmith to pay him the $500 on demand.

The practice of exchanging deposit receipts instead of gold resembles a well-known practice in use today—namely, that of exchanging checks instead of the actual currency on deposit in banks. Thus, the deposit receipt was the forerunner of the present-day check. Of course, the check is a bit more convenient because it can be made out in any denomination. Eventually, people realized this, and deposit receipts were made more flexible. With more widespread use, deposit receipts, or checks, became a widely accepted form of money.

So far we have taken the goldsmith analogy to the point where it is just one step removed from the modern bank. The evolutionary process became complete when goldsmiths began to give out deposit receipts instead of gold when making loans. It is easy to visualize how this practice got started. Consider a person who wished to make a $500 purchase but had to borrow this amount. When the loan was obtained, one option would be for the borrower to hand the gold back to the goldsmith and receive a deposit receipt. After all, we would not expect the borrower to risk carrying the gold around any more than the people who originally deposited it. It would be simpler for the goldsmith to issue the borrower a $500 deposit receipt that in turn could be used to make a purchase. Eventually this was done. These deposit receipts that were given out to borrowers were as good as gold for making purchases.

We have now taken the goldsmith to the point where he was doing essentially the same things as the modern commercial bank does. First, he took in deposits; second, he made loans; and third, he issued and honored deposit receipts that in effect became money. Let us now take a brief look at the commercial banking system as it exists today in the United States.

COMMERCIAL BANKS

Commercial banks engage in three primary activities: (1) they take money for safekeeping, (2) they offer checking account services, and (3) they make loans. As we will see later, the latter characteristic in conjunction with the fractional reserve requirement has an important bearing on the money supply.

Banks that received their charter from the federal government are called national banks, and those operating under a state charter are known as state banks. All of the national banks are required to hold membership in the Federal Reserve System; that is, they must buy stock in the system. Each state bank is free to choose whether or not it wishes to be a member of the Federal Reserve System.

All member banks are required to hold a certain fraction of their deposit liabilities on reserve as cash in their vaults or on reserve in the Federal Reserve bank in their district. This fraction, called the *reserve ratio*, varies between demand and time deposits and by size of deposit. The Federal Reserve Board of Governors has the authority to change these reserve ratios over a fairly broad range, although this power is seldom used. Nonmember state banks also must maintain reserves against their deposits. These reserves are kept in the reserve city banks, which are large banks located in the financial districts of major cities. In a sense, these large reserve city banks act as Federal Reserve banks for the smaller "country" banks.

It is probably assumed by many people that legal reserve requirements were set up to protect depositors. No doubt they have this effect, but an equally valid reason for having legal reserve requirements is to provide a means for the Federal Reserve system to have some control over the maximum amount of bank loans and thus over the maximum quantity of money in the economy.

Before discussing commercial bank transactions, it is necessary to have some understanding of the Federal Reserve System. We will see that some commercial banks' transactions directly affect one or more Federal Reserve banks.

THE FEDERAL RESERVE SYSTEM

Between 1776 and the early 1900s, banking in the United States was a highly decentralized and relatively unregulated industry. While the banking industry was a source of considerable controversy over this period and attracted its share of unscrupulous people, commercial banks should receive at least part of the credit for the tremendous growth and development that the United States experienced during its first 150 years. Banking institutions evolved and changed to meet the needs of the people not only in the new lands that were settled but also in the new industries that came into being during this time. This is not to say that the United States experienced smooth, uninterrupted growth during its first century and a half of existence. Indeed, as history books record, many "panics" or recessions occurred along the way. When the country was largely agricultural, crop failures, bumper harvests, and the normal cyclic behavior of the livestock industry introduced an element of instability in the economy. Of course, other nonagricultural industries also experienced periods of rapid growth and decline, which introduced another element of instability.

Although banks should not be held responsible for the normal growth and decline of industries, it became evident that they did not help maintain a stable economy and may have contributed to the instability. For example, during expansionary periods, banks faced a strong demand for their loans, and banks obliged by increasing loans. But as we will see shortly, this action increased the money supply, which augmented the boom and ensuing inflation. On the other hand, during recessionary periods, banks, along with businesspeople, became pessimistic about the future and reduced their loans outstanding. This in turn reduced the money supply, which contributed to a still further reduction in economic activity.

During certain periods within the year, the banking community also experienced shortages and surpluses of money. For example, during the Christmas shopping season, the volume of business activity rises substantially and more money is needed to carry out these transactions. Unless there is a corresponding increase in money supply, money becomes "scarce" and interest rates rise. As a result, there may be an unnecessary curtailment of economic activity. Similarly, during slack periods of the year, mainly during the first quarter, the supply of money that would fulfill the demand without a rise in interest rates during the peak season would be too large, resulting in unnecessary instability in the money market.

Because of these seasonal fluctuations in the demand for money, it became clear that the country needed an agency that could provide an "elastic" currency, that is, a money supply that could expand and contract with the seasonal fluctuations in the economy. Thus, the need for a central bank became evident because of the "perverse elasticity" of money that accentuated booms and recessions and also because of the need for a greater elasticity of the money supply during peak and slack periods within the year.

Between 1873 and 1907, the United States experienced five serious panics with many bank closings. Following the 1907 panic, Congress brought forth the Federal Reserve Act, which was signed by President Woodrow Wilson on December 13, 1913. This act created the Federal Reserve System. Understandably, there was a great deal of reluctance on the part of bankers to create a strong, centralized banking authority located in Washington. Yet the inadequacy of a completely decentralized banking system was recognized. As a result, the Federal Reserve System was set up as somewhat of a compromise between a more centralized government bank, such as the Bank of England or Bank of France, and a totally private banking system.[1]

To maintain some form of decentralization, the country was divided into 12 Federal Reserve districts, each having a Federal Reserve bank. Several of the Federal Reserve banks have one or more branches located in other cities of the district. The Federal Reserve System is supervised by a seven-member Board of Governors located in Washington, D.C. The Board of Governors is assisted by a Federal Advisory Council and a Federal Open Market Committee. As the name implies, the Advisory Council advises the Board of Governors on monetary policy. The Open Market Committee buys and sell securities, which, as we will see later in the chapter, affects the quantity of money in the economy.

Federal Reserve banks are sometimes called quasi-public banks because they are owned by member banks but controlled by the Board of Governors. The Board of Governors is really a government agency, because the members are appointed by the president of the United States.

Federal Reserve banks also have been called "banker's banks" because they perform essentially the same functions for commercial banks as commercial banks do for private individuals. You and I, for example, cannot walk into a Federal Reserve bank and make a deposit or negotiate a loan. But these services are available to commercial banks that are members of the Federal Reserve System. We will see later why a commercial bank might be in need of a loan. The U.S. Treasury also maintains a deposit in the Federal Reserve System, so in a sense the "Fed," as it is often called, serves as the bank for the federal government.

We can obtain a better idea of the economic characteristics of the Federal Reserve System by looking at the balance sheet for the entire system, shown below.

On the asset side, the largest item is securities. Mainly these are U.S. government bonds issued by the Treasury. The Open Market Committee is continually buying and selling securities, which we will see has an important bearing on the quantity of money in the economy. Gold certificates represent the stock of gold held by the U.S. government. The loans item represents short-term credit extended to commercial banks that are members of the Federal Reserve System for the purpose of bolstering their reserves.

---

[1] For a detailed description of the Federal Reserve System and its functions, see U.S. Board of Governors of the Federal Reserve System, *The Federal Reserve System: Its Purposes and Functions* (New York: AMS Press, 1976).

Consolidated Balance Sheet of the Federal Reserve System as of
December 31, 1989 ($ Billions)

Assets		Liabilities + Net worth	
Cash	0.5	Reserves of member banks	38.3
Gold certificates	11.1	Treasury deposits	6.2
Securities	228.4	Federal Reserve notes	241.7
Loans to banks	0.5	Other liabilities and	
Other assets	63.9	net worth	18.2
	304.4		304.4

Source: *Federal Reserve Bulletin*, March 1990, Table A-10.

On the right side of the balance sheet, the three items listed represent liabilities of the Federal Reserve. Commercial banks that are members of the Federal Reserve System are required to keep a certain fraction of their deposit liabilities on reserve, either in their respective Federal Reserve banks or as vault cash in their respective banks. Member bank reserves represent liabilities of the Federal Reserve System because these funds are held in trust for the commercial banks and may be relinquished at any time. Treasury deposits represent the checking account money the federal government has on deposit for the purpose of paying its bills. Federal Reserve notes, the largest single liability item, is the official name of the paper currency used today in the United States.

COMMERCIAL BANK TRANSACTIONS

In order to understand how the banking system can alter the quantity of money in the economy, it is first necessary to understand the nature of transactions that take place within the banking community. We already have caught a glimpse of the banking world in our discussion of the goldsmith at the beginning of the chapter. As we proceed, you will probably note a resemblance between the modern commercial bank and the ancient goldsmith. It will be easier to understand banking transactions if we start with the most basic—the deposit of cash by a customer—and then move on.

1. Deposit of $10,000 Cash by a Customer. Suppose, to make the example more meaningful, you decide to open a bank. After receiving your charter, you rent some facilities and obtain some of the basic equipment used by a bank, which among other things might include a vault and some conservative clothing. On your first day of operation, a local businessperson brings in $10,000 in cash and wishes to establish a checking account in your bank.

Our main interest at this point is how this transaction affects your balance sheet. The $10,000 in cash that has come under your control becomes an asset of your bank. In the following balance sheet, we refer to this cash deposit as total reserves. Of course, we know a balance sheet must balance, so at the same time there is a corresponding increase in the liabilities side. This is accomplished by increasing the demand deposit (checking account) item by $10,000. Bear in mind that demand deposits represent a liability to you because you may be required to pay this amount to your customer at any time. To simplify the arithmetic, assume the required reserve ratio is 0.20, or 20 percent, so that, along with the $10,000 increase in demand deposits, your required reserves increase by $2,000 (0.20 × $10,000). Thus, out of the $10,000 deposit of cash, $2,000 is taken up by required reserves and the remaining $8,000 becomes "excess reserves." (In the following balance sheets, we show only the changes that take place, in order to concentrate on the particular transaction at hand.)

Deposit of $10,000 in Cash by a Customer

Assets	Liabilities + Net Worth
Total reserves (cash) + 10,000	Demand deposits + 10,000
Required reserves +2,000	
Excess reserves +8,000	

Notice in this transaction that you have not yet created any money. The cash that has come into your bank is now removed from the money supply (only cash outside of banks is considered part of the quantity of money), but this has been offset by the increase in demand deposits. The quantity of money in the economy has changed in composition, from cash to demand deposits, but not in total amount.

2. Deposit of Required Reserves in Federal Reserve Bank.   Assume you are a member of the Federal Reserve System and decide to deposit the entire amount of required reserves in the Federal Reserve bank in your district. In this transaction, only the Federal Reserve balance sheet is affected, because your reserves remain the same. You still have $10,000 in total reserves: $2,000 in the Federal Reserve bank and $8,000 in your vault.

Federal Reserve Balance Sheet
Deposit of $2,000 Required Reserves
in the Federal Reserve Bank

Assets	Liabilities + Net Worth
Cash + 2,000	Member bank + 2,000
	reserves

3. A $1,000 Check Is Drawn on Your Bank.   It is reasonable to suppose that your depositor will begin to write checks against her account. Suppose she buys $1,000 worth of supplies and pays for the purchase by writing a check. Naturally, the supplier will soon after deposit this check in his account, which we will assume is in some other bank (call it Bank B). We will see that this transaction affects the balance sheets of three banks: your bank (call it Bank A), the Federal Reserve, and Bank B.

Your depositor will have her checking account balance reduced by the amount of the check. But how will you know she has written a check? The procedure followed is for Bank B to first add $1,000 to the supplier's checking account and offset this by adding $1,000 to the reserve entry in its balance sheet. Then the check goes to the Federal Reserve bank, which adds to or credits Bank B's reserves by $1,000 and subtracts from or debits your reserves (Bank A) by a like amount. This service that the Fed provides for its members is referred to as a "clearinghouse" function. The Federal Reserve bank then sends the canceled check back to you, which informs you that your depositor should have her checking account reduced by $1,000 and that your reserves in the Federal Reserve are reduced by the same amount. Last, you send the canceled check back to your depositor, so she knows her account has been reduced. The effects of the entire transaction of a $1,000 check drawn on Bank A is summarized by the balance sheets below:

Bank A

Assets		*Liabilities + Net Worth*	
Reserves	− 1,000	Demand deposits	− 1,000

Federal Reserve

Assets		*Liabilities + Net Worth*	
		Bank A reserves	− 1,000
		Bank B reserves	+ 1,000

Bank B

Assets		*Liabilities + Net Worth*	
Reserves	+ 1,000	Demand deposits	+ 1,000

Note that all three balance sheets continue to balance after the transaction is complete. It is always a good idea to represent commercial bank transactions by balance sheets because they provide a good check on one's accuracy. If the balance sheets do not balance after working through the transaction, you have made an error. Unfortunately, the converse is not true; erroneous balance sheets can still balance.

Assuming that the original $10,000 depositor is the only person who has put money into your bank, the $1,000 check has reduced your total demand deposits and reserves to $9,000. With a 20 percent reserve ratio, this means your required reserves drop slightly, to $1,800, and that your excess reserves are reduced to $7,200 ($9,000 − $1,800). It is reasonable to believe that before long your depositor also would bring checks into your bank that were drawn on other banks. These checks would replenish your reserves at the Fed and increase your bank's demand deposits.

So far we have not created any new money. The practice of writing checks just transfers demand deposits from one bank to another. In the above example, your bank lost $1,000 in demand deposits, but Bank B gained a like amount.

MONEY CREATION

Being a banker, you naturally are eager to make loans because the interest return on money lent out is a prime source of income for most banks. The first question is: How much can you loan out? Let us suppose that checks coming into your bank have offset checks going out. Thus, your balance sheet shows $10,000 in demand deposit liabilities and $10,000 in total reserves as illustrated in the top balance sheet that follows. The required reserve ratio of 0.20 tells you that 20 percent, or $2,000, of the $10,000 demand deposits must be kept on reserve either in your vault or at the Federal Reserve bank. Thus, the remaining 80 percent, the $8,000 excess reserve, represents the value of new loans that can be made to the public.

Consider next what happens when a likely prospect comes along in need of an $8,000 loan, say, to build an addition to his home. He signs a promissory note agreeing to pay you certain specified interest and payments on the principal. In return you set up a checking account for him. The moment you set up this checking account, you in effect create $8,000 in additional money. Demand deposits are money. Thus, banks create money by making loans.

So far, you have added $8,000 to the demand deposits item in your balance sheet. Now you have a total of $18,000 in demand deposits in your bank, backed up by $10,000 in reserves. This situation is depicted in the middle balance sheet below. But notice that at this point you still have excess reserves. Under the 0.20 reserve ratio you are required to have only $3,600 in reserves, but you still have $10,000. What happened? Did we make a mistake?

The answer is no, because as soon as this $8,000 loan is spent (checks are written against it) you must expect that these checks will be deposited in some other bank. And, as you recall from the check-writing transaction of the previous section, a check drawn against your bank reduces your reserves at the Fed by the amount of the check. Suppose, then, that the entire loan is spent by writing a single check, say, in payment to a contractor. If the contractor deposits this check in another bank, Bank B, the Fed reduces your reserves by $8,000 (you better be sure you have $8,000 at the Fed) and increases the reserves of Bank B. The end result of the loan process, as it affects your bank, is shown on the bottom balance sheet.

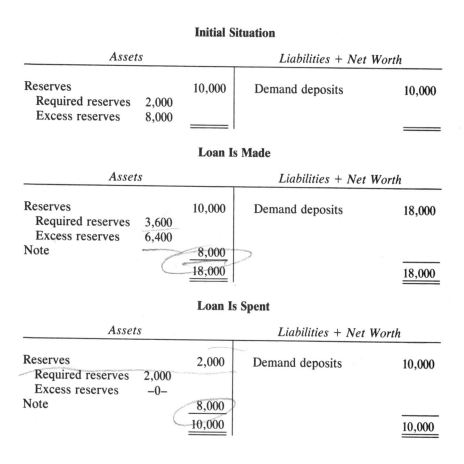

Initial Situation

Assets			*Liabilities + Net Worth*	
Reserves		10,000	Demand deposits	10,000
Required reserves	2,000			
Excess reserves	8,000			

Loan Is Made

Assets			*Liabilities + Net Worth*	
Reserves		10,000	Demand deposits	18,000
Required reserves	3,600			
Excess reserves	6,400			
Note		8,000		
		18,000		18,000

Loan Is Spent

Assets			*Liabilities + Net Worth*	
Reserves		2,000	Demand deposits	10,000
Required reserves	2,000			
Excess reserves	–0–			
Note		8,000		
		10,000		10,000

In this example, we assumed that the demand deposits were created at the time of the loan. We could have assumed instead that the borrower took the money in cash, say, 80 crisp $100 bills. You still would have created $8,000 in additional money, because cash inside banks is not considered part of the money supply whereas cash outside banks is a part of the money supply. Eventually, the contractor who received the $8,000 would take it to a bank for deposit, thus exchanging cash for demand deposits. So we end up at the same place regardless of whether we assume the loan goes out as a check or as cash.

MULTIPLE EXPANSION

The story of your loan does not end when the $8,000 check is cleared against your bank. Let us now go to Bank B, the contractor's bank. When the check has cleared, the Fed increases Bank B's reserves by $8,000 and at the same time Bank B's demand deposit item is increased by the same amount. But if Bank B receives $8,000 in new demand deposits and reserves, we know part of this $8,000 will be excess reserves. Operating under a reserve ratio of 0.20, 20 percent of the $8,000, or $1,600, represents required reserves. The remainder, $6,400 in this example, is excess reserves available to be loaned. Assume Bank B makes a $6,400 loan.

So far, in these first two rounds of the multiple expansion process, a total of $14,400 in new money has been created—$8,000 with your original loan and $6,400 with Bank B's loan. There is no reason the multiple expansion process has to stop here. We could carry it to Bank C and then round after round to infinity. But by now you probably see what is going on. When a check comes into a bank, the bank acquires some excess reserves, which enable it to increase its loans. Of course, the amount of the loan and the demand deposits created become smaller and smaller the further the process is carried. The multiple expansion is summarized in Table 18–1.

Notice the similarity between the multiple expansion process here and the multiplier discussed in Chapter 11. Rather than carrying the process out to infinity, which becomes a bit tedious before long, we can use a simple formula to determine the maximum amount the money supply could increase. Recall from Chapter 11 the following expression that gives the sum of an infinite convergent series.

$$1 + X + X^2 + X^3 + \cdots + X^n = \frac{1}{1 - X}$$

In this case, $X = 1 - R$ where R is the reserve ratio. Thus,

$$\frac{1}{1 - X} = \frac{1}{1 - (1 - R)}$$

But

$$\frac{1}{1 - (1 - R)} = \frac{1}{R}$$

because the ones cancel out.

Therefore, to find the ultimate expansion of the money supply stemming from an influx of new excess reserves, we multiply the original increase in excess reserves by (1/Reserve ratio). In the example, $R = 0.20$, so the "money multiplier" is (1/0.20) or 5. Thus, the sum of the right-hand column in Table 18–1 is equal to (1/0.20) × $8,000, or $40,000.

The multiple expansion process also can work in reverse; that is, a decrease in excess reserves can bring about a multiple contraction of the money supply. For example, suppose the borrower pays back the $8,000 loan. You decrease his checking account by $8,000 and give him the note. Now you have "destroyed"

TABLE 18–1   Summary of the Multiple Expansion Process

New Total Reserves	Excess Reserves, Loans Made, Dollars Created
Bank A, $10,000	$ 8,000 = 1 × $8,000
Bank B, 8,000	6,400 = 0.80 × 8,000
Bank C, 6,400	5,120 = (0.80)² × 8,000
.	.
.	.
.	.
To infinity	$40,000

$8,000. If you do not relend the $8,000, the total money supply in the country will decline by $(1/R) \times \$8,000$. This happens because Banks B, C, D, and so on, lose reserves as checks are drawn against them. In the process, they lose reserves and must contract their loans outstanding also. Lest you receive the impression, however, that the entire banking system revolves around your bank, remember that every commercial bank in the country has the same option of renewing or not renewing loans.

It is necessary to mention also that the full multiple expansion or contraction takes place only if the participating banks are "fully loaned up" at all times; that is, they keep no excess reserves. In reality, though, most banks try to retain some excess reserves rather than operating right at the margin. Generally, if banks face a strong demand for loans and high interest rates can be obtained, they tend to operate with less excess reserves than when the loan business is sluggish and interest rates are low. If a bank happens to find itself with less than the legal reserves, it can in an emergency borrow from the Federal Reserve bank in its district, although the Fed tends to discourage habitual borrowers.

The multiple expansion or contraction process is not likely to approach an infinite number of rounds. However, the major change in the money supply comes during the first few rounds. In the example above, the first three rounds alone created $19,520, or almost half the ultimate expansion. The multiplier of $(1/R)$ provides an upper bound to how much the money supply will expand or contract for a given change in excess reserves. At the same time it is important to recognize that in working through the multiple expansion process, we used a required reserve ratio of 0.20 purely to simplify the arithmetic. The actual ratio is much lower than this, particularly for time deposits. The time deposit reserve ratio of 3 percent, or 0.03, gives rise to a $33 maximum expansion in the money supply for each $1 increase in excess reserves. Hence, the actual money multiplier is likely to be considerably larger than the value of 5 we have been working with.

BOND PURCHASES

A commercial bank with excess reserves on its books may choose to purchase bonds rather than make direct loans to individuals or businesspeople. All banks like to diversify their portfolios and purchase a variety of earning assets with their excess reserves. Government bonds—federal, state, or municipal—are a popular investment for banks. The bonds may be purchased directly from the issuing agency or from a second party who happens to be holding them. Either way, the purchase of a bond by a bank has the same effect as making a loan—it creates money.

This will be easiest to see if we go back to our original example before your bank made the $8,000 loan. Instead, suppose you purchased $8,000 in bonds held by a bond dealer. Once you have the bonds, you give her an $8,000 check. In the process, you have created $8,000 in new money. As soon as the bond dealer deposits the $8,000 check in another bank, this bank receives an increase in its deposits and excess reserves, and off we go again on the same multiple expansion process. Thus, the purchase of bonds from an individual by a commercial bank increases the nation's money supply the same as if the bank made loans.

SUMMARY OF COMMERCIAL BANK TRANSACTIONS

In this chapter, three basic bank transactions have been discussed. These are summarized below, along with each one's effect on the nation's money supply.

Transaction	*Change Money Supply?*
Depositing currency	No
Writing checks	No
Making loans (or buying bonds)	Yes

AN IMPLICATION OF FRACTIONAL RESERVE BANKING

By now you probably realize that a bank does not hold in cold storage, so to speak, all the money that has been brought in for deposit. A certain fraction, the required reserves, must be held; but the remainder, or excess reserves, can be used to make loans or purchase bonds. As pointed out at the beginning of the chapter, a bank is able to operate with fractional reserves because on any one day deposits and withdrawals tend to cancel out.

There have been times, however, when depositors became fearful that their banks would close and they would lose their hard-earned cash. In the early 1930s, for example, when a rumor started in town that the bank was about to close, depositors rushed in to draw their money out. When this happened, it was inevitable that the bank would close because no bank retained all the money that had been deposited. Therefore, if a significant fraction of a bank's depositors wanted their money, the bank had no choice but to close its doors. If enough of a bank's depositors became convinced that a bank was going to fail, it failed.

After the financial crisis of the early 1930s, the Federal Deposit Insurance Corporation (FDIC) was set up. Now each depositor is insured up to $100,000, so there is no need for most people to fear losing their deposits. From time to time we still hear of people keeping their money in a mattress or some such hiding place because they distrust banks. No doubt a good share of this distrust was built during the Great Depression.

SUMMARY

The ancient goldsmith was the forerunner of the modern commercial bank. The practice of check writing began when deposit receipts were used to make purchases rather than the actual gold. Modern commercial banks engage in three major activities: (1) accepting deposits, (2) offering checking account services, and (3) making loans. No new money is created by the first two. Banks create money by making loans. Each bank must keep a fraction of its deposits on reserve. These are called *required reserves*. The remainder, called *excess reserves,* can be loaned out. Because every deposit creates excess reserves, a given increase in excess reserves results in a multiple expansion of the money supply equal to $1/R$ times that increase, where R is the required reserve ratio. Banks also create money by purchasing bonds. Because banks lend a large part of their deposits, they could not pay off all of their depositors on a given day.

YOU SHOULD KNOW

1. What a balance sheet is, and what each side represents.
2. Why assets always equals liabilities plus net worth.
3. Who the first bankers were.
4. Why part of the gold on deposit could be loaned out, and what this practice is called now.
5. The similarities between modern commercial banks and the ancient goldsmiths.
6. How national banks differ from state banks.
7. What the reserve ratio is.
8. Why the Federal Reserve System was established.

9. How to represent the deposit of cash and the writing of checks on a bank's balance sheet.

10. How banks create money.

11. How to represent the making of a loan on a bank's balance sheet.

12. What the money multiplier is, and how it is calculated.

13. Why a bond purchase by a bank is similar to making a loan.

14. The main implication of fractional reserve banking.

QUESTIONS

1. *a.* Construct a balance sheet for an individual from the following information: house, $100,000; car, $5,000; loan on house, $50,000; loan on car, $2,000; money in bank, $3,000; other assets, $6,000.
   b. Why should a balance sheet always balance?

2. *a.* How was it possible for the goldsmith to lend part of the gold on deposit?
   b. How did this practice benefit all parties concerned—that is, depositor, goldsmith, and borrower?

3. *a.* Why was it more convenient to use deposit receipts than gold to pay for purchases?
   b. What modern commercial instrument took the place of the early deposit receipt as a medium of exchange?

4. Why was the Federal Reserve System established?

5. *a.* Using a balance sheet, show what happens when an individual deposits $100 in his or her checking account at a commercial bank.
   b. How much of this $100 could the bank lend out if the reserve ratio were 0.15?

6. *a.* Using balance sheets, show what happens when an individual writes a $100 check on his or her account. Include the deposit of the check in the recipient's account.
   b. Is any money created in the above transactions? Explain.

7. *a.* Construct a balance sheet for a commercial bank showing that it has $10 million in deposit liabilities and $10 million in total reserves.
   b. How much could the bank lend out if the required reserve ratio were 0.20?
   c. If the bank makes the loan stipulated in part *b* above, how much, if any, new money is created? Explain.
   d. How much new money could be created by the banking system from the original excess reserves if all banks are fully loaned up?

SELF-TEST

1. In a balance sheet, which of the following is true?
   a. Assets = Liabilities + Net worth.
   b. Net worth = Assets + Liabilities.
   c. Liabilities = Assets + Net worth.
   d. all of the above.

2. Balance sheets always balance because _____ is calculated as a residual.
   a. assets
   b. liabilities
   c. net worth
   d. liabilities + net worth

3. The ancient goldsmiths discovered that part of the gold entrusted to their safe-keeping could be loaned out because:
   a. people never came back to draw out their gold.
   b. on most days, deposits tended to equal withdrawals.
   c. an ounce of gold is an ounce of gold, that is, it is a homogeneous commodity
   d. b and c

4. The practice of lending out part of the gold (money) on deposit is now called:
   a. fractional reserve banking.
   b. counterfeiting.
   c. usury.
   d. monetizing the debt.

5. When people began to exchange deposit receipts rather than gold, it began a practice known today as _____ .
   a. counterfeiting
   b. fraud
   c. fractional reserve banking
   d. check writing

6. As opposed to state banks, national banks:
   a. must maintain 100 percent reserves against deposits.
   b. must own stock in and be a member of the Federal Reserve System.
   c. do not have to maintain reserves against deposits.
   d. must keep a higher proportion of their deposits on reserve.

7. Commercial banks are required to keep a certain proportion of their deposits on reserve in:
   a. their own vaults.
   b. the Federal Reserve System.
   c. reserve city banks (for smaller state banks).
   d. all of the above.

8. The Federal Reserve System was established in _____ to:
   a. 1913; reduce fluctuations in the nation's money supply.
   b. 1913; provide for an elastic currency.
   c. 1930; to insure bank deposits.
   d. a and b.

9. The largest single asset of the Federal Reserve System is:
   a. securities.
   b. Federal Reserve notes (paper money).
   c. loans to member banks.
   d. gold certificates.

10. The largest single liability of the Federal Reserve System is:
    a. securities.
    b. Federal Reserve notes (paper money).
    c. loans to member banks.
    d. gold certificates.

11. The deposit of $1,000 cash in a checking account by a customer of a commercial bank increases demand deposits by _____ , total reserves by _____ , and required reserves by _____ . (Assume the required reserve ratio is 0.20.)
    a. $1,000; $1,000; $200
    b. $200; $1,000; $200
    c. $800; $1,000; $200
    d. $200; $800; $1,000

12. When a person with a checking account in Bank A writes a $100 check on his or her account and gives the check to someone who has an account in Bank B, Bank A's reserve account in the Federal Reserve is _____ by _____ while Bank B's account is _____ by _____ .
    a. increased; $80; decreased; $80
    b. decreased; $80; increased; $80
    c. increased; $100; decreased; $100
    d. decreased; $100; increased; $100

13. A commercial bank can lend its:
    a. total reserves.
    b. excess reserves.
    c. required reserves.
    d. demand deposits.

14. When a bank makes a $1,000 loan and the borrower receives the money in the form of additional deposits in his or her checking account, the bank's _____

item on the asset side of the balance sheet increases by _____ and the bank's _____ item on the liabilities side increases by _____ .

a. demand deposit; $1,000; promissory note; $1,000
b. promissory note; $1,000; demand deposit; $1,000
c. demand deposit; $800; promissory note; $800
—d. promissory note; $800; demand deposit; $800

15. Commercial banks create money by:
   a. counterfeiting.
   b. making loans.
   c. honoring checks.
   —d. accepting cash in exchange for an increase in a customer's demand deposits.

16. If the borrower described in question 14 took the loan in the form of cash rather than as an increase in checking account balance, _____ new money would be created by this transaction.
   a. no
   b. $800 of
   c. $1,000 of
   d. $5,000 of

17. A commercial bank is fully loaned up when:
   a. it has zero required reserves.
   b. required reserves equal excess reserves.
   c. it has zero excess reserves.
   d. total reserves equal deposit liabilities.

18. If the loan described in question 14 above was the first step in the multiple expansion process through the banking system, a total of $ _____ in new money could be created. (Assume the required reserve ratio is 0.20 and all banks are fully loaned up.)
   a. 1,000
   b. 4,000
   c. 2,500
   d. 5,000

19. Commercial banks also can create money by _____ bonds. The only difference between this and the loan transaction discussed in question 14 is that _____ rather than _____ are increased on the asset side.
   a. selling; bonds; notes
   b. buying; bonds; notes
   c. selling; notes; bonds
   d. buying; notes; bonds

20. One implication of fractional reserve banking is that banks cannot:
   a. make loans.
   b. buy bonds.
   c. pay off all their depositors on any given day.
   d. pay off all their depositors ever.

Part VIII

Monetary Policy and Problems

Chapter 19

Monetary Policy

OVERVIEW

Monetary policy deals with how the government can promote full employment without inflation by its power to regulate the money supply and influence interest rates. Monetary policy is analyzed with each of the four models presented earlier—Keynesian, aggregate demand–aggregate supply, rational expectations, and the new quantity theory.

MONETARY POLICY DEFINED

We now come to the second major tool used by the government to promote full employment without inflation—monetary policy. *Monetary policy* is defined as the deliberate action of the government or monetary authority to manage the supply of money and the interest rate with the goal of achieving and maintaining full employment without inflation. In the United States, the monetary authority is the Federal Reserve System. An important group within the Federal Reserve System is the Open Market Committee. This committee, which is made up largely by the Federal Reserve Board of Governors, is responsible for deciding on the timing and magnitude of Federal Reserve purchases and sales of government securities in the securities market. As we will see shortly, this is the major tool the Fed uses to influence the quantity of money in the economy.

MONEY VERSUS THE INTEREST RATE

The effect of money and the interest rate on the economy has been subject to a great deal of controversy among economists and government policy makers, extending from the Great Depression to the present. One major point of contention has been the appropriate indicator for monetary policy. In deciding on the correct monetary policy to follow, should the major indicator be the interest rate or the quantity of money? During much of the history of monetary policy in the United States, it appears that the interest rate has served as the prime guideline for action, although in recent years there seems to have been a shift in emphasis toward the money supply as the appropriate indicator for policy.

If one looks back over time, it becomes evident that the money rate of interest tends to rise during inflationary times and to fall during periods of depressed economic activity, such as the Great Depression. For example, from 1929 to 1939, the years spanning the Great Depression, the nominal rate of interest on four-to-six-month prime commercial paper decreased from 5.85 percent to 0.59 percent, respectively. In contrast, from 1972 to 1981, a time of inflation, this same rate of interest more than tripled from 4.69 percent to 14.76 percent.[1] Does it follow, therefore, that if the government took action to reduce the interest rate during inflations and to increase it during recessions, these problems would be reduced? No. Such action would make matters even worse. It is important to recognize that the nominal rate of interest depends very much on inflation or the absence of it. As pointed out in Chapter 6, the interest rate is high during inflation because lenders need to get a higher rate of interest to compensate them for the loss in purchasing power of their money. Also, borrowers are willing to pay a higher rate because they know they will pay back the loans in "cheap dollars." Conversely, the interest rate becomes lower in periods of relatively stable prices and still lower when prices are declining as in the Great Depression. Now lenders are willing to accept a lower rate of interest because their money will not be depreciating in value when it is loaned out. Also, borrowers are less willing to pay a high rate of interest since they will have to pay back the loans with relatively valuable dollars.

Consider what would happen if the government tried to lower the rate of interest during an inflation by increasing the rate of growth of the money supply. The immediate result might be some reduction in the interest rate as money became still more plentiful in the loan market. But in the long run, the increase in the rate of growth of the money supply would cause even more inflation. Consequently, interest rates would increase to even higher levels. There is much confusion over the relationship between rates of growth of the money supply and money rates of interest. In the short run, an increase in the rate of growth of the money supply may lower interest rates temporarily because of the larger supply of money in the loan market. But the long-run effect of such action will be just the opposite, namely, to increase nominal rates of interest to still higher levels because of the increase in inflation.

Attempts to raise the interest rate during a recession by reducing the rate of growth of the money supply also would have a destabilizing effect. Initially, the interest rate would increase as money became even more scarce, but then as

---

[1] *Economic Report of the President,* 1969, p. 290, and 1982, p. 310.

prices began to fall the interest rates would fall to still lower levels. Of course, such a restriction in the money supply would cause even more unemployment. It is not likely the government would make the mistake of reducing the rate of growth of the money supply during a recession, at least now.

The preoccupation with the nominal rate of interest by the Federal Reserve has led to much confusion about the appropriate monetary policy and at times has been used to justify an erroneous policy. For example, during the Great Depression, the Fed pointed to the falling money rate of interest as an indication that money was plentiful. We know now that because of the substantial decline in the money supply from 1929 to 1933, money was far from plentiful. The nominal rate of interest declined during the 1930s in large part because of the decline in the price level.

A similar kind of error was made by the people who called for an increase in the rate of growth of the money supply when interest rates were high during the inflationary years of the 1970s and early 1980s. As will be discussed in the next chapter, the evidence suggests that the Federal Reserve would have had more success in achieving a stable economy of full employment without inflation if it had tried to stabilize the rate of growth of the money supply rather than the nominal rate of interest. If the Fed were successful in stabilizing the growth of the money supply, the interest rate also would become more stable.

PRIMARY TOOLS OF MONETARY POLICY

The Federal Reserve System is the monetary authority in the United States. Since monetary policy is largely a matter of regulating the money supply, let us explore next the tools available to the Fed to carry out this task. Essentially the Fed has three primary tools: (1) open-market operations, (2) changes in the required reserve ratio of commercial banks, and (3) changes in the discount rate that commercial banks pay to borrow from the Federal Reserve.

1. Open-Market Operations. This refers to the purchase and sale of government bonds by the Federal Reserve bank. It is the most important means that the Fed uses to change the money supply. The phrase *open market* refers to the purchase or sale of bonds to bond dealers in the bond market.

Consider first an open-market sale of $1,000 of a bond to a bond dealer. To pay for the bond, the dealer writes a $1,000 check against his or her account in a commercial bank. When the check clears, the Fed deducts $1,000 from the bank's reserve account at the Fed. In turn, the bank deducts $1,000 from the bond dealer's checking account balance. When this occurs the nation's money supply decreases by $1,000.

If the reserve ratio is 0.20, required reserves of the commercial bank decline by $200 and excess reserves go down by $800. The $800 decline in excess reserves causes a multiple contraction of the nation's money supply—a $4,000 decline if the reserve ratio is 0.20 ($1/.20 \times 800 = \$4,000$). Thus, the initial $1,000 decline plus the $4,000 multiple contraction makes for a $5,000 total decrease in the nation's money supply resulting from the initial $1,000 bond sale.

The opposite occurs when the Fed purchases bonds. In this case, the bond dealer receives a check for the amount of the bond, which in turn is deposited in a commercial bank. This results in an increase in the money supply. Then because of the new excess reserves created, the banking system can make new loans, which in turn causes a multiple expansion of the money supply. The amount is comparable to the multiple contraction discussed above. An easy way to remember the direction of change of the money supply is that an open-market sale of bonds pulls money out of the economy in exchange for bonds, and an open-market purchase injects money into the economy, again in exchange for bonds.

2. Changes in the Required Reserve Ratio. Recall from the discussion of banking in Chapter 18 that commercial banks are required to hold a certain fraction of their deposits on reserve, either as cash in their own vaults or as money in a reserve account in their Federal Reserve bank (if the bank is a member of the Federal Reserve System). By changing the legal reserve ratio, the Fed can change the amount of bank loans and thus change the amount of money in the economy. Remember that banks create money by making loans.

In the examples of Chapter 18, we assumed for convenience of computation a required reserve ratio of 0.20, meaning that commercial banks are required to keep 20 cents on reserve against each dollar of demand deposits. Thus, $1,000 of total reserves in the banking system can support $5,000 in demand deposits $[(1/R) \times \$1,000]$, assuming the multiple expansion process has run its course and banks are fully loaned up. Now if the Fed should reduce the required reserve ratio to, say, 0.10, this same $1,000 in total reserves could support $10,000 in total deposits. Banks could in this case increase loans and thus increase demand deposits. On the other hand, an increase in the reserve ratio would require banks to contract their deposits for a given amount of reserves. Thus, a decrease in the required reserve ratio increases the nation's money supply, and an increase decreases it. The Federal Reserve rarely changes the required reserve ratio. Even a small change in the ratio has a large impact on the banking system and causes major adjustments.

3. Changes in the Discount Rate. The discount rate is the rate of interest that the Fed charges member banks when these banks obtain loans from the Fed to bolster their reserves. Occasionally, a commercial bank will find itself dangerously close to the upper limit of its loans (given its reserves) or actually over the limit, especially during peak lending periods. In this situation, the commercial bank can temporarily increase its reserves by borrowing reserves from the Fed.

The Fed generally changes the discount rate in conjunction with a large open-market transaction. Suppose there is inflationary pressure in the economy that prompts the Fed to make a large open-market sale in order to reduce reserves and the money supply. The resulting tight money situation and high interest rates provide banks with an incentive to borrow from the Fed in order to maintain reserves so that loans need not be reduced greatly. This is just good business. But to make it less profitable for banks to borrow for reserves, the Fed will raise the discount rate along with the open-market sale. Similarly, when the Fed wants to stimulate bank lending, it can reduce the discount rate to make it more profitable for banks to borrow to obtain reserves.

SECONDARY TOOLS OF MONETARY POLICY

The items discussed in the previous section are the three main tools the Federal Reserve can use to regulate the supply of money in the economy and thus to influence economic activity. The Fed also has a number of other means to influence economic activity that we might mention briefly. First, there is the idea of *moral suasion,* sometimes called *jawbone control.* These terms describe attempts by the Fed to influence commercial bank lending by persuasive means. For example, during inflationary times, the Fed might frown on excessive borrowing by a bank that tries to expand its reserves. Similarly, during recessionary times, the Fed might extol the virtues of a vigorous lending policy on the part of banks.

The Fed also can influence economic activity by what is known as *selective credit controls.* For example, the Fed regulates the length of the repayment period on installment loans. If people are required to repay a new car loan in, say, 24 months as opposed to 36 months, fewer people will buy new cars. Another device is the regulation of margin requirements on stocks. If, for example, the margin requirement is 60 percent, a person need pay only 60 percent of the price of the stock from his or her own money and is allowed to borrow the remaining 40 percent.

MONETARY POLICY IN THE CONTEXT OF THE SIMPLE KEYNESIAN MODEL

The fact that the simple Keynesian model contains no information on the monetary sector of the economy limits its usefulness as a device to analyze the effects of monetary policy. However, it is possible to present an intuitive idea of how monetary policy affects the economy in the context of this model.

It is easiest to trace the effects of a change in the money supply in the simple model if we view the process as sort of a chain of causation. To begin, suppose the Fed makes a large open-market purchase. From our past discussion, we know that this action increases money and bank reserves. With increased reserves banks can expand their loans.

However, in order for banks to induce individuals and businesses to borrow more, they will probably have to lower their interest charges. A reduction in the

interest rate provides an incentive for business firms to borrow for new investment projects such as buildings, machines, and equipment. Lower interest rates
also provide an incentive for consumers to save less and spend more, particularly
on consumer durables, such as autos and appliances. In the simple model, this
increase in spending would be represented by an upward shift in the aggregate
expenditures function.

Our knowledge of the multiplier process tells us that new spending will increase
by some multiple of the initial increase in consumption and investment and give
rise to an increase in equilibrium NNP. We can summarize the chain of causation
as follows:

Increase in $M \rightarrow$ Decrease in $i \rightarrow$ Increase in I and $C \rightarrow$ Increase in
aggregate expenditures $\rightarrow$ Increase in equilibrium NNP

FIGURE 19–1   Monetary Policy in the Context of the Simple Keynesian Model—
Correcting for Unemployment and Inflation

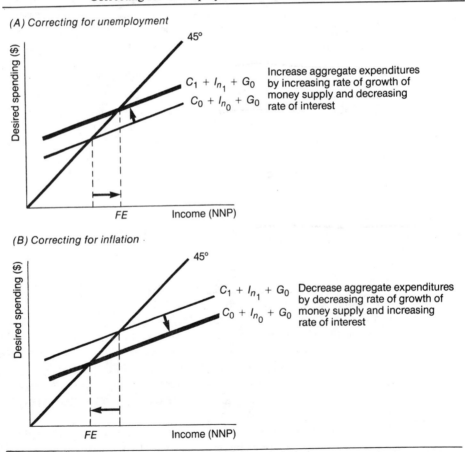

(A) Correcting for unemployment

45°

$C_1 + I_{n_1} + G_0$ Increase aggregate expenditures
$C_0 + I_{n_0} + G_0$ by increasing rate of growth of
money supply and decreasing
rate of interest

Desired spending ($)

FE   Income (NNP)

(B) Correcting for inflation

45°

$C_1 + I_{n_1} + G_0$ Decrease aggregate expenditures
$C_0 + I_{n_0} + G_0$ by decreasing rate of growth of
money supply and increasing
rate of interest

Desired spending ($)

FE   Income (NNP)

Just the opposite would occur in the case of an open-market sale of bonds. The resulting decrease in money and reserves leads to an increase in the interest rate. Then, as investment and possibly consumption decline, the aggregate expenditure function shifts down, resulting in a decrease in equilibrium NNP.

The effect of monetary policy can be illustrated on the familiar Keynesian diagram shown in Figure 19–1. Figure 19–1A again represents unemployment. Here the appropriate monetary policy would be to increase the rate of growth of the money supply so that the interest rate declines and shifts aggregate expenditures upward. In the case of the inflationary situation illustrated by Figure 19–1B, the appropriate monetary policy would be to reduce the rate of growth of the supply of money, thereby increasing the interest rate, shifting aggregate expenditures downward, and reducing the equilibrium NNP.

We cannot be as precise in predicting the ultimate effects of monetary policy, however, as we were able to be with fiscal policy. Recall that by using the multiplier, we were able to predict to the exact dollar how much of a tax or government spending change was needed to match the equilibrium NNP with the full-employment level. In order to make such precise predictions for monetary policy, we would need two additional pieces of information. First, we would have to know how much an open-market purchase or sale of bonds would change the interest rate. Second, information would be needed on how much investment or consumption changes in response to a given change in the interest rate.

Economists have been able to gather a little information on the response of investment to changes in the interest rate, although the general area of the relationship between interest rate changes and spending changes is still subject to considerable uncertainty. Even less is known about the impact of an open-market purchase on the interest rate and the process that occurs in the economy when the interest rate changes.

MONETARY POLICY IN THE CONTEXT OF THE AGGREGATE DEMAND–AGGREGATE SUPPLY MODEL

The economic rationale underlying the impact of change in the money supply in this model is similar to that of the Keynesian model. An increase in the money supply, for example, lowers interest rates, at least initially, and stimulates private consumer and investment spending. This, in turn, causes an increase in aggregate demand. Such a policy would be called for during a time of unemployment, shifting aggregate demand from AD_0 to AD_1 in Figure 19–2.

This model also indicates what happens to the price level under various policy changes. If short-run aggregate supply is close to horizontal, as might occur in a time of high unemployment, there will be relatively little increase in the price level. Conversely, if *SRAS* is comparatively steep, an increase in aggregate demand causes an increase in the price level (inflation).

An inflationary problem calls for the opposite monetary policy. However, rather than decreasing the money supply in absolute terms, a more reasonable

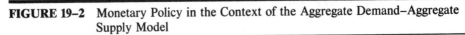

FIGURE 19–2   Monetary Policy in the Context of the Aggregate Demand–Aggregate Supply Model

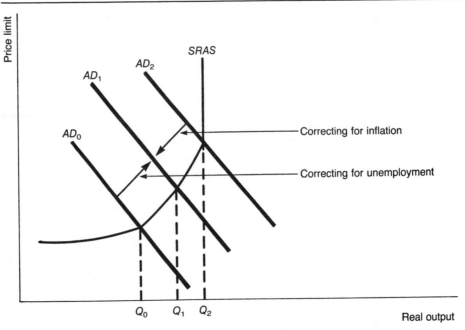

policy would be to reduce the rate of growth of the money supply. The last time the money supply decreased in absolute terms for any length of time in the United States was during the Great Depression. Notice also that the vertical axis shows the price level and not the rate of inflation. Therefore, a shift down and to the left by aggregate demand implies that the price level, not just the rate of inflation, will decline. From this standpoint, the model yields unreasonable results. In an attempt to reduce inflation, the Federal Reserve would never try to roll back the price level. The last time the United States experienced a prolonged decrease in the price level was during the Great Depression.

MONETARY POLICY IN THE CONTEXT OF RATIONAL EXPECTATIONS

Recall from Chapter 14 that, according to the rational expectations hypothesis, government attempts to "fine tune" the economy by means of fiscal policy will at best have only a short-term effect on unemployment and at worst can cause inflation and perhaps even more unemployment in the future when the government tries to slow down the inflation. The same argument applies to monetary policy. The long-run Phillips curve diagram of Figure 13–3 provides the framework for the analysis of monetary policy as well as that of fiscal policy, at least for the rational expectations theory.

Consider first an attempt by government to stimulate the economy by increasing the rate of growth of the money supply. The resulting increase in the price level is at first mistaken by business firms to be an increase in the demand for their particular product. They hire more workers, and the unemployment rate declines temporarily as the economy moves up along a specific short-run Phillips curve. But as wage earners and union leaders recognize that the price increases are widespread across the economy, they press employers for wage increases in order to regain the reduction in real wage rates. The level of unemployment then increases, and the economy comes to rest once again at the natural rate of unemployment but on a higher short-run Phillips curve corresponding to a higher expected rate of inflation. After repeated attempts to stimulate the economy by means of monetary policy, people soon learn what the government is doing and react simultaneously or even in advance of the policy action. In this case, the main effect of this policy is to just move the economy up to higher and higher short-run Phillips curves without any pronounced reduction in unemployment even in the short run.

As pointed out previously, sooner or later inflation, rather than unemployment, will come to be viewed as the main problem. Now the government will reduce the rate of growth of the money supply. As the inflation rate subsides slightly, employers mistake the slowing down of price increases as a softness in the demands for their particular products. Consequently, they lay off people and unemployment increases. Then as unions and wage earners slacken their demands for pay hikes, unemployment eases back down to the natural rate after a time. But during the adjustment period, the economy still suffers from inflation and high unemployment.

Advocates of the rational expectations hypothesis argue that the unemployment consequences of reducing inflation could be mitigated or even eliminated if the government were to announce its intentions of reducing the rate of growth of the money supply. In this case, employers need not lay off employees because of the mistaken belief that the demand for their product had decreased, nor would employees press for as large a pay increase because of the anticipated slowing down of inflation. If the government could convince people of its actions so that expectations were altered, the economy could move down along the vertical long-run Phillips curve without experiencing a period of high unemployment.

MONETARY POLICY IN THE CONTEXT OF THE NEW QUANTITY THEORY

Recall from Chapters 9 and 17 that the impact of changes in the money supply on the economy is expressed in the quantity theory by the quantity equation of exchange, $M \times V = P \times Q$. The quantity theory is perhaps most useful for

TABLE 19–1 Indexes of Total Real Output and Money in the United States, Selected Years, 1949–1989 (1949 = 100)

Year	Real Output	Money	Year	Real Output	Money
1949	100	100	1979	301	1,012
1959	147	201	1984	333	1,604
1969	221	398	1985	323	1,732
1974	253	614	1989	373	2,173

Source: Real output figures from *Economic Report of the President*, 1969, p. 228, and 1990, p. 303.

identifying the main source of inflation and providing a policy prescription to deal with this problem. According to the quantity equation of exchange, if M grows more rapidly than Q, inflation is inevitable, providing V does not decrease when M increases.

Figures on the relative growth of Q and M in the United States from 1949 to 1989 are presented in Table 19–1. The Q in this table is represented by total real GNP as reported by the Department of Commerce. GNP is converted to an index by dividing the series of numbers by the 1949 value. The index makes it easier to compare the growth of real output with the growth in money over the period. The broad definition of money (M_2) is used as the M figure. It is converted to an index also by dividing the series of numbers by the 1949 value of M_2.

As indicated by the figures in Table 19–1, total real output in the U.S. economy increased by 3.7 times between 1949 and 1989. However, the nation's money supply increased over 21 times during this period. Thus, the nation's money supply grew at a much faster rate than did real output. Since V has remained relatively constant (Table 9–1), the quantity equation predicts that the nation should have experienced inflation, which it did.

One might ask: Why did the government (or the Federal Reserve) increase the money supply so much more than the growth in real output? The most likely reason is the deficit spending of the federal government. The Fed had no other reason to expand the money supply as rapidly. By purchasing many of the bonds issued by the Treasury, the Federal Reserve caused large increases in the money supply. And as predicted by the quantity theory (both original and new) as well as the other theories discussed, excessive growth of the money supply causes inflation.

SUMMARY

Monetary policy is the deliberate attempt by the monetary authority, the Federal Reserve System in the United States, to maintain full employment with stable prices by controlling the rate of growth of the money supply and interest rates.

The Federal Reserve can change the money supply by buying and selling government bonds (open-market operations), changing the reserve ratio, and changing the discount rate. Open-market operations is the primary tool. In the context of the simple Keynesian model, a change in the rate of growth of the money supply is perceived to affect the economy by changing the rate of interest, which in turn changes spending. The advantage of the aggregate demand–aggregate supply model over the Keynesian model is that the price level is shown explicitly. According to the rational expectations model, increasing the rate of growth of the money supply to decrease unemployment can only temporarily have the desired effect. In the long run, the result will be increased inflation. As predicted by the quantity theory, the fact the U.S. money supply grew more rapidly than real output during the post-World War II period resulted in higher prices, that is, inflation.

YOU SHOULD KNOW

1. The definition of monetary policy.
2. How maintaining a stable interest rate can destabilize the economy.
3. The three primary tools of monetary policy, and which is used the most.
4. The secondary tools of monetary policy.
5. How money is perceived to affect the economy in the context of the simple Keynesian model.
6. How monetary policy is used to correct for unemployment and inflation in the context of the simple Keynesian model.
7. How monetary policy is used in the context of the aggregate demand–aggregate supply model.
8. How money affects the economy in the context of the new quantity theory.
9. Why the United States experienced inflation during the 1949–89 period.

QUESTIONS

1. During inflationary periods, the nominal rates of interest rise while during recessions they fall. Would you advocate, therefore, that the Federal Reserve act to stabilize interest rates in order to stabilize the economy? Explain why or why not.
2. Describe how an open-market sale of government bonds affects the nation's money supply. An open-market purchase?
3. Besides open-market operations, what other measures are available to the Federal Reserve to change the nation's money supply?
4. In showing the effects of monetary policy, what information can be obtained from the aggregate demand–aggregate supply model that cannot be obtained from the simple Keynesian model?
5. *a.* According to the rational expectations hypothesis, is it possible for the government to reduce unemployment by increasing the rate of growth of the money supply? First consider a situation where the policy change is unexpected and then where it is expected.

   b. According to the rational expectations

hypothesis, is it possible to reduce inflation without increasing unemployment? Explain.

6. *a.* According to the quantity theory of money (original and new), what is the leading cause of inflation?

b. Is this theory consistent with the evidence? Explain.

SELF-TEST

1. Monetary policy is defined as the use of _____ and _____ to maintain full employment without inflation. Monetary policy is carried out by _____ .
   a. money; interest rates; Congress and the president
   b. money; interest rates; the Federal Reserve
   c. taxes; spending; Congress and the president
   d. taxes; spending; the Federal Reserve

2. Nominal or money rates of interest tend to _____ during recessions and _____ during inflationary times. Using monetary policy to temporarily increase interest rates during recessions and decrease rates during inflation would _____ the economy.
   a. rise; fall; stabilize
   b. fall; rise; stabilize
   c. rise; fall; destabilize
   d. fall; rise; destabilize

3. The immediate effect of increasing the rate of growth of the money supply during an inflationary period is to _____ interest rates. The long-term effect is to _____ because of the _____ in the rate of inflation.
   a. decrease; decrease them even more; decrease
   b. increase; increase rates; increase
   c. decrease; increase rates; increase
   d. increase; increase them even more; increase

4. Which of the following tool(s) is (are) available to the Federal Reserve to change the nation's money supply?
   a. Open-market operations
   b. Change the required reserve ratio
   c. Change the discount rate
   d. All of the above

5. Of the tools mentioned in question 4, which is used the most?
   a. Open-market operations
   b. Change the required reserve ratio
   c. Change the discount rate

6. If the Fed wishes to increase the nation's money supply, it will _____ government bonds. If the required reserve ratio is 0.20, a purchase (sale) of a $1,000 bond will increase the nation's money supply by $ _____ after the multiple expansion has run its course.
   a. purchase; 5,000
   b. purchase; 4,000
   c. sell; 5,000
   d. sell; 4,000

7. The discount rate is the rate of interest that _____ charges _____ .
   a. the Federal Reserve; commercial banks that borrow reserves
   b. the Federal Reserve; its most-favored borrowers
   c. the Treasury; the Federal Reserve
   d. the Federal Reserve; the Treasury

8. If the Federal Reserve wishes to increase the nation's money supply, it will commonly _____ the discount rate in conjunction with a large open-market _____ .

    a. increase; sale
    b. decrease; sale
    c. increase; purchase
    d. decrease; purchase

9. Moral suasion refers to effort by the Federal Reserve to convince member banks to:
    a. refrain from morally questionable lending practices.
    b. borrow less from the Fed.
    c. borrow more from the Fed.
    d. do what the Fed wants them to do.

10. In the context of the simple Keynesian model, an unemployment problem would call for a(n) _____ in the money supply, causing interest rates to _____ and aggregate expenditures to _____ .
    a. decrease; decrease; increase
    b. decrease; increase; decrease
    c. increase; decrease; increase
    d. increase; increase; decrease

11. In the context of the simple Keynesian model, an inflation problem would call for a(n) _____ in the money supply, causing interest rates to _____ and aggregate expenditures to _____ .
    a. decrease; decrease; increase
    b. decrease; increase; decrease
    c. increase; decrease; increase
    d. increase; increase; decrease

12. In the context of the aggregate demand–short run aggregate supply model, an inflationary situation calls for a(n) _____ in the money supply, causing interest rates to _____ and _____ to _____ .
    a. increase; increase; aggregate demand; increase
    b. decrease; increase; aggregate demand; decrease
    c. increase; increase; aggregate supply; increase
    d. decrease; increase; aggregate supply; increase

13. According to the aggregate demand–short run aggregate supply model, the action called for in question 12 will result in:
    a. a decrease in the price level.
    b. a decrease in the unemployment rate.
    c. an increase in the price level.
    d. *a* and *b*

14. In the context of the rational expectations hypothesis, an increase in the rate of growth of the money supply will _____ decrease unemployment if the policy is _____ .
    a. temporarily; expected
    b. permanently; expected
    c. temporarily; a surprise
    d. permanently; a surprise

15. According to the rational expectations hypothesis, the action described in question 14 will in the long run _____ but leave _____ unchanged from its natural rate.
    a. increase unemployment; inflation
    b. decrease unemployment; inflation
    c. increase inflation; unemployment
    d. decrease inflation; unemployment

16. In the context of the rational expectations hypothesis, inflation _____ be brought under control without causing increased unemployment if the government _____ the people of (with) its policy objectives.
    a. can; convinces
    b. cannot; convinces
    c. can; surprises
    d. cannot; surprises

17. Between 1949 and 1989, real output in the United States increased _____ fold while the money supply increased over _____ times. According to the new quantity theory, an inevitable consequence of this development was an increase in _____ .
    a. 3.7; 21; prices

b. 21; 3.7; prices

c. 3.7; 21; unemployment

d. 21; 3.7; unemployment

18. The large increase in the nation's money supply during the post-World War II period is most likely due to:

a. the Fed's desire to cause inflation.

b. the Fed's desire to cause unemployment.

c. printing money to finance deficits.

d. inadequate data on the nation's money supply.

Chapter 20

Problems of Monetary Policy

OVERVIEW

Similar to fiscal policy, monetary policy also has its problems. A major problem is timing. In reference to this problem, the issue of whether the Federal Reserve should attempt to engage in an active money policy is discussed. Also, the main distinction between the Keynesians and monetarists is clarified. The chapter concludes with a discussion of how deficits of the federal government can cause both inflation and unemployment.

INTRODUCTION

The policy prescriptions for the use of monetary policy to deal with unemployment and inflation problems do not differ markedly among the various schools of thought discussed in the preceding chapters. Granted, some are more optimistic about the ability of monetary policy to do the job than others. But by and large, there is not a lot of disagreement that an unemployment problem calls for stepping up the rate of growth of the money supply, and inflation calls for the opposite. Lest these policy prescriptions give the impression that eliminating unemployment and inflation is a simple task, it is necessary to consider some of the main problems of carrying out such policy.

TIMING PROBLEMS

Whatever model one uses to prescribe monetary policy, the problem of timing must be faced. There are two timing problems: (1) when to take corrective action and (2) when the action has its impact on the economy.

FIGURE 20–1   The Timing of Monetary Policy

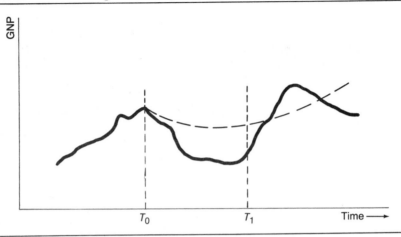

The first problem stems from the difficulty of discerning a temporary fluctuation in economic activity from the start of a recession or inflationary spiral. Because of the political implications of rising unemployment or inflation, there is a great deal of controversy regarding the state of the economy. At the first glimpse of rising unemployment, the political party that is not in power generally calls for a change of policies and leadership, claiming the country is headed for a deep recession. On the other hand, the party in power is likely to argue that the economy is experiencing a temporary downturn and soon will recover to its former state of high employment. It is evident, then, that the monetary authority cannot expect to always please both political parties at once, nor should it try. From this standpoint, it is perhaps fortunate that the Federal Reserve Board of Governors is an autonomous body, to some extent shielded from conflicting pressures of the political parties.

But the Fed is still faced with the problem of when to act. It must be aware, too, that action at the wrong time can be worse than no action. For example, if the Fed steps up the rate of increase of the money supply in a mistaken belief that the economy is headed for a downturn, the result could be a needless inflation in the months and possibly years to come. Or if it sharply curtails the rate of increase of the money supply, thinking that inflation is upon us when it is not, the result may well be a needless increase in unemployment in the future. As illustrated in Figure 20–1, the correct time to undertake an expansion of the money supply or increase its rate of growth—that is, engage in an "easy money" policy—is at time T_0. Or if the economy is headed for an inflationary spiral, such as at T_1, the models imply that the Fed should cut back on the rate of growth of the money supply—that is, engage in a "tight money" policy. The object of these policies is to smooth out the fluctuations in the economy, as illustrated by the dashed line beginning at T_0 in Figure 20–1.

LAGS IN THE EFFECT OF MONETARY POLICY

The second timing problem stems from the time it takes for changes in the money supply to affect economic activity. If there is a lag between policy action and its effect, one has to be mindful of the possibility that the impact of the policy will not come at the time desired. For example, suppose the economy is headed for a downturn as illustrated at time T_0 in Figure 20–1. If the increase in the rate of growth of the money supply is not felt by the economy until time T_1, the result may be a worsening of the inflation problem that the economy will experience after T_1.

Friedman presents evidence that the lags in the effect of monetary policy are both long and variable.[1] In other words, the lag may be 6 to 12 months at one time and 24 to 36 months or longer at another time. The reasons for the long and variable lags are not well understood or agreed upon. One might expect that the lag would have something to do with the time it takes for the multiple expansion (or contraction) process to work itself out through the economy. For example, as banks gain new reserves during an expansionary phase, it takes time to find and screen suitable borrowers. Borrowers also must be willing to take on new debt. If the economy has been in a recession and businesspeople are still pessimistic about the future, they are not so likely to negotiate new loans as during a more optimistic time. Recall that it is the making of loans by commercial banks that results in the multiple expansion. Thus, the willingness of business firms to borrow will influence how quickly an expansionary monetary policy affects the economy and how large the impact is.

In the case of an anti-inflationary monetary policy where the Federal Reserve sells bonds and reduces commercial bank reserves, there seems to be a more immediate reaction in the economy. When loan money becomes scarce and interest rates increase, industries that are dependent on borrowed funds, such as construction, seem to be affected quickly and significantly. Layoffs occur, affecting other industries, such as appliance and lumber. Thus, it is not unreasonable to believe that the lag between monetary policy action and its effect may be different both within an expansionary phase and between expansionary and restrictive monetary policies.

RULES VERSUS DISCRETION: THE FRIEDMAN PROPOSAL

Because of the long and variable lags in the effects of monetary policy, Friedman has proposed that the monetary authority would have a greater stabilizing effect on the economy if it would follow a simple rule of increasing the money supply

---

[1] Milton Friedman, "The Lag in the Effect of Monetary Policy," *Journal of Political Economy* 68 (December 1960), pp. 617–21.

about 4 to 5 percent per year to keep up with a growing economy instead of periodically "stepping on the gas" and then "slamming on the brakes" in response to downturns and upturns in economic activity.

Notice, however, that Friedman is not saying that monetary policy is of little importance. Rather, he is saying that money is so important that large fluctuations in the money supply cause large and damaging fluctuations in economic activity. Friedman argues that following his simple rule would have promoted much more stability in the economy than we experienced with the Fed's attempts to lean against the wind.

MONETARY INSTABILITY

The monetary instability that Friedman was concerned about is illustrated in Table 20–1. During the 1959–79 period, the annual rate of growth of the money supply ranged from 2.1 to 13.7 percent. In more recent years, coinciding with Paul Volcker's chairmanship of the Federal Reserve Board of Governors, and continu-

TABLE 20–1 Year-to-Year Percent Changes in the U.S. Money Supply, M_2, 1959–1989

Year	Change	Year	Change
1959	2.1%	1975	12.6%
1960	4.9	1976	13.7
1961	7.4	1977	10.6
1962	8.1	1978	8.0
1963	8.4	1979	8.0
1964	8.0	1980	8.9
1965	8.1	1981	10.0
1966	4.5	1982	8.8
1967	9.2	1983	11.8
1968	8.0	1984	8.3
1969	4.1	1985	8.5
1970	6.6	1986	9.5
1971	13.5	1987	3.5
1972	13.0	1988	5.5
1973	6.9	1989	4.8
1974	5.5		

Source: *Economic Report of the President*, 1990, p. 371.

ing under Alan Greenspan, the money supply growth rate has stabilized some-what. Economists who advocate a steady growth of the nation's money supply can point to the control of inflation, the decrease in unemployment, and continued economic growth during the mid- to late 1980s as a consequence of this policy.

ADJUSTMENT PROBLEMS

Reducing the rate of growth of the money supply to counteract inflation generally is not costless. The evidence gathered over the past several decades suggests that slowing down inflation invariably causes increased unemployment. Some rational expectations advocates argue that this need not occur if people expect the inflation rate to subside when the government says it will. But if the inflation has persisted for an extended period and the earlier government pronouncements have not been followed through, skepticism will prevail. As a consequence, people will expect a continuation of inflation until they are shown that the government, or Federal Reserve, means business. They become believers only after the actual inflation rate begins to decline. But this decline in inflation creates imbalances between wages and prices, with wages going up too much in anticipation of continued inflation. Therefore, production costs increase more rapidly than sales, causing a decline in profits and layoffs of personnel. It may take a period of several years of high unemployment to squeeze out inflation, which amounts to a high adjustment cost to the economy.

MONETARISTS VERSUS KEYNESIANS

Monetarists have been described as economists who believe that "money matters." That is, they maintain that changes in the money supply have significant repercussions on economic activity, definitely on prices but also on real output and employment. Keynesians, on the other hand, have not been as convinced that changes in the money supply have such an important impact. The intensity of this debate appears to have subsided in recent years with some coming together of the two schools of thought. There remains, however, a subtle difference between how changes in the money supply are perceived to affect the economy in the Keynesian model and in the new quantity theory. In the Keynesian model, changes in the money supply cause changes in the interest rate, which in turn cause changes in consumer and investment spending. In the new quantity theory, money supply changes are perceived to have a more direct impact on spending by altering the balance between actual K and desired K, as explained in Chapter 17.

This distinction can be a problem for carrying out monetary policy. Even if both camps agree in the direction of change, there will continue to be some dis-agreement on how much to rely on monetary policy. It appears that monetarists still advocate a relatively stable money growth policy, following Friedman. Keynesians tend to be more activist in their orientation, preferring to regulate the growth of the money supply depending on current economic conditions. A similar distinction could be made for fiscal policy.

HOW FEDERAL DEFICITS CAN CAUSE INFLATION AND UNEMPLOYMENT

For the purpose of exposition, it has been convenient to separate the discussion of fiscal policy from monetary policy. However, in reality, fiscal policy is likely to have an important bearing on the rate of growth of the money supply. This is particularly true when the federal government runs deficits. If the government incurs deficits in the process of increasing its spending (or cutting taxes), then you recall from Chapter 15 that one way to finance these deficits is to "print money." In this process, the Treasury sells bonds, most likely to a bond dealer. When the Federal Reserve clears the check written by the bond dealer, it prints the corresponding figures in the Treasury's checking account at the Fed. The Treasury can then write checks on these added numbers in its account for the purchase of goods and services, the same as if these numbers were new $10 and $20 bills, hence the term *printing money.*

The key transaction in the process of printing money to finance deficits is when the Federal Reserve buys bonds back from bond dealers. Now the money supply is increased, not only because of the increase in demand deposits in commercial banks when the Federal Reserve pays for the bonds but, more important, because of the multiple expansion process that occurs due to the increase in excess reserves.

When Paul Volcker became chairman of the Fed's Board of Governors, the Fed's policy of purchasing the bonds issued by the Treasury changed. This forced their sale to U.S. citizens and foreign buyers. In order to sell large amounts of bonds to these groups, interest rates had to be made attractive. But the higher interest rates had a negative impact on industries such as construction and automobiles, which depend on credit to sell their products. In turn, this caused increased unemployment.

We see, therefore, that federal deficits need not cause inflation if the bonds are sold to U.S. citizens or foreign buyers. However, the adjustment from printing money to selling bonds to the other two groups of buyers is most likely to cause unemployment, as occurred in the early to mid-1980s. Thus, federal deficits can cause both inflation and unemployment, but at different times. Also, there remains the danger that continued growth in the national debt may at some time in the future cause a reversal of the Fed's policy and rekindle inflation.

If the national debt grows so large as to require a substantial share of the government's tax revenue to pay the interest and the bonds coming due, there will be much pressure on the Fed to buy more bonds, thereby printing money.

Inflation will resume, which in turn will lower the real value of bonds outstanding. Thus, inflation can be used as means of paying off the national debt. The people who own government bonds and other assets that have a fixed face value, such as money, end up paying the debt because of the decline in the real value of these assets.

PRICE AND WAGE CONTROLS

During periods of excessive inflationary pressure, many governments have resorted to price and wage controls in an effort to stem the upward spiral of prices. In the United States, price and wage controls have been instituted generally in times of armed conflict in an effort to hold down the increase in prices. The stringent controls instituted during World War II and the somewhat more flexible controls put into effect in August 1971 are two examples. Price and wage controls have precipitated a substantial amount of controversy among economists, political leaders, and the general public. Thus, it will be useful to review some of the arguments in favor of controls, together with some of the problems that controls bring about.

Those who favor price and wage controls tend to place relatively little faith in the ability of traditional fiscal and monetary policies (such as reduced government spending, higher taxes, or tight money) to do the job. Some who favor controls may grant that traditional policy might eventually stem inflation but argue that the time required is too long or the unemployment effects too severe to be acceptable to the general public.

It is argued also that controls can help to break the inflation psychology that people may have acquired during a prolonged period of inflation. If anti-inflationary policies, such as a tax increase or a reduced rate of money creation, accompany the controls, the momentum of inflation is more quickly checked. In this case, unions are not likely to be as demanding in asking for future wage increases, and people in general need not be as concerned about getting rid of their cash by purchasing real assets that rise in value with the price level. Thus, pressure for price increases is eased somewhat in both the labor and product markets. With an ease in wage demands, employers are likely to be more willing to retain or hire employees, thus easing the unemployment problem brought on by restrictive fiscal or monetary policies.

Economists who oppose price and wage restraints point out that the imposition of controls does not remove the basic cause of inflation. They argue that inflation is caused basically by excessive growth in the money supply due in large part to deficit spending. Hence, the imposition of price and wage controls may suppress the symptoms of inflation but does not remove its underlying cause.

It is argued as well that unless price and wage controls are applied universally, those prices or wages that are not affected will grow even more rapidly. In other words, it would be something like squeezing a balloon—if you push in at one place, it will bulge out at another. But if all prices and wages are frozen, then the economy is placed in a sort of straitjacket. That is, there is no way for consumers to provide signals to producers through the price system.

Resources are allocated in a market economy mainly on the basis of market prices. If the price of one product rises relative to others, it is a signal to producers that consumers desire more of this product relative to others. Producers, in attempting to increase profits by producing more of the higher-priced product, at the same time satisfy the desires of consumers. Similarly, if the price of a resource increases, producers have an incentive to economize on its use by substituting lower-priced resources in its place. Thus, the imposition of price and wage controls takes away the allocating function of product and resource prices.

A second problem encountered with price and wage controls is that they result in shortages in the product and resource markets, which in turn lead to rationing and black-market activities. These undesirable side effects of price controls can be demonstrated by the market demand and supply diagram developed in Chapter 4. Recall that one of the main demand shifters is a change in money income. An increase in money income resulting from an increase in the money supply causes the demand for most goods to increase or shift to the right, as shown by Figure 20–2. Recall as well that a major supply shifter is a change in the prices of resources. During inflation, the increase in prices of labor, capital, and raw

FIGURE 20–2   Illustrating the Effect of Inflation and Price Controls

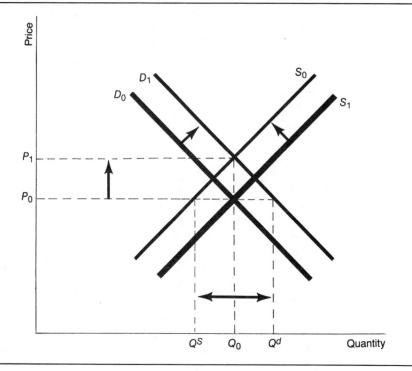

materials causes the supply curve of products to decrease—that is, shift to the left. The increase in demand and decrease in supply both contribute to the increase in the market equilibrium prices of goods and services. As shown by Figure 20–2, the new higher price is equal to P_1.

If the market is "frozen" at P_0 or prohibited by law from increasing, a shortage will occur. Notice at the new demand and supply curves that quantity demanded, Q^d, is greater than quantity supplied, Q^s, at the original or controlled price P_0. This in turn creates a shortage equal to the difference between Q^s and Q^d. If wages are controlled also, the shift to the left by the supply curve would not be so large because costs would not increase as much. But, the costs of raw materials can still increase, which would increase costs for some industries. But even if the supply curve does not shift to the left, there still will be a shortage caused by the difference between Q_0 and Q^d. Because of the resulting shortages, consumers turn to the black market, paying prices higher than the legal maximum. The longer the price controls remain in effect and the wider the gap between Q^d and Q^s becomes, the greater is the incentive to buy and sell on the black market. As the resulting shortages increase, the pressure on market price to increase continues to grow. Eventually, all countries that have attempted to prevent inflation by price controls have been forced to allow prices to rise to their market equilibrium levels.[2] Moreover, when price controls are relaxed, prices tend to shoot up rapidly to catch up to their higher equilibrium levels. Also, the decline in the quantity supplied that occurs during price controls causes prices to rise even more than they would have risen without the controls.

Price indexes, such as the CPI, that reflect prices during periods of price controls measure the legal or controlled prices, not the black-market prices. As a result, the removal of price controls and the subsequent upward spurt of the price index may give the appearance that the controls have been successful in preventing inflation, and that the inflation has recurred with the removal of controls. In reality, the price index fails to measure black-market prices and the continual upward pressure on prices during the period the price controls are in effect.

Although it is generally not reported in history books, the imposition of the price controls by the commonwealth of Pennsylvania on the commodities purchased by the American Revolutionary Army during the winter of 1777–78 nearly caused the demise of George Washington's army at Valley Forge.[3] Price controls caused severe shortages of food, as farmers either held back the sale of

---

[2] For an account of the results of wage and price controls in Western European countries since the end of World War II, see Lloyd Ulman and Robert J. Flanagan, *Wage Restraint: A Study of Income Policies in Western Europe* (Berkeley: University of California Press, 1971). According to the authors, the various wage and price policies in various countries have exhibited a common characteristic: "periods of effectiveness were typically short lived; they were frequently followed by wage and price explosions which sometimes blew up the policies themselves" (p. 223).

[3] Robert L. Schnettinger and Eamonn F. Butler, *Forty Centuries of Wage and Price Controls* (Washington, D.C.: Heritage Foundation, 1979).

food at prices they considered unfair or sold the food to the British, who paid in gold. The intent of the price controls was to reduce the cost of maintaining the Revolutionary War. But the result was the near defeat of that army.

SUMMARY

Although there is general agreement that the rate of growth of the money supply should be increased during a time of higher unemployment and decreased during inflation, a number of problems confront policy makers. The correct timing of monetary policy is difficult because the economy does not grow in a smooth fashion and because the lag in the effect of monetary policy is both long and variable. As a result, Friedman has argued that the money supply should be increased within a relatively narrow range of 4 to 5 percent per year. Attempts to reduce inflation traditionally have brought increased unemployment. Monetarists believe money matters, while Keynesians are less convinced. Federal deficits cause inflation if the bonds are purchased by the Federal Reserve bank and can cause unemployment if they are sold to U.S. citizens or foreign buyers. Attempts to control inflation by price and wage controls result in shortages and black-market activities and have never worked in the long run.

YOU SHOULD KNOW

1. The two main timing problems that must be overcome in order to carry out a successful monetary policy.
2. Why the lag in the effect of monetary policy creates a timing problem.
3. Why Professor Friedman advocates a steady growth in the money supply rather than an activist monetary policy.
4. The U.S. record of monetary stability.
5. Why a slowing in the rate of growth of the money supply tends to increase unemployment.
6. The difference between the monetarists and the Keynesians.
7. How federal deficits can cause inflation and unemployment.
8. The meaning of the term *printing money* to finance deficits.
9. When price and wage controls are most likely to be imposed.
10. The main consequences of price and wage controls.

QUESTIONS

1. Cite the major timing problems that confront the successful implementation of monetary policy.
2. It has been argued that the economy would become more stable if the Federal Reserve

Open Market Committee were replaced by a computer. Why?

3. If the country is experiencing a high rate of inflation and the Federal Reserve reduces the rate of growth of the money supply,

what are the immediate or short-term effects of this policy likely to be? Long-term effects?

4. Some economists have argued that a nation need not experience inflation even though the federal government incurs deficits.
   a. Is there any evidence to suggest this might be true?
   b. If it is true, how must the deficit be financed?

5. How can federal deficits cause inflation? Unemployment?

6. Should the blame for the rapid increase in the U.S. money supply and the resulting inflation during the 1960s, 1970s, and early 1980s be placed entirely on the Federal Reserve? Explain.

7. a. What happens to the market demand and supply of goods during inflation?
   b. What happens if the government attempts to control inflation by wage and price controls?

SELF-TEST

1. The timing problem(s) that confront(s) the successful implementation of monetary policy is (are):
   a. when to take action.
   b. when the action affects the economy.
   c. the time it takes action to be passed by Congress.
   d. a and b.

2. The problem(s) cited in question 1 occurs because:
   a. the lag in the effect of monetary policy is both long and variable.
   b. the lag in the effect of monetary policy is short and predictable.
   c. the economy does not grow in a smooth fashion.
   d. a and c.

3. If the Fed mistakenly increases the growth of the money supply thinking that _____ is at hand when it is not, the result could be needless _____ in the future.
   a. unemployment; unemployment
   b. unemployment; inflation
   c. inflation; unemployment
   d. inflation; inflation

4. Milton Friedman argued that monetary policy _____ be used to "fine-tune" the economy because:
   a. cannot; changes in the money supply have little impact on economic activity
   b. cannot; the lag in the effect of monetary policy is both long and variable.
   c. can; the lag in the effect of monetary policy is short and predictable.
   d. can; change in the money supply have a major impact on economic activity.

5. Because of the problem cited in question 4, Friedman has argued that the nation's money supply should:
   a. be used to "fine-tune" the economy, stepping up the rate of growth during times of increased unemployment and reducing it during inflation.
   b. be increased a constant 4 to 5 percent per year to keep step with a growing economy.
   c. remain constant so as not to destabilize the economy.
   d. be allowed to find its own level in the money market.

6. During the 1959–79 period, growth of the money supply was relatively _____ from _____ to _____ percent per year.
   a. stable; 4; 5
   b. unstable; 4; 5

c. stable; 2; 14

d. unstable; 2; 14

7. Starting with Paul Volcker's reign as chairman of the Federal Reserve Board of Governors, and continuing under Alan Greenspan, growth of the nation's money supply _____ .

   a. stabilized
   b. destabilized
   c. ceased
   d. increased dramatically

8. Evidence gained during the past several decades suggests that slowing the rate of growth of the nation's money supply in an effort to control inflation causes:

   a. even more inflation.
   b. an increase in unemployment.
   c. a decrease in unemployment.

9. _____ argue that the problem cited in question 8 need not occur if:

   a. Monetarists; people can be convinced that the government will stop inflation.
   b. Rational expectations advocates; people can be convinced that the government will stop inflation.
   c. Keynesians; people are surprised by the government's policy.
   d. Rational expectations advocates; people are surprised by the government's policy.

10. When inflation subsides, it is common for wages to _____ relative to prices, causing _____ unemployment.

    a. decrease; decreased
    b. increase; increased
    c. decrease; increased
    d. increase; decreased

11. Monetarists have been described as those who believe that _____ . Keynesians traditionally have been _____ convinced of the importance of money.

    a. money does not cause inflation; more
    b. money does not cause unemployment; more

c. money matters; less

d. money doesn't matter; more

12. In the simple Keynesian model, money is viewed as affecting the economy through the _____ . In the new quantity theory, money affects the economy by:

    a. imbalance of desired K and actual K; the interest rate.
    b. the interest rate; the imbalance of desired K and actual K.
    c. government; the marketplace.
    d. the marketplace; the government.

13. When the government bonds issued by the Treasury are purchased by _____ , the practice is called *printing money* to finance deficit.

    a. U.S. citizens
    b. foreign investors
    c. the Federal Reserve
    d. Congress

14. The consequence of printing money to finance deficits is:

    a. unemployment.
    b. inflation.
    c. deflation.
    d. stagflation.

15. When efforts to control _____ that resulted from printing money are carried out, _____ tends to increase.

    a. unemployment; unemployment
    b. inflation; inflation
    c. unemployment; inflation
    d. inflation; unemployment

16. When Paul Volcker became chairman of the Federal Reserve Board of Governors, the Fed _____ its purchase of bonds issued by the Treasury. As a consequence, the bonds had to be sold to domestic and foreign buyers, causing interest rates to _____ and unemployment to _____ .

    a. increased; decrease; increase
    b. decreased; increase; decrease
    c. decreased; increase; increase
    d. increased; decrease; decrease

17. Those who favor wage and price controls to control inflation put relatively _____ faith in traditional monetary and fiscal policies to do the job. In part, they argue these policies:
    a. little; take to long to work.
    b. much; work too fast to be socially acceptable.
    c. little; work too fast to be socially acceptable.
    d. much; take too long to work.

18. During inflation, demand _____ and supply _____ . Both shifts cause prices to _____ .
    a. increases; increases; increase
    b. decreases; decreases; decrease
    c. increases; decreases; increase
    d. decreases; increases; decrease

19. Critics of wage and price controls point out that they:
    a. have never worked.
    b. cause shortages.
    c. result in black markets.
    d. all of the above.

Part IX

Income Redistribution

Chapter 21

Sources and Measures of Income Inequality

OVERVIEW

In this and the next chapter, we turn our attention to the issue of income redistribution. Because of the various factors discussed at the beginning of this chapter, the natural outcome of economic activity in a free society will be income inequality. The remainder of this chapter discusses the various measures of income inequality and the extent of poverty in the United States.

INTRODUCTION

In the preceding chapters, the discussion focused on the problems of unemployment and inflation and what can be done to avoid or reduce these problems. This part will dwell on the distribution of income and policies aimed at changing the distribution. In a sense, the preceding chapters also were implicitly concerned with this issue. Unemployment reduces the income of the unemployed relative to employed people. Inflation also affects the income distribution. People whose incomes rise less rapidly than the price level or who hold assets that do not rise with the price level (money and bonds) suffer a reduction in income and wealth in relative and/or absolute terms.

SOURCES OF INCOME INEQUALITY

It will be useful at the outset to briefly review the reasons incomes differ among people. Basically, there are two broad reasons: (1) differences in labor earnings and (2) differences in earnings of capital. A more detailed coverage of the labor and capital markets is presented in the companion micro text, but an intuitive explanation of these markets will suffice at this point. Let us consider first the sources of differences in labor earnings. There are two: (1) differences in wages or salaries and (2) differences in hours worked. Wages or salaries differ for a variety of reasons. Perhaps most obvious are differences due to skills. Other things equal, highly skilled people tend to earn higher incomes than those with few skills. Skilled people are more productive than unskilled individuals, which makes it possible for them to earn higher salaries, and the extra income compensates for the expense of schooling or training necessary to acquire skills. Of course, innate differences among people allow some to acquire certain skills easier than others. This is especially true in music, art, athletics, and mathematics, to name a few. Experience also counts. People with many years of experience tend to earn more than newcomers because of skills acquired through years of experience and/or because of greater responsibility of the job. This is particularly true of highly skilled occupations. In relatively unskilled occupations, experience tends to make less of a difference in wages. Working conditions also influence wages. Jobs that involve harsh working conditions or are located in remote areas generally pay higher wages than those with pleasant working conditions or located in desirable locations. Discrimination can also affect wages, resulting in lower incomes for members of minority groups. Given a person's wage or salary, the number of hours worked also will influence income. Some people moonlight, working two or three different jobs, while others may be content with a part-time job, taking instead satisfaction from more leisure or time with their family. There are others who are unable to find a job because of unemployment or are unable to work because of physical or mental disability.

Differences between people in the amount of capital owned and in the rate of return on capital also create income inequality. People acquire capital by saving part of their income and/or by inheriting it, usually from parents or other family members. For a given rate of saving, a high-income person will acquire more capital than a low-income individual; for a given income, a person who saves a large fraction of that income will accumulate more capital than a spendthrift. In addition, capital is transferred from one generation to another by inheritances, after inheritance taxes. Finally, the income of owners of capital will depend on its rate of return; high rates of return yield a higher income to those people having the necessary skills to manage capital and willingness to put forth the effort. The willingness to bear risk also influences the rate of return or income from capital. High-risk ventures may pay off handsomely or they may fail. Those people with the good luck, effort, and skills to succeed end up with more income than those who fail.

It is evident from the preceding discussion that the natural outcome of a market economy will be one where incomes are distributed unequally. From the beginning of civilization, societies have wrestled with the problems of what and how much, if anything, should be done to bring the income distribution toward more equality. There can never be complete agreement on these questions because people differ in their preferences for social action. Many people argue that society has an obligation to help its less fortunate members and should therefore take some income away from higher-income people in order to bring the poor up to a higher standard of living. Others maintain that it is not equitable to deprive hard-working and talented people of their earnings.

It is evident that in the United States, and perhaps in most countries, the majority of people feel that society should take some action to alter the income distribution toward more equality. This desire is reflected by the various government programs and policies designed to take money away from high-income people in order to provide some help to those with low incomes. Much of the discussion in the next chapter will cover these policies and programs along with some of the problems or side effects they cause.

POVERTY DEFINED

At first glance, it may seem odd to be concerned with such a seemingly obvious definition. Surely, you might say, the poor are the people with little money. In general terms you would certainly be correct—additional cash in the pockets of the poor would go a long way in alleviating poverty. But how much additional cash? How low does a family's income have to be before the family is considered poverty stricken?

In 1989, the government considered an income of about $12,000 per year to be the "poverty line" for a family of four. A single individual living alone with an income of about half this amount would be considered to be on the edge of poverty. We should remember that the demarcation line that defines the so-called poor is used purely for convenience of definition. A family a few dollars over the line is really not much better off than a family a few dollars below, although the former is not defined as poor, whereas the latter is.

The definition of poverty has changed over the years, partly because of inflation and partly because of general economic growth. In the early 1960s, for example, when the nation became acutely aware of the poverty problem, a $3,000 income per year for a family of four was considered to be the cutoff point. Back in the late 1920s and early 1930s, families with $3,000-per-year income would have been considered well off. The poverty line then was less than $2,000 per year. If we compare the United States with most other nations, a $12,000 per year equivalent level of purchasing power would be considered quite comfortable. In the less developed countries where the average income may be $200 to $300 per year, the equivalent of a $12,000 yearly income in current U.S. purchasing power would be considered a mark of absolute affluence.

It is quite evident, then, that poverty is a relative thing. Its definition depends to a large extent on the public conscience. As the nation's overall average income rises, so does the accepted demarcation line between the "rich" and "poor."

Even recognizing the tendency for the definition of poverty to change over the

---

TABLE 21-1 Estimated Annual Budget Cost for a Moderate Living Standard in Urban United States, 1989*

Single person, under 35 years old	$12,345
Husband and wife, under 35 years old:	
No children	16,658
One child under 6 years	20,676
Two children under 6 years	23,058
Husband and wife, 35–54 years old:	
One child, 6–15 years	27,665
Two children, older 6–15 years of age	27,680
Three children, oldest 6–15 years of age	37,140

* Adjusted 1967 data, using the increase in the consumer price index between 1967 and 1989 as adjustment factor.

Source: *U.S. Statistical Abstract*, 1969, p. 349.

years and from country to country, the selection of a single number to represent the poverty line is a gross oversimplification. Perhaps most important is the need to recognize the variety of circumstances and environments in which people find themselves. For example, we would expect a family with young children to require more income to maintain a certain living standard than a couple with no children.

Looking at Table 21–1, it appears that despite the old cliché, two *cannot* live as cheaply as one. However, comparing the single person with the married couple, it does appear that two living together can live more economically than two living separately. Also, as shown in Table 21–1, families with older children have to spend considerably more than families with younger children to maintain the same standard of living.

Although the living costs quoted in Table 21–1 provide for a standard of living much above the poverty level, they do make it clear that different family circumstances require different incomes to reach a comparable living standard. For example, a family with three teenage children requires over twice the income of a childless couple to attain the same living standard, and over three times the income of a single person.

Place of residence also affects the amount of income required to attain a given living standard. The Social Security Administration has estimated that living costs for farm families are about 30 percent lower than the corresponding figures for urban families, although this estimate may be too low. The Bureau of the Census estimates farm living costs to be 15 percent lower than the corresponding figure for urban families. Also, living costs in small towns tend to be 10 to 15 percent lower than those in large cities. Probably the main difference is in housing. Housing costs and rents tend to be higher in large cities than in small towns and rural areas.

PERMANENT INCOME

In the discussion so far, we have considered income only during a given year. If a family's income is below the poverty line for a particular year, the family is considered poor. But even taking into account the complexities mentioned in the previous section, defining poverty by a single year's income still involves some problems. We must consider as well variation or changes in income. Perhaps the most noticeable problem here is the year-to-year fluctuation in income. Consider two comparable families: One has a steady $14,000-per-year income and the other has an income that fluctuates from, say, $8,000 per year to $22,000 per year every other year. Over a period of 10 years, the $14,000 per year family is never included in the poverty group if the cutoff point is $12,000 per year. On the other hand, the second family would fall within the poverty group in 5 of the 10 years, even though its average income over this 10-year period would have been $15,000 per year—$1,000 per year higher than the first family.

Thus, the incidence of poverty, as poverty is currently defined, can be reduced simply by reducing the variability of income. Indeed, the second family actually could suffer an absolute reduction in average income over a number of years and still be defined as "better off" simply because it escapes the every-other-year poverty classification. But it is not clear that the second family would consider itself better off with a $1,000 per year smaller, although less variable, income.

A related problem, and perhaps even more important, is the way in which a family, or person, views its long-term income potential. Many college students, for example, do not consider themselves poverty stricken even though their incomes might place them in this category. They know that in a few years or less, they will be able to enjoy a substantial increase in income. Thus, college students tend to enjoy a higher standard of living than, say, ghetto dwellers with comparable incomes but little or no hope of ever improving their lot. There can be little doubt, too, that the psychological effect of having a low income is much different for a college student than for a ghetto dweller. The hope of someday breaking out of one's poverty conditions makes these conditions somewhat more bearable. In a sense, poverty is a state of mind as well as the state of one's bank account.

The fact that people tend to look at their long-run earning potential in making consumption decisions probably makes current expenditures on consumption a better measure of poverty than current income. For example, if you have a current income of $8,000 per year but expect to be making $25,000 per year in two years, your current consumption per year is likely to be larger than someone who expects little or no increase in income. The idea that long-run average income, or permanent income as it is called, is an important determinant of current consumption was first expressed by Friedman in his book *The Theory of the Consumption Function*. This idea is referred to as the permanent-income hypothesis.

Another reason for paying attention to current expenditures instead of current income as a measure of poverty is to take account of people who live off their savings. This is particularly important for retired people. For example, it is not uncommon to observe an older person or couple selling some property or stocks to pay for medical care, buy a new car, or take a trip. Indeed, people save during their lifetime for these purposes. This is not to say, however, that there is no need to be concerned about poverty among older people. The point is that there is a great deal of difference between a couple who has $8,000-per-year income and zero savings or wealth, and a couple who has the same income but $200,000 in savings or wealth. One might raise the question: Would it be fair for society to exclude the second couple from welfare benefits if they have lived frugally and saved while the first couple did not?

THE DISTRIBUTION OF INCOME IN THE UNITED STATES

As one might expect, poverty is closely related to the distribution of income. If everyone had the same income, the question of poverty would not be likely to come up; everyone would be equally rich or equally poor, whichever you prefer. The fact that incomes do differ means that someone must be on the lower end of the income scale. Therefore, in measuring the extent of poverty, it is useful to look first at the distribution of income.

The figures in Table 21–2 show the percent of families within the various income brackets. Note in particular the large reduction in the percent of families falling in the below $5,000-per-year-income category (in constant 1988 dollars) between 1950 and 1970. This reflects the strong economic growth that occurred

TABLE 21–2 Percentage Distribution of Money Income of Families in the United States, Selected Years (constant 1988 dollars)

Annual Income Level	1950	1970	1980	1988
Under $ 5,000	13.9%	3.2%	3.4%	4.0%
$ 5,000 to 9,999	16.9	7.2	7.6	6.8
10,000 to 14,999		8.3	9.4	8.8
15,000 to 24,999	69.2	20.3	19.6	17.8
25,000 to 34,999		21.9	19.3	16.9
35,000 to 49,999		21.6	21.0	20.0
50,000 and over		17.4	19.7	25.7
Median family income	$16,326	$30,084	$30,182	$32,191

Source: U.S. Bureau of the Census, *Current Population Reports*, Series P-60, no. 166, "Money Income and Poverty Status in the United States: 1988," October 1989, p. 36.

during the 1950s and 1960s. The incomes of both the rich and poor increased. A reversal of the trend occurred during the latter half of the period, 1970 to 1988. The slowdown in economic growth, the increased unemployment during the 1980s, and the loss of the relatively good paying jobs in manufacturing caused a slight increase in the percent of families in the below-$5,000 category during this time. During the 1980s, there was a substantial increase in the percent of families in the $50,000-and-over-annual-income category. However, the percent of families in the under-$5,000 category also increased, although by a much smaller amount. The widening gap between the low- and high-income people suggests a trend toward more inequality in U.S. income distribution.

The figures in Table 21–3 provide a clearer picture of the U.S. income distribution. If one were to rank all of the families in the country from the lowest to the highest income, Table 21–3 indicates that in 1987 the lowest 20 percent of the families received 4.6 percent of the nation's income. In contrast, the 20 percent of the families having the highest income received 43.7 percent of the country's income. Whether one considers this income distribution too unequal or inequitable is a matter of opinion. The United States ranks slightly below the average in terms of income equality among the world's industrialized nations. However, as will be shown in Chapter 26, the world's less developed countries have even less equality in their income distributions than the United States and the other high-income nations.

Perhaps most disturbing is the trend toward less income equality in the United States after 1970. Since then, the share of the nation's income going to the poorest families has declined, while the high-income-family share has increased. This is a reversal of the trend that existed from 1950 to 1970 when incomes became slightly more equal. As mentioned, the slowing of economic growth in the 1970s, higher unemployment during the 1980s, and the loss of good-paying jobs in manufacturing appear to be reasons for the reversal of the 1950–1970 trend toward more equality.

TABLE 21–3 Percentage Share of Total Before-Tax U.S. Money Income Received by Each Fifth of Families, Selected Years

Family Group	1950	1970	1980	1987
Lowest fifth	4.5%	5.4%	5.1%	4.6%
Second fifth	12.0	12.2	11.6	10.8
Third fifth	17.4	17.6	17.5	16.9
Fourth fifth	23.4	23.8	24.3	24.1
Highest fifth	42.7	40.9	41.6	43.7

Source: U.S. Bureau of the Census, *Current Population Reports,* Series P-60, no. 162, "Money Income of Households, Families, and Persons in the United States: 1987" February 1989, p. 42.

THE LORENZ CURVE

Economists have long used a device to describe the nation's income distribution that is perhaps a bit more illustrative than numbers, such as those shown in Table 21–3—a device called the *Lorenz curve* after the man who developed it. The Lorenz curve is obtained by plotting the cumulative percentage of the nation's income against the cumulative percentage of the nation's families or individuals receiving this income. Income is represented on the vertical axis of the diagram and households or individuals on the horizontal axis, as shown in Figure 21–1.

Perhaps the easiest way to understand the Lorenz curve is to ask: What would the curve look like if the nation's income were distributed in a perfectly equal manner? In other words, suppose everyone received the same income. In this case, 20 percent of the nation's families would receive 20 percent of the income, 40 percent would receive 40 percent of the income, and so on. Plotting these figures on a Lorenz curve diagram would result in a straight, upward-sloping line, as shown in Figure 21–1.

No nation, of course, exhibits a completely equal distribution of income. The lowest 20 percent of the families receive substantially less than 20 percent of the

FIGURE 21–1 The Lorenz Curve

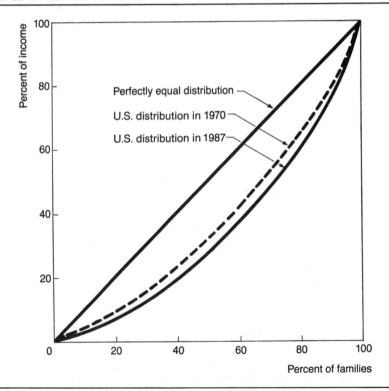

income, whereas the highest 20 percent of the families receive much more than 20 percent of the income. What does the Lorenz curve look like in a situation such as this? If we plot the percentage of income received by the lowest 20 percent of the families, say, in the United States for 1987, we go up on the vertical axis to only 4.5 percent according to the figures in Table 21–3. Proceeding on, we see that the cumulative income of the bottom 40 percent of the families, as shown in Table 21–3 for 1987, amounts to 15.4 (4.6 +10.8) percent of the total income for that year. Hence, in plotting this combination, we choose the point that corresponds to 40 percent on the horizontal axis and 15.4 on the vertical axis. If we continue on in this manner for the 60 and 80 percent points on the horizontal axis, we obtain points that also lie below the straight, bisecting line. By connecting these points, we obtain the Lorenz curve. Note that this curve lies below the straight line that depicts perfect equality.

We can conclude therefore that the more unequal the distribution of income, the more curvature there will be in the Lorenz curve. If all the income of the country were received by just one family, the curve would be a vertical line extending up from the 100 percent point in Figure 21–1. By the same token, if there is a trend toward a more equal distribution of income, the Lorenz curve will flatten out and move closer to the straight, bisecting line. However, there appears to have been a trend toward a less equal distribution of income in the United States between 1970 and the late 1980s. Thus, the Lorenz curve is somewhat flatter for 1970 than for 1987. This is illustrated in Figure 21–1, where the 1970 Lorenz curve lies closer to the perfect equality line than the 1987 curve.

THE GINI RATIO

Economists sometimes use another term to describe the distribution of income— the *Gini ratio* or *Gini coefficient*. The Gini ratio is derived from the Lorenz curve diagram and is defined as the ratio of the area between the Lorenz curve and the perfect equality line to the total area below the perfect equality line. In terms of Figure 21–2, it is the ratio of area *A* over the total area *A + B;* that is, the Gini ratio is equal to $A/(A + B)$.

The size of the Gini ratio or coefficient can vary from zero to one. As a nation moves closer to perfect equality in its income distribution, the Gini ratio will approach zero. This occurs because area *A*, the numerator in the fraction, becomes smaller and smaller as the Lorenz curve becomes flatter and approaches the perfect equality line. At the extreme of perfect equality, area *A* disappears or becomes zero, which means the value of the fraction becomes zero. Conversely, as a nation moves toward complete inequality of the income distribution, the Lorenz curve approaches the boundaries of the rectangle and area *B* grows smaller and smaller. At the extreme of complete inequality, area *B* disappears, so the ratio is equal to A/A or one.

Nations that have a relatively low Gini ratio have relative equality in their distribution of income. The advantage of using the Gini ratio is that it enables us to

FIGURE 21-2 Deriving the Gini Ratio

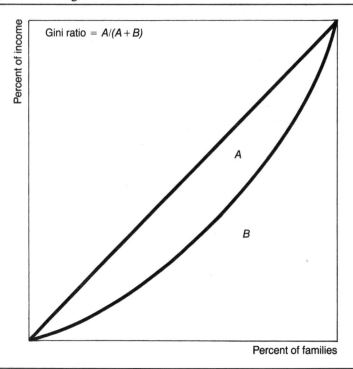

Gini ratio $= A/(A + B)$

Percent of income (vertical axis)

Percent of families (horizontal axis)

describe a nation's income distribution by a single number rather than a series of numbers, such as in Table 21–3, or a diagram, such as Figure 21–2. The Gini ratio also can be used to describe the income distributions of smaller groups of people, such as states or municipalities.

POVERTY IN THE UNITED STATES

Before turning to the policies and programs aimed at reducing poverty, it will be useful to take a brief look at the extent of poverty in the United States and how it has changed over the years. Each year the Department of Commerce establishes an income level that represents the dividing line between the poor and everyone else. This income is sometimes called the *poverty line*. It is determined by the amount of income necessary to purchase the essentials such as food, housing, transportation, and clothing that would provide a family with a "lower" living standard as defined by the Department of Commerce. This income level varies by family size and place of residence—such as, farm versus city. The poverty line for an urban family of four for selected years is presented in Table 21–4 along with the

TABLE 21–4 The U.S. Poverty Line and Percent of Families below the Line, 1959–1985 (Defined for Urban Families of Four People)

Year	Poverty Line (Current Dollars)	Percent of Families Below Poverty Line
1959	$ 2,973	22.4%
1964	3,169	19.0
1969	3,743	12.1
1974	5,038	11.6
1979	7,412	10.7
1984	10,609	11.6
1988	12,092	10.4

Source: U.S. Bureau of the Census, *Current Population Reports*, Series P-60, no. 166, "Money Income and Poverty Status of Families in the United States: 1988" (Washington, D.C.: U.S. Government Printing Office, October 1989), p. 88.

percentage of families in this category having incomes below that level. The poverty line has been moving upward in recent years primarily because of inflation. It is encouraging to note that the percentage of families falling below the poverty line declined by nearly half between 1959 and 1969. However, relatively little improvement is evident between 1969 and 1988. In fact, between 1979 and 1983 (not shown), there was some regression because of the recession and increased unemployment during the early 1980s.

It is important to recognize, however, that the incidence of poverty (percentage of families falling below the poverty line) varies considerably among families according to circumstances. As shown in Table 21–5, poverty is most prevalent among minority families, families having a female head, those having a head under 25 years of age, families headed by a person with a low level of schooling, families with many children, and families where the head is unemployed. The incidence of poverty is about the same for farm and nonfarm people, however.

SUMMARY

Incomes differ among people because of differences in labor earnings and differences in earnings from capital. Labor earnings differ because of differences in wage rates and hours worked. Wage rates differ because of a variety of factors including skills, working conditions, and discrimination. In 1988, the poverty line for a family of four was $12,092 per year. People tend to regulate their consumption according to permanent, or long-run expected, income. During the

TABLE 21–5   Selected Characteristics of Families in Relation to the Incidence of Poverty, 1988

Selected Characteristic	*Percent below Poverty Line*
1. Race and sex of householder:	
White—all families	7.9%
White—female head	26.5
Black—all families	28.2
Black—female head	49.0
2. Age of householder:	
15 to 24 years	29.7
25 to 34 years	15.0
35 to 44 years	9.2
45 to 54 years	6.9
55 to 59 years	7.1
60 to 64 years	8.4
65 and over	6.6
3. Educational attainment of householder:	
Elementary	15.8
High school	8.9
College	3.5
4. Size of family:	
2 persons	8.5
4 persons	9.9
6 persons	20.8
7 persons or more	32.3
5. Employment status of householder:	
Employed	5.5
Unemployed	34.4
6. Place of residence:	
Farm	10.6
Nonfarm	10.4

Source: U.S. Bureau of the Census, *Current Population Reports*, Series P-60, no. 166, "Money Income and Poverty Status of Families in the United States: 1988" (Washington, D.C.: U.S. Government Printing Office, October 1989), p. 68.

1970s and 1980s, the U.S. income distribution became somewhat less equal. The lowest fifth of families receive less than 5 percent of the nation's before-tax income, while the highest fifth receive over 40 percent. The Lorenz curve is obtained by plotting the cumulative percentage of the nation's income against the cumulative percentage of families, or individuals, receiving this income. The more equal the income distribution the closer the Lorenz curve is to the straight perfect equality line. The Gini ratio is obtained by dividing the area between the Lorenz curve and the perfect equality line by the total area below the perfect equality line. Poverty is most prevalent among minorities, young parents, people with low levels of schooling, large families, and the unemployed.

YOU SHOULD KNOW

1. Why incomes differ among people.
2. Why labor earnings differ among people.
3. Why wages and salaries differ among people.
4. The problems of defining poverty.
5. Why living costs differ among families.
6. The definition of permanent income.
7. The U.S. income distribution, and whether it has changed over time.
8. How the Lorenz curve portrays the nation's income distribution.
9. How the Gini ratio is computed, and how it relates to the Lorenz curve.
10. How the percent of families living below the poverty line in the United States has changed over time.
11. The characteristics of people most likely to be below the poverty line.

QUESTIONS

1. *a.* What factors account for differences in the income among people?
   b. Do you think society should try to attain a more equal distribution of income than would occur naturally? A lot more or just somewhat more? Defend your view.
2. The words *unequal* and *inequitable* are commonly used interchangeably to describe a particular income distribution. Do they mean the same thing? Explain.
3. *a.* Should people who have lived frugally all their lives and amassed considerable savings be excluded from welfare benefits if their income places them in the poverty class after they have retired? Defend your position.
   b. Should people who have squandered their money on high living during their working years rather than saving for old age be eligible for welfare benefits

after they have retired? Defend your position.
4. Most full-time college students earn a level of income (through part-time and/or summer work) that places them in the poverty class. Yet most college students probably do not consider themselves poverty stricken. Why not?
5. Why are current expenditures a better measure of poverty than current income?
6. *a.* According to the official income statistics, the rich are getting richer and the poor are getting poorer. True or false? Explain.
   b. Why do the official income distribution figures likely understate the equality of income in the United States?
7. Using a Lorenz curve, illustrate what you believe to be the income distribution among college students as compared to the income distribution for society at

large. Which group would have the highest Gini ratio?

8. *a.* What are the characteristics of a family that stands the greatest chance of being poor?

b. What characteristic is most commonly shared by poor people (besides not having money)?

SELF-TEST

1. Differences in income among people can be traced to differences in:
   a. labor earnings.
   b. earnings of capital.
   c. neither *a* nor *b.*
   d. a and b.

2. Differences in labor earnings among people can be traced to differences in:
   a. wages and salaries.
   b. hours worked.
   c. neither *a* nor *b.*
   d. a and b.

3. Differences in wages and salaries among people are due to differences in:
   a. acquired skills through education or training.
   b. inherent skills.
   c. working conditions.
   d. all of the above.

4. Differences among people in the earnings of capital are due to differences in:
   a. labor earnings and inheritances.
   b. willingness to save.
   c. rates of return on capital
   d. all of the above.

5. In the late 1980s, the poverty line for an urban family of four was about $ _____ of income per year.
   a. 3,000   *c.* 12,000
   b. 5,000   *d.* 20,000

6. Over the years, the nominal income poverty line has been increasing due to:
   a. inflation.
   b. economic growth.

c. the trend toward smaller families.
   d. a and b.

7. The cost of achieving a given standard of living differs among people due to differences in:
   a. family age and size.
   b. place of residence (urban versus rural).
   c. neither *a* nor *b.*
   d. a and b.

8. Differences in living costs between urban and rural areas are due primarily to differences in _____ costs.
   a. food   *c.* clothing
   b. housing   *d.* gasoline

9. The disadvantage of using current income to measure poverty is _____ . A more accurate indicator would be:
   a. income variation; wealth
   b. income variation; consumer expenditures
   c. cost-of-living variation; wealth
   d. cost-of-living variation; consumer expenditures

10. Permanent income is:
    a. the guaranteed minimum wage.
    b. earnings from capital, particularly land.
    c. long-run expected income.
    d. current income deflated by the CPI.

11. Most college students earn incomes from part-time and/or summer employment that places them in the poverty class. Yet most college students probably do not consider themselves poverty stricken because:

a. their permanent income exceeds their current income.

b. their current income exceeds their permanent income.

c. most do not receive financial help from parents.

d. living costs for students are lower than for employed people.

12. In constant 1988 prices, the proportion of families in the United States having annual money income under $5,000 _____ from 1950 to 1988. Most of the change occurred between:
    a. more than doubled; 1950 to 1970
    b. more than doubled; 1970 to 1984
    c. decreased by more than 50 percent; 1950 to 1970
    d. decreased by more than 50 percent; 1970 to 1988

13. From 1970 to 1988, median family income in the United States _____ in real terms.
    a. more than doubled
    b. declined by nearly one half
    c. increased slightly
    d. more than tripled

14. If U.S. families are ranked by income, the lowest fifth received about _____ percent of the 1987 income, while the highest fifth received about _____ percent.
    a. 10; 23   *c.* 15; 8
    b. 5; 44   *d.* 2; 50

15. Between 1950 and 1970 the distribution of income in the United States became slightly _____ equal. Between 1970 and 1987, it became slightly _____ equal.
    a. more; less   *c.* more; more
    b. less; more   *d.* less; less

16. It is likely that college students have more equality of incomes than the population as a whole. If so, the Lorenz curve for college students would:
    a. lie above the Lorenz curve for the total population.
    b. lie below the Lorenz curve for the total population.
    c. correspond to the perfect equality line.
    d. correspond to the two axes of the diagram.

17. Given the situation described in question 16, the Gini ratio for college students would be:
    a. larger than the ratio for the population as a whole.
    b. smaller than the ratio for the population as a whole.
    c. equal to zero.
    d. equal to one.

18. In 1979, about _____ percent of all families had incomes below the poverty line. During the early 1980s recession, this figure _____ .
    a. 17; increased   *c.* 11; increased
    b. 17; decreased   *d.* 11; decreased

19. In 1988, the percent of families falling below the poverty line was about _____ of what it was in 1959.
    a. twice   *c.* triple
    b. three times   *d.* half

20. The family characteristic that exhibits the highest incidence of poverty is:
    a. white-female head.
    b. black-female head.
    c. reside on farms.
    d. elementary level of education for household head.

Chapter 22

Poverty Programs and Problems

OVERVIEW

This chapter discusses the various programs and policies that have been implemented to help low-income people, along with the main side effects or drawbacks of each. The chapter concludes with a discussion of the negative income tax.

IMPLICIT PROGRAMS THAT HELP THE POOR

Before considering the more explicit poverty or income redistribution programs, we ought to mention that the extent of poverty is influenced by other circumstances in the economy as well.

A. Economic Growth

Although we do not generally consider economic growth as a program to help the poor, there can be no doubt that the across-the-board increase in incomes has greatly reduced the extent of poverty in the United States and in the other more highly developed nations of the world. This was clearly shown in Table 21–4, where the incidence of poverty during the 1960s was reduced by about half. Remember, too, that these figures are based on a current definition of poverty. Had we used the poverty definition from the 1930s, the incidence in 1989 would have been even lower, indeed almost nonexistent.

B. Full Employment

Since poor people make up a disproportionately large share of the unskilled labor force, a rise in unemployment hits poor people hardest. In the discussion of unemployment in Chapter 5, it was pointed out that the unskilled tend to be the first laid off. The unemployment rate among blue-collar workers rises faster than that for all workers during a recession, despite the fact that the blue-collar category includes many skilled artisans who do not face as great a threat of layoffs. Thus, during recessions the poor tend to be hurt the most.

C. Stable Prices

The presence of an unexpected high rate of inflation also hurts the poor; indeed it is likely to *make* some people poor. Those who keep a relatively large share of their assets in the form of cash, savings deposits, bonds, or life insurance policies are made relatively poorer by inflation. Contrary to popular opinion, poor people tend not to be large debtors. Because unexpected inflation helps debtors at the expense of creditors, the poor as a group tend to end up relatively worse off during inflation. Retired people living off monetary savings or relatively fixed incomes also experience a reduction in the purchasing power of their incomes.

D. Public Education

Although we may not think of public education as a policy or program to help the poor, there can be no doubt that such has been the case. The relationship of education to poverty is very clear. If we take a cross section of poor people, we find them in many different situations. Some are white, others black; some live in big cities, others in small towns or on farms. We find the poor in every region of the country and from divergent backgrounds. Indeed, the poor are far from a homogeneous group. If we tried to find a common characteristic that fit most poor people, aside from a lack of money, probably the closest we could come would be their low level and poor quality of education.

The relationship between income and education is illustrated by Table 22–1. Here we see that the median income of females is over $10,000 per year greater for those with four or more years of college than those with a high school education. For males, this difference is over $14,000 per year. The difference is even greater for those lacking a high school diploma.

The fact that income bears a close positive relationship to education does not guarantee, however, that large numbers of poor people can use education to escape from poverty. Education is a costly activity and not many poor people could afford to purchase much if they had to pay the full cost. Thus, if education is to be a major means of escape from poverty, a share of its cost must be borne by

TABLE 22–1 Relationship between Median Annual Income and Education in the United States, 1988

Educational Level	Females	Males
8 years or less	$ 5,205	$ 9,922
1 to 3 years high school	6,295	14,067
4 years high school	9,748	21,186
1 to 3 years college	13,367	25,397
4 or more years college	20,465	35,697

Source: U.S. Bureau of the Census, *Current Population Reports,* Series P-60, no. 151, "Money Income and Poverty Status in the United States: 1988," March 1989, p. 42–43.

the public. In public elementary and high schools, the entire operating costs are financed by tax revenues. In public colleges and universities, student tuition generally covers a third or less of the operating costs of the institutions, with tax revenue covering most of the remainder. There can be little doubt that the long history of public education in the United States has contributed to the upward mobility of people coming from poor families, resulting in a more equal income distribution. If all education had to be paid for by the parents of school-age children and young people, children from low-income families would have less chance of breaking out of the low-income level. This is not to say that publicly financed education should result in perfect equality of income, but it should be regarded as a major factor that moves the income distribution in the direction of more equality.

The use of publicly financed education has become a widely accepted means of achieving more income equality probably because it tends to provide equality of opportunity as opposed to equality of income. Taxpayers seem more willing to help people who in turn will help themselves than to transfer income directly to low-income people who many taxpayers may believe are unwilling to work and improve their lot in life.

Despite generous public support of educational institutions in the United States, it has been argued that the poor and lower middle class still subsidize the college education of higher-income people. The argument has some validity. Low-income people pay taxes to support public colleges and universities but utilize these institutions to a much smaller extent than the higher-income people. This is especially true for poor people among minority groups.

One way to make education more accessible and responsive to poor people is for the government to directly support or subsidize people (students) rather than educational institutions. One proposal is to give students vouchers that they could "spend" at the educational institution of their choice. This would also create some competition between educational institutions, which in turn should promote greater efficiency and higher quality of services provided.

In recent years, a number of states have adopted an open enrollment program whereby students have a choice of public schools. This program moves part of the way toward a voucher system. However, open enrollment does not include private schools. Thus, parents who send their children to private schools have to pay twice for education—once as taxes to support public schools and again as tuition in the private schools.

In states where open enrollment is available, choices of people are still quite limited because of waiting lists of students trying to get into the better schools. There is some incentive for the poorer public schools to try harder to retain students in order to retain their support. However, the better schools, usually those in the higher-income suburbs where enrollment already is at capacity and classrooms are crowded, do not have much incentive to acquire students from poorer schools and poorer neighborhoods. Thus, the open enrollment program has not been very effective in improving the quality of education for those who receive the poorest quality schooling, mainly students from low-income neighborhoods or communities.

EXPLICIT PROGRAMS TO HELP THE POOR

We turn now to programs and policies designed specifically to alter the income distribution toward more equality.

A. Minimum Wage Laws

Since poor people tend to be on the low end of the wage scale, minimum wage laws affect the poor primarily. At first glance, it may appear that minimum wage laws are a boon to poor people. After all, if a poor person cannot be paid less than $3.50 per hour, say, income will be higher than if the person's wage were $2.50 per hour. It should be kept in mind, however, that the higher minimum wage can benefit poor people only if they are working. If the market wage is lower than the minimum wage, the inevitable result will be a reduction in employment opportunities for people at the low end of the wage scale, mainly teenagers and unskilled workers. As wages increase because of minimum wage legislation, employers find it more profitable to substitute machines for labor, thereby eliminating some low-paying jobs. It can be argued, therefore, that minimum wage laws work to the detriment of low-income people by making it more difficult for them to find jobs. The high rate of unemployment among teenagers is a case in point.

B. Farm Programs

Since poverty still exists on farms and in rural areas, various farm programs designed to bolster farm incomes have been implemented. In large part, these programs have taken the form of supporting the prices of various agricultural products above their free-market levels. Again, it may appear reasonable to believe that such a program would benefit poor farmers. If a farmer can receive $5 per bushel for wheat, for example, his income ought to be higher than if $4 per bushel were received. But one of the problems of such a program is that the setting of a support price higher than the market level reduces the quantity demanded of farm products and increases the quantity supplied, causing a surplus. In order to reduce the magnitude of surplus, the government sets limits on the use of land or pays farmers to take land out of production.

Once the surplus products have accumulated in government hands, the government frequently tries to dispose of them by subsidizing their export on the world market. This lowers the world market price, making it more difficult for farmers in poor countries who do not receive a support price to compete. As a result, this dumping of surplus products on the world market retards the development of agriculture in the less developed countries.

In addition to the surplus problem, the removal of land from production encourages farmers to use more chemicals and fertilizer as substitutes for land. This in turn results in more water pollution as the chemicals either seep into the groundwater or run off with the surface water. Also, land retirement programs make it more difficult for small towns in rural areas to survive. If the land isn't farmed, the business places in these towns are not able to sell inputs to farmers or market their products. Many are forced out of business, further reducing the viability of rural communities.

Another drawback of farm programs is that they help large, high-income farmers to a greater degree than they help small, poor farmers. A little simple arithmetic makes this point clear. A small farmer who produces 1,000 bushels of wheat for sale will gain $1,000 extra income if the price of wheat is raised from $4 to $5 per bushel by the support price. But the large farmer who sells, say, 40,000 bushels of wheat per year gains $40,000 in extra income from the program.

In 1987, 30 percent of the $22.4 billion in farm subsidies went to 4 percent of the farmers, having an average net income exceeding $100,000 per year and a net worth of nearly $850,000.[1] Clearly, farm programs have increased income inequality in the United States. A large share of the payments goes to people with two to three times the average income of taxpayers.

While on the topic of farm income, the idea of parity price should be explained. The *parity price* of a commodity is the price that farmers would have to receive for that item in order for it to have the same purchasing power as in some base period. For example, if the price of wheat in the base period was $1 per bushel and the

---

[1] *Government and Commerce,* February 24, 1990, p. 582.

prices of goods and services that farmers buy increased by eight times from the base period to the current year, then the 100 percent of parity price of wheat in the current year would be $8 per bushel. In using the parity concept, the 1910–14 base period invariably is used. The use of this base is not purely accidental because these years have come to be known as the "golden age of agriculture." During this period, agricultural product prices were relatively high in comparison with the prices of goods and services purchased by farmers.

The goal of some farm groups is to raise farm prices to 100 percent of parity. In other words, they would like a given "bundle" of farm products to be able to buy as much now as in 1910–14. Since that time, it has been rare for farm products to approach 100 percent of parity. In the post–World War II years, farm products have commonly sold in the range of 60 to 90 percent of parity.

Aside from the fact that 1910–14 was an unusually profitable period for agriculture, one might think that the goal of 100 percent of parity would be a reasonable one to strive for. However, this goal has not been attainable during the post–World War II period, and it is not likely it will be attained in the foreseeable future. The main reason is that the index of prices paid by farmers, constructed by the U.S. Department of Agriculture, does not fully reflect quality improvements in the inputs purchased by farmers. Consequently, this index is biased upward, which in turn makes the 100 percent of parity price too high. At a full 100 percent of parity, farmers would be able to buy more goods and services per unit of product than in the 1910–14 period. An attempt by the government to support farm product prices at 100 percent of parity would inevitably result in large surpluses of unsold products. In the case of dairy products, price supports at levels below the 100 percent of parity market still have resulted in huge surpluses of dairy products. The consequences of price supports are discussed more thoroughly in Chapter 13 of the micro text.

C. Welfare Programs

Included under this general heading are a variety of programs specifically designed to help poor people, such as Aid to Families with Dependent Children (AFDC), hospital and medical care for the poor, school lunches, food stamps, and public housing. Although these programs undoubtedly help the poor, they have undergone a growing amount of criticism in recent years. Despite substantial increases in per capita real income over the past 20 to 25 years, welfare programs have been increasing and costing more and more each year. Moreover, taxpayers complain that not enough of the welfare funds reach poor people; too much is eaten up by highly paid administrators in the welfare bureaucracy or goes to high-income professionals, such as physicians and lawyers. The present welfare programs also give rise to a number of undesirable side effects.

For example, there is the built-in incentive for breaking up families. Poor families with several children find that the income of the wife and children can be doubled in many instances if the husband leaves home and the family goes on welfare. Consider, for example, a man with a wife and two children who earns $700 per month. If the husband and wife separate, the wife may then become eligible for welfare payments under the AFDC program. In many states, the welfare payments would be as high as the husband's take-home pay. As a result, the family (husband plus wife) could double its income by the husband leaving home. This provides a rather strong incentive for families to separate, at least for the purpose of applying for welfare. It also acts as a strong disincentive for families to reunite once they have separated.

In addition, the program takes over the support of many children born to unwed mothers. This is not to criticize these people for taking advantage of the program. But it is unlikely that society would consciously design a program that promotes the breakup of families or pays young unwed mothers to have more children. Yet this is what society has done in the current welfare programs. This is not to say that *all* single-parent families have resulted from a desire to benefit from the program. But the large increase in single-parent families coinciding with the inception of the AFDC program makes it hard to believe that the program is neutral in its effect on family behavior. Any program that increases the number of children growing up without both parents while shifting the cost of rearing them to society leaves a great deal to be desired.

D. Social Security and Unemployment Insurance

These two programs are more straightforward and less controversial than the ones we have just discussed. Perhaps the major criticism of the social security program is that it has elements of a 100 percent tax phenomenon. If a retired person wants to supplement his or her income with part-time work, the individual must be careful not to earn over the allowable maximum, or else the social security benefits will be lost. If these benefits are lost, it is equivalent to a 100 percent tax on wage income over the cutoff point. Surprisingly, there is no limit on the amount of income that can be earned from capital in being able to qualify for benefits.

E. Progressive Income Tax

As explained in Chapter 16, a progressive income tax is one that levies higher tax rates on high incomes than on low incomes. In the United States, the degree of progressivity has been reduced somewhat in the 1986 tax law. Conceptually, a progressive tax is an effective method of redistributing income. First, it reduces the after-tax income more for high-income people than it does for those with low incomes. Second, if some of the money collected as taxes is used for helping low-income people, the disparity in the living standard between rich and poor is further reduced.

THE NEGATIVE INCOME TAX

First proposed by Milton Friedman in his 1962 book, *Capitalism and Freedom,* the negative income tax has been called a number of things including "income maintenance" or a "family assistance plan." The proposal is surprisingly simple. If society is really serious about helping poor people and wants to help them in the most efficient way possible, the best way is for the government to supplement their incomes by a so-called negative tax—a payment from the government to the poor.

Perhaps the easiest way to understand how the negative income tax plan might work is to look at a specific example. Suppose that under the ordinary income tax schedule, a family of four could earn up to $10,000 per year without paying any federal income tax. Let us consider the case of a poor family of four with a total income of $6,000 per year. This family would file an income tax return reporting that it had an income deficit of $4,000. Let us assume that the negative tax rate or the refund rate is 50 percent. In this case, the family would receive a $2,000 check (0.50 × $4,000) from the government, which in a sense is a negative tax. Thus, the family would end up with a total income of $8,000: $6,000 from its initial income plus $2,000 in negative taxes.

It is important to recognize, too, that the negative tax rate must be something less than 100 percent. In other words, the government would not make up the entire difference between a family's initial income and the zero tax income ($10,000 in our example). For example, suppose the family had an opportunity to earn an extra $1,000, so that its initial before-tax income would increase to $7,000. With a $3,000 deficit, the government would pay $1,500, giving the family a total income of $8,500: the initial $7,000 plus the $1,500 negative tax. In this second case, the family's after-tax income would have increased to $8,500. If the government had made up the entire difference between the $10,000 base and the family's actual income, the total income would have been $10,000 in both cases. Thus, there would be no incentive for the family to earn additional income if it remained below $10,000. But as long as the negative tax law is less than 100 percent, the family still has an incentive to earn money on its own. Of course, the negative tax rate and the base zero-tax income can be set at any level desired as long as the rate is kept below 100 percent. The 50 percent rate and $10,000 income are just examples. Additional refinements could be built into the plan, such as allowing deductions from actual income for such things as medical expenses above a certain level before calculating the negative tax.

The arguments in favor of the negative tax are quite convincing. First, it would be possible to eliminate or at least reduce the variety of present programs that are overburdened with administrative expense and often treat different groups unequally. The negative income tax would not suffer from either of these shortcomings. Second, poor people would not have to suffer the indignities and degradation that they are now subject to in the welfare schemes that label the poor in full view of their neighbors. Also, programs that dole out a few dollars for this and a few dollars for that treat the poor as if they were second-class citizens who could not be trusted with money. To be poor is bad enough, but to suffer the indignities of the present welfare setup is more than some can bear.

Granted, the negative income tax scheme does present some problems. Probably the major concern of middle- and high-income taxpayers is that the assurance of a guaranteed annual income might prompt people with low-paying jobs to simply quit working and live off the taxes of employed people. However, the less than 100 percent negative tax rate feature would mitigate this problem, since a family always would have a higher net income by working than by not working. The present welfare programs are more open to this criticism. If a welfare recipient chooses to work, AFDC and other welfare payments stop. For people with few skills and low earning ability, joining the labor force at a low wage can decrease income. In such cases, there is not much incentive to get off the welfare rolls and go to work. With the negative income tax, recipients always end up with more money by working than not working.

The way in which people might spend the money received from negative tax payments also troubles some people. What is to stop poor people from buying alcohol, football tickets, and color television sets with their extra income (that is, from acting like middle-class Americans)? Our willingness to provide welfare for low-income people appears to be influenced by what the recipients get from the welfare. Necessities such as food and shelter are most desired, as evidenced by the food stamp, AFDC, and public housing programs.

Yet this is a somewhat naive approach. If a poor family receives $100 worth of food stamps or subsidized housing, this leaves $100 more of its own money with which to buy such nonessentials as mentioned above. Also, providing welfare "in kind" rather than in money is not likely to maximize the welfare of the recipients for a given budgetary cost. Items that are given free or at a reduced price will of course be accepted but may not be what the family would have bought had they received an equivalent amount of cash. If what they would have bought is different, we can infer that the payment in kind is less desirable than the cash. For example, which would you prefer: $10,000 of rent for low-income housing or $10,000 in cash? The provision of low-income housing also has a tendency to create ghettos, something that could be avoided if low-income people were given an equivalent amount of money even in the form of housing stamps and were free to live where they chose.

The cost of a negative income scheme is regarded by some as being out of the realm of possibility. Naturally, if the minimum income level were set high, the cost would be high. But this is not the question. The relevant question is whether the amount society decides to spend on welfare, say, $200 billion, can be more efficiently spent by the current setup or by the negative tax scheme. There can be little doubt that the negative tax scheme would be more efficient and equitable. We could avoid a large part of the welfare bureaucracy that has grown up over the years, giving this money directly to poor people. Moreover, we could be sure that the poor would receive the benefits and in ways that would not degrade them or label them as second-class citizens.

If a negative income tax plan were ever put into effect, it would be important to design it in such a way that families would not have an incentive to separate, such as occurs under the AFDC program. One way of removing such an incentive would be to require the husband to pay as taxes the equivalent of his wife's negative tax payment when he files his income tax at the end of the year. In this case, the family would receive the same income regardless of whether they stayed together or separated. In fact, there would be an incentive to stay together in this case because a family living in one location should be able to live more economically than one living in two locations.

SUMMARY

Although they are not regarded as poverty programs, economic growth, full employment, stable prices, and public education enhance the ability of low-income people to improve their income and standards of living. Minimum wage laws, farm programs, welfare programs, social security, and the progressive income tax are the main explicit programs designed to help low-income people and reduce the inequality of income. Drawbacks of these programs include higher unemployment from minimum wage laws; the greatest aid to large, high-income farmers from farm programs; the large public bureaucracy and incentives to break up families from welfare programs; and a high effective tax from social security on retired people who wish to work. A negative income tax has been proposed as an efficient way to redistribute income.

YOU SHOULD KNOW

1. The four implicit programs that help the poor.
2. The relationship between education and income.
3. The five explicit programs that help the poor.
4. Why minimum wage laws increase unemployment, and who are most affected.
5. Why farm programs mainly help large, high-income farmers.
6. Why welfare programs promote the breakup of low-income families.
7. How the social security program can tax income of semiretired people at a 100 percent rate.
8. How the progressive income tax is perceived to reduce income inequality.
9. How a negative income tax might work.
10. The main advantages of a negative income tax, and why it is not widely accepted.

QUESTIONS

1. Discuss how each of the following circumstances help low-income people.
   a. economic growth
   b. full employment
   c. stable prices
2. Virtually all societies have utilized public

education as a way to help low-income people.

a. What evidence is there to suggest that education reduces poverty?

b. Why is public education looked on as a more desirable way of helping poor people than welfare programs?

3. a. Describe the mechanism of providing public education through the voucher system.

b. Would the voucher system help low-income people? Explain.

4. Cite the undesirable side effects of each of the following programs aimed at helping low-income people:

a. Minimum wage laws.

b. Farm programs.

c. Welfare programs.

5. In what way does the social security law require recipients of social security benefits to pay a 100 percent tax on income earned over a certain level?

6. What are the two ways that a progressive income tax can help low-income people move closer to the standard of living of high-income people?

7. a. Describe the mechanics of helping low-income people by a negative income tax.

b. What would be the advantage of such a system?

c. Why has it not been more favorably received?

SELF-TEST

1. The economic condition(s) most conducive to reducing poverty in a country is (are):

a. inflation.

b. economic growth.

c. full employment.

d. b and c.

2. The characteristic that is most common among poor people is:

a. old.

b. reside in rural areas.

c. low level and poor quality of schooling.

d. reside in large cities.

3. Society has attempted to increase the educational levels of young people by:

a. publicly financed educational institutions.

b. lowering entrance requirements for students from low-income families.

c. establishing private schools.

d. all of the above.

4. During the late 1980s, females with four or more years of college on the average earned over _____ more per year than those with a high school education. For males, the difference was _____ per year.

a. $5,000; $10,000   c. $13,000; $20,000

b. $10,000; $14,000   d. $17,000; $25,000

5. In general, the highest-quality public schools are found in:

a. rural areas   c. rich communities.

b. large cities   d. poor communities.

6. The main problem of using a legislated minimum wage to increase incomes of those with low earnings is:

a. it creates a shortage of skilled workers.

b. it increases unemployment among low wage earners.

c. many employers do not comply with the law.

d. it increases unemployment among skilled workers.

7. Efforts to increase the incomes of farm people have been primarily:
   a. price supports on farm commodities.
   b. price supports on land.
   c. price controls on inputs used by farmers.
   d. minimum wage legislation.

8. The main drawback(s) of farm programs is that:
   a. they create food shortages.
   b. they create surpluses of farm commodities.
   c. most of the help goes to the largest and most prosperous farmers.
   d. *b* and *c*.

9. Parity prices of farm commodities are those prices that give the commodities the same purchasing power they had in:
   a. 1910–14.   c. 1940–44.
   b. 1930–34.   d. 1980–84.

10. The drawback(s) of using parity prices as an indicator of purchasing power of farm commodities:
    a. The base period has come to be known as the "golden age of agriculture."
    b. Quality of inputs has increased.
    c. Inflation has occurred.
    d. *a* and *b*.

11. Undesirable side effects(s) of the AFDC program:
    a. promotes breakup of families.
    b. increases the incentive for unwed mothers to have children.
    c. keeps couples together that would be happier if they separated.
    d. *a* and *b*.

12. Drawback(s) of the social security program:
    a. Much of the money goes to highly paid administrators.
    b. It levies a 100 percent tax on income of semiretired people who work and earn over a certain amount.

    c. The poorest people receive the lowest payments.
    d. *b* and *c*.

13. The progressive income tax can be used to increase equality of incomes by:
    a. taking a larger percent of the income away from the rich than from the poor.
    b. spending the tax collections on programs that help poor people.
    c. the loopholes that exist in the tax law.
    d. a and b.

14. A negative income tax is:
    a. a tax on losses.
    b. a tax on poor people.
    c. a payment from the government to poor people.
    d. a payment from the government to rich people.

15. If the zero-tax income is $10,000 per year a family that earned $5,000 per year on its own would have a total income of _____ if the negative tax rate were 50 percent.
    a. $7,500   c. $6,500
    b. $5,000   d. $4,000

16. Incentives to earn income would be maintained under a negative tax scheme if the negative tax rate were _____ 100 percent.
    a. equal to
    b. less than
    c. greater than

17. Advantages(s) of a negative income tax:
    a. It is an efficient way of helping low-income people.
    b. It provides help to those who need it.
    c. Recipients can buy the goods and services that maximize their utility.
    d. All of the above.

18. Drawback(s) of a negative income tax:
    a. It is inefficient.
    b. It is thought to reduce work incentives.
    c. Society prefers to transfer necessities such as food and shelter to low-income people rather than money.
    d. *b* and *c*.

Part X

International Trade and Exchange Rates

Chapter 23

International Trade

OVERVIEW

We now turn our attention from the national to the international economy. The main objective of this chapter is to provide an understanding of why international trade benefits all nations. In the following chapter, we consider exchange rates between currencies—how they are determined and how they affect trade.

THE BASIS FOR TRADE

Perhaps the easiest way to understand the basis for trade is to consider why each of us as an individual engages in trade. If people did not trade with each other, everyone would have to be self-sufficient. The extreme inefficiency of self-sufficient people is well documented throughout history, starting with the cave dwellers. It did not take people, even the most primitive people, long to discover that by specializing in one or a few activities, their total productivity could be increased greatly. For example, in tribal societies, it is well known that certain people made the utensils, others hunted, and still others cared for the domestic animals and crops. These people knew that the output of the entire tribe was increased when even a modest amount of specialization took place.

The opportunity to increase output also accounts for present-day trade between people, whether it be people in the same neighborhood or people of different regions of a country or different countries. In the United States, for example, it would be foolish for people in the northern part of the nation to attempt to grow their own citrus fruits; the output of the entire nation is increased when people in the South and West produce the nation's fruit, part of which is traded with the people of the North for items produced there. A trade barrier between North and South surely would reduce the output of the entire country, because each region would have to undertake production for which it is not well suited. The same reasoning applies to trade between countries. (In the discussion that follows, we will speak of international trade as trade between two countries. But in reality, it is trade between people living within different national boundaries.) If the United States attempted to produce its own coffee, for example, it would have to forgo the production of a relatively large amount of other products because of the resources that would have to be devoted to relatively inefficient coffee production.

The examples in the preceding paragraph illustrate what is perhaps the most obvious reason for the increase in total output or productivity resulting from trade—differences in climate or natural resources. Citrus fruits and coffee require special climates, so it makes sense to produce these products in the areas that have the appropriate climate. Similarly, the extraction of minerals or petroleum can take place only where nature provides these resources. Other examples include location of a fishing industry in a specific area due to the proximity to a large body of water, or the existence of lumbering due to abundant tree growth. It would not make much sense for the Great Plains to produce lumber and the Northwest to produce corn, for example.

In addition to differences in the natural endowment, specialization and trade take place because of the past establishment of traditions and institutions that favor a certain industry. For example, Taiwan has become well known for its light manufacturing industries; Germany, for its machines and tools; Sweden, for its high-quality steel; and Switzerland, for its watches. Traditions of workmanship and knowledge are passed down from generation to generation, giving the nation or region a distinct advantage in certain kinds of production.

The existence of a particular industry often gives rise to other supporting industries and institutions. For example, trade centers or markets are established where buyers and sellers can get together. Financial institutions develop that cater to a particular industry because of the specific knowledge required. If a large share of the people are employed by an industry, it is common for the public schools to offer training that is specifically applicable to the industry. Economists refer to the increase in productivity that occurs because of the formation of other supporting industries or institutions as *external economies*. In other words, an industry may become more productive as it becomes larger because of the existence of other supporting industries and institutions.

It is sometimes argued that the people of certain regions or nations have some innate ability or characteristic that makes them better suited for certain occupations. For example, the Japanese have gained a reputation for being nimble and able to assemble tiny components of their products. The Germans and Swiss, on the other hand, are often thought of as processing a characteristic of preciseness that makes them well qualified to produce tools and instruments. It is not clear whether such traits are inherent in the population or learned or acquired through generations of people doing the jobs that require these traits. At any rate, if differences in skills among populations do exist, regardless of whether they are inherent or acquired, it is reasonable to expect that a nation or area will be better off if it accentuates the activities that it does comparatively well.

COMPARATIVE ADVANTAGE

It is easy to see how specialization and trade can be beneficial to areas or nations because of special advantages in the production of certain goods or services. As mentioned, these advantages may stem from climatic conditions, natural resource endowments, human skills, and so on. It is possible, however, to find areas or even nations that seem to have been "shortchanged" by nature and as a result do not possess special advantages vis-à-vis other areas or nations. In these cases, will there be any incentive for the more productive nations to trade with their less productive neighbors? After all, in order to have trade between two nations, or even two people, it is necessary for both to gain from the transaction. If one trader gains and the other loses, the loser will refuse to trade.

We are indebted to one of the classical economists, David Ricardo, for first shedding light on this question. Using the production of cloth and wine in Portugal and England as an example, Ricardo demonstrated that even though Portugal might be able to produce each unit of wine and cloth more "efficiently" than England, it still was to the advantage of Portugal to engage in trading these two commodities with England. The incentive for trade to take place in this situation is much less obvious than the examples we discussed earlier, where each country has a natural advantage in one of the commodities.

The key to understanding the basis for trade in this latter situation is found in the concept known as *comparative advantage.* Perhaps the easiest way to understand this concept is to construct a simple example. Let us use the United States and United Kingdom as our two countries, and fish and chips (potatoes) as the two products. If you wish you may assume that the United States is more efficient in both, or vice versa. We will see later any difference in the level of absolute efficiency between the two countries does not affect the outcome.

Table 23–1 is a production possibilities schedule showing various possible combinations of output of the two goods for the two countries. Notice that when chips are increased in each country, the output of fish declines, and similarly if more fish is produced, the quantity of chips must decline. This tells us that each country has a limited amount of resources and each cannot simultaneously increase the production of both commodities.

The opportunity cost of producing each commodity in each country can be computed from the figures in Table 23–1. For example, if the United States wishes to increase its chips output from 0 to 150 million tons, it must give up 50 million tons of fish $(100 - 50 = 50)$. Recall from Chapter 3 that the cost on a per-ton basis can be determined by applying the following simple formula:

$$\text{Give up/Get} = 50/150 = 1/3$$

In this case, the United States must give up one-third ton of fish per ton of chips. To keep the example simple, constant opportunity costs are assumed so that the same cost is obtained moving from possibility B to C.

In the United Kingdom, the opportunity cost of increasing chip production is obtained in the same manner. Again moving from possibility A to B, the cost per

TABLE 23–1 Example of Production Possibilities Schedules for Fish and Chips in the United States and United Kingdom (millions of tons)*

	United States		United Kingdom	
Possibility	Fish	Chips	Fish	Chips
A	100	0	40	0
B	50	150	20	10
C	0	300	0	20

* These figures represent an example only and are not intended to reflect actual production in the two countries.

ton of chips is two (20/10 = 2). Notice that the cost of producing extra chips is relatively expensive in the United Kingdom compared to the United States, two in the United Kingdom, one third in the United States.

The cost of fish is obtained in a similar manner. Moving from possibility C to B of Table 23–1, the United States must give up 150 chips (300 − 150) to obtain 50 fish. Applying the above formula, the cost of an extra ton of fish is 3 tons of chips. In the United Kingdom, the cost of producing an extra ton of fish is one-half ton of chips. Notice in this case, the cost of producing more fish is relatively expensive in the United States (three) compared to the United Kingdom (one half). The following table summarizes these costs. Notice that for each country, the cost of chips is the reciprocal of the cost of fish, and vice versa.

	United States	United Kingdom
Cost of an extra ton of chips in terms of fish given up	1/3 ton of fish	2 tons of fish
Cost of an extra ton of fish in terms of chips given up	3 tons of chips	1/2 ton of chips

From these figures, we can say that chip production is relatively efficient in the United States because a small amount of fish must be given up to produce an extra ton of chips. In international trade terminology, the United States has a *comparative advantage* in chips. Conversely, the United Kingdom has a comparative advantage in fish because the amount of chips given up per ton of fish is small. *Comparative advantage* means that the opportunity cost of producing an extra unit of a product is smaller than in another country. Climate and natural resources are important determinants of a country's comparative advantage. For example, Saudi Arabia has a comparative advantage in oil vis-à-vis most other nations.

THE GAINS FROM TRADE

So far we have illustrated a situation where the United States has a comparative advantage in chips and the United Kingdom a comparative advantage in fish. So what? We will show that each country can have more of both products by specializing to a certain extent in the production of the good in which it has a comparative advantage and trading part of the increased output of that good to the other country. The only thing required for this little sleight of hand is that the price paid by each country for the imported good is less than the opportunity cost of producing it at home.

Let us suppose that the world market price of fish and chips is one-for-one. That is, the price of a ton of fish equals the price of a ton of chips. This price is a good deal for both countries. To produce an extra ton of fish in the United States, three tons of chips must be given up. By trading chips for fish, only one ton of chips must be given up. For the United Kingdom, the trading price also is a good deal. Domestically, the United Kingdom must give up two tons of fish to obtain an extra ton of chips. But the United Kingdom can buy chips by exchanging only one ton of fish per ton of chips. Hence, there is a mutual advantage for both countries to trade.

In establishing the trading price, the exporting country must receive a higher price than it can obtain at home, otherwise it has no incentive to sell abroad. By the same token, the importing country must be able to buy from abroad at a lower price than exists at home in order to have an incentive to do so. The world market for commodities will establish prices within a range that makes trade mutually beneficial to both trading partners.

Let us now illustrate how both countries can end up with more of both products after trading. As an initial situation, suppose both countries are producing at possibility B, as shown by Table 23–1. The corresponding output figures are shown in the first line of Table 23–2. Now let us suppose that each country specializes to a certain extent in the product for which it has a comparative advantage—chips in the United States and fish in the United Kingdom. Let the United States increase

TABLE 23–2 Illustrating the Gains from Trade

	United States		United Kingdom	
	Fish	*Chips*	*Fish*	*Chips*
Before trade	50	150	20	10
Specialize	− 5	+ 15	+ 12	− 6
Net	45	165	32	4
Add imports	+ 10			+ 10
Subtract exports		− 10	− 10	
After trade	55	155	22	14

its chip production by 15 million tons. Because of the opportunity cost of one-third ton of fish per extra ton of chips, the United States reduces fish output by 5 million tons. By the same token, let the United Kingdom increase fish output by 12 million tons. Because of the one-half opportunity cost, 6 million tons of chips are given up.

Now let trade take place, at the one-for-one price. Assume the United States exports 10 of the 15 million extra tons of chips and imports 10 million tons of fish. The United Kingdom will in turn have 10 million extra tons of chips and 10 million less tons of fish. The trade is summarized in Table 23–2.

Notice that both countries have more of both products after trade than before. This outcome may at first appear a bit "fishy." After all, there has been no increase in the total resources in each country. The increased output occurs because each country can specialize in what it does best by trading with the other country.

INCOMPLETE SPECIALIZATION

In order to simplify the above example, a number of complicating factors were omitted. First, as mentioned, constant opportunity cost was assumed. In reality, the opportunity cost of increasing the output of each product in both countries could be expected to increase as resources not well suited to either fish or chip production were drawn into each. At low levels of fish production, the United States may well produce fish domestically cheaper than it could buy them abroad. The same is true of chips (potatoes) in the United Kingdom. Thus, even with trade, it is not unusual for nations to produce a portion of imported products domestically.

Transportation costs also are important in determining the extent of international trade. If transport costs more than offset comparative advantage, trade will not take place. This is particularly true of heavy or bulky products. We do not observe much international trade in cement blocks, for example.

The absolute size of a country and the per capita income of its inhabitants also can be expected to influence the degree of specialization. As you would expect, large nations such as the United States tend to be much more diverse in terms of climate and natural resources than smaller nations. Much of the trade between states within the United States would be international trade if the country were made up of a number of smaller countries. In addition, a small nation, even if it specializes in a particular product, may not be able to satisfy the total demand of a large nation. Hence, the larger country may have to produce a portion of the product domestically in addition to importing in order to satisfy the total demand for it.

The extent of a nation's trade with other countries is influenced also by political and military considerations. It the government of one nation is not on speaking terms with the government of another nation, trade between the two countries is not likely.

National policies aimed at achieving self-sufficiency are common, particularly among developing nations. The implication is that a nation is better off if it produces most of everything it consumes. As we saw in the preceding section, this will not be true if the nation has a comparative advantage in one or more products. Of course, the advantage of trading diminishes a great deal when one trading partner abruptly refuses to buy or sell. This problem has come to the surface a number of times in recent years. For example, the Arab oil embargo led many Americans to believe that self-sufficiency is better than trade because we could at least be assured of supplies. The same was true of other nations when the U.S. government temporarily prohibited exports of certain agricultural products during 1974 and 1975, and again during the Carter administration's embargo of agricultural exports to the Soviet Union. In order for trade to flourish, it must take place under conditions of trust where trading partners allow themselves to be dependent on each other. Unfortunately, in the arena of international politics, trust and the willingness to depend on other nations probably are the exception rather than the rule.

PRIVATE GAINS AND LOSSES FROM TRADE

In our previous discussion, we stressed that society as a whole gains when nations tend to concentrate their production on goods and services they produce comparatively well and trade the excess for goods that other nations can produce more cheaply (in terms of other goods given up). However, we should point out that specific individuals or groups within an economy are likely to reap economic gains from trade and other groups are likely to suffer losses.

It is relatively easy to see how profits can be made. Suppose some enterprising U.S. citizen, on reading international price quotations, notices that the price of a ton of chips in the United Kingdom is equal in value in two tons of fish, but the cost of chips in the United States is only equivalent to one-third tons of fish. What a splendid opportunity to make a profit. The entrepreneur can buy chips in the United States at the relatively low price (one-third ton of fish) and sell them in the United Kingdom for the relatively high price (two tons of fish). After paying transport and marketing costs, the difference in the net price between the two countries can still yield a tidy profit.

The same thing can be done with fish, buying them cheap in the United Kingdom and selling them high in the United States. At some point, the profit margin will disappear as the increased demand for chips in the United States (for the export market) drives their price up, and the increased supply of fish in the United States (from abroad) drives its price down. The same is true in the United Kingdom, as the fish price increases and the chips price decreases there.

In addition to import and export firms that can earn profits from trade, several other groups are affected. Chip producers in the United States will benefit from the export market, as will the fishing industry in the United Kingdom. On the other hand, the fishing industry in the United States and chip producers in the United Kingdom will not welcome trade because the inflow of cheap foreign goods lowers domestic prices and takes part of their market. In spite of the benefits to consumers of both products in both countries (recall that both countries can have more of both products), it is common for adversely affected industries to petition their respective governments to limit the entry of cheap foreign goods. It will be useful to briefly explain the effects of trade barriers and analyze some of the arguments used to justify such barriers.

QUOTAS AND TARIFFS

As the name implies, a *quota* simply limits the amount of a good that can be brought into a country. A quota may be set up to exclude a good entirely or to allow the import of a certain maximum amount per year. A *tariff,* on the other hand, is a tax on an imported good. As a result of tariffs, the prices of imported goods to domestic consumers are increased over what they would otherwise be. And the higher prices discourage domestic buyers from purchasing imported articles. Thus, quotas and tariffs both reduce trade. The following are some of the more common arguments used to justify trade restrictions.

1. Tariffs as a Revenue Source.   Governments generally are on the lookout for sources of revenue, particularly for ways to "fleece the goose with the least amount of squawking." It might seem logical, therefore, to impose a tax on foreign producers; that is, let foreigners help pay the country's taxes. But in reality the people of the nation imposing the tariff end up paying the equivalent of the tax anyway because of the higher prices they pay for the imported items. Also, the reduction in imported goods that results from the tariff makes it necessary for consumers of the importing country to use relatively more of the higher-priced domestically produced goods.

2. Tariffs to Equalize for Low-Cost Foreign Labor.   A common argument for tariffs in the United States is that the wages of labor in foreign countries are but a fraction of U.S. wages and, therefore, foreign products can be made more cheaply and drive U.S. products off the market. A basic flaw in this argument is that it makes no mention of why U.S. workers receive higher wages. In market economies, the wage of a worker is determined ultimately by his or her productivity. If a person is paid $60 per day, that person has to produce at least $60 per day in order for the person's employer to pay this wage.

Workers in other nations who happen to be paid a fraction of U.S. wages find themselves in this unhappy situation because their output is small—a fraction of the output of U.S. workers. Mainly this stems from the fact that low-paid foreign workers have a relatively small amount of capital (machines, tools, and so on) to work with. Also, their skills may be less sophisticated than those of U.S. workers. Both of these factors explain why foreign workers, especially those in the less developed countries, earn such low pay. The main point is that well-paid labor does not necessarily imply high-cost products. The important factor in determining the cost of a product is the price of labor and capital in relation to their productivities.

A U.S. worker may earn three times the pay of a foreign worker, but if the person's contribution to output is more than three times that of the foreign worker, the U.S. worker is actually the cheaper of the two. It appears, however, that during the 1970s, wages in the United States increased to such high levels in certain industries that the products of these industries were no longer competitive with those of foreign producers. During the early 1980s, for example, wages plus fringe benefits averaged about $19 per hour in the U.S. auto industry compared to about $8 per hour for Japanese automakers. Since Japanese automobile factories were even more automated and modern than U.S. factories at that time, it became cheaper to produce cars in Japan than in the United States. An industry can easily lose its comparative advantage if its costs increase more rapidly than costs in other countries.

It is of interest to note also that low-wage countries have gained a comparative advantage vis-à-vis the United States in the production of labor-intensive items, such as the assembly of electronic components. Other aspects of production of modern electronic products may still take place in the United States, however, where the technological base still gives it a comparative advantage.

If nations were to impose tariffs to offset lower wages in other countries, trade between countries would be greatly diminished because of the reduction or elimination of comparative advantage. In other words, the argument for a tariff to offset low wages in other countries, carried to its logical conclusion, implies the elimination of international trade to the detriment of all concerned.

3. The "Infant Industry" Argument.

Sometimes nations attempt to justify tariffs on foreign products in order to reduce competition for a newly established domestic industry. The argument is that small industries should be given protection until they can grow large enough to take advantage of economies of scale and thus produce at a lower cost in the future.

The problem with this argument is that an industry should not come into existence until it can earn a rate of return on its capital that is comparable to other nonsubsidized industries. If the return on its capital is lower, the economy could enjoy a larger real output by investing in other industries. For example, if the rate of return on other additional investment in the economy is 15 percent, then the rate of return on the infant industry over the long run should also be at least 15 percent. It it takes a tariff to achieve a 15 percent return, we know that the true rate of return is less than that, indicating the economy is not investing its resources wisely. If the return is relatively high, as is often implied, then is should not need a tariff to become established. The high profits in the later years should be great enough to compensate for any losses in its early years.

4. Tariffs for Retaliation.

It has been argued that although tariffs and quotas on imports are undesirable, a nation often is forced to retaliate against other nations that have set up trade restrictions of their own. But it can be argued that a government that retaliates by increasing its tariffs really does not have the economic well-being of its people in mind. The imposition of a tariff by a nation reduces the products coming into that country, thereby reducing the total amount of goods and services available to its people. The fact that one government chooses to reduce the economic well-being of its people is not a good reason for another government to follow suit. Retaliatory tariffs are analogous to two governments trying to best each other, each saying, "I can deprive my people of more things than you can deprive yours of."

5. "Buy American."   Frequently we see bumper stickers or advertisements urging us to buy American-made products. Apparently, the objective is to keep foreign products out while providing employment for U.S. workers. However, it is necessary to keep in mind that thousands of U.S. workers are employed in industries producing for foreign markets. Unless we buy from other countries, they cannot buy from us. Without trade, some of the workers in export industries would have to find jobs in other industries. So it is not clear that workers in these industries end up any better off in the long run.

Even if jobs are saved, one should ask, At what cost? It is estimated that when the Japanese "voluntarily" limited their exports of cars and light trucks to the United States because of congressional threats of retaliation, car prices in the United States increased by an average of $3,000 per vehicle over what they would have been.[1] As a result, American consumers ended up paying $350 million per year more for their cars. Even if 10,000 jobs were saved, which is unlikely due to the resulting decrease in exports, the estimated cost to U.S. consumers was $35,000 per job per year.

The "buy American" slogan also is used as an argument for keeping American dollars at home. Yet, as pointed out in Chapter 17, money is just a convenient tool for exchanging goods and services. The important things are the real goods and services that are available to society, not the number of pieces of paper called money that it has. The amount of money in a society can be increased simply by the government's cranking up the printing presses.

In our discussion so far, we have not presented a convincing argument for tariffs and quotas, but we cannot deny that they are extremely popular throughout the world. Thus, there must be some reason for having them. To be perfectly honest, tariffs and quotas can result in a short-term gain for specific industries. In our fish and chips example, the entrance of foreign fish into the United States or foreign chips into the United Kingdom probably would have reduced the price of fish in the United States and the price of chips in the United Kingdom, or at least kept prices lower than they would otherwise be. By placing tariffs or quotas on these products and reducing imports, U.S. fish producers and U.K. chips producers probably would enjoy higher prices.

Thus, when advocating trade restrictions, industry spokespersons should, to be honest, admit that tariffs or quotas will help them by keeping the prices of their

---

[1] Todd G. Bucholz, *New Ideas from Dead Economists* (New York: New American Library, 1990).

products higher than they would otherwise be. Efforts to increase tariffs or lower quotas often increase during downturns in economic activity, as observed in the early 1980s in regard to Japanese cars. The object is to keep out foreign products so as to maintain higher domestic sales. Granted, it is in the interest of industry representatives or union leaders who represent the labor in industries that face foreign competition to try to keep out foreign products. We should not expect businesspeople who face declining sales or union members whose jobs are in jeopardy to think first of society's welfare. But the government should.

It should be stressed also that trade restrictions are likely to provide only short-term benefits to the industries they are designed to help. In the long run, many of the people in the protected industries probably would have been better off to leave and enter industries in which the nation has a comparative advantage. By doing so, their incomes might be increased even more because of their greater productivity in other lines of work. Tariffs and quotas often delay adjustments that eventually come about in the long run.

A more subtle, but economically justifiable, argument for a trade barrier on a particular item can be made if a country either buys or sells a large share of the world's production of the commodity in question. The underlying economic rationale for the argument is presented in more advanced international trade courses, but a brief intuitive explanation will be helpful here.

Consider first a nation that sells a relatively large share of the world's output of an item, such as Brazil in the case of coffee. By restricting exports, Brazil is able to significantly decrease the quantity of coffee exchanged on the world market and therefore drive up the price it receives for coffee. As a result, Brazil as a country is able to enjoy higher total profits from its export trade. Keep in mind that this is a case of placing a barrier on exports rather than on imports. Most of our previous discussion centered on the latter.

A case can be made for taxing or placing a quota on an import if the nation buys a substantial share of the world's output of the item. In this case, the resulting decrease in the quantity imported depresses the world price and as a result the price paid for the item by the importing country will be lower than if free trade were allowed. However, in order for such a situation to arise, the country in question must consume a substantial portion of the world's consumption of the product. Since consumption patterns of nations tend to be more homogeneous than production patterns, it is extremely difficult to find examples where a single importer can have a significant impact on the world consumption of a product. Certainly this argument could not be used to justify the major portion of import trade barriers that nations have set up.

We should caution, too, that in the cases of these justifiable export or import barriers, the benefits will extend only so far. By placing the barrier too high, the nation can be made worse off than it would have been with no barrier. It should also be kept in mind that the barriers just discussed are justifiable only from the standpoint of the country in question. Those nations that must pay a higher price for products they buy or receive a lower price for products they sell do not, of course, benefit from such barriers.

DUMPING

Occasionally, a nation will try to sell more of its products abroad by setting the export price lower than its domestic price, with the government reimbursing producers for the difference. This practice has come to be known as *dumping* and has been associated in the post-World War II years with agricultural products by the United States and some of the other more highly developed nations. In their attempt to support prices of agricultural products, the governments of these nations have been forced to buy the resulting surplus. Then, in an attempt to dispose of the surplus, the government sells it abroad at a reduced price or gives it away, usually to developing nations. The U.S. Public Law 480 program is a good example.

At first glance, it might appear that such a practice works to the advantage of all concerned. Consumers of the developing countries receive free or low-priced food, which in many cases has helped them avoid starvation or at least severe malnutrition, and the governments of the developed nations have been able to put the surplus to good use. But there have been a couple of undesirable side effects. First, producers of comparable products in other exporting nations suffer a reduction in the demand and price of their products. For example, Canadian wheat producers do not greet subsidized wheat sales by the United States with much enthusiasm.

A second problem, and perhaps even more important, is that producers in the recipient nations face a depressed market for their output because of the free or cheap products coming in under such programs. This in turn tends to retard the development of domestic agriculture in the recipient nations.

In more recent years, the charge of dumping has been levied against other nations by certain groups in the United States because of a belief that these nations have been selling manufactured products on the U.S. market at prices lower than their production costs. Such a practice would not likely persist, however. Firms do not stay in business very long by selling below cost. Of course, their own governments could subsidize these firms by making up the difference between their domestic price and the U.S. price, except that their taxpayers would end up subsidizing U.S. consumers. Again, such a practice is not likely to enjoy much popularity among foreign taxpayers, even though U.S. consumers should not complain.

U.S. TRADE

It will be of some value to look briefly at the magnitude and characteristics of U.S. trade with other nations. The figures in Table 23–3 provide an indication of the magnitude of U.S. exports and imports. In most years during the 1930–70 period, the United States exported a larger value of merchandise to other countries than it bought from them. However, this pattern changed in the 1970s when U.S. imports exceeded exports by a substantial amount, due mainly to the increase in prices of oil imports.

TABLE 23–3   U.S. Exports and Imports of Merchandise, Selected Years (1989 prices)

Year	Exports ($ millions)	Imports ($ millions)	Imports as a Percent of GNP
1930	$ 23,804	$ 18,804	3.4%
1940	29,981	19,098	2.7
1950	42,607	38,357	3.2
1960	66,715	50,475	2.9
1970	111,259	104,196	4.2
1980	333,353	363,755	9.2
1989	361,872	475,120	9.1

Source: *Federal Reserve Bulletin,* respective years.

Also notice the small quantity of imports relative to GNP at least before 1970. Even in 1989 imports were less that 10 percent of GNP. Most Americans, it appears, do ''buy American.'' In fact, U.S. citizens consume a small share of their total goods and services in the form of imported items compared with most other nations of the world. We should not conclude from these figures, however, that Americans are more isolationist or distrustful of foreign goods than other people. For it is necessary to bear in mind that the United States is a large and diverse nation compared with most other countries. A good deal of the trade that takes place between regions or states in the United States would be considered international trade in other countries. Notice, however, that the share of imports in GNP increased substantially between 1970 and 1980. But this figure stabilized during the 1980s. Also significant is the substantial reduction of exports from 1980 to 1985 (not shown). We will return to this point in the next chapter.

A country is said to have a ''favorable'' balance of trade if it sells more to other countries than it buys from them; that is, if exports exceed imports. It is perhaps unfortunate that this term came into such general use because it does not have much if any economic justification. As mentioned in Chapter 7, the error of this thinking is made clear by considering the limiting case where a nation sells everything it produces to other countries but buys nothing in return, leaving exactly zero goods and services for the people to consume—not a very ''favorable'' situation to say the least.

BALANCE OF TRADE VERSUS BALANCE OF PAYMENTS

In discussing international trade and finance, it is necessary to distinguish between a nation's balance of trade and its balance of payments. The balance of trade can be thought of simply as the difference between exports and imports of merchandise. As shown in Table 23–4, the United States in 1989 imported $475.1 billion of merchandise while exporting $361.9 billion, leaving a balance of trade deficit of

TABLE 23–4   U.S. Balance of Trade and Balance of Payments, 1989 ($ billions)

Exports of merchandise	+ 361.9
Imports of merchandise	− 475.1
Balance of trade	− 113.2
Investment earnings, net	+ 76.2
Grants, pensions, and other transfers	− 4.0
Military transactions, net	− 5.7
U.S. government grants	− 10.2
Other	+ 26.3
Balance of payments	− 30.6

Source: *Federal Reserve Bulletin*, May 1989, p. A-55.

$113.2 billion. However, it should be noted that considerably more money flows between countries than is due to merchandise trade alone. Two important items are U.S. spending on investments in other countries and income from such investments flowing back into the United States. There are also monetary flows because of foreign investment in the United States and income received from this capital. In 1989, the amount of money flowing into the United States because of investments in other countries was $ 76.2 billion more than the amount flowing out due to foreign investments in the United States. This item along with the "other" category, reduced the balance of trade deficit somewhat, leaving a balance of payments deficit of $ 30.6 billion in 1989.

SUMMARY

Differences in natural resources and climate account for much of the trade that takes place among nations, although culture, tradition, and educational differences also are important. A country has a comparative advantage in the production of a product if it gives up less of other products to produce it than another country. The total output available to the consumers of two countries can be increased if each country specializes to some extent in the production of the goods in which it has a comparative advantage, exporting the excess of production over consumption to other countries and importing more of the goods in which it does not have a comparative advantage. It is common for countries to restrict imports from other countries because of the added competition with domestic producers, even though consumers benefit from the imports. Balance of trade refers to the difference between merchandise exports and imports. Balance of payments includes both merchandise and monetary flows.

YOU SHOULD KNOW

1. The underlying basis for all trade.
2. What the more obvious reasons for international trade are.
3. The meaning of comparative advantage, and how to determine which country has a comparative advantage.
4. How to calculate opportunity cost.
5. How to determine the price range for imports and exports between two countries.
6. Why international trade increases the output available to both trading countries.
7. Why countries do not specialize completely.
8. Who gains and who loses from trade.
9. What is a tariff, and who advocates tariffs.
10. The main reasons given to justify tariffs, and whether they are valid.
11. The definition of dumping and who has done it.
12. The fraction of U.S. imports to GNP, and how this has changed.
13. The difference between balance of trade and balance of payments.

QUESTIONS

1. What are the more obvious reasons for international trade to take place?
2. Consider the following production possibilities schedules for radios and rice in the United States and Japan.

	United States		Japan	
Possibility	Radios	Rice	Radios	Rice
A	400	0	400	0
B	200	400	200	100
C	0	800	0	200

   a. Calculate the cost of radios per unit of rice in both countries.

   b. Calculate the cost of rice per unit of radios in both countries.

   c. Which country has a comparative advantage in radios? In rice?

3. In order for trade to take place, in what range must the trading price of radios be? The price of rice?
4. Using an appropriate price from the preceding answer, show how trade can increase the amount of both goods in both countries.
5. *a.* Who benefits from the trade discussed in question 4? How?

   b. Is anyone harmed by this trade? Explain.

6. A popular bumper sticker urges us to "Buy American—your job depends on it." How valid is this argument? Explain?

SELF TEST

1. Trade among people eliminates the need _____ and therefore _____ production.

   a. to be self-sufficient; increases

   b. to be self-sufficient; decreases

   c. for money; increases

   d. for money; decreases

2. The most obvious reason for trade to take

place between regions or countries is differences in:

a. political systems.
b. language.
c. educational levels.
d. climate and natural resources.

3. Specialization by a country or a region in the production of certain goods can increase total output because of:

a. natural resources.
b. acquired skills.
c. supporting institutions.
d. all of the above.

4. In order for trade to take place between two parties, _____ must gain.

a. both
b. one
c. neither

5. David Ricardo, one of the classical economists, was able to show that trade between two countries benefits _____ even if one was less efficient in the production of everything.

a. neither country
b. the most efficient country
c. the least efficient country
d. both countries

6. A country has a comparative advantage in the production of a commodity if it _____ than another country.

a. gives up more of another commodity
b. gives up less of another commodity
c. uses less resources to produce it
d. uses more resources to produce it

Answer questions 7–14 from the following production possibilities table.

	United States		*Japan*	
Possibility	*Radios*	*Rice*	*Radios*	*Rice*
A	500	0	200	0
B	250	750	100	50
C	0	1,500	0	100

7. The cost of producing one more unit of rice in the United States is _____ unit(s) of radios. The cost in Japan is _____ unit(s) of radios.

a. 250; 200
b. 500; 100
c. 3; 1/2
d. 1/3; 2

8. The cost of producing one more unit of radios in the United States is _____ unit(s) of rice. The cost in Japan is _____ unit(s) of rice.

a. 3; 1/2
b. 1/3; 2
c. 750; 50
d. 1,500; 100

9. According to these figures, the United States has a comparative advantage in _____ and Japan has a comparative advantage in _____ .

a. rice; radios
b. radios; rice
c. rice; rice
d. radios; radios

10. If trade takes place between the two countries, the United States would buy _____ and sell _____, while Japan would buy _____ and sell _____ .

a. rice, radios; radios, rice
b. radios, rice; rice, radios
c. rice, radios; rice, radios
d. radios, rice; radios, rice

11. In order for trade to take place between the two countries, the trading price of radios would have to be less than _____ rice in the United States and greater than _____ rice Japan.

a. 3; 1/2
b. 2; 1/3
c. 3; 1/3
d. 2; 1/2

12. In order for trade to take place between the two countries, the trading price of rice would have to be greater than _____ radio(s) in the United States and less than _____ radio(s) in Japan.

a. 3; 1/2
b. 2; 1/3
c. 1/3; 2
d. 2; 1/2

13. It would be possible to show that, after trade, consumers in the United States would have _____ rice and _____ ra-

dios and consumers in Japan would have _____ rice and _____ radios.

a. more; fewer; less, more
b. less; more; more, fewer
c. more; more; more, more
d. less; fewer; more, more

14. Efforts to restrict trade between two countries would come mainly from U S. _____ and Japanese _____.

a. rice producers; radio producers
b. radio producers; rice producers
c. rice consumers; radio consumers
d. radio consumers; rice consumers

15. A tariff is a _____ on imports. It _____ trade by _____ the cost of imported commodities.

a. subsidy; increases; decreasing
b. tax; decreases; increasing
c. subsidy; decreases; increasing
d. tax; increases; decreasing

16. Import tariffs that are intended to protect domestic jobs can cost jobs because they tend to:

a. increase imports.
b. decrease imports.
c. increase exports.
d. decrease exports.

17. Dumping exists when a government _____ exports. In recent times, this has

most commonly occurred in the _____ trade.

a. taxes; petroleum
b. subsidizes; petroleum
c. taxes; agricultural
d. subsidizes; agricultural

18. In the late-1980s, imports into the United States amounted to _____ percent of GNP.

a. more than 50   c. more than 25
b. less than 10   d. less than 5

19. A favorable balance of trade is said to exist when exports are _____ than imports. This situation _____ the amount of goods available to consumers.

a. greater; decreases
b. less; decreases
c. greater; increases
d. less; increases

20. Balance of payments:

a. is the monetary value of the balance of trade.
b. includes balance of trade plus monetary flows between countries.
c. excludes balance of trade and includes monetary flows between countries.
d. is balance of trade corrected for inflation.

Chapter 24

Exchange Rates

OVERVIEW

Everyone who has traveled to another country knows that before making a purchase in that country, their home currency must first be exchanged for the currency of the host country. The same is true of firms doing business in other countries. The main objectives of this chapter are to show how exchange rates are determined and how changes in exchange rates affect the prices of internationally traded goods and services.

EXCHANGE RATES DEFINED

An *exchange rate* is the number of units of one currency that it takes to buy a unit of another currency. For example, if the rate of exchange between the German mark and U.S. dollar is two to one, it takes two marks to purchase a dollar, or 50 cents to purchase a mark. Or we could say that the exchange rate is the price of one currency in terms of another currency. For each nation's currency, there exists an exchange rate between it and the currencies of other countries.[1]

In order to fully appreciate the role of exchange rates in international trade, it will be necessary to study in somewhat more detail the import and export markets for internationally traded goods and services. After gaining an understanding of these markets, we will be in a better position to understand how exchange rates are determined and why they change.

---

[1] For quotations of recent exchange rates see the *Federal Reserve Bulletin*, published monthly by the Federal Reserve System. Many daily newspapers also report current exchange rates.

IMPORT AND EXPORT MARKETS

Recall from Chapter 4 that in each market there is a demand for a good or service and a supply of that good or service. Also recall that we represented demand by a downward-sloping line, indicating that people buy more when price declines (other things being equal). Similarly, supply was represented by an upward-sloping line, which implies that producers place larger quantities on the market at progressively higher prices.

It will be easier to understand international markets if we utilize specific examples. As the two countries, let us consider the United States and Germany. Also, let us consider two products: U.S.-produced feed grains exported to Germany and German-produced Volkswagens imported into the United States. Thus, we will be dealing with two markets in the United States—one from the standpoint of U.S. importers of Volkswagens and the other from the standpoint of U.S. exporters of feed grains. Both the import price of Volkswagens and the export price of feed grains are quoted in terms of dollars. The markets are illustrated in Figure 24–1.

At first glance, the import and export markets appear no different from the domestic markets discussed in Chapter 4. Both demand curves are downward sloping, indicating that U.S. consumers buy more Volkswagens when their dollar price declines and that German farmers buy more U.S. feed grains when the price they pay declines. Similarly, both supply curves are upward sloping, indicating

FIGURE 24–1   Markets for Imports and Exports in the United States

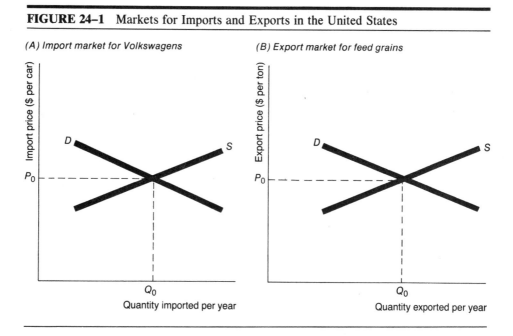

(A) Import market for Volkswagens

(B) Export market for feed grains

that at higher prices more Volkswagens will be supplied to the United States and more feed grains to Germany. And each market has an equilibrium price and quantity, as shown on the diagrams.

However, the markets for internationally traded commodities are not quite as simple as domestic markets. The complication enters because of the need to consider the price of each currency in terms of the other—that is, the exchange rate. As we will see in a moment, changes in the exchange rate shift the demand and supply curves of internationally traded commodities and as a result alter the prices paid by consumers of imported items and the prices received by producers of exported goods.

As an example, let us consider the effect of the decrease in the value of the dollar relative to the German mark on the dollar price paid and the mark price received for Volkswagens imported into the United States from Germany. To make the example a bit more specific, suppose the price of the dollar decreases from four marks per dollar to two marks per dollar. (We will see shortly how this change could come about.) Let the supply curve S_1 in Figure 24–2 represent the supply of Volkswagens for U.S. consumers if the exchange rate is four marks per dollar. This supply curve tells us that Volkswagen is willing to supply Q_1 cars at a price of $6,000 per car. At the four marks per dollar exchange rate, the Volkswagen company receives 24,000 marks per car at the Q_1 level of sales in the United States.

Notice, however, that when the exchange rate falls to $2:1$ (two marks per dollar) Volkswagen would have to receive $12,000 per car in order to still receive 24,000 marks per car. In other words, in order for Volkswagen to be willing to continue supplying Q_1 cars, the U.S. price per car would have to increase to

FIGURE 24–2   The Effect of a Decrease in the Exchange Rate on the Dollar Price Paid and Mark Price Received for Volkswagens

Exchange rate	Marks received	Dollars paid
2:1	24,000	12,000
2:1	17,400	8,700
4:1	24,000	6,000

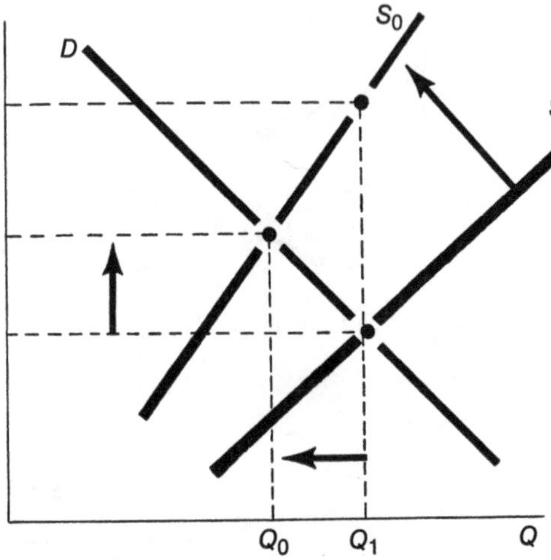

$12,000 per car. This means the supply curve facing U.S. consumers shifts upward and to the left (decreases) as a result of the decrease in the exchange rate (shown by S_0 in Figure 24–2).

The decrease in the supply of Volkswagens increases the dollar price paid for Volkswagens and decreases the number of Volkswagens imported, as shown by Figure 24–2. However, the dollar price paid for Volkswagens does not increase as much as the vertical shift in the supply curve. This is because the demand curve is downward sloping. U.S. consumers are not willing to pay $12,000 per car and still buy Q_1 cars per year. The market equilibrium price of $8,700 per car in this example is what people are willing to pay at the given level of demand and supply.

Perhaps even more surprising, the mark price received by Volkswagen for each car declines from 24,000 marks at the 4 : 1 exchange rate to 17,400 at the 2 : 1 rate. In order for Volkswagen to continue to receive 24,000 marks per car, the dollar price would have to increase to $12,000, which it does not. Hence, the decrease in the value of the dollar causes an increase in the dollar price paid for Volkswagens and a decrease in the mark price received by the company.

As one might expect, the decrease in the value of the dollar also influences the demand for U.S. products exported to Germany. Consider as an example the export demand for feed grains facing U.S. producers. At the original 4 : 1 exchange rate, the demand for U.S. feed grains is denoted by D_0 in Figure 24–3. This demand curve tells us that German buyers are willing to pay $200 per ton at Q_1 tons purchased per year. At the 4 : 1 exchange rate, this translates into 800 marks per ton. When the exchange rate falls to 2 : 1, German buyers should still be willing to pay 800 marks per ton for Q_1 tons. But notice that 800 marks per ton at

---

FIGURE 24–3   The Effect of a Decrease in the Exchange Rate on the Dollar Price Received and Mark Price Paid for U.S. Feed Grains

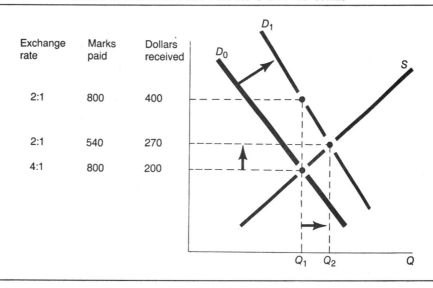

Exchange rate	Marks paid	Dollars received
2:1	800	400
2:1	540	270
4:1	800	200

the 2:1 exchange rate translates into $400 per ton at Q_1 tons. Thus, the export demand for U.S. feed grains shifts upward and to the right (increases) as the result of a decrease in the exchange rate, as shown by Figure 24–3.

It is also interesting to note that the dollar price received by U.S. producers does not increase by the full vertical shift in the demand curve. If the supply curve is upward sloping, the equilibrium price increases in this example from $200 to $270 per ton. At the 2:1 exchange rate, German buyers are able to purchase Q_2 tons at 540 marks per ton. Thus, the decrease in the exchange rate increases the dollar price received by U.S. producers but decreases the mark price paid by German buyers.

In the preceding example, we have shown the outcome of a decrease in the value of the dollar. The same analysis can be applied to a decrease in the value of any other currency in other countries. Also, the opposite outcome will prevail in the event of an increase in the value of the dollar. Now the supply of foreign goods to U.S. buyers increases while the demand for U.S. goods exported abroad decreases.

FOREIGN EXCHANGE MARKETS

Since an exchange rate can be defined as the price of one currency in terms of another, it is reasonable to believe that currency prices are determined in foreign exchange markets, similar to the way goods and service prices are determined in goods and service markets. Moreover, we can identify both a demand for and a supply of currencies. In terms of the example in the previous section, there would be a demand for U.S. dollars in Germany in order to pay for the feed grains imported from the United States. Similarly, there would be a supply of dollars in West Germany from the purchase of Volkswagens by U.S. consumers.

The demand for and supply of U.S. dollars in Germany is illustrated in Figure 24–4. The price of U.S. dollars is quoted in terms of marks per dollar. The more marks per dollar, the greater the value of the dollar, and vice versa. The quantity axis shows the number of dollars exchanged per year. Notice too that the demand for dollars is represented by a downward-sloping line, indicating that more dollars will be demanded as the price of dollars declines. The supply of dollars is represented by an upward-sloping line, indicating that the number of dollars supplied will increase as the price of dollars increases. Also, there is an equilibrium price and quantity corresponding to the intersection of these two curves.

An intuitive feeling for why the demand curve for dollars slopes down and the supply slopes up can be gained by calling to mind why dollars are demanded and supplied on the foreign exchange market. Dollars are demanded by foreign buyers of U.S. products. The higher the price of the dollar, the higher the prices of U.S. products; hence, a smaller number of dollars will be demanded to buy these products. Dollars are supplied by U.S. buyers of foreign products. The higher the price of the dollar, the cheaper these products, and more dollars will be supplied to buy these products.

In the example depicted by Figure 24–4, the equilibrium price of the dollar is two marks per dollar. At the relatively high three-mark price, Q_2 dollars are supplied while Q_0 dollars are demanded. Consequently, there will be a surplus of dollars on the foreign exchange market. As German dollar holders place these surplus dollars on the market in an attempt to exchange them for marks, the price of the dollar will have to decline in order to entice holders of marks to exchange marks for dollars. As is true of any market, the surplus causes downward pressure on price. The exchange rate continues to decline until it reaches the intersection of the dollar demand and supply curves. As the price of the dollar declines, recall that imports of German products into the United States are reduced and exports of U.S. products into Germany are increased. These changes cause more dollars to be demanded and fewer dollars to be supplied, which brings the foreign exchange market into equilibrium. The opposite would occur if the exchange rate were one to one. Now there would be a shortage of dollars, causing a price increase. The resulting changes in the import and export markets would increase the quantity of dollars supplied and decrease the dollars demanded until equilibrium was again reached.

FIGURE 24–4   Demand for and Supply of Dollars in Germany

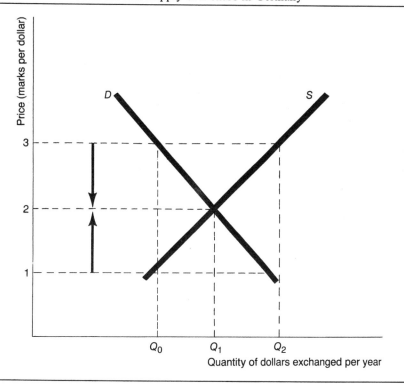

Be aware that shifts in the import demand or export supply can occur for reasons other than changes in the exchange rate. For example, inflation in the importing country can increase the import demand for products from abroad. Other things being equal, this will increase the supply of the nation's currency in the foreign exchange market, which in turn will result in a decrease in the equilibrium price of the currency. Thus, it is well to keep in mind that changes in the exchange rate affect the import and export markets, and autonomous changes in the import or export markets in turn affect the foreign exchange market. It is also necessary to bear in mind that the supply of dollars to foreign currency markets depends not only on merchandise imports into the United States but also on such things as expenditure by U.S. firms for plant and equipment in other countries, expenditures by U.S. tourists, and U.S. military spending abroad.

DEFICITS AND FOREIGN EXCHANGE MARKETS

In the discussion of fiscal policy, we noted that government bonds can be sold to foreign investors. Such bonds can be an attractive investment for these investors if the interest rate quoted on the bonds is relatively high. This describes the situation in the United States during the early to mid-1980s. When the Federal Reserve changed its policy of purchasing so many of the bonds issued by the Treasury, this left two groups of buyers: (1) U.S. citizens and (2) foreign buyers.

It became apparent that U.S. citizens were not prepared to buy all these bonds without extremely high real rates of interest. As it was, the real rates of interest in the early 1980s were the highest they had been for 50 years. These high real rates served as a strong pull for foreign funds coming into the United States. Indeed, it was fortunate for the United States that foreign investors financed a large share of U.S. deficits during the 1980s. Without these extra funds, it is likely that real rates of interest in the United States would have gone even higher, further dampening private consumer and investor spending and causing even more unemployment. But the reliance on foreign funds was not without its costs.

In order for foreign investors to purchase U.S. bonds, they first had to buy U.S. dollars. This caused an increased demand for dollars, which in turn increased the price of dollars in the foreign exchange market. The higher price of dollars vis-à-vis foreign currencies had two effects: (1) the supply of foreign goods to U.S. consumers increased, and (2) the demand by foreign buyers for U.S. goods decreased.

These changes had rather widespread repercussions throughout the U.S. economy. U.S. consumers enjoyed lower prices of imports, which no doubt helped dampen the inflationary pressure in the country. However, as U.S. consumers and business firms turned to buying more foreign goods, the domestic demand for U.S. products declined. This contributed to the unemployment problem. In addition, the demand by foreign countries for U.S. goods decreased because of the strong dollar. This also contributed to the U.S. unemployment problem. Between 1980 and 1985 the real value of U.S. exports decreased and imports increased.

Another outcome of the reliance on foreign funds to finance U.S. deficits is that by the latter part of the 1980s, the United States became the largest debtor nation in the world (in absolute terms). In time the "chickens will come home to roost." U.S. taxpayers will be called on not only to pay for goods consumed in the present, but also for goods consumed in the past. And these dollars will be going to citizens of other countries.

THE POST–WORLD WAR II INTERNATIONAL MONETARY SYSTEM

Previously we presented the process of adjustment that would occur if the actual exchange rate between two currencies were different from its equilibrium value. In so doing, we essentially showed how market rates of exchange are determined. However, it is necessary to qualify the preceding discussion by pointing out that during the early part of the post–World War II period, the exchange rates between the currencies of the major trading nations were for the most part set by government decree rather than by freely functioning foreign exchange markets. A bit of background will be useful at this point.

In an effort to promote confidence and stability in the international monetary system in the upcoming post–World War II period, a conference of allied nations was held at Bretton Woods, New Hampshire, in 1944. As an outgrowth of this conference, an international organization known as the International Monetary Fund (IMF) was established. Among other things, each member nation of the IMF agreed to maintain specified rates of exchange between its currency and all other currencies. This was to be accomplished by buying or selling its own currency in the foreign exchange market whenever the exchange rate deviated from the "parity rate" by 1 percent, or by making its currency convertible into gold or other reserve assets at the request of another member nation or official institution. As it turned out, countries other than the United States maintained or attempted to maintain the official exchange rate by buying or selling their currencies for dollars, while the United States attempted to maintain a parity between the dollar and gold or other reserve assets tied to gold by offering to sell gold to qualified buyers at a fixed $35 per ounce price. (We will discuss the role of gold and the problem of maintaining adequate reserves shortly.)

The IMF permitted member nations to alter the prices of their currencies in terms of gold (and other currencies) should they encounter a prolonged period of balance of payments disequilibrium. If a nation were running persistent balance of payments deficits, it would likely devalue its currency. *Devaluation* means that the nation increases the price of gold vis-à-vis its currency. For example, the United States devalued the dollar in 1971 by changing the price of gold from $35 to $38 per ounce, and again in 1973 by increasing the gold price to $42.22 per ounce. Another way of looking at devaluation is that it decreases the price of currency vis-à-vis gold. If other currencies stay tied to gold, it reduces the price of the currency in question relative to other currencies. Recall that this devaluation reduces the supply of imports to a nation while it increases the demand for its exports. And this in turn increases the quantity demanded of the currency in the foreign exchange market while decreasing the quantity supplied, to bring the balance of payments closer to equilibrium.

Occasionally, a nation revalued its currency upward against gold and other currencies, as West Germany, Japan, and a few other nations did in 1971. This has an effect opposite to that of devaluation, in that it decreases the demand for the country's exports and increases the supply of its imported goods.

In practice, member nations of the IMF have adjusted the value of their currencies rather infrequently. Indeed, the United States held to the $35 per ounce gold price from 1934 to August 1971. The rather inflexible exchange rates during the post–World War II period gave rise to a growing balance of payments deficits for the United States, shrinking U.S. gold reserves (from $23 billion in 1952 to $10 billion in 1972) and leaving an increasing number of U.S. dollars in foreign hands. During the 1960s, it became increasingly apparent that a realignment of currency values against each other and against gold was the only permanent solution to the disequilibrium in the international money markets. Clearly, the dollar was overpriced vis-à-vis gold and other currencies. Finally, in August 1971, the United States stopped the sale of gold for $35 per ounce and called for a meeting of IMF nations. As a result of this meeting, the dollar price of gold was increased to $38 per ounce. The currencies of the other major trading nations also were appreciated in value relative to the dollar and relative to gold. The realignment of currencies in the 1971 meeting has come to be known as the Smithsonian Agreement.

It was soon evident that the currency and gold price realignment coming out of the Smithsonian Agreement did not bring the IMF parity prices in line with equilibrium prices of currencies in the foreign exchange markets. Indeed, the United States experienced an even larger balance of payments deficit in 1972 than in 1971. This culminated in yet another devaluation of the dollar in 1973, from $38 to $42.22 per ounce of gold.

The second devaluation of the dollar still did not bring the dollar price down to the foreign exchange market equilibrium. The disequilibrium seemed to be widest in the case of the dollar versus the West German mark and the Japanese yen. Even after the second devaluation, the governments of these countries were forced to buy billions of dollars in order to support the mark and yen price of the dollar. And each time the United States devalued the dollar, these governments (really, their taxpayers) lost large sums of money. For example, suppose the German government purchased 1 billion U.S. dollars at four marks per dollar in order to keep the price of the dollar from falling below this level. Let us say that after the devaluation of the dollar, the parity ratio became 3.6 marks per dollar. Now the people who sold the 1 billion dollars to the German government had the option of buying them back for 3.6 billion marks. If they did, the outcome was that the German government was left with 400 million fewer marks in its treasury after the U.S. devaluation than before it. The 400 million marks represented a profit to speculators at the expense of German taxpayers.

Needless to say, any government can soon be expected to grow weary of losing these amounts of money just to support the price of another nation's currency.

Hence, it was not long after the 1973 dollar devaluation that most of the major trading nations of the world "floated" their currencies vis-à-vis the dollar—that is, allowed the dollar to find its own level on the foreign exchange markets of the world. Although the 1973 float technically was a violation of the IMF rules, it had been done before. Canada, for example, allowed the Canadian dollar to float for extended periods during the 1950s and 1960s, and Britain had already floated the pound in mid-1972.

In the years preceding the float, other governments, particularly West Germany and Japan, supported the price of the U.S. dollar vis-à-vis their respective currencies by purchasing large quantities of dollars that had accumulated in their countries. In the process of buying dollars, these governments injected large amounts of their own currencies into their respective economies. It is reasonable to expect, therefore, that these countries would experience inflation shortly after these purchases, which they did.

The U.S. dollar, of course, was not always overvalued. Indeed, during the time of the so-called dollar crises in Europe and Japan that we have just discussed, the dollar in some countries was undervalued by the official rate of exchange. This was true in many of the developing countries (especially those experiencing high rates of inflation), the Soviet Union, and its Eastern European satellites. For example, in the 1970s, the official exchange rate between rubles and dollars in the Soviet Union was roughly one for one. However, if one knew the right people in Vienna or Moscow, a person could obtain about five rubles for the dollar. Thus, the official price of the dollar was set substantially below the price that would have prevailed in a freely functioning foreign exchange market.

The practice of maintaining an artificially low price of foreign currencies can be expected to result in a black market in these currencies. It is easy to see how much more a dollar will buy in the Soviet Union if you can obtain five rubles per dollar on the black market as opposed to the one-for-one official rate of exchange. By the same token, Soviet citizens have an incentive to buy these high-priced dollars if they can buy goods on their black market with the dollars that they could not buy with rubles.

THE ROLE OF FLOATING EXCHANGE RATES

The problems brought on by attempting to maintain official exchange rates that are different from the equilibrium rates established by freely functioning foreign exchange markets have prompted many economists to argue for a system of floating exchange rates. As mentioned, under such a system, the price of each currency in terms of other currencies would be allowed to find its own level in foreign exchange markets. Moreover, the price of each currency would be allowed to change in response to changes in the demand and supply of the currency in question.

The most compelling reason for allowing exchange rates to float is that they automatically correct for imbalances of trade. For example, if a country experiences persistent balance of payments deficits, that is, it buys more from abroad than it sells, there will be a buildup of its currency in the foreign exchange market. As the price of this country currency declines, the prices it pays for imports increase and the prices it receives for exports also increase. This causes the country to decrease its imports and increase its exports, closing the gap between imports and exports.

The opposite occurs if a country experiences a balance of payments surplus such as Japan during the 1980s. In this case, the country's currency will appreciate in value, causing the prices of its exports to increase and the prices of its imports to decrease. This change diminishes exports and increases imports, again bringing trade into balance. Of course, this adjustment process may take several years to work itself out.

Under a system of floating exchange rates, a nation that experiences a rate of inflation that is higher than those of its trading partners will experience a decline in the value of its currency in the foreign exchange market because there will be more units of its currency in existence relative to other currencies. This should be looked upon as an advantage rather than a drawback of floating exchange rates. Even though domestic prices will increase during inflation, the prices of goods exported to other nations need not increase (in terms of other nations' currencies) because other nations will be able to buy more units of the inflated currency with each unit of their own currencies.

GOLD—THE INTERNATIONAL MONEY

Gold long has been used as an international money to settle accounts between nations. Perhaps the easiest way to see how gold is used is to consider a simple example. Suppose that during a given year, U.S. citizens purchase $1,800 million worth of goods and services from Germany, while Germany buys $1,400 million from the United States. When the books are balanced at the end of the year, financial institutions in Germany find they have 400 million more U.S. dollars at the end of the year than at the beginning. It is possible that these financial institutions will decide to hold these extra dollars as added U.S. dollar reserves. However, if its dollar reserves are deemed adequate or excessive, the German central bank may decide to exchange these dollars for gold.

Under the rules of the IMF, member nations were obliged to sell gold at the specified price. And this is what the United States did during much of the 1950s and 1960s. Foreign nations accumulated dollars because of the U.S. balance of payments deficits and proceeded to exchange billions of these excess dollars for gold. Moreover, the more certain that foreign dollar holders became that the United States would have to devalue the dollar sometime in the near future, the more incentive they had to exchange dollars for gold. For example, by exchanging $35,000 at the $35 per ounce price, a foreign bank or firm received 1,000 ounces of gold. Exchanging the same $35,000 after the price of gold increased to $38 reduced the gold received to 921 ounces. Thus, if one wanted to exchange surplus dollars for gold, it clearly was better to do it before devaluation than after. As the run on gold continued into the 1970s, the United States government suspended the convertibility of the dollar into gold in August 1971. We should also point out that the U.S. dollar (and to a lesser extent the pound sterling) has been used to supplement gold as international money.

Because of the substantial increase in world trade since the end of World War II, the demand for international reserves also has increased. The supply of gold, on the other hand, grew to a much smaller extent during this time. Thus, the market equilibrium price of gold increased accordingly, breaking the $100 per ounce level in the European gold market in 1973. At that time, the official price of gold was $42.22 per ounce in the United States. Because the official price of gold was held substantially below the free-market price in terms of dollars, a "shortage" of gold developed; that is, a greater quantity of gold was demanded than was supplied, at least in reference to dollars.

Because of the large difference between the market price of gold and the official price in the early 1970s, it became apparent that the only lasting solution to the world gold shortage was to allow the price of gold to seek its own market equilibrium. In late 1974, just before it became legal for U.S. citizens to own gold (the first time since 1934), the dollar price of gold exceeded $180 per ounce on the European gold market. Because U.S. citizens turned out to be less inclined to buy gold than many European speculators anticipated, the world market price of gold sagged a bit during the mid-1970s but rebounded to about $800 per ounce in the late 1970s before declining to about half that in the mid-to-late 1980s. The price of gold closely follows expected inflation.

SPECIAL DRAWING RIGHTS (SDRs)

In an attempt to "demonetize" gold, the IMF created in 1968 a new international money called *special drawing rights* (SDRs), sometimes called "paper gold." These SDRs were created to take the place of gold or other reserve currencies (mainly the U.S. dollar) in settling accounts between nations. The motive here was to create a true international currency that would be free from the influences of private supply and demand fluctuations (as gold) and from changes in domestic monetary policies (as the dollar or pound sterling).

In later years, much of the early enthusiasm over SDRs faded. When faced with the choice of being paid in gold or pieces of paper printed by the IMF, most creditor nations understandably prefer the real thing. Also, the so-called world gold shortage that existed in the early 1970s has disappeared, as one would expect when the price of gold was freed from its artificially low level. At $400 to $500 an ounce, a little gold goes a long way.

SUMMARY

An exchange rate is the units of one currency it takes to purchase one unit of another currency. Prices of imported and exported goods are established in markets by demand and supply. A decrease in the value of the dollar vis-à-vis other currencies decreases the supply of foreign-produced goods imported into the United States. This causes an increase in the dollar price paid for these goods and a decrease in the foreign currency price received. A decrease in the value of the dollar also increases the demand for products exported by the United States. This causes an increase in the dollar price received and a decrease in the foreign currency price paid for these commodities. Under a system of floating exchange rates, the prices of currencies are established in foreign exchange markets by demand and supply. A currency is demanded for the purpose of buying goods or securities from that country. A currency is supplied by the purchasers of goods from other countries. The sale of bonds by the United States to foreign buyers in the 1980s increased the demand for dollars and increased the price of dollars. Floating exchange rates serve as an automatic adjustment mechanism to balance of payments surpluses or deficits. Gold is used to settle accounts among nations. A shortage of gold occurred in the early 1970s because its official price was held below its market price.

YOU SHOULD KNOW

1. The definition of exchange rates.
2. How prices of imports and exports are determined.
3. How a change in the value of a nation's currency affects the supply of its imports.
4. What happens to the dollar price paid for imports from Germany and the mark price received for these goods when the dollar decreases (increases) in value vis-à-vis the mark.
5. How a change in the value of a nation's currency affects the demand for its exports.
6. What happens to the dollar price received and the mark price paid for U.S. exports to Germany when the dollar decreases (increases) in value vis-à-vis the mark.
7. Why dollars are demanded in foreign exchange markets.
8. Why dollars are supplied in foreign exchange results.
9. How the U.S. government deficit has affected the price of the dollar in foreign exchange markets.
10. How foreign governments kept the price of the dollar artificially high during the 1960s and early 1970s, and the consequence of this policy.
11. How the United States kept the price of gold artificially low during the 1960s and early 1970s, and the consequence of this policy.
12. The meaning of floating exchange rates, and how they correct for imbalances of international trade.
13. How gold is used as an international money.
14. Why special drawing rights were created.

QUESTIONS

1. *a.* What happened to the supply of Volkswagens to U.S. consumers when the dollar increased in value vis-à-vis the German mark in the early 1980s?

   b. What happened to the dollar price paid and the mark price received for Volkswagens?

2. *a.* What happened to the demand for U.S.

agricultural products by German buyers when the dollar increased in value?

    b. What happened to the mark's price paid and dollar price received for these products?

3. *a.* Why are dollars demanded in foreign exchange markets?

    b. Why are dollars supplied in foreign exchange markets?

    c. Explain how exchange rates between dollars and foreign currencies are established in foreign exchange markets.

4. If countries that export goods to the United States experience inflation, then the United States also will experience inflation because these goods will cost more in terms of U.S. dollars. True or false? Explain.

5. How were the large deficits of the federal government related to the strong U.S. dollar in the early to mid-1980s? What were the consequences of the strong dollar?

6. In the Soviet Union and other Communist nations as well as in many less developed countries, U.S. tourists often are approached by locals with an offer to buy dollars at exchange rates higher (more favorable to U.S. citizens) than the official rates. What is this a symptom of?

7. *a.* Suppose a country is experiencing persistent balance of payments deficits. What will happen to the value of its currency in the foreign exchange market, and how will this change correct the imbalance of trade.

    b. Follow similar reasoning for a country that experiences a long-term balance of payments surplus.

8. *a.* During the 1960s and early 1970s there was a "shortage" of gold in the world. But in the 1980s, the shortage disappeared. Why?

    b. At the current price of gold, what are you worth if you are worth your weight in gold?

SELF-TEST

1. The exchange rate between U.S. dollars and German marks is given in terms of:
    a. dollars(s) per mark.
    b. marks per dollar.
    c. one for one.
    d. *a* and *b*.

2. Prices of internationally traded commodities are determined by:
    a. import and export markets.
    b. the International Trade Commission located in Geneva, Switzerland.
    c. importing countries.
    d. exporting countries.

3. A decrease in the value of the dollar in terms of German marks causes the _____ for(of) goods imported from Germany to _____ .
    a. demand; decrease
    b. demand; increase
    c. supply; decrease
    d. supply; increase

4. The situation described in **question 3** causes the dollar price paid for imports to _____ and the mark price received to _____ .
    a. increase; increase
    b. increase; decrease
    c. decrease; decrease
    d. decrease; increase

5. A decrease in the value of the dollar in terms of the German mark causes the _____ for(of) goods exported to Germany to _____ .
    a. demand; decrease
    b. demand; increase
    c. supply; decrease
    d. supply; increase

6. The situation described in question 5 causes the dollar price received for exports to _____ and the mark price paid to _____ .
   a. increase; increase
   b. increase; decrease
   c. decrease; decrease
   d. decrease; increase

7. In general, a decrease in the value of the currency of a country is _____ for producers who sell on the export market and _____ for consumers of imported commodities.
   a. good; good   c. good; bad
   b. bad; bad   d. bad; good

8. Foreign exchange markets determine the prices of:
   a. commodities.   c. gold.
   b. currencies.   d. brokerage fees.

9. Dollars are demanded on foreign exchange markets by _____ buyers of _____ products and securities.
   a. foreign; U.S.   c. foreign; foreign
   b. U.S.; foreign   d. U.S.; U.S.

10. The higher the price of the dollar, the _____ the prices of U.S. products to foreign buyers, and the _____ the number of dollars demanded.
    a. higher; smaller   c. higher; larger
    b. lower; larger   d. lower; smaller

11. Dollars are supplied on foreign exchange markets by _____ buyers of _____ products.
    a. foreign; U.S.   c. foreign; foreign
    b. U.S.; foreign   d. U.S.; U.S.

12. The higher the price of the dollar, the _____ the price of foreign products to U.S. buyers, and the _____ the number of dollars supplied.
    a. higher; smaller   c. higher; larger
    b. lower; larger   d. lower; smaller

13. Foreign investors who purchased U.S. government bonds issued to cover the large deficits of the early 1980s first had to buy dollars. This increase in the demand for dollars _____ the value of the dollar and _____ the quantity of U.S. exports.
    a. increased; increased
    b. decreased; decreased
    c. increased; decreased
    d. decreased; increased

14. The situation described in question 13 also _____ the _____ for(of) foreign products on the U.S. market.
    a. decreased; demand
    b. decreased; supply
    c. increased; demand
    d. increased; supply

15. The situations described in questions 13 and 14 _____ unemployment and _____ inflationary pressure.
    a. increased; increased
    b. increased; decreased
    c. decreased; increased
    d. decreased; decreased

16. If a country runs persistent balance of payments deficits causing a buildup of its currency in the foreign exchange markets, the price of its currency will _____ , which in turn will _____ its exports and _____ its imports, eventually bringing trade into balance.
    a. rise; increase; decrease
    b. rise; decrease; increase
    c. fall; increase; decrease
    d. fall; decrease; increase

17. From the end of World War II to the early 1970s, foreign exchange rates were established by:
    a. foreign exchange markets.
    b. government decree.
    c. the World Bank.
    d. the International Monetary Fund.

18. During the 1960s, it became evident that dollars were _____ in terms of German and Japanese currencies, and gold was _____ in terms of dollars.
    a. undervalued; undervalued

b. overvalued; overvalued

c. undervalued; overvalued

d. overvalued; undervalued

19. Foreign governments, mainly Germany and Japan, kept the price of the dollar artificially high by _____ dollars, while the United States kept the price of gold artificially low by _____ gold.

    a. selling; buying   *c.* selling; selling

    b. buying; selling   *d.* buying; buying

20. The situation described in question 19 caused an _____ of dollars in foreign hands, which in turn caused an _____ of gold into (from) the United States.

    a. accumulation; inflow

    b. accumulation; outflow

    c. outflow; inflow

    d. inflow; inflow

21. Black markets in dollars spring up in countries that attempt to keep the price of the dollar artificially _____ . In these countries, prices paid by U.S. tourists are artificially _____ .

    a. high; high   *c.* low; low

    b. low; high   *d.* high; low

22. Floating exchange rates exist when:

    a. exchange rates are set by the Department of the Navy.

    b. currencies are printed on waterproof paper.

    c. exchange rates are set by foreign exchange markets.

    d. currencies are transported between countries by air freight.

23. If a nation experiences a persistent balance of payments deficit, the value of its currency will _____ , causing its imports to _____ and its exports to _____ , thereby correcting the trade imbalance.

    a. decrease; increase; decrease

    b. decrease; decrease; increase

    c. increase; increase; decrease

    d. increase; decrease; increase

24. During the 1960s, there was a shortage of gold in the world because:

    a. its price was kept artificially low.

    b. its price was kept artificially high.

    c. gold mining was disrupted during World War II.

    d. gold fields were exhausted.

25. If gold sells for $500 per troy ounce, a person weighing 150 pounds is worth $ _____ if he or she is "worth his or her weight in gold." (There are 12 troy ounces per pound).

    a. 9,000   *c.* 900,000

    b. 9 million   *d.* 1.2 million

26. Special drawing rights were established in the 1960s to reduce the _____ of gold. They are sometimes called _____ gold.

    a. surplus; fools'

    b. shortage; paper

    c. surplus; paper

    d. shortage; fools'

Part XI

Economic Growth
and Development

Chapter 25

Economic Growth

OVERVIEW

In this chapter and the next, we consider the growth and development of nations. The material in the present chapter provides a general picture of how the rich nations got to be where they are. The following chapter focuses more on the problems of achieving economic growth in the poorer nations.

ECONOMIC GROWTH DEFINED

In this chapter, we will look briefly at the relatively recent phenomenon of economic growth. We say "recent" because from the standpoint of world history, several thousand years elapsed during which the economic well-being of most of the world's population remained at a relatively low level. In the developed nations of the world, the largest share of economic growth has taken place within the past two centuries.

At the outset, it will be useful to define rather specifically what is meant by economic growth. We will define *economic growth* as a long-run sustained increase in the per capita real output of a society. Occasionally, growth is defined in terms of the total output of a nation, but for our purposes, growth in the per capita context will be the most useful concept. For lack of a better measure, real output generally is gauged by one of the output measures discussed in Chapter 7 (GNP, NNP, and so on) adjusted by changes in the general price level. However, we should keep in mind the biases of these measures also discussed in Chapter 7.

GROWTH AND THE QUALITY OF LIFE

Until the 1960s and 1970s, most people thought of economic growth as a desirable goal. In fact, throughout a large part of the post–World War II period, nations seemed to have been engaged in a contest to see who could grow the most rapidly.

The contest was especially noticeable between the communist or centrally planned economies (mainly the Soviet Union, mainland China, and their satellites) and the nations that have more decentralized economic systems characterized by relatively free markets. The outcome of this contest is no longer in doubt.

This is not to say that economic growth has now become undesirable. Most nations still rank economic growth as a high-priority goal. But in recent years, in the United States at least, a growing number of people have begun to question the wisdom of striving for a high rate of growth. They point to the growing amount of resource scarcities, pollution, congestion, and social instability as the consequences of growth. Some have even suggested that a more desirable goal should be a no-growth economy, implying that the United States is rich enough already.

Upon closer examination of their argument, it becomes apparent that the advocates of a no-growth economy really do not mean that at all. What they appear to be saying instead is that people now are consuming enough automobiles, appliances, luxuries of various types, but not enough of other things, such as clean air and water, a chance to see the blue sky once in a while, and the opportunity to enjoy more peace and serenity. In other words, the no-growth advocates really want growth in the output of such things as pollution control devices and parks—goods and services that improve the environment.

Perhaps a reason for some of the confusion about a no-growth economy is that many things that people once considered "free" goods, such as clean air and water, blue skies, green grass, and the sight of a bird, now are no longer free. In an industrialized society, many of these items have become economic goods in the sense that alternative goods and services must be given up to obtain them. For example, if we want clean air and water around industrial cities, some of the resources that formerly were devoted to the production of industrial products now must be devoted to the production of pollution control devices.

There may be a few people who would be willing to give up some of their present consumption to obtain more quality in their environment. Surely there are more people, however, who would prefer to retain their present level of consumption and obtain a higher quality of environment through the growth of the economy. Indeed, it seems reasonably safe to say that most people in the United States would prefer both more conventional goods and services and a higher-quality environment. This is particularly true of low-income people.

This point is more clearly seen by observing conditions in the poorer, or less developed, nations of the world. Not only do most people in these countries have substantially fewer conventional goods and services to consume than people in the United States and other developed nations, but they also live in a much more polluted environment. Thus, economic growth for most people of the world has meant an increase in both conventional goods and the quality of the environment as well as more leisure time and better health to enjoy the environment. In some of the poorest nations, economic growth still is a matter of life and death because of the necessity of increasing per capita income to avoid starvation.

Perhaps the main point to be made here is that there is really no contradiction between economic growth and quality of life. It is the phenomenon of economic growth that has freed humans from a lifetime of struggle against famine, disease, and the elements and allowed them to set their sights on a more comfortable, more enjoyable, and longer existence.

NEW TECHNOLOGY AND THE UNEXPECTED DIVIDEND

Ever since the publication of *Essay on the Principle of Population* in 1798 by Thomas Malthus, the Malthusian doctrine of ever-expanding population pressing against limited food supplies has been a major concern of people. Having the benefit of nearly 200 years of hindsight, we can now say that Malthus's dire predictions have not materialized, at least not for the United States and the more highly developed nations of the world. Instead of famine, the major agricultural problems of these nations have been overproduction and food surpluses. Why have these nations managed to escape the plague of long-run diminishing returns in the production of food? We know that their populations have grown considerably and that their total land areas have remained about the same or have even declined. For example, in 1950, the total land in farms in the United States (50 states) amounted to 1,162 million acres. By 1969, this figure had been reduced to 1,064 million acres. In 1983, the federal government paid farmers not to grow crops on 78 million acres of farmland.

It is interesting to note that the number of people engaged in the production of agricultural products also has declined substantially in the United States. At the end of World War II (1946), employment in agriculture totaled 8.3 million people. By 1989, farm employment had been reduced to 3.2 million people. These substantial reductions in both land and the number of farmers become even more impressive when we consider that the total U.S. population increased from 141 million people in 1946 to more than 248 million in 1989. Thus, we see that in the United States, not only has a given land area supplied the food for a greatly increased population, but also the amount of land used to produce food and the number of farm people have declined. For the United States, at least, Malthus could not have been more wrong.

But we are still faced with the question of why Malthus was wrong. First, we should bear in mind that Malthus considered only two major resources in the production of food—land and labor. What he failed to consider was the host of new resources or inputs that have come on the scene since his time. Here we have in mind such things as new, improved varieties of crops like hybrid corn, better and cheaper sources of commercial fertilizer, new and improved pesticides and herbicides, and the tremendous increase in tractors and equipment of all kinds. In addition, and perhaps most important, people themselves have become a new and improved resource because of the increased skills they have acquired through research and education. These new resources, along with greater knowledge, have enabled mankind to greatly increase the production of food from a given land area.

We should not criticize Malthus too severely for failing to foresee the additional output that new technology has made possible. During his lifetime, the primary inputs in the production of food were labor and land. Diminishing returns will occur in any situation where there is the mere application of additional labor to a fixed amount of land. It is only the application of additional, complementary resources that makes labor and land more productive, thereby offsetting the phenomenon of diminishing returns. The law of diminishing returns is still a useful concept in the study of microeconomics.

You may have recognized also that Malthus's pessimistic predictions about the future of mankind have been more nearly borne out in the less developed nations of the world. In many of these nations, food shortages and malnutrition have continued to be the major problems. In these nations, millions of people perish each year because of lack of food. We will return to a more thorough discussion of this problem and that of achieving economic growth in the less developed nations in the next chapter.

TECHNOLOGICAL CHANGE

Our discussion thus far has centered mainly on the effects of new technology on the production of food, particularly in reference to the Malthusian doctrine of diminishing returns. We should be aware, however, that new technology has had pronounced effects on virtually every sector of the more highly developed nations. The developed nations are characterized by the widespread use of new technology.

The utilization of new and improved resources to achieve a larger level of output in the economy has come to be known as *technological change*. For a long time, economists have been aware of increased output that could not be explained by the increased use of conventional resources, such as land, labor, and traditional forms of capital. The additional or unexplained output was then attributed to the phenomenon of technological change. However, the more basic question still remains: What are the causes or sources of technological change? Using the phrase *technological change* as a label for the additional or unexplained output is really nothing more than giving a name to our ignorance.

In more recent years, economists have begun to address themselves to the basic question of identifying the sources of technological change. There is still a great deal to be learned in this area, but at the present it is possible to at least make some general statements. At the most general level, we can say that the basic source of new technology, or technological change, is new knowledge. By unlocking some of the secrets of the universe, humans have been able to create new inputs or resources that complement or replace traditional resources and increase the total output of goods and services. Hence, it has become possible to increase output without increasing the use of traditional resources. Thus, we observe an increase in output per unit of input because measures of total inputs do not reflect the improved quality of inputs or the completely new inputs that have come on the scene.

THE PRODUCTION AND DISTRIBUTION OF KNOWLEDGE

At this point, it is legimate to ask: What are the sources of new knowledge? The nations that have been most successful in acquiring new knowledge have done so through formal, structured research and development. Humans have learned a few things in their normal day-to-day activities, but the contributions of learning by doing have been relatively small compared with the contributions of scientists and engineers.

An important step in the acquisition of new knowledge by a society is the transmission of this knowledge from research workers to the general public. Knowledge that exists only in the minds of scientists or perhaps in scientific journals is of little value to society until it is disseminated to the general public and put to widespread use.

The dissemination or "trickling down" of new knowledge is in most cases a complex process. New knowledge seems to first find its way into professional journals, then into textbooks, most likely at the upper levels of school first and then gradually into society as graduates begin to utilize it. For example, the concept of hybridization developed by Mendel was understood only by professional geneticists not too many years ago. Now it is found in undergraduate biology texts and is common knowledge to plant breeders. As knowledge becomes more widely known and accepted, it seems also to become simplified, so that what was initially understood only by a few scientists and teachers later becomes understandable to more and more of the general public, provided, of course, the knowledge proves useful to the public.

COSTS OF ECONOMIC GROWTH

Recall that there are two basic kinds of goods and services produced in every society: (1) consumption goods and (2) investment goods. If a society insisted on producing only consumption goods and services—that is, if people did not save any of their income—there would be no resources available for investment goods. And, according to the preceding discussion, there would be no chance for economic growth to occur. The fact that most societies have chosen to devote a portion of their resources to the production of investment goods means they have decided to forgo a certain amount of their present consumption in order to have more consumption goods in the future.

Thus, in one sense, we can consider the cost of economic growth as the consumption goods and services we have to give up in order to undertake investment. As members of the present generation, we should be thankful that past generations decided to forgo part of their possible consumption goods in order to produce investment goods, or we would probably still be living in caves, cloaked in animal skins, and sustaining ourselves on roots and raw meat.

The fact that a certain amount of present consumption must be given up in order to achieve economic growth presents a serious problem to the less developed nations. If the major part of a nation's resources is required to produce just the necessities of life—food, clothing, shelter—there is not much chance to forgo consumption goods in order to invest. And if investment is small, the resulting economic growth will be small. Since the end of World War II, many of the developed nations have attempted to provide investment goods, such as technical assistance (knowledge) and a small amount of machinery and other forms of nonhuman capital, to their less developed neighbors, but progress has been slow.

In recent years, there has been an increase in concern over what might be considered another cost of economic growth, namely the pollution, congestion, social unrest, and other problems that accompany an industrialized society. Part of the difficulty, which we alluded to at the beginning of this chapter, involves obtaining a meaningful measure of economic growth. If in fact the environment has deteriorated significantly over the years, then using GNP to gauge the economic well-being of society will result in an overstatement of economic growth. However, as mentioned, this does not mean economic growth is undesirable. In order to obtain a more pleasing environment without giving up the consumption goods and services we now have, we must have continued economic growth.

CAPITAL AND GROWTH

Although economists still have a lot to learn about economic growth, it can at least be said that growth will not occur without an increase in the amount of resources or inputs per worker; output cannot increase without more inputs. In order to increase per worker inputs, there must first be investment. We continue to define *investment* as the production of new capital. Capital serves to augment labor, thereby increasing the productive capacity of the economy. All capital can be divided into two broad categories: (1) nonhuman capital and (2) human capital. As the name implies, *nonhuman capital* consists of all the buildings, machines, tools, infrastructure, and so forth, that human beings utilize in the production of goods and services. *Human capital* is the knowledge and skills acquired by people that enable them to also increase their output.

The difference between the richest and poorest countries in output and capital inputs per worker is shown in Table 25–1. Output (GDP) per worker is over 25 times greater in the five richest countries of the world than in the five poorest.[1] Notice that the stock of nonhuman capital per worker in the richest countries is 47 times greater than the corresponding figure for the poor countries. Using years of schooling as a proxy for human capital, the difference is not so great at the first and second levels of schooling (elementary and secondary), averaging 3.8 times more for the rich countries. The greatest difference between the two groups is in the third

---

[1] GDP is gross domestic product. It is equal to GNP minus payments to other countries for resources contributed by these countries.

TABLE 25–1   Relationship between GDP per Worker and Capital, 1980 (Constant 1985 Prices)

	GDP	Nonhuman Capital	Human Capital (years of schooling per worker)	
	(dollars per worker)			
A. Five richest countries			1st and 2nd levels	3rd level
Norway	37,100	149,400	9.13	.369
Canada	34,800	129,700	9.65	.746
United States	34,200	126,800	10.40	1.283
France	32,400	126,200	9.81	.467
Sweden	30,700	127,900	8.80	.553
Average	33,840	132,000	9.56	.684
B. Five poorest countries				
Malawi	1,600	2,900	2.04	.004
Rwanda	1,500	1,300	3.63	.005
Zaire	1,400	5,300	5.04	.020
Upper Volta	1,200	2,500	.71	.003
Mali	900	1,900	1.14	.007
Average	1,320	2,780	2.51	.008

Source: Willis Peterson, "Rates of Return on Capital: An International Comparison," *Kyklos* 42 (1989), pp. 203–17.

level of schooling—85 times. The third level of schooling (college and professional training) probably is the best indicator of the level of technology utilized by a society.

TRADE AND GROWTH

In a previous chapter, we demonstrated that all nations benefit by trade. Yet, most nations have set up trade barriers, thereby reducing the actual benefits received from trade. This appears to be especially true among the world's less developed countries (LDCs). Typically, these countries have levied high import duties on goods coming into the countries, required foreign firms to acquire licenses to import, or established quotas. Also, it has been common for LDCs to levy taxes on their own exports, which reduced the net, after-tax price received by the producers. Mainly, export taxes affected agricultural products.

The motivation for trade barriers set up by LDCs varies among countries, although two appear to stand out: (1) protection of domestic industry and (2) conservation of foreign exchange. The first is essentially the infant industry argument. The danger is that without foreign competition, such industries may never "grow up." They remain inefficient and technologically retarded to the detriment of the consumers in these countries. Imports are an important source of new capital and technology as well as consumer goods. Their importance is illustrated by Table 25–2, showing the relationship between the degree of openness of various developing countries and their rate of economic growth. The most open economies have experienced the highest rate of growth, and the most closed, the lowest growth rates.

The conservation of foreign exchange, the second major reason for import barriers, is thought to be necessary because developing countries have a hard time selling their products in the world market. Mostly they have primary products to sell, which have suffered a long-run decrease in real prices except for a brief period in the mid-1970s. However, the foreign exchange problem is worsened by taxes

TABLE 25–2   Trade and Growth, 1973–1985 (percent change in per capita real GNP per year)

Outward-Oriented				Inward-Oriented			
Strongly		*Moderately*		*Moderately*		*Strongly*	
Singapore	6.5%	Malaysia	4.1%	Cameroon	5.6%	Bangladesh	2.0%
Hong Kong	6.3	Thailand	3.8	Indonesia	4.0	India	2.0
S. Korea	5.4	Tunisia	2.9	Sri Lanka	3.3	Dom. Rep.	0.5
		Brazil	1.5	Pakistan	3.1	Ethiopia	−0.4
		Turkey	1.4	Yugoslavia	2.7	Sudan	−0.4
		Israel	0.4	Colombia	1.8	Peru	−1.1
		Uruguay	0.4	Mexico	1.3	Tanzania	−1.6
		Chile	0.1	Philippines	1.1	Argentina	−2.0
				Kenya	0.3	Zambia	−2.3
				Honduras	−0.1	Nigeria	−2.5
				Senegal	−0.8	Bolivia	−3.1
				Costa Rica	−1.0	Ghana	−3.2
				Guatemala	−1.0	Madagascar	−3.4
				Ivory Coast	−1.2		
				El Salvador	−3.5		
Average				Nicaragua	−3.9		
	6.1		1.8		.7		−1.2

Source: *The Economist*, 4 July–10 July, 1987. Adopted from World Bank data.

levied on exports in many LDCs. This policy reduces the profitability of producing products that can be sold in the world market.

INTERNATIONAL COMPARISONS

At this point, it will be useful to compare the records of various nations in achieving economic growth. In Table 25–3 we present the 1987 per capita GNPs for 17 representative countries, ranging from the most highly developed to the least developed. The average annual growth in per capita GNP in dollars per year assuming the 1965–87 percentage growth rates continue, also is shown.

There are two major points to be gleaned from Table 25–3. First, notice the extreme variation among countries in the per capita output of goods and services. The people fortunate enough to be born in the nations on the upper end of the

TABLE 25–3 Estimates of Average per Capita Gross National Product in U.S. Dollar Equivalents, 17 Selected Countries and Growth per Year

Country	1987	Average Annual Growth ($ per year)
United States	$18,530	$278
Japan	15,760	662
Sweden	15,550	280
Canada	15,160	409
West Germany	14,400	360
Austria	11,980	371
United Kingdom	10,420	177
Brazil	2,020	83
Mexico	1,830	46
Thailand	850	33
Philippines	590	10
Haiti	360	2
Pakistan	350	9
India	300	5
Niger	260	− 6
Zambia	250	− 5
Zaire	150	− 4

Source: World Bank, *World Development Report,* 1989, pp. 164–65.

income scale enjoy over 50 times the annual output of goods and services available to the people of the poorest nations.

The second point is the wide variation among countries in the annual growth of per capita GNP shown in the second column. Again in this case, the people living in the richest nations have been able to achieve much larger annual increases in per capita output than the inhabitants of the less developed countries. People living in the richest countries can look forward to more than $300-per-year increases in incomes during the 1990s, whereas the inhabitants of the poorest nations can expect less than $10-per-year increases. Some countries such as the Niger, Zaire, and Zambia are even worse off, experiencing a decrease in per capita GNP. Thus, the income gap between the rich and poor nations grows larger each year. In order for the poor nations to catch up, they must achieve a larger average annual absolute growth than their richer neighbors. Considering their small base values of per capita GNP, this requires an extremely high percentage rate of growth—something most poor nations have not been able to achieve. In a relative sense, at least, it appears that the rich are getting richer and the poor are getting poorer, as far as nations are concerned.

SUMMARY

Economic growth is a long-run sustained increase in per capita output of goods and services. It is commonly measured by real GNP. Economic growth can enhance the quality of life and the environment by making it possible for society to produce environmental goods such as clean air and water. Malthus's prediction of mankind living on the edge of starvation has not come true in the developed countries because of new technology that increased land and labor productivity. In order to achieve economic growth, society must allocate resources to the production of capital goods. The five richest countries of the world have almost 50 times more nonhuman capital per worker than the five poorest. The difference is even greater for human capital at the third level of schooling. Nations that have opened their economies to trade have been more successful in achieving growth than those who have not. The absolute increase in GNP per capita has been greater for the rich than for the poor countries, resulting in an ever-widening gap between them.

YOU SHOULD KNOW

1. The definition of economic growth.
2. How economic growth can enhance the quality of life and the environment
3. What Thomas Malthus did not foresee.
4. What technological change is.
5. The basic source of new technology.
6. The main sources of new knowledge.
7. The costs of economic growth.
8. The source of economic growth.
9. The two broad categories of capital.
10. The differences between the rich and poor countries in capital per worker.

11. How trade influences economic growth.
12. The difference between the rich and poor nations in the annual increase in per capital GNP.

QUESTIONS

1. Is economic growth inconsistent with a clean and healthful environment? Explain.
2. *a.* Why have Malthus's predictions not been borne out in the so-called developed nations?
   b. In which group of countries have Malthus's predictions come closest to being fulfilled? Why?
3. A large proportion of the world's poor people live within 20 degrees north and 20 degrees south of the equator. Do you think this is purely accidental, or could there be a reason for this phenomenon? Explain.
4. *a.* What is technological change?
   b. What is the basic source of new technology?
   c. What is the main source of new knowledge?
5. *a.* Why is investment required for economic growth to occur?
   b. What are the two main types of investment required for economic growth?
   c. In which area do LDCs lag the most?
6. Many of the less-developed countries of the world have enacted policies that restrict trade.
   a. What has been the motivation for these policies?
   b. What effect have these policies had on their economic growth? Explain.
7. If poor nations are not able to achieve higher percentage rates of growth than the rich nations, what will happen to the income gap between the two groups? Has this happened?

SELF TEST

1. Economic growth is generally defined as an increase in _____ output and is measured by _____ .
   a. total; real GNP
   b. per capita; real GNP
   c. total; nominal GNP
   d. per capita; nominal GNP

2. If people desire a cleaner environment, without economic growth, they must be willing to:
   a. starve.
   b. reduce output of conventional goods.
   c. suffer increased unemployment.
   d. accept more inflation.

3. In order to attain a cleaner environment without giving up conventional goods, _____ must occur.
   a. a shift from a market to a centrally planned economy
   b. a shift from conventional goods to environmental goods
   c. economic growth
   d. economic decline

4. Quality of life generally is the highest in countries that have:
   a. achieved economic growth.
   b. not modernized.
   c. adopted a centrally planned economic system.
   d. an abundance of natural resources and a warm climate.

5. In 1798, Thomas Malthus predicted that by now most people in the world would be:
   a. living on the edge of starvation.
   b. millionaires.
   c. unemployed.
   d. knee-deep in food.

6. Malthus's prediction has come closest to being correct for:
   a. the less developed countries
   b. the market economies.
   c. the centrally planned economies.
   d. all countries.

7. Malthus's prediction about the shortage of food in the world has not come to pass in the developed countries because of their:
   a. abundance of high-quality land.
   b. low population densities.
   c. use of new inputs in agriculture.
   d. propensity to diet, eating less and less.

8. A name for our ignorance is:
   a. IQ.
   b. economic growth.
   c. technological change.
   d. diminishing returns.

9. The source of technological change is:
   a. the government.
   b. new or improved inputs.
   c. conventional inputs.
   d. outer space.

10. The source of new or improved inputs is:
    a. the earth.   c. new knowledge.
    b. the stars.   d. the government.

11. The source of most new knowledge is:
    a. research and development activities.
    b. everyday activities.
    c. happy accident.
    d. the classroom.

12. Without economic growth, nations that want to increase capital must:

a. suffer from unemployment.
b. reduce consumption.
c. increase consumption.
d. suffer from inflation.

13. The largest difference between the richest and the poorest nations is:
    a. nonhuman capital.
    a. first and second levels of schooling
    c. third level of schooling.
    d. population density.

14. In order for a nation to increase its per capita output, it must increase per capita:
    a. inputs.
    b. land area.
    c. natural resources.
    d. rainfall.

15. Nations that have been most successful in achieving economic growth are:
    a. strongly outward oriented.
    b. moderately outward oriented.
    c. moderately inward oriented.
    d. strongly inward oriented.

16. In terms of dollars per year, the richest nations of the world increase their annual per capita GNP by about $ _____ per year, while the average annual growth of the poorest nations is about $ _____ per year.
    a. 300; 10   c. 30; 10
    b. 10; 300   d. 10; 30

17. In terms of absolute income levels, the:
    a. poor nations are falling farther and farther behind the rich nations.
    b. poor nations are catching up and will surpass the rich nations by the year 2025.
    c. poor nations are maintaining about the same distance behind the rich nations.

Chapter 26

Economic Development

OVERVIEW

In this chapter, we focus more specifically on the developing countries, or as they are sometimes called the less developed countries (LDCs). Specifically, we look at what needs to be done to achieve development and the problems that have to be overcome or at least dealt with.

THE LESS DEVELOPED COUNTRIES

Because of the extremely low level of per capita output in the less developed countries (LDCs), together with their relatively small annual growth, the problem of achieving economic growth is both more critical and more perplexing than is the case in the richer nations. The general statements about the sources of new knowledge and the need to invest in activities that increase knowledge and education as well as the need for new forms of nonhuman capital to achieve economic growth apply to both the developed and less developed nations. However, because of the critical nature of the problem in the less developed nations, it will be useful to consider these in somewhat more detail.

First, we should bear in mind that the attainment of economic growth is a matter of life and death for the poorest people living in the world's poorest nations. Without food today, there is no tomorrow to enjoy the fruits of economic progress. It becomes apparent, then, that less developed nations are faced with a dilemma. The acquisition of new knowledge, increasing the level of education, and the production of new forms of nonhuman capital are long-run phenomena, taking perhaps several generations to bear significant results. Yet there is a critical short-run problem of staving off famine. An adequate diet is necessary for people to be able to work and be reasonably productive.

To survive the difficult short-run future, most less developed nations have attempted to adapt the knowledge and technology of the developed nations to their situations. These efforts have been moderately successful. Certain knowledge (for example, the concept of hybridization, the technology for harnessing power such as electricity, the internal combustion engine, jet propulsion, and the know-how for nitrogen fixation and chemical production) can be applied in any locality. On the other hand, certain technology, particularly that which is biological in nature such as new varieties of crops, must be developed in the area in which it is to be utilized. Varieties of hybrid corn that produce record yields in Iowa fare no better, and sometimes fare worse, than traditional varieties in Mexico and Argentina.

It is important also to consider the profitability of new types of technology. It is a mistake to conclude that new inputs or resources that are profitable in the developed economies also will be profitable in the underdeveloped countries. A major consideration is differences in wage rates between nations. Laborsaving technology that is profitable in countries where labor is relatively scarce and wages are high will be unprofitable in countries where labor is abundant and wages low.

AGRICULTURAL DEVELOPMENT

Agriculture is by far the dominant industry in the less developed nations of the world. It is common to observe between two thirds and three fourths of the total population of the LDCs directly engaged in agriculture. In contrast, farmers constitute about 2 percent of the population in the United States. As a general rule, the poorer the nation, the larger is the proportion of the population engaged in agriculture. This is not particularly surprising. The first order of business in staying alive is to obtain nourishment. Once food requirements are met and surpassed, some of the people engaged in food production can leave agriculture to produce such things as better housing, medical care, transportation, and the host of items that contribute to a higher standard of living.

This phenomenon has happened in the United States and the other more highly developed nations of the world.[1] At the time of the American Revolution, the United States was as much an agricultural nation as most LDCs are today. But as the nation developed, a progressively smaller share of the population produced food and a progressively larger share produced other things.

It is apparent, therefore, that agricultural development is of major importance in

---

[1] An exception would be a nation that retains a relatively large agricultural sector but trades its excess agricultural commodities with other nations for industrial goods. Denmark and New Zealand are examples.

the overall development of the LDCs. Unless their major industry can become more productive, there is little chance of releasing people from agriculture to produce more of the other amenities of life or to trade agricultural products for industrial products produced by other nations.

Unfortunately, there is no simple formula that a nation can follow to rapidly increase the productive capacity of its agriculture. The process is relatively slow and is likely to differ among countries. About all we can do here is to present some ideas that appear to have general application across various situations.[2]

The sources of economic growth presented in the previous chapter apply to agricultural development in particular as well as to overall economic growth and development. The key is making high-payoff investments, but the question is where these investments are to be found. From past experience, we can say with some confidence that they are not found in the production of more traditional inputs, such as bullocks or wooden plows. Although additions to these inputs provide some increase in food and fiber production, the increase will be relatively small.

The investments that give rise to new nontraditional inputs, particularly new varieties of crops, fertilizer, and irrigation facilities, appear to have paid off handsomely in the LDCs. Because plants can produce carbohydrates and protein more efficiently than animals, crops have been utilized more as a direct source of food in the LDCs than in the developed nations. Unfortunately, because of differences in soil, day length, temperature, and so forth, it usually is not possible to relocate proven varieties of crops from one nation to another, or even from one locality to another. As a result, investments first have to be made in research facilities that can develop new varieties suited for a particular area. The International Rice Research Institute in the Philippines and the Rockefeller corn and wheat programs in Mexico, headed by Dr. Norman Borlaug (recipient of the Nobel peace prize for his efforts), have been particularly successful in this endeavor.

New varieties of crops with high-yield potentials usually cannot reach their potentials, and may not even achieve the yields of traditional varieties, without increased fertilization. Thus, investments are required in fertilizer production facilities, or imports of plant nutrients must be increased. In many parts of the world, irrigation water must be supplied in order for crops to approach their yield potential. North America and Europe are somewhat unique in that a large share of agricultural production can be carried on under conditions of natural rainfall. Many of the less developed nations do not have this advantage.

The application of fertilizer and water to improved varieties of crops may also

[2] For additional reading on the problem of agricultural development, see T. W. Schultz, *Transforming Traditional Agriculture* (New Haven, Conn.: Yale University Press, 1964); A. W. Mosher, *Getting Agriculture Moving* (New York: Agricultural Development Council, 1966); and Y. Hayami and V. W. Ruttan, *Agricultural Development: An International Perspective* (Baltimore: The Johns Hopkins Press, Revised edition, 1985).

require a change in production techniques. For example, increasing the fertility of the soil, as well as adding water, usually intensifies the weed problem. So farmers must become better managers and in a sense become a "new input" themselves. Greater use of agricultural chemicals, mainly herbicides and insecticides, also may be required to control weeds and insects. More plant food and greater yields produce a more favorable environment for yield-reducing weeds, insects, and plant diseases. The timing of planting and harvesting also tends to become more critical with the higher yielding varieties.

The gradual shift from a subsistence type of agriculture (where farmers produce mainly for their own use) to a commercial agriculture (where a greater portion of the output is sold) requires additional transportation and marketing facilities. So additional investments generally are required in these areas. In the United States and many other developed nations of the world, farmers have formed cooperatives to market their products. Farmers in LDCs also are turning in this direction. There is not much incentive for farmers to increase production by adopting new varieties and other new inputs unless they can be reasonably sure they can sell their added output for a profit. However, if there are profits to be made in buying from farmers and selling in urban markets, we can be sure that entrepreneurs will emerge to perform this service, provided the government allows this activity to take place.

It is quite common in LDCs for governments to restrict competition while giving monopoly power to government agencies both in the purchase of agricultural products and in the production and sale of inputs for agriculture, such as fertilizer and seeds. A common outcome of this situation is lower-than-market prices paid to farmers for their products and higher-than-world prices charged for the inputs. This phenomenon is due in part to attempts by governments to obtain revenues from the profits of these purchases and sales. But it may also be due to inefficiency stemming from the monopoly position of the government agencies. In either case, farmers are poorly served; they receive low prices for their products and pay high prices for the inputs they purchase. Even when governments allow competition to prevail, the same outcome may result if taxes are levied on exports and imports. The general result of the disincentives faced by farmers is a retardation of agricultural development, and sometimes famine for the entire country. We will return to this issue in a later section.

INDUSTRIAL DEVELOPMENT

Although the LDCs by their nature are highly agricultural, the industrial or nonagricultural sector offers the greatest potential for growth. As implied in the previous section, the industrial sector must provide an increasing proportion of inputs utilized in the agricultural sector, such as machinery, tools, chemicals, fertilizers, and transportation facilities and equipment. One characteristic of a modern agricultural sector is that a large share of its inputs is produced off the farm. In other words, growth in the farm supply industries is an important determinant of growth in agriculture.

In addition to providing new, nontraditional inputs for agriculture, the industrial sector must provide many of the inputs for its own production of consumer goods. Industrial inputs, such as machinery, tools, buildings, and chemicals, are themselves the output of the industrial sector. As the economy grows, the industrial sector faces an ever-increasing demand for consumer goods of all types: housing, clothing, shoes, furniture, refrigerators, stoves, air conditioners, automobiles, radios, and television sets, to name a few.

Since industrial technology is not as location-specific as agricultural technology, it is somewhat easier for industrial firms in the LDCs to draw upon the technological base of the developed nations. However, a major difficulty of transferring industrial technology from the developed to the less developed nations stems from the wide difference between the two in wage rates relative to the price of capital. In the less developed nations, wage rates tend to be low relative to the price of capital. The opposite is true in the developed nations. Because labor is relatively cheap in the LDCs, production should utilize more labor relative to capital in order to minimize costs. As a result, the production processes of the developed nations cannot (or at least should not) be exactly reproduced in the LDCs if the LDCs wish to utilize their abundant supply of labor and minimize costs. The same holds true for agriculture as far as the substitution of machines for labor is concerned.

The kinds of products demanded and produced in the LDCs also differ from those of the developed nations. Instead of expensive accessory-laden automobiles designed to cruise at 70 miles per hour down a four- or six-lane expressway, they need motorbikes and relatively cheap, rugged cars that can maneuver down narrow, often unpaved roads. In general, their demand is mainly for relatively simple items that can be operated and repaired without a high degree of engineering skill.

By the same token, the manufacturing establishments themselves tend not to be large and highly sophisticated. Much of the manufacturing in the LDCs is carried out in relatively small establishments or machine shops, many employing no more than 5 to 10 people. Each establishment may produce a simple final product or a single component of a final product. The phenomenon of subcontracting is quite common in the LDCs. Basically, it allows specialization of functions by employees without requiring the firms to be large. It is easy to underestimate the entrepreneurship of small businesspeople in the LDCs. If there are profits to be made, someone is usually there to take advantage of the situation.

Another problem of industrial development in the LDCs is the mobilization of sufficient funds to finance business firms. The most efficient way to draw together funds is by a stock market. Without a stock market, firms have to utilize borrowed funds to a large extent, which in turn places relatively low limits on firm size unless the owner already is wealthy.

The entrance of multinational firms into the LDCs provides another source of financing industrial development. Usually these firms provide the plant, equipment, and management while employing domestic labor and raw materials. This kind of arrangement can work to the benefit of both the firm and the LDC. The firm taps a relatively cheap source of labor, and possibly raw materials, in producing a product that can be sold for a profit in the LDC itself or can be shipped to another even more profitable market. The people of the LDC, on the other hand, gain some additional industrial output or the means to buy such output on the world market.

Some LDCs have become more nationalistic, purposely making it more difficult for foreign firms to carry on business in their countries. In certain cases, the firms' assets have been expropriated by their host country. Whether or not the charges of exploitation and the like levied against the firms involved are justified is a question we cannot answer here. It appears, however, that banishment of a foreign firm by a host LDC does not, in general, further the economic development of the country in question. The country obtains some physical assets, which in most cases it could have purchased in the world market, but loses the management skills provided by the firms. The latter input is usually the most difficult to come by in an LDC. When the risk of expropriation increases, foreign firms may insist on a higher rate of profit in order to write off their assets in a shorter time.

INFRASTRUCTURE: DEVELOPMENT AND FINANCE

By *infrastructure*, we have in mind a network of transportation and communication facilities, together with such public utilities as electricity, telephone, water supply, and waste disposal. Although the major cities in most LDCs (with the exception of the very poor districts) in general have modern and adequate infrastructures, the same usually is not true for the interior or rural regions. Such an imbalance of infrastructure contributes to the uneven growth pattern in LDCs. Their major cities become hardly distinguishable from New York, Chicago, or Los Angeles, while the interior lags a hundred years or more behind, not only in terms of per capita income but also in terms of public conveniences, such as paved roads, public transportation, electricity, telephones, radio and television, and waste and sewage disposal—services people take for granted in the large cities or in the developed nations. Understandably, this situation contributes to increased migration from the backward areas to the cities, further aggravating the congestion and unemployment problems of the cities.

It is one thing to say that the interior needs roads, bridges, electric and telephone lines, and railroads; it is another thing to supply these facilities. Although their construction usually is in the hands of the government of the LDC, they still require the use of scarce resources. In order to buy these resources, either domestically or abroad, the government must acquire the money. The question is: Where and how?

Most LDCs have a small number of relatively rich (and influential) families that certainly could afford to pay more taxes to provide more government revenue. However, these families often have gotten to be rich because of special favors or tax advantages bestowed by past or present governments. And if the rich still enjoy considerable influence in the government, it is not difficult to understand why the government is reluctant to soak the rich.

Even if the government were to substantially increase the taxes paid by rich or high-income people, the total tax take may not increase substantially because the rich are relatively few in number. Certainly the added taxes would not meet the demand for infrastructure development. This leaves the poor (the vast majority of the people) and a small but growing middle class (if the nation is growing). Not even the most heartless of governments is eager to tax the poor, which puts the major share of the tax burden on the middle class, usually the top-level civil service, management, and professional people in the large cities. But the ability to tax these people also is limited. For one thing, the income tax laws of most LDCs tend to have rather large loopholes. Also, the tradition of paying income taxes is not well established, so that tax evasion is a major problem. Moreover, an excessive rate of taxation dampens private incentive. Since these people are relatively mobile and usually can earn higher incomes in the developed nations, the LDCs certainly cannot afford to lose their services by taxing them out of the country. These people also are not likely to be very happy about paying a major part of the cost of infrastructure development in the interior. They are not likely to see much, if any, personal benefit from this public expenditure unless they are planning to migrate to the interior, which is unlikely.

Because of the problems of taxing income, governments of LDCs have turned more to taxes on internationally traded commodities. These taxes are the easiest to collect. All the goods are funneled through one or at most a few ports of entry, so evasion is relatively difficult. It is not uncommon to observe taxes on certain imports equal to their world market prices, especially on so-called luxury items, such as automobiles and appliances. Because the higher-income people buy these items, it is one way of taxing the rich. However, the low- and middle-income people are at the same time deprived of these commodities because their prices are driven up so high by the taxes.

Since exports also are easy to tax, they too provide a tempting source of government revenue. Because the LDCs are highly agricultural, exports are heavily weighted with these commodities. The major difficulty with export taxes is that they lower the price received by domestic producers of the items. As a consequence, their profitability is reduced and output is less than it would otherwise be. In view of the importance of agricultural development in the LDCs, these taxes leave much to be desired.

As explained previously, governments can spend more than they take in by tax revenues. Part of the deficit can be made up by selling government bonds and part by issuing new currency. In most LDCs, the latter means of financing a deficit has been more popular than the former, and by now it is clear that large increases in the money supply result in high rates of inflation. However, inflation also amounts to a tax on holders of money, so the government still is left with the two alternatives of taxing or borrowing.

Funds for infrastructure development also may be obtained by borrowing (or gifts) from governments of developed nations or international lending agencies such as the World Bank. Loans and interest must be paid eventually, but payment can be postponed until the government of the LDC is in a better position to raise the revenue, perhaps from a broader tax base.

The debt problems now faced by many LDCs, especially in Latin America, illustrate the limitation of this source of funds. The increase in interest rates on these loans coupled with the decrease in prices of primary products (agriculture, mining, and petroleum) that reduced export earnings are the main underlying reasons for these problems. Countries that find themselves with a heavy debt burden will not be eager to borrow further.

EDUCATION: DEVELOPMENT AND FINANCE

Much of what we said about infrastructure development and finance applies also to education. People living in the major cities generally have access to at least average-quality public or private schooling, again with the possible exception of the very poor. In the rural areas, if schools even exist, the quantity and quality of schooling obtained by the people tend to be much lower than those in the major city or cities. In rural areas, it is not uncommon to see only one third to one half of the children in school, with the number falling to 10 to 15 percent for young people of high school age. Nor is it uncommon to find two thirds to three quarters of the adult population illiterate in rural areas.

We should be careful, however, not to equate illiteracy with lack of intelligence. There is no reason to believe that the average level of innate intelligence (however measured) is lower for populations with a low level of schooling than it is for people living in the developed nations. Nor should we be so presumptuous as to believe that people with little or no schooling cannot learn. Granted, the ability to read facilitates further learning, but learning also can take place by oral communication and observation. Experience has shown that illiterate farmers can and do adopt new inputs or techniques from their better-schooled neighbors, from farm supply firms, or from extension agents if the techniques or inputs are profitable. Similarly, new factory workers grasp what they need to know after a few weeks on the job. This is not to downgrade the importance of education; we argue only that economic growth can take place without waiting several generations for the major portion of the population to become literate.

In the area of education, the first order of business is to bring all children who are capable of learning up to the level where they can read and write with some facility; perhaps up to the equivalent of an eighth-grade education in the United States. This should enable them as adults to learn new things more easily and also make it possible for increasing numbers to obtain the equivalent of high school, college, or professional training.

Investment in human beings, like investment in infrastructure, requires scarce resources, namely teachers and school facilities. Someone has to pay for these resources. If they are to be provided by the government, the government must first acquire the necessary funds. It is not necessary to restate the problems discussed in the previous section in regard to obtaining tax revenue.

Assuming that some resources are allocated to education, it may be another matter to obtain teachers. Since relatively few people have advanced through the equivalent of the high school level, few are available as teachers. Those who have completed the necessary training are likely to prefer life in the major city rather than in the countryside. Thus, wages probably will have to be higher in the interior in order to attract teachers away from the advantages of the city. The opposite is usually the case.

Assuming that teachers and facilities can be provided, there has to be demand for the education. Parents with little or no schooling may not recognize the importance of educating their children beyond their level even if the education is free. The problem is that the education will not in general be free to the parents, because after the age of 9 or 10 children become economic assets to peasant farmers. If the children are in school, they cannot be contributing to the family income, which is likely to be extremely low as it is. The problem can be reduced somewhat by dismissing school during times of peak labor demand (such as planting and harvesting) and holding classes when the children are less in demand at home. To ensure anything near universal attendance, schooling probably has to be made mandatory up to a minimum level, such as the sixth or eighth year.

The cost of education increases as a greater proportion of young people go on to high school and college. In part, this is due to more expensive (more highly trained) teachers and facilities. But even more important is the increase in forgone earnings (loss of output) that is incurred as young people attend school rather than enter the labor force. Although the absolute size of these earnings may be small relative to earnings forgone by comparable students in developed nations, they often make a substantial difference in the amount of food and clothing the students and their families can enjoy. Consequently, the value of forgone earnings is likely to be even more important to young people in LDCs, particularly to students from rural areas, than to students from high-income families in the developed nations.

In many developing nations, particularly the Latin American countries, a large proportion of college students hold full-time jobs during the day and attend classes in the evening. Although this practice reduces forgone earnings, it also reduces students' study time considerably and therefore reduces the quality of their education. Similarly, many college professors in these countries hold full-time positions in the government, the professions, or the business world, as well as teaching. Again, this limits the time teachers can spend in preparing for classes and in keeping up with new developments in their professions. The necessity for college professors to hold other jobs stems largely from the low salaries they receive relative to what they could earn in other occupations that require comparable training. Low salaries also deter capable people from entering the teaching profession, which in turn holds the quality of education below what it would otherwise be.

THE AGRICULTURAL ADJUSTMENT PROBLEM

In the event that the LDCs can overcome the problems we have been discussing and start down the road of sustained growth, some other problems will be encountered because of that growth. A major one is the agricultural adjustment problem—the movement of a substantial share of the population out of agriculture into the industrial and service trades.

As the industrial sector of a nation begins to develop, the opportunity cost of farm labor (wages in the nonfarm sector) increases relative to the cost of machinery services.[3] This provides an incentive for farmers to increase the amount of machinery relative to labor. To effectively utilize this machinery, they must farm larger areas. The pull of higher nonfarm wages draws people off of farms, leaving the land in fewer but larger farms.[4] As farms grow larger, farm people are able to utilize more machines and increase their incomes along with people working in nonfarm occupations. Thus, when nonfarm incomes are low, farms will be small, and when development occurs, farms increase in size. If land is very expensive as in Japan and Western Europe, it is common to observe relatively small farms with farm people augmenting their income from nonfarm jobs.

The migration from agriculture usually begins with young people who have just completed their educations and are embarking on their careers. Next in line are the small farmers who find their meager incomes becoming smaller relative to nonfarm wages. But, in order to leave agriculture, one must find a job in another occupation. This is where the problem begins.

Although the industrial sector is likely to be expanding in a growing economy, it may not be expanding fast enough to absorb the large influx of farm people. As a result, unemployment grows in the cities. Shanty towns made of tin and cardboard inhabited by the poor, unemployed new arrivals from the countryside begin to spring up. It is unlikely that the already hard-pressed government can provide many public services such as waste disposal and health and education services. Because of the crowded and unsanitary conditions, disease and malnutrition are common.

Some of the more fortunate and able-bodied migrants find jobs in factories and shops. Others find temporary employment, usually in the service trades. Selling newspapers, shining shoes, operating a taxi, and working as a maid or gardener are some of the common means of earning enough to stay alive while searching for more permanent employment.

Despite low incomes in agriculture, some people choose to remain on their farms. Usually, these are the older farmers who are too young (or too poor) to retire but too old or unskilled to find employment in the cities. As a result, they continue to work their small plots until they eventually pass from the scene.

What can be done to alleviate the agricultural adjustment problem? One thing the government can do is to ensure freedom of entry into all occupations or training programs for all who have the necessary skills or capabilities. There is a natural tendency for unions representing the skilled trades to restrict entry into their respective occupations. This is usually accomplished by regulating the number of people who can enter the training program—either apprenticeships or

---

[3] Yoav Kislev and Willis Peterson, "Prices, Technology and Farm Size," *Journal of Political Economy*, 90 (June 1982), pp. 578–95.

[4] Willis Peterson and Yoav Kislev, "The Cotton Harvester in Retrospect: Labor Displacement or Replacement," *Journal of Economic History*, 46 (March 1986), pp. 199–216.

formal schooling. By so doing, unions limit the supply of labor and raise the wages of those lucky enough to be established members.

Powerful industrial unions also can make it more difficult for farm people to obtain work in the unskilled and semiskilled occupations. If these unions under threat of strike can obtain a union wage that is substantially above the free-market wage, employers will attempt to substitute machines for labor. Even if the established union members can retain their jobs, the newly arrived and inexperienced ex-farmers will have a more difficult time obtaining jobs at the comparatively high union wage.

A similar effect can be created by a government-imposed minimum wage if it is above what would prevail in a relatively free labor market. Here again, employers are motivated to substitute machines for labor. A high wage does not do a worker any good if the person cannot find a job at that wage.

Sometimes governments of LDCs have made the agricultural adjustment problem worse than it need be by subsidizing the purchase of agricultural machinery, particularly for large farmers. The subsidy often takes the form of providing low-interest credit for buying farm equipment. In this case, the large farmers are induced to substitute machines for labor. The combination of relatively high minimum (or union) wages and subsidized farm machinery squeezes poor farm laborers or small farmers from two directions, leaving them unable to find employment in agriculture or in industry.

Governments could also take an active role in providing information to farmers on job vacancies in the cities. Many farm people probably migrate with the expectation of finding jobs that do not exist. If information were available on actual opportunities, or if farm workers could be hired before they migrate, the time spent living in slum conditions while looking or waiting for a permanent job could be eliminated or at least shortened for many.

The preceding discussion is not intended to convey the impression that a nation would be better off if farm people remained on farms. It is precisely the movement of people off the farms that provides the wherewithal for a nation to increase its output of goods and services. If a nation requires 70 to 80 percent of its people to produce food, it cannot produce much of anything else; hence, the country remains poor. The vast array of goods and services, such as housing, medical care, education, roads, transportation, and energy, that are produced by former farmers or descendants of farmers is what distinguishes rich from poor nations. This points up the key role that agriculture plays in overall economic development. Without agricultural development, there is not much chance for people to leave agriculture since food ranks number one on the list of essentials to stay alive.

THE POPULATION PROBLEM

Improvement in the economic well-being of the average person in a developing country depends on two factors: (1) growth in the total output of the economy and (2) growth in the population of the country. The per capita output of a nation can increase only if total output increases more rapidly than population. If population is growing at the same rate as total output, the economic well-being of the average person remains unchanged. Per capita output can be increased by a reduction in the population growth or by an increase in the rate of growth of total output.

An unfortunate characteristic of most less developed nations is that they exhibit a relatively high population growth. As more and more people press against the land area and other resources of these nations, the pessimistic predictions of Malthus are more nearly borne out. Hence, in recent years, there has been an increased awareness of the need for the LDCs to practice some form of population control.

The extent of the population problem in the less developed nations is illustrated in Table 26–1. Notice that the average population growth rate of the group of representative less developed nations shown in the right-hand column is over seven times the average population growth rate of the selected group of developed countries shown in the left-hand column.

Although we still have much to learn about population theory, a few factors seem to be important in determining or influencing population growth. Taking into account migration between countries, a nation's population growth depends both on its death rate and on its birthrate. If the birthrate is larger than the death rate, obviously population grows.

One of the important factors contributing to the spurt of population growth in the LDCs, particularly during the years following World War II, was the drop in infant mortality due to the availability of new drugs and better medical care. Families that had 8 to 10 babies with the expectation of 4 or 5 dying as infants found their family size increasing as fewer died than expected. However, a lower infant mortality need not lead to a preference for larger families. But during the time it took parents to become adjusted to the lower death rate among infants, population grew rapidly.

Assuming that families eventually return to a so-called equilibrium family size, it is likely that this size will still be substantially larger for the LDCs than for the

TABLE 26–1   Annual Population Growth Rates, 14 Selected Countries, 1980–1987

Developed	Percent	Less Developed	Percent
Austria	0.0	Brazil	2.2
Canada	1.0	Colombia	2.3
West Germany	−0.1	India	2.1
Japan	0.6	Kenya	4.1
Sweden	0.1	Mexico	2.2
United Kingdom	0.1	Pakistan	3.1
United States	1.0	Zambia	3.4
Average	0.39		2.77

Source: World Bank, *World Development Report*, 1989, pp. 214–15.

developed nations. Why? There probably are a number of reasons, both economic and noneconomic. We still have much to learn about the factors determining family size. However, it does appear that one important economic factor is the price (or cost) of rearing and educating a child.

The price, or total cost, of rearing a child depends on a number of items. Most obvious is the cost of food, clothing, and medical care. Education also is a major item that includes out-of-pocket costs (tuition, books, and so on) as well as forgone earnings. For poor rural families in LDCs, the forgone earnings to the family become important rather early in life. As mentioned earlier, a child going to school cannot be working in the fields. In fact, it is very likely that many children in LDCs turn out to be an economic asset to their parents rather than a cost. In contrast, children reared in cities, particularly in developed nations with child labor and minimum wage laws, do not have as many opportunities to contribute to the family income.

Another less obvious cost is the time spent by the mother in rearing the child. For a mother living on a farm in an LDC, this cost is not so important because she takes the child with her to work. But this time cost is quite important for a highly educated woman in developed nations. The reduced birthrate in the United States during the post–World War II period might be attributed to the increased educational levels and employment opportunities for women outside the home, thus raising the price of children.

Because of these factors, the price or cost of a child is least in rural areas of LDCs. And with a low price, we might expect that more will be demanded, which seems to be the case. The price of children in a nation tends to rise as a greater proportion of the children are reared in cities. So we might expect some tendency for the birthrate to fall in the LDCs as people migrate from rural areas.

Recent advances in birth control technology have made it easier for parents to voluntarily limit the size of their families. But, this is no guarantee that parents will want to do so, especially low-income parents in rural areas. Considering that such action may constitute a short-run economic loss to these parents, we have little basis for optimism. Also, children tend to be a major source of old-age assistance for parents in LDCs. If governments of the LDCs are determined to reduce population growth, they may have to institute policies that make children less essential for survival of parents in their old age.

THE HUNGER PROBLEM

It is estimated that 15 million people in the world's poorest nations die each year from the direct or indirect effects of hunger or malnutrition.[5] This amounts to over 40,000 per day; in the hour or so it takes to read this chapter, over 1,600 people will have died from lack of food. A large percentage of these people are children

---

[5] The Hunger Project, *Ending Hunger: An Idea Whose Time Has Come* (New York: Praeger, 1986).

below the age of five who are more susceptible to disease because of their weakened condition. The hunger toll is even higher than the death figures indicate. Millions of children who survive grow into adulthood with impaired mental capacity because of childhood malnutrition. And millions more suffer a lifetime of blindness or other physical ailments for the same reason.

Up until the late 1980s, it was thought that the main cause of hunger in the LDCs was an inability to produce enough food because of their primitive agriculture. Considerable effort by the world's developed countries was, and still is, directed at improving agricultural productivity in the LDCs. While these efforts are laudable, little improvement in the world hunger problem has been achieved. In fact, by the early 1990s, there were more hungry people in the world than ever before.

It should also be noted that a primitive agriculture does not necessarily imply an unproductive agriculture, at least from the standpoint of land productivity. If one were to rank the world's nations according to total agricultural output per hectare of land, some of the world's poorest nations would rank relatively high. Bangladesh, for example, has nearly three times the annual output per hectare of the United States. The United States ranks about midway among the world's nations in agricultural output per hectare.[6] In general, nations having high population densities and located in regions of high rainfall, and utilizing extensive irrigation, exhibit high land productivities. Of course, the low-income nations do not have high labor productivities because of low wage rates and a small amount of capital per worker.

It has become evident that the primary cause of world hunger is a demand problem stemming from a lack of purchasing power of the poor rather than a supply problem.[7] In countries where the average per capita GNP averages $100 to $300 per year, in comparison to the U.S. average of over $20,000, a large segment of the population does not have enough income to buy sufficient food. Increasing land productivity has little effect on the ability of these people to buy food.

A recent proposal for attacking the world hunger problem from the demand side has been put forth.[8] Essentially, it calls for a transfer of purchasing power from the world's high-income nations to the poorest people in the world's low-income nations. Instead of giving cash, the transfer would be in the form of international food stamps, a commodity-specific money. It is estimated that world hunger could be virtually eliminated for about the same amount of money spent on farm-income support programs in the world's high-income countries and the various food aid programs of these countries. Because of the predicted growth in the world demand for food, farm prices in the developed countries are estimated to increase 30 to 35 percent, making the traditional price and income support programs

---

[6] Willis Peterson, "International Supply Response," *Agriculture Economics,* 2, no. 4 (December 1988).

[7] World Bank, *Poverty and Hunger* (Washington, D.C.: World Book, 1986).

[8] Willis Peterson, "International Food Stamps," *Food Policy,* 13, no. 3 (August 1988).

unnecessary. The expected increase in the prices of agricultural products in both the donor and recipient countries would stimulate their farm sectors as well as their farm supply industries. As a result, economic growth should increase, particularly in the LDCs where agriculture is a big part of the economy.

The predicted results of an international food stamp program are in sharp contrast to traditional food aid programs, such as the U.S. PL 480 program. Shipping free or subsidized food to poor countries depresses their domestic farm prices, which retards development of their agricultural sector as well as the industries that sell goods and services to agriculture.

THE FOREIGN EXCHANGE PROBLEM

We argued that the key to economic growth in the LDCs is in the use of new, nontraditional inputs. However, in large part, the knowledge and the facilities to produce these inputs do not exist in the LDCs. Thus, it is necessary for the LDCs to either purchase these inputs from the developed nations or import equipment and the technical know-how in order to produce them domestically. For most LDCs, both lines of action generally are followed, but in either case, foreign currencies (or gold) are required to make such purchases. The needed foreign exchange is obtained mainly by selling to the developed nations.

What do the LDCs have to sell that the developed nations want to buy? A few of the more fortunate LDCs have petroleum. Other LDCs have mineral deposits. But for the most part, the LDCs are agricultural. One might expect the LDCs to have a comparative advantage in agriculture vis-à-vis the developed nations. However, because of the low per capita food output in the LDCs, there is little surplus that can be exported. Some exceptions are the specialty crops such as coffee, sugar, tea, bananas, and citrus fruits. But in the case of livestock products and food and feed grains, the agricultural industries of the developed nations seem capable of satisfying their domestic demands and producing surpluses.

Many LDCs, therefore, are caught in a situation where they are buying more from the developed nations than the developed nations are buying from them. The inevitable result is a drawing down of the international reserves of these countries. Hence, they must limit their imports of new inputs or facilities and live within their means. This limits their ability to buy new inputs required for the development process.

In recent years, some of the LDCs have been able to earn foreign exchange through the export of labor-intensive industrial products, such as clothing, shoes, radios, and electronic components. South Korea and Taiwan have been especially successful in this area. However, this requires some development of the industrial sector and a growing productivity of the agricultural sector in order to maintain food production with less labor. Of course, if the LDCs can buy some of their food and feed grains from the developed nations more cheaply than they can produce these products themselves, labor can (and should) be withdrawn from agriculture in order to increase the output of manufactured goods for export to the developed nations.

Thus, we observe a rather curious and unexpected phenomenon of the LDCs exporting manufactured products to the developed nations in return for agricultural products. However, this phenomenon is not so surprising if we keep in mind that the manufactured goods exported by the LDCs tend to be labor-intensive and that the food and feed grains are produced in the developed nations under capital-intensive techniques.

This is not to say that the developed nations will someday revert to an agricultural status, with the LDCs becoming industrial. It is not likely that even the productive agriculture of the developed nations can supply the food of the two thirds of the world's population that reside in the LDCs. In order for the people of the LDCs to enjoy some of the fruits of their growing industrial sectors, most will have to increase the productive capacity of their agricultural sectors as well. Otherwise their agricultural output will continue to decline as people are drawn into the industrial sector. As a result, more and more food will have to be imported, most likely at increasing prices, which have to be paid for by exports.

INCOME DISTRIBUTION

A convenient measure of a nation's income distribution is its Gini ratio. Recall that the smaller the Gini ratio, the more equal the income distribution. A country where everyone had the same income would have a Gini ratio of zero. Conversely, the higher the Gini ratio (the closer to one) the more unequal the income distribution.

As shown by the figures presented in Table 26–2, the high-income countries have the smallest average Gini ratio, that is, the most equal income distribution. The U.S. Gini ratio is 0.392, just slightly below the high-income country average in terms of income equality. The middle-income countries have the highest Gini ratios, which implies they have the least equality of incomes. The average Gini ratio for the low-income countries falls between these two but closer to the middle-income group.

Why does the income distribution become more equal as nations develop? One explanation is that when a country is poor, income differences stem mainly from differences in the ownership of property. Since the ownership of property is

TABLE 26-2   Average Gini Ratios*

Low-income countries	.468
Middle-income countries	.504
High-income countries	.371

* Calculated from World Bank data, mid-1980s figures.

highly unequal, incomes also will be unequal. In agrarian societies, ownership of land and animals has a large influence on income distribution. T. W. Schultz, a Nobel prize recipient for his work on human capital, argues that as a nation develops, human capital (education) grows relative to nonhuman capital (property).[9] Therefore, a greater share of income is earned from ownership of skills or human capital in the more highly developed countries. Since human capital is distributed more equally among the population than nonhuman capital, or property, the income distribution in the high-income nations is more equal than it is in the poor nations.

In the middle-income or newly industrialized countries (NICs), the income distribution tends to become less equal as indicated in Table 26–2. In these countries, it appears that nonhuman capital or property at first grows relative to the growth in human capital. Wealthy entrepreneurs and a prosperous middle class emerge. Then, in the later stages of development as education becomes more accessible and affordable to the poor, human capital begins to grow relative to property, and incomes begin to exhibit less inequality.

ECONOMIC INCENTIVES AND GOVERNMENT POLICIES

One of the lessons that has been learned about the people living in the LDCs is that they respond to economic incentives as much as people living in the developed nations. An explanation sometimes given for the existence of the LDCs is that their people lack the ambition or the motivation to better their lot and prefer instead the "simple life." The stereotyped native sleeping in the shade of a palm tree is sometimes used to represent this attitude.

Yet the more we learn about the LDCs, the more apparent it becomes that the vast majority of their people, whether rural or urban, take advantage of opportunities to increase their incomes. Farmers readily adopt new higher-yielding varieties of crops, apply commercial fertilizer if it is profitable, and switch to crops that provide the greatest profits. By the same token, rural people migrate to cities in search of higher-paying occupations and urban workers sell their services to employers who pay the highest wages. People in the LDCs, as everywhere, attempt to spend their incomes on goods and services that provide the most for the money. Trite phrases such as "the Protestant ethic" or "the work ethic" no longer can be used to explain differences in income among nations.

The desire to increase one's income is the basic prerequisite for economic growth. Such a desire among the people of the LDCs provides a strong positive force for economic growth and development. At the same time, the desire for personal gain is often misdirected or controlled by various government policies.

Many LDC governments have enacted "cheap food" policies whereby the prices of agricultural products have been held below world market levels. This has

---

[9] Theodore W. Schultz, *Investing in People* (Berkeley: University of California Press, 1980).

been accomplished by various methods, including the use of price controls on food, the imposition of special taxes on agricultural exports, and the creation of government marketing boards with monopoly privileges that allow them to pay farmers lower prices than would exist in free markets. It has been estimated that prices received by farmers in LDCs relative to purchased inputs such as machinery and fertilizer are substantially lower than in the developed countries.

Economists as well as international development and lending agencies have urged LDC governments to reform their price and trade policies in order to bring their domestic prices in line with the world market. This is easier said than done. In the world's poorest nations, commonly referred to as the *third world,* prices of agricultural products and food relative to wage rates and per capita incomes are already three times greater than in the world's high-income nations. Thus, LDC governments are in no position to make food even more expensive for a large segment of their people. It is not that food is high priced relative to the world market but rather because per capita incomes are so low, $300 per year or less.

As pointed out previously, even at the low price of food in the poor nations, over 40,000 people die each day from the direct or indirect effects of malnutrition because they cannot afford to buy sufficient food for their families. This is hard to envision for most middle- and high-income people living in rich countries.

The cheap food policies of LDC governments can be viewed as a compromise between low output prices relative to purchased inputs and high output prices relative to wages and per capita incomes. This creates a dilemma for these countries. The low output/purchased input price ratio inhibits the use of modern inputs and retards economic growth. But raising this price ratio would make food even less affordable to the poorest people. It is a catch-22 situation. Food prices are low because people are poor. People are poor because food prices are low. Low food prices inhibit the use of modern inputs in agriculture and retard economic growth.

The proposed international food stamp program is envisioned as a means of alleviating the short-run hunger problem while promoting long-run economic growth. Because of the increased food purchasing power of the poorest people in the third world, the demand for food would increase, leading to more favorable agricultural prices and greater use of modern inputs. Farmers and people living in rural areas of the high-income countries also would benefit because of the increase in the export demand for agricultural products to feed people in the third world.

Whether such a program stands a chance of being adopted is an open question. International development agencies are now well established and generously funded, spending about $60 billion per year but apparently without much impact on poor people.[10] By and large, most development assistance is government-to-government. It is not clear that either donor or recipient governments, or development agencies, are willing to change their approach toward one that helps poor people directly.

---

[10] Graham Hancock, *Lords of Poverty* (New York: The Atlantic Monthly Press, 1989).

ECONOMIC STABILITY

In the preceding discussion, we argued that investment is the key to economic growth, particularly investment in people or facilities to produce new, nontraditional inputs for factory or farm. In a decentralized free-market economy, a person must be reasonably certain that a profitable return will be forthcoming before he or she is willing to invest. In an economically unstable society, the uncertainty associated with the future is increased.

One common source of uncertainty in the LDCs is inflation, especially fluctuating rates of inflation, and the controls that usually accompany it. Inflation creates uncertainty because prices do not all rise at the same rate and, more important, the rate at which they will rise is unknown. If one borrows money at a 20 percent rate of interest, a rate not uncommon in the LDCs, it makes a big difference whether the future rate of inflation is 10 percent or 30 percent. In the former case, the real rate of interest is +10 percent, while in the latter it is −10 percent. If one could be sure the inflation rate would be 30 percent or higher, the chances would be good that the investment would be profitable. It does not take much skill to make money when borrowing at a negative real rate of interest, providing loan money can be found.

It is well to keep in mind that an inflation rate figure such as 30 percent is an average annual increase of all prices included in the price index. Not all, or even any, prices have to rise by 30 percent.[11] Some prices may increase 40 to 50 percent, while others may rise only 10 to 20 percent. If the product to be produced is among the latter group and the inputs to be bought are among the former, the chances of making profits are diminished. The imposition of government controls on prices also influences the profitability of investment. If the price of the product is controlled more tightly than the prices of the inputs, again profits are diminished.

If business is carried on in the international market, exchange rate fluctuations become important. If inflation is higher domestically than in countries where the product is sold, the local currency will probably become overvalued vis-à-vis other currencies and the product may become too expensive to compete in foreign markets.

Thus, you can see that inflation and changes in government-controlled prices make it difficult to predict conditions very far into the future. One never knows whether an investment will make a million or force the person into bankruptcy. For people who like to avoid risk of this nature and magnitude, it is often wisest to buy consumer durables such as automobiles and housing. The prices of these items tend to be fairly responsive during inflation. They can be especially attractive if purchased with borrowed funds that carry a nominal rate of interest that is less than the rate of inflation.

---

[11] You may have heard of the man who drowned while attempting to walk across a river that was on the average six inches deep.

SUMMARY

Economic growth is a matter of life and death for many people in the LDCs because of low incomes and an inability to buy food for their families. Agriculture is the dominant industry in LDCs. Industrial development is a prerequisite for agricultural development because industry supplies many of the inputs employed by a modern agriculture. Except in the major cities, infrastructure in the LDCs is relatively primitive or lacking. Educational institutions also are lacking, particularly in rural areas and for the poor. As countries develop, farm people leave agriculture for jobs in the nonfarm sector. The low-income countries exhibit higher rates of population growth than the rich countries. The hunger problem is really a poverty problem because of an inability of the poor to buy food. Income distribution tends to be less equal in the middle-income countries. In order for people to work hard and invest for the future, they must have the incentive of personal reward for themselves or their families. High and fluctuating rates of inflation and unstable governments increase uncertainty and reduce investment.

YOU SHOULD KNOW

1. Which industry is dominant in the economies of the less developed countries.
2. How such countries can increase agricultural output.
3. Why industrial development is required for agricultural development.
4. Why it is not possible to transfer industrial technology intact from the developed to the less developed countries.
5. The definition of infrastructure, and the main reason it is lacking in LDCs.
6. The problems of increasing the level of education in the LDCs.
7. Why the number of farms decrease and farm size increases as development occurs.
8. Which countries have the highest population growth.
9. Why children are the least expensive in rural areas of LDCs.
10. The basic reason for widespread hunger among people in the LDCs and what might be done about it.
11. Why LDCs have a foreign exchange problem, how they have attempted to solve this problem, and the undesirable side effects.
12. How income distribution is related to the level of development.
13. Why the income distribution tends to be more equal in the developed countries than in the low-income nations.
14. Why LDCs have low food prices and how this affects development.
15. Why economic stability enhances economic growth.

QUESTIONS

1. As a nation develops, the proportion of the population engaged in agricultural production invariably decreases.

   a. What causes this decrease in the number of farm people?

   b. Is this phenomenon desirable for a

country or should every effort be made to keep people on farms? Explain.

2. Why is industrial development important for the development of agriculture?

3. A problem common to many LDCs is the exodus of people from rural areas into large cities, resulting in overcrowded slum areas and the host of problems that come with these conditions. What can LDC governments do to alleviate these problems?

4. It might be argued that children are less expensive for rural families in LDCs than anywhere in the world. Why?

5. For many years, the world's developed nations have attempted to reduce the hunger problem in the poorest nations by donating or selling food to them at subsidized prices.

   a. What has been the effect of this practice

on the development of agriculture in the recipient countries?

   b. How would the proposed international food stamp program differ in its effect on agriculture in the recipient countries?

6. *a.* Why have LDC governments adopted policies that maintained the prices of agricultrual products in their countries below world market levels?

   b. What dilemma do third-world countries face in changing their policies?

   c. How would an international food stamp program help third-world countries overcome this dilemma?

7. *a.* Inflation is a common problem in LDCs. Why?

   b. How does inflation affect development?

SELF-TEST

1. For the poorest people in the poor countries, the most immediate problem is to obtain:
   a. a job.
   b. enough food to stay alive.
   c. clothing.
   d. housing.

2. It is not always possible to transfer technology from the developed to the less developed countries because of differences in:
   a. climate and environment.
   b. relative input prices, mainly capital versus labor prices.
   c. educational levels.
   d. all of the above.

3. In LDCs, the majority of people are:
   a. unemployed.
   b. employed in manufacturing.
   c. employed in agriculture.
   d. employed in the service trades.

4. If the majority of people must be employed in agriculture to produce a nation's food:
   a. not much else can be produced.
   b. there will be food surplus.
   c. there will be famine.
   d. there will be a large industrial sector producing inputs for agriculture.

5. Investments in agriculture that yield the highest payoffs tend to be:
   a. in new, nontraditional inputs.
   b. those that increase crop production.
   c. those that increase livestock production.
   d. nonexistent.

6. The shift from a subsistence to a commercial agriculture requires:
   a. supporting farm supply industries.
   b. transportation and communications facilities.
   c. markets for farm products.
   d. all of the above.

7. Compared to the developed countries, prices received by farmers in LDCs are relatively _____ , and prices paid for inputs tend to be relatively _____ .
   a. high; low
   b. low; high
   c. high; high
   d. low; low

8. The condition described in question 7 tends to _____ the development of agriculture in LDCs and causes food _____ .
   a. promote; shortages
   b. retard; shortages
   c. promote; surpluses
   d. retard; surpluses

9. Industrial technology is _____ location specific than agricultural technology and is therefore _____ to transfer from the developed countries.
   a. more; harder
   b. less; easier
   c. more; easier
   d. less; harder

10. Multinational corporations that locate branches in LDCs provide _____ and _____ to the host countries and utilize _____ and _____ of these countries.
    a. labor; raw materials; capital; management skills
    b. labor; management skills; capital; raw materials
    c. capital; management skills; labor; raw materials
    d. capital; labor; management skills; raw materials

11. The main problem of providing infrastructure in LDCs is:
    a. technology.
    b. deciding what is needed.
    c. getting people to accept it.
    d. paying for it.

12. LDCs that borrowed heavily during the 1970s experienced great difficulty in paying back their loans because of the _____ in prices of primary products and _____ in interest rate.
    a. increase; decrease
    b. decrease; increase
    c. increase; increase
    d. decrease; decrease

13. Providing high-quality education to the majority of students is most difficult in:
    a. rural areas.
    b. large cities.
    c. the suburbs.
    d. small towns.

14. As development occurs, the opportunity cost of farm labor _____ relative to the cost of machinery services. This leads to _____ mechanization and _____ farms.
    a. decreases; less; smaller
    b. increases; more; larger
    c. decreases; more; larger
    d. increases; less; smaller

15. Conditions that have intensified the agricultural adjustment problem are:
    a. powerful industrial unions.
    b. minimum wage.
    c. lack of skills and information by rural people.
    d. all of the above.

16. Children are least expensive in:
    a. rural areas of LDCs.
    b. large cities of LDCs.
    c. rural areas of developed countries.
    d. large cities of developed countries.

17. Birthrates are highest in:
    a. rural areas of LDCs.
    b. large cities of LDCs.
    c. rural areas of developed countries.
    d. large cities of developed countries.

18. The main cause of hunger and malnutrition in the world's poorest nations is _____ . A program that could greatly reduce world hunger at an affordable price is:

a. poverty; international food stamps.

b. poverty; increased food shipments.

c. low crop yields; more technical aid.

d. low crop yields; increased food shipments.

19. Anticipated effects of an international food stamp program are:

    a. lower incidence of hunger and malnutrition in the less developed countries.

    b. higher rate of economic growth for the recipient countries.

    c. higher prices and a greater volume of exports by farmers in the developed, food surplus countries.

    d. all of the above.

20. In the early stages of development, a nation's income distribution tends to become _____ equal. As economic growth continues, the income distribution becomes _____ equal.

    a. more; less

    b. less; more

    c. more; more

    d. less; less

21. The asset that grows in relative importance as a nation develops is _____,

making the income distribution _____ equal.

    a. nonhuman capital; more

    b. nonhuman capital; less

    c. human capital; more

    d. human capital; less

22. Prices of agricultural products relative to the prices of purchased inputs are _____ in third-world nations compared to the developed countries. Compared to wages and per capita income, agricultural product prices are _____ in third-world countries.

    a. lower; higher

    b. higher; lower

    c. lower; lower

    d. higher; higher

23. The practice of printing money to finance government spending in LDCs produces _____ , which in turn _____ uncertainty of investment projects.

    a. unemployment; decreases

    b. inflation; decreases

    c. unemployment; increases

    d. inflation; increases

Glossary

A

aggregate demand   A negative relationship between the price level and real output demanded.

aggregate expenditure function   The relationship between actual income and desired spending by consumers, investors, and government.

asset   Anything of value.

autonomous investment   Investment spending that is assumed to remain constant at varying levels of income.

average propensity to consume (APC)   Annual consumption expenditure divided by disposable income. APC = C/DI.

average propensity to save (APS)   Saving divided by disposable income. APS = S/DI.

B

balance sheet   A listing of assets, liabilities, and net worth, and their values. Assets equal liabilities plus net worth.

balanced-budget multiplier   Equal to one under the assumptions of the simple Keynesian model.

benefits of holding money   Convenience and security.

Bretton Woods Agreement   Established fixed exchange rates among nations in 1944.

broad definition of money (M_2) M_1 plus savings accounts balances, including money market funds.

C

cheap food policies   Polices such as price controls on food or taxes on agricultural exports that maintain the price of food below the world market.

classical economics A name given to economic thought starting with Adam Smith's *Wealth of Nations* (1776) and extending up to the 1870s. Concerned mainly with macroeconomic issues.

Combination Laws Outlawed unions in England during the time of the classical economists.

commercial banks Includes those institutions that offer checking account services.

comparative advantage The nation that gives up the least amount of another good to produce an extra unit of the good in question has a comparative advantage in that good.

concave to the origin A line that bends out from the origin and decreases at an increasing rate.

constant opportunity cost The amount of one good that is given up to obtain an additional unit of another good remains the same as the maximum output of the good being increased is approached.

constant price or dollars Value figures deflated by a price index such as the CPI.

consumer price index (CPI) The cost of a "market basket" of selected goods and services in the current year divided by the cost of the same items in a base year and the answer multiplied by 100.

consumption function Relationship between income and consumption.

convex to the origin A line that bends in toward the origin and decreases at a decreasing rate.

Corn Laws Tariffs on imports of agricultural commodities in England during the time of the classical economists.

cost of holding money The value of services forgone by not owning nonmonetary assets (opportunity cost).

current year prices or dollars Undeflated value figures.

curvilinear positive relationship A curved, upward-sloping line that increases at either an increasing or decreasing rate.

curvilinear negative relationship A downward-sloping line that decreases at either an increasing or a decreasing rate.

D

demand A negative relationship between price and quantity.

devaluation Reduction in the value of one currency relative to another.

diminishing marginal utility of money The extra satisfaction received from each additional dollar becomes smaller as income increases.

discount rate The interest rate paid by commercial banks when borrowing money from the Federal Reserve bank to augment their reserves.

discouraged worker effect People who have dropped out of the labor force because of a lack of job opportunities.

discretionary fiscal policy   Refers to specific legislation that changes government spending or taxes in response to an unemployment or inflation problem.

disguised unemployment   Causes the unemployment rate to understate the unemployment problem. Includes underemployment and the discouraged worker effect.

disposable income (DI)   PI minus personal income taxes.

dumping   When a government subsidizes the sale of a good in the world market at a price lower than its cost of production at home.

E

economic growth   Sustained increase in real output of society. Also defined as a sustained increase in per capita real output.

employment rate   Percentage of the adult population, age 16–64, that is employed.

equilibrium income   Where there is neither an unintentional building up or drawing down of inventories. Corresponds to the income level where the aggregate expenditure function intersects the 45-degree line.

equilibrium price   That price where there is neither a shortage nor a surplus of a product. Corresponds to the intersection of the demand and supply curves.

exchange rate   The number of units of one currency that is exchanged per unit of another currency.

expenditure components of GNP   Includes consumption, gross investment, and government spending $(C + I_g + G)$.

F

Federal Deposit Insurance Corporation   An agency of the federal government that insures bank deposits to $100,000 in case of bank failure.

fiscal policy   Attempt by government to promote full employment without inflation through its spending and taxing powers.

fixed exchange rates   Where exchange rates are set by government decree.

flat rate tax   The tax rate remains constant at all income levels.

floating exchange rates   Where exchange rates are determined by foreign exchange markets.

forced saving   The use of tax funds to finance public investment.

fractional reserve banking   The bank holds less than 100 percent of its deposits. The remainder is loaned out or invested in securities.

frictional unemployment   Percentage of the labor force temporarily out of work because of adjustments in the economy and people changing jobs.

full employment   Everyone who wishes to work at a prevailing wage rate can find a job for which he or she is qualified.

G

Gini ratio The ratio of the area between the Lorenz curve and the perfect equality line over the total area below the perfect equality line.

government spending multiplier (M_g) The number of dollars of increased spending in the economy resulting from \$1 increase in government spending. $M_g = 1/1 - MPC$.

Gresham's law Bad money drives out good money.

gross national product (GNP) Total of all final goods and services produced in the economy over a period of time.

H

human capital Skills and knowledge possessed by people.

I

import substitution policies Policies to limit imports in order to provide a less competitive environment for domestic industry and save on foreign exchange.

income and employment theory Deals with the effects of government spending and taxation.

income components of GNP Includes wages, interest, rents, and profits (WIRP).

income in kind Goods and services obtained through government programs free of charge or at a reduced cost.

income velocity A measure of income such as GNP divided by money.

increase (decrease) in demand Buyers take a larger (smaller) quantity off the market at a given price. Corresponds to a shift to the right (left) of the demand curve.

increase (decrease) in quantity demanded Movement down (up) along a demand curve.

increase (decrease) in quantity supplied Movement up (down) along a supply curve.

increase (decrease) in supply Sellers place a larger (smaller) quantity on the market at a given price.

increasing opportunity cost The amount of one good that is given up to obtain an additional unit of another good becomes larger and larger as the maximum output of the good being increased is approached.

inflation A sustained increase in the general price level.

infrastructure The network of transportation and communication facilities together with public utilities such as electricity, telephone, water supply, and waste disposal.

K

K value The proportion of income held as money. Reciprocal of velocity.

Keynesians Economists who believe changes in the money supply are secondary in importance to changes in government spending and taxation.

L

Labor Theory of Value   Goods are exchanged in proportion to the amount of labor required to produce them. Proposed by Karl Marx.

Laffer curve   A backward-bending line showing the relationship between tax rates and tax revenue.

laissez-faire   A policy whereby the government exercises a minimum of intervention in the economy.

less developed countries(LDCs)   Countries with relatively low per capita output or income compared to the richer nations.

liability   Creditor's claim on the assets.

linear negative relationship   A straight, downward-sloping line.

linear positive relationship   A straight, upward-sloping line.

long-run aggregate supply   A vertical line showing the same output at various possible price levels. No money illusion assumed.

long-run Phillips curve   A vertical Phillips curve extending up from the natural rate of unemployment

Lorenz curve   A line showing the relationship between the cumulative percentage of the nation's income against the cumulative percentage of income recipients.

lump sum taxes   Tax collections are assumed to remain constant at varying levels of income.

M

macroeconomics   Concerned mainly with the economy as a whole, particularly with the problems of unemployment and inflation.

Malthusian Doctrine   Population will expand more rapidly than food supply unless checked by starvation and disease.

marginal propensity to consume (MPC)   Change in consumption expenditures divided by the change in disposable income. MPC = $\Delta C / \Delta DI$.

marginal propensity to save (MPC)   Change in saving divided by change in disposable income. MPS = $\Delta S / \Delta DI$.

marginal tax rate   The tax rate on an extra dollar of income.

mercantilism   Preclassical economic thought that served to justify the policies that gave special privilege to a select few.

microeconomics   Deals with consumer and producer behavior and how prices are established in markets.

monetarists   Economists who believe change in the money supply have a pronounced impact on economic activity.

monetary policy   An attempt to promote full employment without inflation by control of the money supply and interest rates.

monetary theory   Deals with the effects of changes in the money supply and interest rates.

monetizing the debt   When the Federal Reserve bank purchases bonds issued by the Treasury. Also called *printing money* to finance deficit.

money creation   Occurs when banks make loans or purchase securities.

money illusion   Resource owners perceive an increase in resource prices but not product prices.

moral suasion   Attempts by the Federal Reserve to persuade commercial banks to follow either a more restrictive or a more expansive lending policy. Called *jaw bone control*.

the multiplier   A $1 increase in spending by one person or group results in a more than $1 increase in spending in the economy. Equals $1/1 - \text{MPC}$.

N

narrow definition of money (M_1)   Currency outside of banks plus checking account balances.

national income (NI)   NNP minus indirect business taxes.

natural rate hypothesis   The argument that the economy always moves toward its natural rate of unemployment after the government attempts to reduce unemployment by stimulating the economy.

natural rate of unemployment   The level of unemployment that will exist in an economy over the long run in the absence of policies that either stimulate or dampen economic activity.

negative income tax   A system where people below a certain income level receive cash payments from the government.

negative relationship   The variables change in opposite directions; when one increases the other decreases.

neoclassical economists   A name given to economic thought starting in the 1870s and extending up to the 1930s. Concerned mainly with microeconomics.

net national product (NNP)   GNP minus depreciation.

net worth   Owner's claim on the assets.

new quantity theory of money   An extension of the original quantity theory. An attempt to explain and predict changes in velocity.

nominal rate of interest   The interest rate quoted on savings accounts or loans.

nondiscretionary fiscal policy   Past legislation that created such programs as unemployment compensation, welfare programs, and the progressive income tax that stabilize the economy. Sometimes called built-in stabilizers.

nonhuman capital   Durable, long-lasting inputs such as buildings, machines, tools, and all forms of infrastructure such as roads, bridges, and communications facilities.

normative economics   Deals with "what should be."

O

open-market operations   Purchase and sale of government bonds by the Federal Reserve.

opportunity cost   That which is given up to obtain more of something else.

P

parity price   The price farmers would have to receive for their products to give them the same purchasing power as they had in 1910–14.

permanent income hypothesis   The idea that current spending on consumer goods and services depends on long-run expected income.

personal income (PI)   NI minus social security taxes, corporate income taxes, and corporate savings plus transfer payments.

Phillips curve   Originally a negative relationship between the rate of change in money wage rates and the unemployment rate. More recently, it denotes a negative relationship between the rate of inflation and the unemployment rate.

positive economics   Deals with "what is."

positive relationship   Both variables change in the same direction; both either increase or decrease.

poverty   Defined as being below a specified level of income, $12,000 for a family of four in the United States in 1989.

primary tools of monetary policy   Open-market operations, changes in the required reserve ratio of commercial banks, and changes in the discount rate.

principle, model, or hypothesis   Other names for theory.

production possibilities curve   A line showing various combinations of two goods that can be produced with a given amount of resources.

production possibilities schedule   A table showing various possible combinations of two goods that can be produced from a given amount of resources.

progressive tax   The proportion of income paid as taxes increases as income increases.

proportional tax   The proportion of income paid as taxes remains constant at all income levels.

Q

quantity equation of exchange $M \times V = P \times Q$.

quota   A limit on the imports of a good.

R

rate of inflation   The percent change in the CPI from one year to the next.

rational expectations   The idea that people attempt to maximize utility given the information at their disposal.

real rate of interest   Money rate minus the rate of inflation.

regressive tax   The tax rate decreases as income increases.

required reserve ratios   The fraction of deposit liabilities that a commercial bank must keep on reserve either as vault cash or deposits in the Federal Reserve (or a reserve city bank).

Ricardian rent   The excess of sales over nonland production costs on land that is more productive than the poorest.

S

Say's Identity   The value of purchases equals the value of sales.

Say's law   Supply creates its own demand.

secondary tools of monetary policy   Moral suasion and selective credit controls.

short-run aggregate supply   A positive relationship between the price level and real output supplied. Implies a money illusion.

slope of a line   Change in the vertical axis divided by change in the horizontal axis, or rise over run.

special drawing rights   An international currency to take the place of gold, also called *paper gold*.

supply   A positive relationship between price and quantity.

supply-side economics   A school of thought that advocates low tax rates to promote economic growth and reduce the deficit.

supply shocks   Changes in short-run aggregate supply due to changes in the amount of resources available to society.

surplus value   According to Marx, the excess of the value of goods produced by labor over their wage.

T

tariff   A tax on imports.

tax multiplier (M_t)   One less than the government spending multiplier under the assumptions of the simple Keynesian model.

technological change   The production and utilization of new and improved inputs.

theory   A statement that contains the important information bearing on a decision or problem.

transformation curve   Another name for a production possibilities curve.

transactions velocity   Total volume of sales in the economy divided by the nation's money supply.

U

underemployment   People having to work in jobs for which they are overqualified.

unemployment rate   Percentage of people in the labor force who are unemployed.

V

value-added   Sales of a firm or industry minus purchases from other firms or industries.

value-added tax (VAT)   A tax on the value added of the firm.

velocity of money   Can be thought of as the average number of times each year each dollar changes hands.

Index
